Rock Climbing
Arizona

Stewart M. Green

FALCON®

GUILFORD, CONNECTICUT
HELENA, MONTANA

AN IMPRINT OF THE GLOBE PEQUOT PRESS

CAUTION
The Globe Pequot Press assumes no liability for accidents happening to or injuries sustained
by readers who engage in the activities described in this book.

♻ Text pages printed on recycled paper.

CONTENTS

ACKNOWLEDGMENTS

I've always enjoyed climbing in Arizona's wide open spaces. One of my first forays was an aborted attempt on the Mitten Thumb with Jim Dunn in 1972. After climbing the first pitch, we stood on a narrow shelf and listened to the distant thump of a drum and decided that a Navajo war party was preparing to capture the piton-festooned infidels on their desert fortress. Afterwards, our big plans for Spider Rock and The Totem Pole fell by the wayside. On succeeding trips to Arizona, however, I sampled the excellent rock and climbing at Granite Mountain, Cochise Stronghold, and Mount Lemmon, finding joy, beauty, and excellent climbing at these marvelous areas.

Writing this select guide to Arizona fell to me after a half-dozen prospective authors dropped the ball, citing too much work and too much time. Putting together a book like this is an immense and complex research project, with lots

Martha Morris seconds *Sweet Surprise* (5.7) on the Loaf, Little Granite Mountain.

of pieces that need to be assembled. This guide took 16 months and over 25,000 miles of windshield time. Every cliff, crag, tower, and butte was visited and documented. Many hours were spent scoping routes and cliffs, talking with local climbers about their beloved crags, and then actually putting hands and feet on the rock.

My sincere thanks and appreciation goes out to all of the climbers who participated in the creation of this weighty and comprehensive tome to Arizona's best climbs. First and foremost, I want to thank Jim Waugh, a long-time Arizona climber, prolific first-ascensionist, X-Games and Phoenix Bouldering Contest organizer, great climbing and hiking partner, and all-around good guy. Jim and Michelle Aubert provided me with a needed home away from home while I worked on this book and sorted life out. Jim's wide knowledge of, and experience at Arizona's crags were invaluable. When I needed a route description, a bit of beta, a suggested rack, or descent information, Jim always had it and graciously shared it with me.

Many thanks also to Marty Karabin, another Phoenix climber who developed many routes in the Queen Creek area and wrote an excellent guide on them. Marty checked access information, route descriptions, topos, and maps, and provided excellent advice on the climbs in the Phoenix area and Baboquivari Peak.

I also greatly appreciate the efforts and comments of Albert Newman and Pieter Dorrestein from Flagstaff. They provided information and criticism on the Flagstaff and Sedona climbing areas. Muchas gracias guys! Many thanks to Rick Donnelly for updated information, comments, and corrections on Granite Mountain and Cochise Stronghold. Also thanks to Eric Scully, the Tucson kid wonder, who gave updated information on Mount Lemmon and posed for photos; Rob Miller for beta on The Pit; Randy Leavitt and Boone Speed for proofing the Virgin River Gorge; Leo Henson, who proofed the Granite Dells; and all the climbers at all the crags who gladly shared beta, rack and route suggestions, and constructive comments. I also appreciate my friends who shared and climbed at many of the areas with me, including Pete Takeda, Beth Renn, Noah Hannawalt, Martha Morris, Jim Waugh, Ian Spencer-Green, Dennis Jump, and Chris Baddams.

Lastly, I thank my friend Martha Morris for all the hard work on the book's artistically drawn topos, as well as the photo topos and maps. Thanks for taking notes and keeping me focused on the task at hand. Thanks also to Falcon Publishing's marketing and editorial staff, with special thanks to John Burbidge and Nicole Blouin for turning a pile of manuscripts, topos, and photographs into this definitive Arizona climbing guide. And to my family, Nancy, Ian, and Brett, thanks for all the encouragement and support.

ARIZONA CLIMBING AREAS

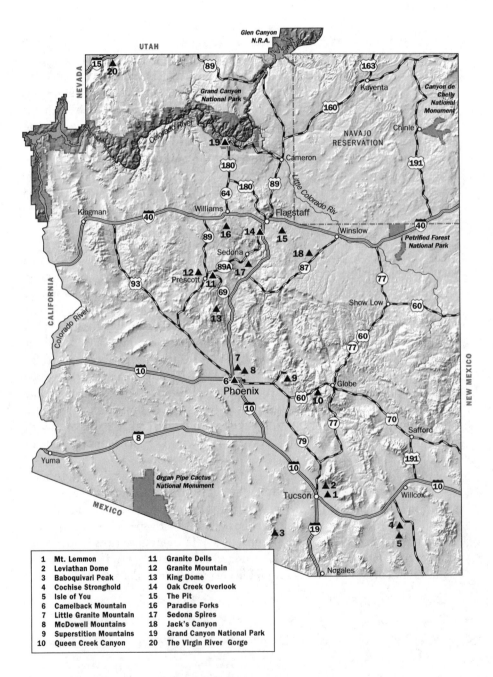

1	Mt. Lemmon	11	Granite Dells
2	Leviathan Dome	12	Granite Mountain
3	Baboquivari Peak	13	King Dome
4	Cochise Stronghold	14	Oak Creek Overlook
5	Isle of You	15	The Pit
6	Camelback Mountain	16	Paradise Forks
7	Little Granite Mountain	17	Sedona Spires
8	McDowell Mountains	18	Jack's Canyon
9	Superstition Mountains	19	Grand Canyon National Park
10	Queen Creek Canyon	20	The Virgin River Gorge

LEGEND

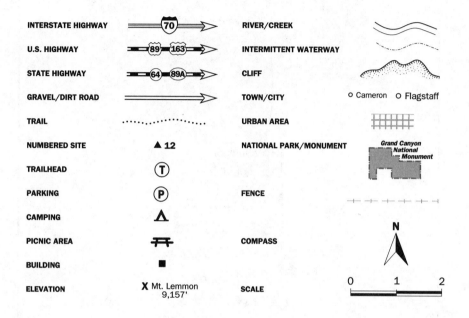

INTERSTATE HIGHWAY	70
U.S. HIGHWAY	89 163
STATE HIGHWAY	64 89A
GRAVEL/DIRT ROAD	
TRAIL	
NUMBERED SITE	▲ 12
TRAILHEAD	T
PARKING	P
CAMPING	⋀
PICNIC AREA	
BUILDING	■
ELEVATION	X Mt. Lemmon 9,157'

RIVER/CREEK	
INTERMITTENT WATERWAY	
CLIFF	
TOWN/CITY	○ Cameron ○ Flagstaff
URBAN AREA	
NATIONAL PARK/MONUMENT	Grand Canyon National Monument
FENCE	
COMPASS	N
SCALE	0 1 2

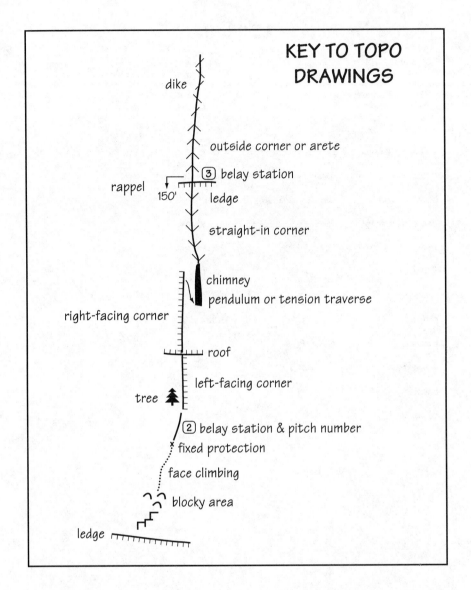

KEY TO TOPO DRAWINGS

dike

outside corner or arete

③ belay station

rappel

150' ledge

straight-in corner

chimney

pendulum or tension traverse

right-facing corner

roof

left-facing corner

tree

② belay station & pitch number

fixed protection

face climbing

blocky area

ledge

lb.	lieback	thin	thin crack(to 1 ½")
chim.	chimney	3rd	class 3
ow	off-width	4th	class 4
HB, RP	very small chocks	KB	knife blade
TCU	small cramming devices	LA	lost arrow

INTRODUCTION

Arizona—there's magic in that name. The word conjures up primeval images: immense, cliff-lined canyons filled with silence and birdsong, salmon-colored sandstone mesas and buttes glowing in the morning sunlight, ancient villages nestled in vaulting caves, stony outwash plains studded with stately columns of cacti, and saw toothed desert mountains outlined against the distant horizon. It's a powerful landscape, and once its timeless, ethereal beauty gets into you, it won't loosen its hold.

Arizona then, starts with its superlative landscape. The brutal land is dominated by a harsh climate, lorded over by the dazzling sun and filled with diversity and extremes. Rock formations of all types—basalt, limestone, sandstone, gneiss, and granite—are scattered across Arizona. This wide variety of rock, coupled with the state's stunning natural beauty, make Arizona an ideal arena for the rock climber.

Numerous vertical challenges and world-class routes hide out in the state's vast reaches. Around the Phoenix metropolis, climbers find exquisite granite crags tucked away on rugged ranges like the McDowell Mountains and adventure sandstone routes up the loose walls at Camelback Mountain. East of Phoenix, there are moderate backcountry routes and pumpy bolted lines up volcanic cliffs in the fabled Superstition Mountains and in Queen Creek Canyon, one of the state's premier sport climbing areas. Around Tucson, climbers can sample edging testpieces on Mount Lemmon, ascend to the holy summit of Baboquivari Peak, and cruise chickenhead-festooned domes at Cochise Stronghold. The Prescott area offers perfect jamming up Arizona's "little big wall" Granite Mountain and the joys of cragging at Granite Dells. Flagstaff, nestled against the San Francisco Peaks, yields countless basalt routes for the energetic climber at the beautiful Paradise Forks and The Overlook. Nearby, Jacks Canyon and The Pit offer bolted sport climbing for both the recreational climber and the honed stonemaster. South of Flagstaff, numerous sandstone towers hide, including The Mace, Arizona's classic spire climb. The Virgin River Gorge, inaccessible from anywhere in Arizona, slices across the state's far northwest corner and offers some of the most difficult routes in the United States.

Rock Climbing Arizona describes 20 of the state's premium climbing areas, guiding the traveling climber to the best and most classic routes. Thousands of routes ascend the cliffs, crags, and towers that are covered here. And climbers, from beginners to aces, will find worthwhile objectives in this outstanding sampling of rocks and routes. In addition to the described crags, Arizona is literally covered with remote, hidden, and little-known climbing areas. While these are not included here, this guide helps you find lots of these backcountry crags by giving information sources and directions. The rest, as always, is up to you.

Rock climbing. It's kind of a crazy thing to do when you think about it. Just like your mother warned you, it can be so easy sometimes to crash and burn. But those of us who pursue the vertical path know that it's more than just a sport or an adrenaline rush. We realize that climbing is a way of life—a way of looking at the world in a very simplistic manner, a way of getting in touch with the grace and beauty of our bodies through pure movement, and a way of releasing our civilized minds and being in the moment. As my son, Ian Spencer-Green, wrote in a letter to one of his sponsors, "Lately I have been training and bouldering a lot—mainly having fun and climbing better than I ever have. I am grateful that I take part in such an incredibly spiritual and rewarding pursuit."

So get out there onto Arizona's rock walls. Find joy in simply moving over stone, in standing on crystal edges on a sunlit face, and in watching vultures wheel skyward on thermals. Sit atop a rounded monolith after a satisfying day of climbing and contemplate the setting sun as it creeps across the hushed desert below you. It's these tender moments of lucidity far from the maddening crowd that we climbers live for. These are the moments when we feel most alive and yes, grateful. Out here on Arizona's rocks, we learn that life itself is a fragile and precious experience and that its vertical world offers us an unparalleled adventure into our consciousness.

CLIMBING HISTORY

One of Arizona's first recorded technical climbing ascents was up Baboquivari Peak in 1898 by University of Arizona professor Dr. R. H. Forbes and Jesus Montoya. After Forbes moved to Arizona in 1894, he became obsessed with climbing this rocky, toothlike peak that towers above southern Arizona. After four attempts, the pair succeeded on a route up the north flank of the mountain. The key was an extendable grappling hook that allowed Forbes to reach past a seemingly blank slab to better holds, a section now rated 5.6. On the summit, they built a huge bonfire to signal their success to friends below. The fire was so large that people in surrounding villages thought that the mountain was erupting.

Rock climbing as a sport in Arizona began in Phoenix after World War II. In 1945, Ray Garner, an ex-Teton climbing guide, taught a climbing class to a Boy Scout troop at Creighton School. Several interested scouts, along with Garner, formed a climbing group they dubbed The Kachinas. Under Garner's watchful eye, The Kachinas developed the cliffs on Camelback Mountain, putting up routes that included *Suicide, Hart Route, Pedrick's Chimney, George Route,* and the *Ridge Route.* They also made the first known ascents of Pinnacle Peak

Jim Waugh pulls pockets up *Casting Shadows* (5.11b) at the Upper Pond Wall in Queen Creek Canyon.

and Tom's Thumb in the McDowell Mountains. Some of the more active Kachinas were Ed George and Ben Pedrick.

Ray Garner also was involved in the 1949 first ascent of The Agathla, an immense volcanic peak on the Navajo Reservation in northern Arizona. Garner, along with Herb Conn and Lee Pedrick, made a reconnaissance climb up the mountain's west face. By afternoon, the trio was so high that they decided to press on to the summit rather than descend and return the next day. They reached the top in the late afternoon and endured a chilly bivouac before rappelling to the cliff's base the next morning.

The 1950s brought an influx of California climbers who bagged some significant sandstone ascents. Bob Kamps, passing through Sedona in the mid-1950s, was impressed with the unclimbed spires around the village. He returned in 1957 with TM Herbert, Dave Rearick, and Yvon Chouinard to bag some first ascents. The best was The Mace, an airy two-summited tower south of Sedona. On a Sunday morning, Kamps, Rearick, and Herbert followed a system of cracks and chimneys to the top of the lower summit, hoping that it would be possible to stem across to the higher summit. They bridged over the four-foot gap between the summits, did an exciting mantle, and stood atop the flat summit. Chouinard missed out on the excitement because he opted to attend Mass that morning.

Four other Californians—Mark Powell, Don Wilson, Jerry Gallwas, and Bill Feuerer (The Dolt)—left their signatures in the summit registers atop Arizona's finest sandstone towers in the 1950s. In 1956, Wilson, Gallwas, and Powell spent four days over Easter vacation climbing chimneys and flared jamcracks with occasional aid moves to the airy summit of 800-foot-high Spider Rock in Canyon de Chelly National Monument. The following year the three, along with Feuerer, ascended the startlingly thin 500-foot-high shaft of The Totem Pole in Monument Valley on the northern Navajo Reservation. The party aided up soft, wide cracks using wide aluminum channel pitons specially made by Feuerer for the ascent. Another important milestone in Arizona climbing came in 1959 when Phoenix climbers Dave Ganci and Rick Tidrick pushed a line up the northeast arête of Zoroaster Temple, a remote peak in Grand Canyon National Park.

The 1960s brought a new generation of climbers to Arizona. In the Phoenix area, Bill Forrest, Doug Black, brothers Lance and Dane Daugherty, and Larry Treiber explored new crags and established numerous new routes. Forrest was particularly active in the Superstition Mountains, putting up scary lines on many pinnacles. Forrest, with partner George Hurley, did Arizona's first grade VI, *The Spring Route*, up Baboquivari Peak in 1968. The Daughertys were both excellent free climbers who pushed Phoenix standards into the 5.9 range. Lance Daugherty, however, was tragically killed in a motorcycle accident in 1968. Treiber established quality routes throughout Arizona into the 1970s, including the Superstitions, Pinnacle Peak, the McDowell Mountains, and Granite Mountain.

Cragging was also a popular pastime in the Tucson area. One of the foremost pioneers was John Rupley, a Shawangunks-trained climber who moved to Tucson in 1961 to pursue biochemical research at the University of Arizona. Through the 1960s, Rupley climbed almost every technical summit along the Mount Lemmon Highway and established many of today's popular classics at places like the Rupley Towers below Windy Point. Ironically, Rupley was more of a mountaineer than a rock jock and viewed outcrop climbing as mere practice for the big mountains.

Granite Mountain, outside of Prescott, was another 1960s discovery. A cadre of local climbers that included Scott Baxter, Lee Dexter, and Tom Taber began putting routes up the smooth granite monolith. These three formed the nucleus of a prolific group of northern Arizona climbers who later called themselves the Syndicato Granitica. The Syndicato members, subsequently including transplanted Rhodesian Rusty Baillie, Karl Karlstrom, and David Lovejoy, pushed Arizona's free climbing standards in the late 1960s and early 1970s with their many ascents on Granite Mountain. Assuming their abilities were below that of other American climbers, they rated their routes with conservatism and modesty. Even today, the mountain is esteemed for its stiff standards.

The 1970s brought free climbing to Arizona in a big way. Besides the explosion at Granite Mountain, local climbers in Tucson and Phoenix pushed standards and routes at their many crags. Phoenix climbers Stan Mish, John Ficker, and Jim Waugh established bold and difficult testpieces throughout the state. Mish's hangdog ascent of *Lost Nuts* at Pinnacle Peak was Phoenix's first 5.12. Waugh developed hard new lines on many Arizona crags, including the Klondyke Wall, Mount Lemmon, and the Superstitions.

Some equally bold climbers were active around Tucson. Mike McEwen eked out several desperate no-pro slab lines in blue Royal Robbins boots in 1971 and firmly established 5.11 in Arizona with free ascents of *Voodoo Child* and *Last Supper* on Mount Lemmon. Dave Baker, Steve Grossman, and Rich Thompson were also very active around Tucson. The beautiful cliffs and domes at Cochise Stronghold in southeast Arizona were explored in the 1970s, and most of today's classics were established. Paradise Forks, in northern Arizona, was discovered in 1979 and quickly became a bastion of traditional climbing ethics, with many difficult crack routes protected only by nuts and cams.

Momentous changes came to Arizona climbing in the 1980s with the widespread use of new protection, including Friends and RPs, and the proliferation of the bolt. A change in ethics regarding the placement of protection bolts and the way routes were established opened up new cliffs in the 1980s and 1990s, like those at Queen Creek Canyon. This ethical debate was not usually polite and reasoned, and often verged on all-out war between traditionalists and sport climbers. At many areas, like Mount Lemmon, bolts were chopped and hangers removed from rap-bolted routes, a practice leading to all kinds of accusations, finger pointing, and name calling. Eventually, cooler heads prevailed and

Arizona climbers and climbing areas have been able to accommodate a mixture of traditional adventure climbing along with bolted, clip-and-go sport routes. A more detailed history of each climbing area, along with significant ascents and activists, is found in each section of this guide.

GEOLOGY AND GEOGRAPHY

Arizona, covering 113,510 square miles, is divided by geographers into two main physiographic regions—the Colorado Plateau in the north half of the state and the Basin and Range Province in the south. The Mogollon Rim, the dividing line between the two, is sometimes added as a third region.

The Colorado Plateau is a remote and rugged landscape of sweeping plains blanketed by sagebrush, towering sandstone cliffs, and deep canyons chiseled by the Colorado River and its tributaries. The bare-bones sandstone, a layer cake of various bands, defines and characterizes the plateau. Some of Arizona's grandest scenery, including the awesome Grand Canyon, Monument Valley, Canyon de Chelly, and the Petrified Forest, is sculpted from the plateau's colorful sandstone strata. Each distinctive sandstone formation—Kaibab, Coconino, Moenkopi, Chinle, Wingate, Kayenta, Navajo, de Chelly, and others—tells a different story of the earth's past.

In the layers hides evidence of emerald tides that washed across ancient sand beaches, vast fields of sand swept into immense dunes by ceaseless winds, twisting rivers that coiled across floodplains and deltas, and the long-extinct life forms that once dominated these lost worlds. Volcanic peaks, like the San Francisco Peaks above Flagstaff, dot the plateau. The Colorado Plateau offers climbers a smorgasbord of routes up frail sandstone towers, towering rock peaks, hidden limestone canyons, and occasional cliff bands of basalt.

The Basin and Range Province, spreading across southern and western Arizona, is a region of broad basins flanked by rugged mountain ranges that tower above the desertlike sky islands. The area not only offers lots of remote wilderness lands but also houses most of the state's population in the Phoenix and Tucson metropolises. Much of the region lies in the Sonoran Desert and is characterized by many species of cacti including the saguaro. Most of southern Arizona's climbing opportunities are on granite cliffs and domes, and volcanic cliffs formed from tuff, breccia, and basalt.

The Mogollon Rim divides the Colorado Plateau from the Basin and Range Province, winding for more than 200 miles across the state's midsection like a long, sinuous snake. The rim, a series of huge escarpments and mountain ranges, forms an ecological transition zone between northern and southern Arizona. Plants and animals from each province mingle here in a biological melting pot. Climbing is found mostly on the basalt cliffs along the rim.

Arizona's diverse topography harbors equally diverse plant and animal communities. Desert shrub, comprised of creosote, sagebrush, saltbush, and cactus, covers 40 percent of the state. Conifer forests, including the world's largest ponderosa pine forest on the Mogollon Rim, blanket 10 percent, while pinyon pine, juniper, and oak woodlands spread across another 25 percent. The grasslands form the remaining 25 percent. These habitats are home for myriad species of animals and birds, including black bear, bighorn sheep, rare Sonoran pronghorn, javelina, mountain lion, many species of rattlesnake, the Gila monster, and tropical birds like the coppery-tailed trogon and thick-billed parrot.

CLIMBING DANGERS AND SAFETY

For those living far from the mountains, the whole notion of rock climbing seems strange, exotic, and dangerous. The flatlander ponders the question "Why?" while the rock climber simply asks, "Why not?" At the root of the question "Why?" lurks a couple of the deepest human fears—falling and heights. Climbers must resolve these fears each time they step off the ground into the vertical rock world. The perils of rock climbing are, however, generally over-rated. The only risks climbers face are those they choose to take. When most climbers choose risk, they do everything possible to mitigate and minimize the danger. Still, H. L. Mencken's observation of hot air balloonists also holds true for climbers. "They have an unsurpassed view of the scenery, but there is al-ways the possibility that it may collide with them."

There is no denying the simple fact that rock climbing is a dangerous activity. Every climber from beginner to ace needs to recognize this fact. Every time you slip on your rock shoes and tie into your harness, you or your climbing partner might die as a direct result of your own actions or by an act of God. Rock climbing, despite all the fun and hype, is a serious business and you need to treat it seriously. The fun quickly drains out of the vertical game when you see your buddy hauled off in a body bag. And almost everyone who has climbed for at least ten years has had a friend die in a climbing or mountaineering related accident.

It is totally up to you how you minimize the risks of rock climbing. If you are inexperienced or out of shape, get help. Don't jump on the sharp end and lead some horrendous runout route because you think you might lose face with your pals. The worst scenario sees *you* in that body bag, or at least hauled off to the hospital with a broken back. Safe rock climbing takes experience, and lots of it. At one time, tyros served an apprenticeship under the watchful eye of a more experienced hand; but now, with the burgeoning growth of rock gyms, those with basic climbing know-how and a handful of hard gym routes under their harness thinks they're rock jocks. But it's just not true.

This guidebook, as well as any other climbing guide or instruction book, is not a substitute for your own experience and your own sound judgment. Do not depend or rely only on the information in this book to get you safely to the top of the crag and back down to your car. Guidebook writing is by necessity a compilation of information obtained by the author through his experience at a given crag, as well as information gleaned from other experienced climbers. Errors can and do creep into route descriptions, topos, gear lists, anchor placements, fixed gear notes, and descent routes and rappels. Things change out there on the rocks. Rockfall might obliterate that crucial set of rappel anchors, or that fixed piton at the 5.11 crux move might have pulled on the last leader fall. You must rely solely on your own experience and judgment to ensure your own personal safety and that of your partners.

Climbing experience is only obtained by getting outside on the rock and doing lots of routes. If you do not have the necessary experience, it is prudent not to attempt serious or long routes, especially in places like Baboquivari. Local guides and climbing gyms operate in many of Arizona's popular climbing areas. Their invaluable services allow you to develop the techniques and wise judgment needed to safely ascend many routes. Guide services and gyms are listed for each area in this book. Also, see the appendix for a complete list of addresses and phone numbers. Before committing your hard-earned cash to a guide service, ask about their experience, accident rates, safety procedures, and class or group sizes. If you have any question about a particular route or cliff, take the time to seek out a local and ask for his or her advice. Most local climbers and guides are happy to give updated ratings, gear lists, and topos to their area's routes.

Ratings of climbing routes are subjective grades and are usually arrived at by a consensus opinion. Use them with caution. Many climbing movements are subject to an individual climber's experience, technique, body type, size, and strength. Some routes may be harder for you than the grade in this book indicates. Again, use your judgment and don't let the rating fool you into thinking a route is easier than it really is. Every effort has been made to designate routes with protection ratings. If no rating is listed, then that route should be safe for anyone with experience in finding and placing protection gear. Both R and X ratings indicate more serious routes, with possible serious injury, groundfall, or even death as the result of a fall. But remember, every route, no matter what the grade, has an X rating if climbing equipment is improperly used, if fixed protection including bolts and anchors fail, or if you do not place and use safe gear.

Climbers who have learned their techniques in climbing gyms should be realistic about their limitations. Climbing at an indoor gym is not a substitute for real rock. Climbing in a gym is a controlled and safe activity. Climbing outside is not safe. Climbing outside requires a lot of judgments and skills that are not learned inside, including rope handling, placing and removing protection, setting up equalized belay anchors, rigging rappel lines and anchors, and doing all the other little things that keep both you and your partner safe on the rocks. Beginning climbers and gym climbers should take special note of route ratings. Gym routes rated with the Yosemite Decimal System do not accurately reflect outdoor ratings. Just because you're a hot 5.12 gym climber doesn't mean you can properly jam and safely protect a 5.9 hand crack. Consider every route you attempt seriously, no matter what the grade. Every experienced climber can relate a horror story from an "easy" route.

Keep safe on the rocks by using common sense. Most accidents and fatalities occur because of bad judgment and improper decisions, and most accidents are preventable. Rely on your own good judgment to evaluate changing conditions. Your safety depends entirely on you. Use the following reminders to avoid accidents:

- Always protect yourself near the start of a route by placing lots of gear or stick-clipping a high bolt to avoid groundfalls.

- Always double-check your tie-in knot and harness before climbing, as well as your harness and rappel device before rappelling.

- Do not climb below other parties. Rockfall can be fatal.

- Do not solo routes (without a rope). Even a 30-foot fall is deadly.

- Do not climb beyond your skill level without proper safety and protection devices.

- Place protection whenever possible to keep yourself and your partner safe.

- Rope up on wet, snowy, or dark descent routes.

- Tie knots in the ends of your ropes to avoid rappelling off the ends of the ropes.

- Tie in properly after completing a sport pitch and double-check your knot and the rope before downclimbing or lowering.

- Remember that the belay is a crucial part of the safety link. Belayers need to be alert, competent, and anchored. Expect and remind your belayer to pay attention while you climb and not to visit with the neighbors or fix lunch.

- Tie a knot in the end of the rope to avoid being dropped by inattentive belayers while they're lowering you.

OBJECTIVE DANGERS

Bad things can happen any time you go rock climbing. Always keep that in mind when you venture out to the crag. Objective dangers, those that you have no control over, are found while hiking to the cliff, climbing your route, descending, and returning to the car. It's a good rule to never consider your climbing day over until you are safely back at your car. Many accidents happen on descents due to rockfall, carelessness, loose rock, inclement weather like rain or snow, and darkness. Always rope up on any descent you are the least bit uneasy about. Pay attention to your intuition.

Albert Newman belays Martha Morris on the first pitch of *Dr. Rubo's Wild Ride* (II 5.9+), Sedona Spires.

Loose rock. The main objective danger is loose rock. Loose blocks and flakes are found on many routes, sitting on ledges or loosely wedged in cracks and chimneys. Use extreme caution around any suspect rock. Falling rock is deadly to your belayer and friends at the cliff's base, and it can even chop your rope. Warn your partners if you feel a block is unstable so they can be prepared for possible rockfall. Thawing and freezing cycles in winter and spring can loosen flakes and boulders on rock walls. The movements of your climbing rope can also dislodge loose rock. Use care when pulling rappel ropes because you can also pull a stone missile down as well. Wear a helmet while climbing and belaying to reduce the risk of serious head injury or death from rockfall or falling. Helmets may not be in fashion, but they're definitely in style if you want to live long and prosper!

Fixed gear. Use all fixed gear with caution. Bolts can shear from the force of a fall. Fixed pitons will loosen due to rock weathering and expansion caused by repeated freezing and thawing. Metal fatigue and age can also affect the useful life of gear. Always back up fixed pro whenever possible, and always back them up at a belay and rappel station. Never rely on a single piece of gear for your personal safety. Always build redundancy into the system so the failure of one part will not affect the overall safety of the system. Never rappel or lower from a single anchor, especially on sandstone or other soft rock, and don't lean straight out on a bolt. The pullout strength of bolts in sandstone is very low. Fatalities occur when a sandstone anchor bolt pulls on a climber. Do not trust your life to questionable anchors or desiccated rappel slings. Don't be so cheap that you're unwilling to leave gear to safeguard your life.

Noxious plants and bugs. Poison oak and sumac, bee and wasp nests, ticks, and rattlesnakes are found at many of Arizona's climbing areas. Poisonous plants cause a severe itching rash that can take weeks to heal. Learn to identify their shiny leaves. Poison oak is often found growing in thickets along the bases of cliffs and in streambeds. Bees and wasps live on many crags. Take note of possible hives and avoid them. Ticks are tiny blood-sucking arachnids that live in brush and woods on lower mountain slopes. They're usually active in spring and early summer. All ticks can carry tick fever, the more serious Rocky Mountain spotted fever, and Lyme disease. Avoid tick-infested areas if possible; otherwise, wear clothing that fits tight around the ankles, wrists, waist, and neck, use lots of bug juice, and always check your clothes and pack before getting into your car. Ticks usually crawl around on you for a few hours before finally settling down for a blood-sucking party, so they can often be found before damage is done.

Snakes. Rattlesnakes are a serious hazard in most Arizona climbing areas, especially during the warmer months. More rattlesnake species are found in Arizona than any other state. They have broad, triangular-shaped heads and a pit in front of each eye (they're pit vipers). The buzz from their tail is unmistakable, and once you've heard the sound it is never forgotten. Remember, though, that rattlesnakes do not always warn before striking. Watch for them along access paths or hiding under boulders and dead brush. They often climb into bushes to get off the hot ground during the day. Watch for snakes when scrambling on easy terrain.

If you encounter a rattlesnake, don't kill it. This is their home and you're the intruder. They don't see a large mammal like you as prey, but are simply protecting themselves. Most bites occur when people attempt to pick a snake up. If you are bitten, get to a hospital as quickly as possible. A snakebite is considered a major medical emergency. In 25 percent of bites, no venom is injected, and in another 25 percent, so little venom is injected that no antivenin is needed for recovery. Do not attempt first aid to a snakebite, do not apply a tourniquet or ice, and do not use a snakebite kit unless absolutely necessary. The wrong treatment can result in the loss of limb or life. Get the victim to the nearest medical help and treat for shock as needed. Keep a good eye on young children in rattlesnake country. A bite is much more serious for a small child than for an adult.

Rattlesnakes are found at almost all of Arizona's crags. One of the most dangerous rattlesnakes is the aggressive Mojave rattlesnake. This snake, *Crotalus scutulatus*, has a very potent venom, making its bite potentially much more serious than the western diamondback, a species it is often confused with. The Mojave grows to 4 feet long and is usually a greenish gray color.

Weather. Lastly, keep a close eye on the weather when climbing. Thunderstorms can build up very rapidly, creating unpredictable weather. Torrential rain and cool temperatures can lead to potentially deadly hypothermia, the lowering of the body's core temperature. Be prepared for wet weather by carrying extra clothes and a raincoat. Heavy rain can also cause severe flash floods. When hiking through narrow canyons, keep an eye on the weather, even if it's miles away, to avoid flood danger.

Also watch for lightning. Climbers and lightning are usually drawn to high points, like the summits of desert towers and cliffs. Be vigilant for lightning whenever a storm is moving your way and retreat at the first sign of lightning. Avoid being on an exposed ridge or summit during a lightning storm. A sign of an impending strike is St. Elmo's Fire, a buzzing of static electricity and your hair standing on end. If you are trapped during a storm, crouch down with your feet close together and use something to insulate yourself from the ground (like a sleeping pad). Move all metal gear as far away as possible. Avoid rappelling during a lightning storm. The electricity can travel down the rope and zap you. The best way to avoid lightning is to use common sense—get the hell off the rock before the storm reaches you.

ACCESS AND ENVIRONMENTAL CONSIDERATIONS

Rock climbers have long been a maverick bunch, doing their own thing at the crags like it was their God-given right. Now, however, climbers have a growing ethical responsibility to minimize their impact on the rock and the surrounding lands, and realize that rock climbing is not a right, but a privilege. The world is a fragile place that is being rapidly damaged by insensitive users, including loggers, miners, ranchers, mountain bikers, horseback riders, rafters, and rock climbers. Climbers should focus on preserving and protecting our unique climbing resources rather than putting up more new routes at tired crags or debating old ethical battles.

The increasing number of climbers in the United States is putting pressures that never existed 20 years ago on crags. Many common rock-climbing practices, such as bolting and aid climbing, are viewed as high-impact activities by management agencies like the National Park Service and Bureau of Land Management. Land managers are required by federal law to protect and preserve the areas that they manage. They are consequently designing comprehensive management plans that regulate recreational land uses such as rock climbing to minimize human impact and preserve the natural resources.

Fortunately, a couple of excellent organizations, The Access Fund and the Rocky Mountain Field Institute, are working with governmental agencies and private landowners to ensure that our precious crags are kept open and generally free from bureaucratic red-tape regulations. Active climber groups in Arizona, including the Prescott Climbers Coalition, work with management agencies, city and county governments, and private owners to keep access open to their crags.

To ensure climbing freedom, we need to adopt an environmental ethic that reflects our concern and love for the rock. We need to be more sensitive and caring toward the nation's limited rock resources and minimize our impact at the crags. We need to establish positive partnerships with landowners and management agencies, as well as climbing organizations, to actively preserve the rock resources. We need to be active stewards and caretakers of our own local areas—think globally, act locally—by investing in what Mark Hesse of the Rocky Mountain Field Institute calls "sweat equity." Devote some time to building proper trails, restoring trampled cliff-base ecosystems, picking up trash at the crags, and replacing colored slings with muted colors. We need to educate ourselves about our areas. Many parklands are set aside to protect specific geological, ecological, or cultural resources. Preservation of these values takes precedence over recreational uses like climbing. Our continued access to these areas depends on our sensitivity to these unique features. We need to make the important decisions regarding rock climbing rather than leaving it to the politicians and political appointees in Washington D.C.

We can begin the process by doing all the little things that add up to a big difference. Look at the various impacts that climbers have at the crags and begin mitigating them by changing your own habits. Here are a few suggestions on how you can help:

- Pick up all your trash at the crags, including cigarette butts, burned matches, tape, soda and beer cans, and candy wrappers.

- Bury human waste away from the base of the cliff or leave it in the open where it will rapidly deteriorate. Burn your toilet paper whenever possible, especially in arid environments. Don't leave human feces on access trails or below routes—as unbelievable as it sounds, it does happen! And use established toilets whenever possible.

- Use existing approach and descent trails. Avoid taking shortcuts on corners and causing additional erosion. Stay off loose scree and talus slopes that easily erode. Soil erosion destroys plants and ground cover. Belay on boulders rather than the lush grass at the base of the wall. Don't chop down trees or tear off branches that might interfere with the first few feet of a route. Use a longer approach or descent route to protect sensitive ecological areas.

- Do not leave cheater slings on bolts or brightly colored slings on rappel anchors. Instead, use slings that match the rock's color. Camouflage bolt hangers with matching paint.

- Respect wildlife closures. Many cliffs in areas like Granite Mountain and Cochise Stronghold are closed for nesting raptors. Climbing near active nests can cause the birds to abandon the site.

- Practice clean camping ethics, especially when primitive camping. Don't rip up trees for firewood, particularly old desert junipers. Put your fire out cold before leaving or going to sleep. Use a stove for cooking. Use only sites that show signs of previous use.

- When accessing canyon country routes, look carefully for existing climbers' paths or follow dry creek beds to avoid damaging vegetation and fragile soils. Hiking in the desert can severely impact the fragile ecosystem. It can take as long as 100 years to recover from even minimal human impacts.

- Avoid biking to reach more distant climbing sites, as mountain bikers have a greater environmental impact than hikers. An exception to this would be biking on an existing roadway.

- Do not climb near or above any Indian rock art or ruined dwellings. It's against both federal and state law to damage rock art panels or ruins, and climbers have damaged some by careless and thoughtless actions.

- Join and contribute money and time to worthwhile climbing organizations like The Access Fund and the Rocky Mountain Field Institute. They are working to keep our climbing areas open and free from cumbersome restrictions.

Ethics. Ethics are at the very heart of our sport. The style we use to climb a route means everything. Every climber and every area has a unique and individual ethic regarding how routes are put up, ascended, and rated. But we need to remember to disagree about ethics only to the point where the rock itself doesn't become an innocent victim of ethical wars and callous egos gone awry. There have been too many bolt wars that solved nothing, but left irreparable damage to the crags. A schism, although slowly healing, has existed in American climbing for the last decade between traditional climbers and sport climbers. This us-versus-them mentality benefits no one. It's best to remember there are only rock climbers. Enjoy the challenges of both schools and leave the petty ethical grievances behind.

The style employed on a route is a personal choice. How you climb is entirely up to you. There is purity, beauty, and adventure in climbing from the ground up, placing gear, routefinding, leaving the topo behind, and accepting what the rock offers for both protection and technique. Many of Arizona's classic routes were put up in this traditional fashion. Modern gymnastic routes require working, memorizing, and hangdogging before the coveted redpoint ascent from the ground to the anchors is achieved. Toproping is a legitimate tactic on some hard routes as well as airy boulder problems. It not only saves the climber from a serious fall, but also saves the rock from extra bolts.

Bolting. Bolting is the most controversial ethical dilemma of modern climbing. Permanent bolts on cliffs have created many of Arizona's popular and newer climbing areas at places like Queen Creek Canyon and Jacks Canyon, which until the last ten years had no climbing tradition. Bolts have also allowed more difficult routes to be climbed in a relatively safe manner, but bolts have also been misused. Some modern crags, the work of Bosch owners gone berserk, are a grid of bolts. These eyesores have angered land managers as well as other users. Other crags have been subjected to bolt wars, with the offended faction either chopping or placing bolts. The placement as well as the removal of bolts, however, doesn't solve the problem, instead it only damages the rock and creates more climbing restrictions. Common sense, dialogue between climbers, and some civil decorum go a long way toward resolving the bolting issue. Many Arizona climbing areas, like the Superstition Wilderness Area, now have limitations on the placement of new bolts. Others have a bolting moratorium that allows for only the replacement of existing, unsafe anchors and bolts. Always check with Arizona land managers to learn about bolting restrictions and concerns.

The Access Fund has worked with many management agencies to resolve the use of fixed anchors, that is bolts, on public lands. Climbers should support the work they have done to create a broad national policy for fixed anchors on our crags. They are working to allow fixed anchors at climbing areas, recommending that their use be determined on an area-by-area basis by climbers who rely on fixed protection and anchors for their personal safety. Climbers, not the government, should bear the responsibility for the placement and upkeep of fixed pro. They are also working to permit the use of fixed anchors in designated wilderness areas to safeguard climbers and to minimize the impact of climbing on soils, vegetation, wildlife, and fragile environments on top of the cliffs.

Climbers who place new bolts and create new routes need to think long and hard about the placement. Toprope the proposed line and see if it is indeed worthy of creation. If it is, place the bolts with sensitivity to minimize rock damage. Do not place bolts next to cracks that accept gear placements. Use the natural line up the rock; don't force it up the hardest, most contrived way because everyone else will undoubtedly follow the natural weakness. End the route or pitch at natural stances or ledges whenever possible. In the end, it really doesn't matter if a route is put in from the ground up or on a rappel rope. The important thing is the safety and proper placement of the fixed pro and the aesthetic qualities of the route. Don't let the ease of rap bolting lead to over-protecting the route, and don't add new bolts to existing lines. Respect the style of the first ascensionists. If you don't have the skills or courage to do the route as it is, then leave it as a future challenge that you'll someday meet with proper respect.

Defacement. Chipping and manufacturing holds is a growing problem on many American crags, including some in Arizona. As climbers push the standards higher, they desire harder routes to test their abilities. As many indoor gym climbers, often newcomers to the climbing world, spread outward from their insulated plywood walls, they see the real rock as a malleable medium ready for their sculpting. They bring a gym ethic—every hold and move is changeable—to the outside rock world. Do not chip or chisel or glue any hold on a route or boulder problem. If you can't do the route with what is already there, maybe you're just not good enough to climb it or maybe that piece of rock just can't be climbed. Save it for the day when you are good enough, when you've worked hard enough, and when you've finally earned the ascent. Chipped routes destroy the future of climbing, especially for the up-and-coming rock stars. Chipped routes reflect egotism, selfishness, and mediocrity.

In the quest for your own personal ethic, remember that neither the rock nor the route belongs to you. You're only a transient traveler across the vertical terrain. Don't allow egotism, ignorance, and arrogance to dictate your ascent style and personal climbing ethic. Be sensitive to both the cliff and the landscape, and consider each route a precious gift for everyone to open and share.

Enough said—let's go climbing!

Using this guide

A locator map at the front of the book shows the general locations of the main climbing areas. Each section is organized with several headings that will give you a variety of information about the area. In the **Overview,** you will get a general description of the area and a brief summary of the climbing history and local ethics. **Trip Planning Information** consists of a condensed summary of specific information on each area. **Finding the area** will give you written directions, and in addition, many cliffs have a road map and/or sketch of the general area. Specific descriptions of the routes are also included, which in most cases are accompanied by photos with overlays or drawn topos identifying routes and showing the locations.

Overview: The Overview describes the setting, type of rock, and climbing. This section also includes recommendations for climbing equipment and some discussion of local climbing history and ethics.

Trip Planning Information: This section offers a brief synopsis of the following categories:

- **Area description:** A brief summary of the area.

- **Location:** Reference to region of the state and largest nearby towns.

- **Camping:** Information on nearby developed campgrounds and suggestions for camping in undeveloped sites. When available, addresses or phone numbers are given.

- **Climbing season:** The best time of year to visit an area.

- **Restrictions and access issues:** Important issues, such as land ownership, parking, safety, and regulations on use.

- **Guidebooks:** Published sources of information for the area.

- **Nearby mountain shops, guide services, and gyms:** The names and location of businesses providing these services. For a full listing of addresses and phone numbers, by town, see Appendix C.

- **Services:** Nearby retail mountain shops, guide services, and gyms.

- **Emergency services:** Hospitals, emergency numbers.

- **Nearby climbing areas:** Other easily accessed climbing areas.

- **Nearby attractions:** Places of cultural, historical or geographical interest.
- **Finding the crags:** How-to-get-there directions starting at the nearest major road and town.

For each cliff, more detailed information is included about location, equipment, approaches, and descents. Routes are listed numerically, with the name and rating followed by a brief discussion of the location and nature of the climb, equipment recommendations, length, and descent information. There is an overview map of each climbing area, and photos and drawings showing cliffs and route locations accompany the descriptions. The **Map Legend** and **Key to Topo Drawings** are located at the front of the book.

There are three appendices at the back of this guidebook. These offer further reading (Appendix A), a rating system comparison chart (Appendix B), and a list of climbing equipment shops, guide services, and gyms (Appendix C). The alphabetical index follows and lists all proper names, including people, climbs, and climbing areas.

A book of this magnitude requires a wide selection of routes of all difficulties and lengths. Errors will creep into route descriptions due simply to the sheer diversity and number of routes detailed here. A wide range of active climbers has carefully checked and double-checked the area and crag descriptions to maximize the book's accuracy. Be forewarned, however, that things on paper aren't always as they are in the real world. Take every route description with a grain of salt. This book is not intended to carry you up any route. It will get you to the base of the cliff and point you in the right direction, but the rest is up to you and your sound decisions. This book is not a substitute for your own experience and judgment.

Almost all of the routes included in this guide are worth climbing. Routes not worth climbing have usually been omitted or described as "not recommended." If a route is especially good, words like "quality" and "excellent" may be included in the route description. These terms are generally subjective opinions that may or may not be true for every climber. Every climber has his or her own unique experience on every route. Star ratings have been deliberately omitted in an effort to avoid queues and a diminished experience for everyone. There are many fine routes in this guide to choose from. You are invited to decide for yourself what looks right and feels best on any given day.

RATING SYSTEM

This book uses the Yosemite Decimal System (YDS), the usual American grading scale, to identify the technical difficulty of the routes. Remember that ratings are subjective and vary from area to area. In this book, we have tried to bring a consensus to the grades, but we relied on previously listed grades for routes in most cases. You will find small rating variances in each area. Some climbs may seem to be more conservatively rated (read harder) than other areas. Easier sport climbs (5.8 to 5.11) seem to be harder to translate to the YDS, although the standard of difficulty on the higher end of the scale is comparable to European grading. Older traditional routes conform to early Colorado and California ratings established at the same time. The present sticky rubber and better pro currently available might make them slightly easier, but climbers will still find them solidly rated.

Some of the older bolted climbs have been retro-bolted, which on some level makes them seem slightly easier. A 5.9 can start feeling like a 5.10 when you're 40 feet up! Use all ratings only as a starting point in any area and expect a one- to two-letter grade, or even a full grade, variation from what you are accustomed to at your home area.

Many of the routes listed also have protection or danger ratings. These routes generally have little or no protection, and a climber who falls could sustain serious injuries or death. R-rated climbs have serious injury potential. X-rated climbs have groundfall and death potential. Remember, however, that every route is a possible R- or X-rated climb.

Mountain travel is typically classified as follows:

Class 1: Trail hiking.

Class 2: Hiking over rough ground such as scree and talus, which may include the use of hands for stability.

Class 3: Scrambling that requires the use of hands and careful foot placement.

Class 4: Scrambling over steep and exposed terrain where climbing difficulty is relatively easy, but a long fall could result in injury because of exposure. The lead climber trails a rope, uses natural formations for protection if available, and is on belay.

Class 5: Climbing on steep and exposed terrain where a fall would definitely result in injury or death. Only the hands and feet are used for upward progress, no direct or artificial aid is employed. Ropes, belays, running belays (protection), and related techniques are used.

The Yosemite Decimal System (YDS) used to rate Class 5 climbing fails to follow mathematical logic. It is now an open-ended scale where the 5 denotes the class, and the difficulty rating is tacked on behind the decimal point, with 5.0 being the easiest and 5.15 (read five-fifteen) being the hardest (to date). When the system was originally developed, 5.9 was the theoretic upper end of the scale. When routes were climbed that were obviously harder than 5.9, higher numbers were then used to denote the difficulty.

When a route has had too few ascents for a consensus or the estimated difficulty rating is unclear, a plus (+) or minus (-) subgrade may be employed (5.9+ or 5.12-, for example). Where there is a consensus of opinion, additional subgrades of a, b, c, and d are used on climbs rated 5.10 and above. Occasionally, two letters may be used, such as 5.12b/c. This is because the grade still requires consensus, is height dependent, or is subject to some other qualifier.

Routes are rated according to the most difficult move. Some climbs may be continuously difficult, seeming harder than other routes that are rated the same but only have one or two hard moves of that grade. In some instances, routes are described as "sustained" or "pumpy" to give an indication of the continuous nature of the climbing. Differences in strength, differences in reach, and distance between protection points may be factors contributing to rating variations. Where these factors seem significant, they are pointed out in the written descriptions.

Aid climbing—using artificial means to progress up the rock—has a different set of ratings. Class 6 is aid climbing, and climbing equipment is used for progress, balance, or rest. Difficulty levels are denoted with a capital letter A followed by numbers progressing from 0 to 5. A capital letter C indicates that the aid placements are "clean aid," and pitons or hammered aid should not be used.

A0: Equipment may have been placed to rest on or to pull on for upward progress.

A1: Solid gear placements and aid slings (etriers) are used for progress because the climbing is too difficult to be free climbed.

A2: Gear placements are more difficult to install and support less weight than an A1 placement.

A3: Progressively weaker placements that are more difficult to install and may not hold even a short fall.

A4: Placements can support body weight only, and long falls can occur.

A5: A series of A4 placements that could result in a fall of 50 feet or longer.

A pitch or rope-length of technical climbing may have a combination Class 5 and Class 6 rating, such as 5.9 A4. This means that the free climbing difficulties are up to 5.9 with an aid section of A4 difficulty. On the route photo overlays and the topo drawings in this guide, the crux (most difficult section) is often marked with the difficulty rating. (Not all crux ratings are marked.)

An additional grade denoted by Roman numerals I through VI is given to some longer routes. This generally refers to the level of commitment in terms of length and time necessary for the climb. Climbers should also consider other factors, such as technical difficulties, weather, logistics, and the approach and descent. Typically a Grade I requires a few hours to complete; Grade II, up to half a day; Grade III, most of the day; Grade IV, all day; Grade V, a bivouac; and Grade VI, two or more days.

An additional "danger" rating may be tacked on to some climbs. Where the protection may not hold and a fall could result in injury or death, an R or X may be added. A route rated 5.9 R may mean that the protection is sparse or "run-out" or that some placements may not hold a fall. X-rated routes have a fall potential that can be fatal. Do not attempt an X-rated route unless you have the confidence and ability to solo the climb safely with absolutely no protection.

See Appendix B for a table comparing the American rating system (Yosemite Decimal System) to the British, French, and Australian systems.

Injuries sustained from falls are always possible, even on routes that can be well protected. This guide does not give a protection rating nor does it provide detailed information on how, when, or where to place protective hardware. Suggested "standard" gear racks are described in the overview for most areas, and individual recommendations on types and sizes of protection that may be useful are made on some climbs.

Be advised that all rack information should be considered the bare minimum required to safely ascend a route. It's up to you to decide if you need more or less gear than is described in the text to safely and properly climb the route. The standard desert rack mentioned in some descriptions is considered to be a couple of sets of Friends or similar-sized camming units, a set of TCUs, a selection of wired Stoppers and Tri-Cams, and some quickdraws. Ultimately, safety and the level of risk assumed are the responsibility of the climber. There's really no such thing as being "too careful."

Sport climbers should eye their prospective route and count the number of bolts. Bolt counts are given for many routes, but things change on the real rock. Some bolts may be hidden, added, subtracted, or miscounted. Always carry extra quickdraws in case the count is wrong or you drop a quickdraw. Remember to consider what you need for the anchors and for lowering. Again, it's always up to you to provide for your own safety. Climb safe, climb smart, and have fun!

Eric Scully on the Mount Lemmon classic *Afternooner* (5.11b).

TUCSON AREA

MOUNT LEMMON

OVERVIEW

Mount Lemmon, the 9,157-foot high point of the Santa Catalina Mountains, towers above Tucson and the surrounding desert basins. The 27-mile Mount Lemmon Highway, winding up the mountain's south flank, offers easy access to literally hundreds of granite and metamorphic rock outcrops scattered across steep mountain slopes. More than 1,200 climbing routes are found on the mountain, making Mount Lemmon one of Arizona's most popular and well-traveled climbing areas. For many climbers, the Lemmon sums up the best of Arizona rock climbing.

Mount Lemmon and the Santa Catalinas are Arizona's "sky islands," mountain ranges that poke up above the low desert. These southern ranges are cool refuges from the lowland heat and harbor diverse communities of plants and animals. The Mount Lemmon Highway climbs more than 5,300 feet and passes through five of North America's seven distinct life zones, making the summit drive a telescoped journey that is the biologic equivalent of traveling from Mexico to Canada.

Mount Lemmon has an equally diverse amount of rock climbing ranging from difficult, bolted clip-ups to multi-pitch traditional classics. Variety is the key word for Lemmon's vertical terrain. The popular and accessible crags offer thuggish face climbs up thin edges, intermittent cracks and corners with occasional jams, and even slabs that require precise technique and balance. Many of the routes here, particularly at Windy Point, are technical and devious. If you're looking for sport routes with lots of jugs, you should avoid Mount Lemmon. Good routefinding and face climbing techniques are needed for a successful Lemmon day, with flakes, edges, and smears linking corners and short cracks together. Some of the lines look improbable until you get your fingers on the holds. There are many bolted sport routes that require only a rack of quickdraws. Other routes are protected by a combination of bolts and gear. To safely climb anything besides bolted lines here, you should be competent at placing protection—

TUCSON AREA

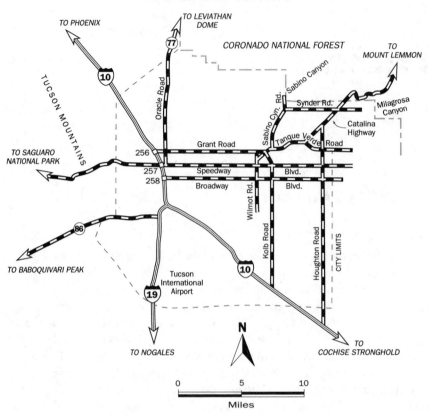

slotting RPs into thin seams, wedging a Tri-Cam into a flared pocket, cramming TCUs into a shallow groove, as well as setting up safe, equalized belay anchors.

Almost all of Mount Lemmon's crags are on the southern slopes of the mountain and lie within a half-hour hike of the highway. Some of the more popular crags include Chimney Rock, a roadside 150-foot-high cliff laced with superb crack routes; the closely spaced crags around Windy Point Overlook; and lots of sport routes at Middle Earth. Many new crags have been developed in the 1990s, including Andy Cook Wall, New York Deli Wall, Obscure Rock with *The Mask of the Red Death* (5.13a), Wall of the Marching Munchkins (a dozen bolted 5.9 to 5.11 routes), The Murray Wall, The Fortress (lots of excellent sport and trad lines), and The Ravelin. Some of these crags, however, are currently closed part of the year for raptor nesting. More backcountry challenges on remote Mount Lemmon cliffs await those willing to do longer approaches. These are beyond the scope of this guide. Intrepid climbers should consult *Backcountry Rockclimbing in Southern Arizona* for details and directions.

MOUNT LEMMON CLIMBING AREAS

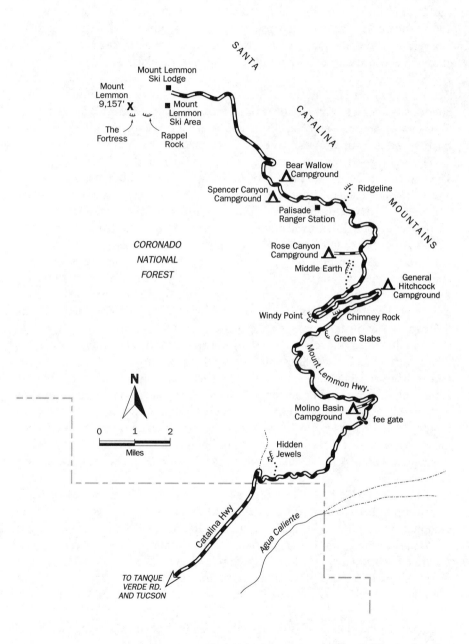

Mount Lemmon Ski Lodge

Mount Lemmon 9,157'

The Fortress

Mount Lemmon Ski Area

Rappel Rock

SANTA

CATALINA

MOUNTAINS

Bear Wallow Campground

Spencer Canyon Campground

Ridgeline

Palisade Ranger Station

CORONADO NATIONAL FOREST

Rose Canyon Campground

Middle Earth

General Hitchcock Campground

Windy Point

Chimney Rock

Green Slabs

Mount Lemmon Hwy.

N

Molino Basin Campground

fee gate

0   1   2
Miles

Hidden Jewels

Catalina Hwy

Agua Caliente

TO TANQUE VERDE RD. AND TUCSON

The Santa Catalina Mountains are composed of granite. Most of the crags are composed of what geologists call the Wilderness Granite, an intrusion of igneous rock that occurred in several episodes between 75 and 25 million years ago. It is called a "peraluminous granite," or a granite enriched with aluminum, and as such, forms sharp outcrops because it is erosion resistant and weathers more slowly than other nearby granites. A distinctive characteristic of Lemmon's granite is the alternating dark and light bands, particularly visible near Windy Point. The dark layers have a high iron and magnesium content, while the light bands are rich in silicon and aluminum. The erosion of Lemmon's towers, hoodoos, and crags is due to differential erosion along joints, cracks, and fractures in the granite. Water attacks the joints using freeze-thaw cycles to further fracture the surrounding rock and widen cracks.

Generally good climbing weather is found year-round on Mount Lemmon. The best time to visit, like the rest of Arizona, is in spring and autumn. March and April are excellent months to climb on Lemmon's crags. Days and nights are mild and dry, although rain showers can occur. Likewise, October and November are ideal, with warm, dry conditions. Summer days can be hot, but it's always cooler than down in Tucson. Plan to climb in the early morning and late afternoon or up high on the mountain. Shady routes are easily found on many cliffs, especially at Windy Point. Localized heavy thunderstorms occur on July and August afternoons. Watch for lightning in exposed areas. Winter days can be cold and even snowy, or warm and dry. Cold spells are usually short-lived and snow quickly melts off the crags.

Climbing history: Technical climbing began on Mount Lemmon in the early 1960s when biochemist John Rupley moved to Tucson in 1961. Rupley, a mountaineer who viewed cragging as simply practice climbing for bigger routes, systematically began bagging unclimbed pinnacles and faces on Mount Lemmon with his wife Ira, Pete Kaiser, and Nick Clinch. He was particularly active in what is now called the Rupley Towers at Windy Point, putting up classic routes including *R-1, R-3,* and *R-4.* Bob Kamps, a traveling California climber, first climbed the popular Hitchcock Pinnacle at Windy Point in 1960 and *Standard Route* on Chimney Rock.

The early 1970s saw a group of young Tucson climbers, including Mike McEwen and Dave Baker, firmly establish Mount Lemmon as Arizona's leading climbing area. McEwen brought 5.11 to the mountain with his leads of *Voodoo Child* and *Last Supper.* Baker did first ascents of many of today's classics like *Jungle Gym* and *Copperhead #5* at Chimney Rock. The late 1970s brought a further renaissance in free climbing style and difficulty with ascents by Rich Thompson and Steve Grossman. Thompson, who was killed in a fall in 1970, established many hard routes and discovered the potential of Reef of Rocks on Lemmon's north flank. Grossman, a talented climber, put up many classics as well as free-soloed many of the mountain's easier routes.

The 1980s saw more exploration of Mount Lemmon's rock potential. Most of the obvious traditional lines, protected by gear and an occasional bolt, were ascended on cliffs and towers. Activists included John Steiger, Paul Davidson, Eric Fazio-Rhicard, and Mike Head, who put up more 5.13s than anyone else. In the late 1980s, sport climbing and rap bolting came to Lemmon, creating new routes and lots of controversy.

Traditional locals felt strongly about the bold ethic established on Mount Lemmon's crags, with most first ascents done ground-up with a minimum of bolts. After several rap-bolted routes were climbed on the Beaver Wall at Windy Point, some by out-of-town climbers including Todd Skinner, Christian Griffith, and Dan Michael, a trio of locals including Steve Grossman removed all the bolts from the wall. This action spurred Tucson climbers to meet at the local mountain shop, The Summit Hut, to discuss their differences on the bolting issue. An uneasy truce was reached and sensible rap bolting continued with some restrictions.

The late 1980s and the early 1990s began a prolific period on Mount Lemmon. Many hard routes were established on crags like New Wave Wall, Big Pine Towers, and the Beaver Wall. Some of the busy climbers were Ray Ringle, Jim Waugh, and Dan Michael. Michael's 1990 ascent of *Hebe* on the Beaver Wall became legendary, with its crimpy, technical moves repelling many excellent climbers until Merrill Bitter finally repeated it in 1998. It's rumored to be Lemmon's hardest route, possibly checking in at 5.14a.

The 1990s have seen continued activity, with local climbers exploring Mount Lemmon's wealth of rock and revisiting many crags that previously had only one or two routes and little recent traffic. Scott Ayers added lots of quality sport lines to Middle Earth, an off-the-beaten-track crag north of Windy Point, while Andy Cook Wall, Obscure Rock, and New York Deli Wall were discovered, bolted, and climbed. The summit crags saw many new, excellent bolted routes added on The Fortress, The Ravelin, and The Murray Wall.

In so many ways, Mount Lemmon is the heart and soul of Arizona rock climbing. The climbing is interesting, technical, and always challenging. The position of the crags is spectacular, with routes often overlooking the mountain-rimmed Tucson basin. The weather is usually perfect for fun-in-the-sun cragging, and the variety of routes make it a haven for the moderate climber. There are numerous lines from 5.7 to 5.10.

Rack: Gear information is listed in many route descriptions. Keep in mind that the specified gear is only a suggestion. Look at your proposed route and decide for yourself what you might need up there. Everyone protects routes differently. The sin is not in taking too much gear, but too little gear. Keep in mind that many Mount Lemmon routes have specific gear needs and if you don't have the right size, you don't have any protection. A traditional rack here requires at least one set of RPs or other brass nuts, a set of wired Stoppers, and a couple of sets of Friends or their equivalent. At least some cams should have flexible stems for horizontal placements. Tri-Cams and an occasional extra-large Camalot are useful on some routes. A single 165-foot rope is standard for

Lemmon. Due to the wandering nature of many routes, however, double-rope technique is sometimes useful to avoid rope drag. If you do climb with a single line, bring some extra 2-foot slings for easier rope management. Most sport routes require only a rack of a dozen quickdraws and a rope. Some older routes have occasional gear placements between widely spaced bolts.

TRIP PLANNING INFORMATION

General description: Excellent face and crack routes ascending numerous and easily accessible gneiss and granite cliffs, walls, and towers along the Mount Lemmon Highway in the Santa Catalina Mountains.

Location: Southern Arizona, just northeast of Tucson.

Camping: The best climber camping is at the six Coronado National Forest campgrounds along the Mount Lemmon Highway. The lower elevation Molino Basin Campground, just past the fee station, is the best place for cool weather camping. Bear Canyon and General Hitchcock campgrounds in Bear Canyon are just down the road from Windy Point. Other higher campgrounds are good in summer when temperatures are hot down low. Bear Wallow Campground is best for the summer crags. The higher campgrounds close in winter.

Climbing season: Year-round. Spring and fall are best, with warm days and cool nights. Summer days are hot in the sun, but shade is easy to find. The crags toward the top of Mount Lemmon are usually cool and pleasant in summer. Winter weather is generally very good, making this a good cold weather destination. It can, however, snow at the higher elevations including Windy Point. The crags on the upper mountain are usually snowed in.

Restrictions and access issues: Mount Lemmon lies within Coronado National Forest. The main restriction is the closure of the summit crags for raptor nesting from February 1 through August 31, or whatever date the Forest Service deems important. This includes The Fortress, The Ravens, Wheeler Wall, San Pedro Overlook, Panorama Wall, and other crags. Check with the Forest Service for current closure dates and information.

Guidebooks: *Squeezing the Lemmon* by Eric Fazio-Rhicard, 1991, is the comprehensive guide and is available in Tucson shops. A new, updated version is supposedly in the works. Inquire at The Summit Hut for information on new areas. Marty Karabin publishes a fold-out topo guide to East Windy Point.

Nearby mountain shops, guide services, and gyms: The Summit Hut and Bumjo's Climbing Shop in Tuscon. Rocks & Ropes is the Tucson gym.

Services: All services are in Tucson, including great Mexican restaurants. Cheap showers are available at Kino Veterans Memorial Center on the south side of Tucson.

Emergency services: Call 911. Kino Community Hospital, 2800 East Ajo Way, Tucson, AZ 85713, 520-294-4471 and Tucson General Hospital, 3838 North Campbell Avenue, Tucson, AZ 85719, 520-318-6300.

Nearby climbing areas: Milagrosa Canyon (sport routes below Mount Lemmon), Reef of Rocks, Sabino Canyon, Esperero Spires, Bear Canyon, Finger

Rock Canyon, Table Mountain, Leviathan Dome, Mendoza Canyon, Kitt Peak, The Dry.

Nearby attractions: Saguaro National Park, Sabino Canyon, Colossal Cave, Tucson Mountain Park, Old Tucson, Arizona-Sonora Desert Museum, Catalina State Park, Fort Lowell Museum, San Xavier Del Bac Mission, Madera Canyon, Santa Rita Mountains.

Finding the crags: Mount Lemmon is easily accessed from downtown Tucson and Interstate 10. The easiest way is via Speedway Boulevard. Exit onto Speedway from Interstate 10 and drive east to Wilmot Road. Turn left on Wilmot and follow to Tanque Verde Road. Follow Tanque Verde to the Catalina Highway (which turns into the Mount Lemmon Highway) and turn left. This road angles northeast and climbs the mountain. A lot of other roads lead to Tanque Verde and the Catalina Highway. Consult a road map of Tucson to figure out the best route from your location.

Detailed directions to each crag are found below. The main areas are at or near the following mileposts on the Mount Lemmon Highway: Hidden Jewels, milepost 1; Green Slabs, milepost 10; Chimney Rock, milepost 11; Windy Point, milepost 14; and Middle Earth, milepost 15.

HIDDEN JEWELS

This area offers a couple of west-facing cliffs perched high above the hairpin turn just past the start of the Mount Lemmon Highway. The cliffs, which lie at a relatively low elevation, are a cool weather alternative when cold and snow envelope the popular cliffs of Windy Point farther up the highway. The Hidden Jewels has great atmosphere, with tall saguaro and cholla cacti scattered over the surrounding mountainsides and distant views across Tucson to Kitt Peak. The cliffs are composed of Catalina Gneiss, a banded metamorphic rock found along the base of the Santa Catalina Range. The routes were developed mostly in 1994 by Jeff Mayhew, Shawn Lowry, and Ryan Murphy.

Finding the cliffs: Drive up the Mount Lemmon Highway for 1.4 miles and park on the left (north) side of the highway in a large pullout. This is the trailhead for Soldier Trail. Follow the steep trail uphill for just over a mile. Where the trail begins to level out, look for cairns that mark a climber's trail going left (west) toward a saddle on the ridge to the left. A large, triangular-shaped rock marks the cutoff. Follow the trail west and northwest through the saddle and onto the west flank of the ridge. The cliffs are reached after about a quarter-mile walk. The path follows a broad shelf between the upper and lower cliffs. A two-bolt rappel station (165-foot, two-rope rappel) is located on the left (south) side of the cliff edge, allowing access to the lower cliff. The path continues contouring north along the shelf to the base of the upper cliff. A rough path also descends to the base of the lower cliff on its north side, below the upper cliff. Allow 20 to 30 minutes to hike to the cliffs from the highway.

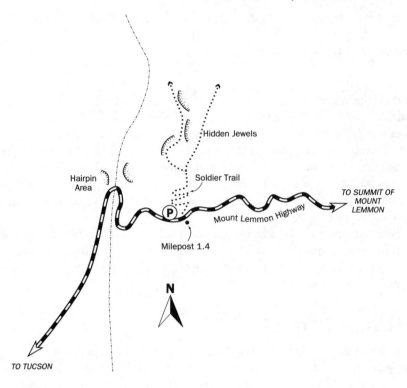

UPPER CLIFF

The upper cliff, facing northwest, is a series of steep faces broken by chimneys and clefts. Three routes are found on two of the buttresses. Routes are listed right to left above the trail.

1. **The Right One** (5.8) Locate an obvious, steep, slabby wall seamed by horizontal bands of strata. This good but serious route ascends the right side of the cliff. Begin by climbing an easy right-facing corner for 20' to a small ledge. Clip a bolt and continue up a shallow, right-facing corner to a thin crack. Free climb straight up past 3 bolts (5.8) before trending up left to the last bolt of Route 2 to a 2-bolt chain anchor just below the top of the cliff. **Descent:** Lower or rappel 95'. **Rack:** Quickdraws, small to medium Stoppers, and TCUs. Use a 200-foot rope.

2. **The Left One** (5.7) Really fun face climbing with a few hard moves and lots of jugs. Begin 10' left of Route 1. Climb awkward rock past a

30

bolt and continue up to a 2-bolt chain anchor (same anchor as Route 1). A couple of the clips are hard for short people. Use a 200-foot rope. 7 bolts. **Descent:** Lower or rappel 95'.

3. **Lazy S** (5.10a) The hardest route on the cliffs and better than it looks. This route ascends the obvious buttress 100' north of Route 2. Begin left of a deep chimney. Climb the right side of a ramp (1 bolt) to the right side of a large roof. Step right around the roof and traverse up left past 3 bolts on the steep headwall above the roof. Pull over a bulge to a narrow ramp and climb up and left on a slab to a juggy finish and a bolted belay atop the cliff. 6 bolts. Use long runners on the 2nd and 3rd bolts. **Descent:** Rappel 100'. **Rack:** Quickdraws, small to medium Stoppers, and cams.

LOWER CLIFF

Access this cliff below the trail by making a 165-foot rappel from bolted chain anchors on the south side of the cliff. Use two ropes and watch for loose rock. Otherwise, hike down a steep path from the north edge of the upper cliff at the end of the access trail. Routes are listed left to right (north to south). Routes 4, 5, and 6 are located on a steep, banded, northwest-facing wall. Routes 7, 8, and 9 are to the south around the edge of a flat buttress on the right wall of a deep chimney/gully system.

MOUNT LEMMON
HIDDEN JEWELS LOWER CLIFF

4. **The Crescent** (5.6) On the left side of the smooth wall. Jam and lieback a right-angling hand crack with good hidden holds to a 3-bolt anchor on a ledge. Loose at top. 45'. **Rack:** Medium to large cams.

5. **Soldier Blue** (5.9+) Superb and varied technical climbing. Begin just right of Route 4. Climb the thin crack with the crux between bolts. End on the ledge with 3-bolt anchor. 2 bolts. 45'. **Rack:** Small wires, TCUs, and a medium cam.

6. **Soldier's Revenge** (5.7) Fun liebacks and jams up the hand and fist crack right of Route 5. Go left at the top to avoid loose blocks. **Descent:** Rap or lower from 3-bolt anchor. **Rack:** Hand-sized cams.

7. **Cactus Corner** (5.8+) South of a square buttress right of Route 6. Begin below the obvious corner just right of a brushy gully. Jam and lieback for 165' up the right-facing corner system to a bolted belay station (also the rap station). Watch for loose rock. **Rack:** Mostly medium to large cams.

8. **Tread Softly** (5.6) A combination of Routes 7 and 9. Begin up *Cactus Corner* onto narrow ledges. Work up right to the 4th bolt on Route 9 and continue up it to the bolted belay station. 165'. **Rack:** Quickdraws and medium to large cams.

9. **Soldier of Contortion** (5.9) Start below a roof 25' right of Route 7. Climb a wide crack to the right side of the roof. Squeeze through a 5.9 roof slot (handjams in back) to a bolt. Work up and left on easier bolted rock broken by ledges to the bolted belay/rappel station. 165'. **Rack:** Stoppers and a good assortment of cams to 4".

GREEN SLABS

The Green Slabs is a popular and easily accessible area. The crag, a southwest-facing collection of slabs and fins, sits above the highway just past milepost 10 and before the road enters Bear Canyon. Some fun, moderate, single-pitch routes ascend excellent granite flakes, edges, and cracks. Most of the routes are protected by a combination of bolts and gear.

Finding the cliff: Park in a pullout on the left (west) side of the highway at milepost 10.1, or just beyond at a couple of right-hand pullouts at mile 10.2. The small pullouts may be full on weekends. The broken cliff is obvious above the road. The five-minute approach follows a steep trail to the base of the cliff. The trail continues uphill along the base on a loose, rocky path. Routes are listed left to right, beginning with the west-facing wall on the west side of the slabs.

MOUNT LEMMON
GREEN SLABS

10. **Missing in Action** (5.7) No topo. Fun and easier than it looks. Walk uphill to the left (north) from the toe of the cliff and along the base for about 100'. This line climbs the steep face just after the trail begins descending from a saddle. Begin on a ledge with trees. Climb the obvious, shallow, right-facing corner and flake system up to a face climbing finish and belay ledge. **Rack:** Good selection of small and medium gear.

11. **Highway Robbery** (5.12a) Start below a smooth face with 2 bolts, 10' left of the obvious banana-shaped, hanging flake. Sketchy face climbing past a bolt to a left-angling crack. Work up crack 5', clip bolt on the right, and continue up crack to easier rock. 45'. **Rack:** Small gear to protect crack above 2nd bolt.

12. **Green Banana Jam** (5.9) Off-width up either of the awkward, curving cracks that form the Green Banana.

13. **Mother Psycho's Little Darlins** (5.12a) Ascends the steep, thin face right of Route 12. Climb thin edges for 25' past 2 bolts to an overhanging flake crack. Head up beautiful plated rock above past 5 bolts to the top of the buttress. 7 bolts. **Rack:** Quickdraws and a medium Friend for the crack.

14. **Banana Cake** (5.7) Excellent climbing but devious pro. Begin at the toe of the buttress just left of a deep chimney. Great climbing on flakes

leads up a narrow ridge that broadens above a short crack to a plated slab. Belay up right on a ledge. **Rack:** Wires and small cams.

15. **Monkey Business** (5.7) Popular. Begin right of the obvious chimney at the toe of the buttress. Climb incipient cracks for 25' to a horizontal crack. Get pro and traverse left into the chimney or continue up the face right of the chimney to a bolt. Continue on to a belay ledge. **Rack:** Small to medium gear.

16. **Here and Gone** (5.8) Walk east up a steep trail to the third buttress. This line ascends the narrow, south face of the buttress. Face climb up a thin, intermittent crack. Follow flakes to a bolt on the left edge about 25' up. Continue up right into a flared corner, which leads to plated rock. Easier climbing leads to top of the buttress and a belay ledge. **Descent:** Walk off ledge and descend the gully to the west. **Rack:** Small and medium gear.

17. **David and Goliath** (5.10c) Hike uphill to the next buttress and begin on its right side. Climb a broken, right-angling, clean crack to a bolt. Pull up on good edges and step right to another bolt. Another bolt leads to slabby rock and a 2 cold-shut anchor on a narrow ledge. **Descent:** Rappel from cold shuts or scramble off right to ledges. **Rack:** Small and medium gear.

18. **Toy Roof** (5.9) This route is on the west face of the next buttress uphill from Route 17. Start up a short hand crack. Move up right from the crack to a bolt on a slab 15' up. Climb up and over a small roof to banded rock and another bolt. Tiptoe up the thin slab above past the 3rd bolt to a horizontal cam placement. Easier rock leads to a good ledge and a 2-bolt anchor. **Descent:** Rappel from bolts or walk off left to gully scramble. **Rack:** Small and medium gear.

CHIMNEY ROCK

Chimney Rock is a superb roadside crag on the west side of Bear Canyon with lots of classic crack routes for the trad freak. Many routes and variations lace Chimney Rock's granite east face. The following are descriptions of the popular, quality routes on the lower left side of the cliff. Consult the comprehensive guide *Squeezing the Lemmon* for more routes and all the variations. The crag, which is sunny on cool mornings and shady on warm afternoons, makes a good year-round cliff. **Rack:** All the described routes are protected by gear. Bring a generous selection that includes RPs, Stoppers, and Friends. A large off-width piece is sometimes needed.

Finding the cliff: Drive up the Mount Lemmon Highway to milepost 11. Chimney Rock looms immediately west above the road. Park in one of the small pullouts

MOUNT LEMMON
CHIMNEY ROCK

walk off back side

walk off

walk off

3rd class

ledge

.5xp
fp

X

X

ow

chimney

X

hands

hands

XX

hands

.9"

hands
in slot

awk

X

squeeze
chimney

19

20

21

22

23 24

25

26

on the right. Parking can be problematic on busy days. Short, two-minute trails access the cliff's base. One trail is on the left side below *George's Buttress* and the other trail is below *Standard Route*. Use caution scrambling above the road; the trail climbs loose, crumbly rock.

19. **George's Buttress** (5.7) The left-most route on the wall. Begin on boulders at the base on the left side of the cliff. Climb easy rock up left into an obvious, left-facing crack system. Jam and lieback up cracks to a large, triangular roof. Traverse right under roof and jam a flared crack to a 2-bolt chain anchor on a ledge. 125'. **Descent:** Rappel to the ground with double ropes.

20. **Mistaken Identity** (5.9) More than just the first ascent party has mistaken this route for *George's Buttress*! Start right of boulders and below a prominent crack system right of a large roof. Jam a hand crack up right to a flared hand and fist crack. Above, traverse 5' left to a shallow, left-angling, thin crack system. Jam and face climb up insecure cracks (5.9) to a small roof. Continue up left to a 2-bolt chain anchor on a ledge (same as Route 19). **Descent:** 1 double-rope rappel from chain anchors to ground. **Rack:** A good selection including RPs, wires, TCUs, and small to large cams.

21. **Stoner's Boner** (5.9) Just right of Route 20. Follow a ramp that leads right into a recess flanked by double cracks. Climb the left crack past a small pine. A finger crack leads to a slot left of a small, blocky roof at the left base of a large phallic flake. Climb the slot, with a hand crack in back, to a small pedestal stance atop the phallic flake. Face climb up left on broken rock to an obvious roof. Lieback around a horn on the right side of the roof and face climb up left to a wide crack. Belay above on a ledge. **Descent:** Walk off to left by scrambling across the ledge.

22. **Centerpiece** (5.10-) Superb, classic, and interesting. Begin behind a large flake boulder at the base of the wall. Follow a left-facing corner (fingers, hands, liebacks) to a 2-foot roof. Handjam and stem over the roof to a squeeze chimney that narrows to fist and hand size. Face climb up steep, knobby rock to the base of an overhanging hand crack. Jam thin hands up the airy crack (5.10-) to a ledge belay. **Descent:** Scramble left on the ledge to walk off. **Rack:** Generous selection of cams. Upper crack takes #2 and #2.5 Friends.

23. **Single Lens Reflex** (5.10-) A quality route with awkward, thought-provoking moves. Scramble onto a large, flat boulder right of Route 22 and belay. Face climb up left on edges and flakes to a left-angling, left-facing corner alongside an inverted spearhead. Lieback and stem

up a finger crack (5.10-) in the awkward, left-facing corner to an obvious, right-angling crack system that leaves the main corner. Follow the finger and hand crack up right to a belay stance with 2 bolts. **Descent:** Traverse the ledge system left to walk off. **Rack:** Generous selection of cams and lots of runners to alleviate rope drag.

24. **Copperhead #5** (5.10) Another good trad route. Begin at the same belay point as Route 23, on the flat boulder. Climb an easy, right-angling crack/ramp for 10' to the base of a right-angling corner. Traverse right 10' on good footholds and follow a flake system up right over a narrow roof to an obvious, left-facing dihedral. Work up to a large pointed flake. Above, move past blocks and cracks. Pull through a small slot to the base of an overhanging, off-width crack. Off-width over the roof (solid 5.10) or pull over with a long reach (5.10-) to a right-facing corner that leads to Garden Ledge. Variations to start are possible. Best is the prominent left-facing dihedral—a thin, fingery lieback (5.10) joins the route about 30' up. **Descent:** Continue up *Standard Route* to the top or traverse straight left along a Class 3 ledge to walk off descent. **Rack:** Lots of cams, including a large Camalot for the off-width section.

25. **Jungle Gym** (5.10d) Good, committing climbing. Begin just uphill to right from Route 24 below a narrow, left-facing corner. Lieback and jam up the corner to awkward crux moves in a flared, insecure crack (5.10+) 25' up. Continue liebacking up left with good footholds to the top of the arching corner. Exit right up a good, short hand crack to a stance. Follow the crack system up right past small bushes to a small roof. Hand traverse left a few feet, pull roof, and jam a short finger crack until it's possible to face climb up left (5.9) over a long, narrow roof to Garden Ledge. Belay on the ledge. **Descent:** Continue up *Standard Route* or traverse left (Class 3) along horizontal crack/ledge to a walk off. **Rack:** Wires, TCUs, and Friends.

26. **Standard Route** (I 5.7) 5 short pitches. An excellent and popular beginner's route. Walk up right along the base of the cliff to a worn staging area. This can also be reached directly by a path from the highway. Begin below a prominent, overhanging flake. **Pitch 1:** Ascend a large boulder to a face with a bolt. Face climb up left, mantling on ledges, to another bolt. Another mantle (5.7) leads to a belay on a good ledge below the flake. 50'. **Pitch 2:** Work up the chimney behind the big flake to a left-facing corner formed by a large block. Continue up a shallow, right-facing corner (5.5) past a couple fixed pitons to Garden Ledge. Many variations to the top can be done from here. The traditional finish is described here. **Pitch 3:** Move the belay to the back, left side of the ledge behind trees. Lieback up a corner on the left edge

of a flake (5.7). Pull past a large, pointed flake onto a terrace with trees. **Pitch 4:** Move the belay quite a bit left to the edge of the left buttress by a long, perched boulder. Follow cracks up right along the edge of the buttress (5.4) to a belay beside a large boulder. **Pitch 5:** A short lead over a bulge (5.6) to the top of the rock. **Descent:** Scramble down the back side to a walk off left. **Rack:** Generous selection of Stoppers and cams.

WINDY POINT

Windy Point, a lofty viewpoint overlooking Tucson, is the focus of Mount Lemmon rock climbing and has the highest concentration of routes in the Tucson area, with more than 200 lines within a 15-minute hike of the parking area. Numerous buttresses, spires, crags, and faces line the steep mountain slopes below the highway as it bends northward at the point. This is the place to sample the best of Tucson's rock, with superb granite, few crowds, and numerous sport and trad routes on a variety of crags. The moderate routes, however, can be busy on weekends.

Finding the crags: The described routes are all on crags east of the Windy Point parking lot, near milepost 14 on the Mount Lemmon Highway. Lots of excellent routes are found on the crags to the west, including the Beaver Wall, South Fin, North Fin, and Mean Mistreater Wall. Check the comprehensive guide *Squeezing the Lemmon* for details and directions.

The crags below Windy Point are initially hard to find. Take your time and carefully study the overview map of the area. Look at the crag descriptions and photo topos, too. Getting to and around the crags can be difficult because of obscure trails and thick underbrush.

HITCHCOCK PINNACLE

This stubby pinnacle towers east above the road and the Windy Point parking area. Several fun, classic routes ascend this popular spire. Access by scrambling east to the base from the parking lot. Approach time is about one minute.

27. **Hitchcocks I** (5.7) Begin below a block on the west side. Climb up and left (5.7) past 2 bolts to the summit and a 2-bolt anchor. **Descent:** Rappel 50' north.

28. **Hitchcocks II** (5.8) Begin below the block on the west side. Climb to the top of the block and work up right past a small roof to the summit. 1 bolt. **Descent:** Rappel 50' north from a 2-bolt anchor. **Rack:** A few pieces of medium pro for short crack.

29. **East Face** (5.10) Face climb over a roof to a bolt and fixed piton.

WINDY POINT

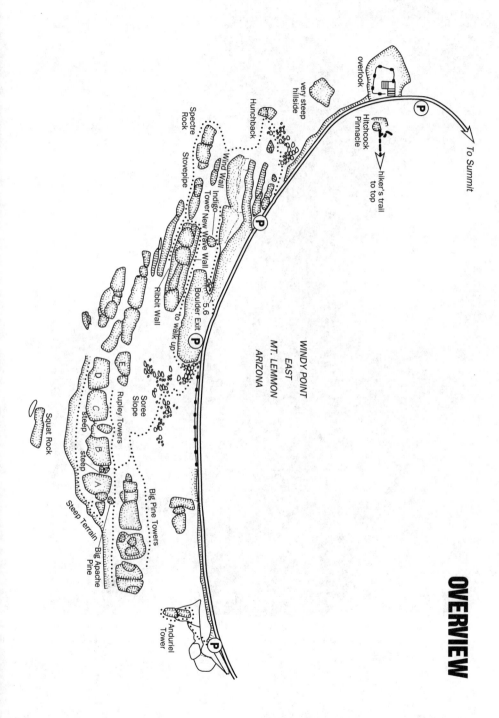

OVERVIEW

overlook

To Summit

Hitchcock Pinnacle

hiker's trail to top

very steep hillside

Hunchback

Spectre Rock

Stovepipe

Wind Wall

Indigo-Tower

New Wave Wall

5.6

Boulder Exit

to walk up

Ribbit Wall

Soree Slope

Rupley Towers

Steep

Steep

E

D

C

B

A

Squat Rock

Steep Terrain

Big Apache Pine

Big Pine Towers

Anduriel Tower

WINDY POINT
EAST
MT. LEMMON
ARIZONA

41

MOUNT LEMMON
HITCHCOCK PINNACLE

X X 2 bolts, chains

X

X

X

up west face
to top

X 28

X

alt. Belay

27
28

29

MT. LEMMON
HUNCHBACK PINNACLE

HUNCHBACK PINNACLE

A good blocky pinnacle below the road about 100 feet east of the Windy Point parking area. Access it down a short trail through broken boulders below milepost 14. Park at the main Windy Point parking area and walk east, or park in the first pullout east of the lot. The trail begins from the west side of the pullout and drops down to the obvious spire. No topo.

30. **Hunchback Route** (5.7+) A short 40-foot route up the west side of the pinnacle. Climb an obvious, right-facing corner past 2 bolts to the airy summit. **Descent:** Rappel from a 2-bolt chain anchor. **Rack:** Small and medium gear.

31. **Green Ripper** (5.12a) A 4-bolt sport route up edges and flakes on the steep, white-striped and lichen-covered east face. 40'. **Descent:** Rappel or lower from a 2-bolt chain anchor.

32. **Hunchback Arête/a.k.a. Steve's Arête** (5.11a) A classic route with good position and perfect photo opportunities. Swing up the gorgeous, overhanging arête on the southeast corner past 4 bolts to anchors. 40'. **Descent:** Rappel from a 2-bolt chain anchor.

33. **Danglefoot Dihedral** (5.10b) Start below the south face left of the *Hunchback Arête*. Work up an 8-foot-long thin crack to 3 bolts on a striped, overhanging wall left of a left-facing corner. 3 bolts. 45'. **Descent:** Rappel from a 2-bolt chain anchor.

Eric Scully hanging out on *Hunchback Arete* (5.11a) at Windy Point.

WIND WALL

A south-facing wall just below the road and a south side pullout. This cliff offers some very good routes, but use caution—protection can be hard to get and ratings may seem sandbagged if you're not used to Mount Lemmon climbing. Topropes can be easily set up from the finlike top of the wall. Access the cliff by descending the path toward Hunchback Pinnacle through boulders below the roadcut and milepost 14; go left (east) down through trees to the cliff's base. Routes are listed left to right.

34. **Baba Rum Raisin** (5.10d R) A face route up the far left margin of the wall. Climb a short crack to a stance, then reach around the corner and clip a bolt. Thin face moves go around the left side of a roof to a large, plated flake. Easier crack and face climbing lead above to the top. **Descent:** Walk off along the top of the wall.

35. **St. Stephen** (5.11a) An excellent and mostly well-protected face route. Begin in an oak clump on the far left side of the wall. Climb up and left over overlaps past bolts. Continue up easier cracks and flakes to the top. 6 bolts. 75'.

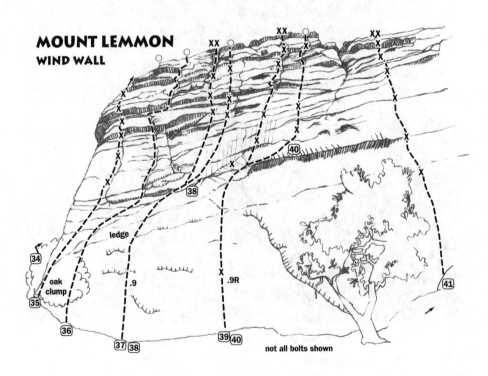

MOUNT LEMMON
WIND WALL

not all bolts shown

36. **Be Here Now** (5.10+ R) Begin at the oaks on the left side. Scramble right onto a ledge below obvious seams. Follow the seams up left, then back right to a final, steep headwall. 75'. **Rack:** Lots of wires and small cams.

37. **Space Cowboy** (5.9+) Recommended fun. Begin 20' right of oak clump. Edge up an easy slab onto a slanting ledge. Face climb up past 3 bolts and enter a right-angle groove. Follow the groove past 1 bolt to a final, water-streaked headwall. Pull past the last bolt to 2-bolt chain and 1-cold shut anchors in an obvious cleft on the cliff rim. 5 bolts. **Descent:** Rappel 75' to ground or walk off right. **Rack:** Small stuff— RPs, wires, and TCUs.

38. **Horton Here's a Who** (5.10) Same start as *Space Cowboy*. Bear right below *Space Cowboy's* 1st bolt and work over beetling bulges past 3 widely spaced bolts to a final mantle over the cliff's lip. 3 bolts. 80'. **Descent:** Walk off to right or rappel from *Space Cowboy's* anchors. **Rack:** Wires, TCUs, and small cams.

39. **Rocket Man** (5.10 R) Hard and serious climbing. Edge (5.9) to the 1st bolt, then easy climbing above leads up right to a bolt. Continue via tricky face climbing over several bulges to the top and a 2-bolt anchor. It's runout and hard to get decent pro between the 3rd and 4th bolts. Final hard section is committing and scary! 7 bolts. **Descent:** Walk off right or rappel from *Space Cowboy's* chain anchor. **Rack:** RPs, wires, and small cams. Pro is devious and hard to find.

40. **Spaceman Spiff** (5.10) Same start as *Rocket Man,* but keep right on a sloping ramp. Follow a right-angling seam/crack past bolts. Finish through an obvious skyline cleft in the rim. 4 bolts. 90'. **Descent:** Walk off right or rappel from *Space Cowboy's* chain anchor. **Rack:** RPs, wires, and small cams.

41. **Deranged of Late** (5.8) A popular moderate up slightly polished granite. Begin next to the twisted lone oak on the right side of the cliff before a grove of trees. Fun climbing up edges and numerous bulges to the top of the cliff. 6 bolts to 2-bolt anchor. 65'. **Descent:** Rappel or lower from the anchor or scramble up to the pullout.

INDIGO TOWER

This small, narrow fin/tower sits in a canyon between the eastern extension of Wind Wall and New Wave Wall, which is to the south. Access it by following a climbers' trail east from Wind Wall or doing a downclimb (5.6) through boulders from the road to the boulder-choked corridor between New Wave Wall and Indigo Tower. The two routes are on the west side of the formation.

MOUNT LEMMON
INDIGO TOWER

42. **Short Wave** (5.9) A fun route up the left arête with delicate, tricky moves down low. 4 bolts to a 2-bolt chain anchor. 40'. **Descent:** Lower from anchors.

43. **Indigo Montoya** (5.7+) A crack to a slot on the right side of the narrow, west face. End at *Short Wave*'s 2-bolt chain anchor. 45'. **Descent:** Lower from anchors. **Rack:** Stoppers and Friends.

NEW WAVE WALL

A superb, north-facing wall with lots of technical new wave routes for the hardman/woman. Good cranking is found during warm weather because the wall gets lots of morning shade. The wall can be too cold in winter. Easiest approach (five minutes) is from between the first and second pullouts east of Windy Point. Scramble over the road embankment and downclimb (5.6) boulders into a boulder-filled corridor below the wall. It can also be accessed from Wind Wall by walking east on a path through trees past Indigo Tower. The wall is to the right. Routes are listed from left to right when facing the wall.

44. **Change in Luck** (5.12a) Begin on the far left side of the face, just right of a deep chimney. Crank past 3 bolts (5.12a) to a kneebar hole. Pull above to a break and another hole. Head left up a black streak to a narrow ledge, step right, clip a bolt on the bulge, and reach the rim at *Skid Mark*'s anchors. Going to anchors is runout. 7 bolts to 2-bolt chain/cold shut anchor. 70'.

45. **Skid Mark** (5.12d) Doesn't see many ascents. Begin with a bouldery start 15' right of Route 44. Thin, technical edging leads up a yellow streak to the horizontal ledge break. Clip the bolt on the bulge and swing up to lip anchors. Runout between the 7th and 8th bolts—bring small gear if you need peace of mind. 8 bolts to 2-bolt chain/cold shut anchor. 70'.

46. **Holey Moley** (5.12a) The New Wave classic with quality, fun climbing. Begin below the obvious hueco hole. Thin face climbing (crux) leads to the hole. Find a kneebar (left leg) rest. Crimps and flakes lead to another rest at the horizontal crack. Pull good flakes up a striped headwall to the lip anchors. 8 bolts to 2-bolt chain/cold shut anchor. Some climbers place a cam after the hueco. 75'.

47. **Sign of the Times** (5.12a) A squeezed route. Start 10' right of *Holey Moley*. Climb thin edges straight up past 5 bolts to a left-angling crack. Clip one more bolt and move to anchors above a small ledge below the top. 6 bolts to 2-bolt chain anchor. 60'.

MOUNT LEMMON
NEW WAVE WALL

48. **New Wave** (5.12c) Classic. Begin off a square boulder at the wall's base. Narrow edges lead past 2 old bolts to a fixed pin at the base of a thin crack. Fingery jams and face holds lead 20' up the crack (small gear and 1 bolt). Where the crack bends left, move straight up past 2 bolts to anchors above a ledge. 5 bolts and 1 fixed piton to 2-bolt chain anchor. 60'.

49. **Tsunami** (5.12b) No topo. Maybe the best route on the wall. Expect tidal waves of stiff crimping. Climb thin, technical edges up the slightly overhanging, banded wall. 9 bolts to 2-bolt chain anchor. 65'.

50. **Electro Magnus** (5.12a) No topo. Brilliant, exposed climbing. Climb the northwest arête on the far right side of the face. 7 bolts to 2-bolt chain anchor. 70'.

51. **Shrieking Chimnoids** (5.7+) No topo. On the narrow west face of the fin. Move up right in a crack and into a chimney that slowly widens. Where it eases back, step left to a 2-bolt chain belay/rap anchor on a blocky ledge or continue up the slab above to the fin summit. **Descent:** Scramble off along the top of the fin to the road. **Rack:** Selection of medium to wide cams.

RIBBIT WALL

The south-facing Ribbit Wall is the analogue to the New Wave Wall because it's on the opposite side of the broad fin. Access the wall by doing the 5.6 downclimb between the first and second pullouts east of Windy Point, walking west down the corridor below the New Wave Wall, and scrambling down and around the west side of the fin to the wall. Otherwise, descend talus from milepost 14 just east of Windy Point, then follow the path through woods past the Wind Wall to Indigo Tower. Scramble down below the end of New Wave Wall. Ribbit Wall is to the left (east). You can scope out the Ribbit routes by climbing on top of a low fin directly south of the wall. Routes are listed from left to right when facing the wall.

52. **Acid Rain** (5.10 R) Face climbing up the left edge of the face. Begin below the southeast arête on the far left margin of the wall. Climb up and over a roof to an overlap with a bolt. Continue up the blunt arête (hard to get pro) to a ledge. Step right to a 2-bolt belay/rap station or continue over the roof above to a low-angle prow. 1 bolt. 135'. **Descent:** Rap 80' from the bolted station or walk off from the summit. **Rack:** Stoppers, RPs, and a good selection of Friends.

53. **West of the Pesos** (5.11c) Thin, continuous climbing. Joins *Two for a Peso* at the 5th bolt. Begin below a small overlap. Climb up left past 2 bolts to a bolt above a narrow roof. Angle up right along incipient cracks to a 2-bolt chain anchor on a ledge. 8 bolts. 120'. **Descent:** Rappel 80'. **Rack:** Quickdraws and small gear.

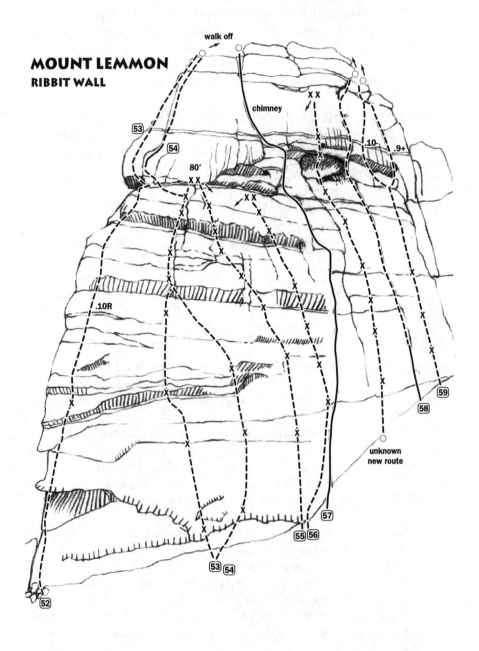

MOUNT LEMMON
RIBBIT WALL

walk off

chimney

53

54

80'

.10-

.9+

.10R

59

58

unknown
new route

57

55 56

53 54

52

54. **Two for a Peso** (5.10) 2 pitches but most climbers only do the first. Excellent, thin face climbing! **Pitch 1:** Same start as Route 53, only edge directly up past 3 bolts, angle up left to bolted incipient cracks, then on to a 2-bolt chain anchor on a ledge. **Pitch 2:** Step left and work up a wide crack over a roof. Follow the crack up right to face climbing and the fin summit. **Descent:** Rappel 80' from the bolted stance or walk off the from summit. **Rack:** Quickdraws for 1st pitch and medium to large Friends for 2nd pitch.

55. **Coyote Business** (5.10c) More fun edging up the banded wall. Begin up the slope from Route 54. Balance and edge up and left to a 2-bolt chain anchor on a ledge. 7 bolts. 65'. **Descent:** Rappel 80'.

56. **Mexican Radio** (5.10b) A great route, but kind of scary getting to the 1st bolt. Begin same as Route 55 but climb up to a thin crack, move up left, and follow a line of bolts to a 2-bolt anchor. 6 bolts. **Descent:** Rappel or lower 55'.

57. **Coati Trot** (5.10a) Same start as Route 55. Follow right-angling cracks (work at getting good pro) up to a cave. Move left, pull up a steep crack out the right side of the cave, and follow a wide crack to the summit. 125'. **Descent:** Walk off. **Rack:** Stoppers, RPs, TCUs, and Friends.

58. **Dog Meat Tacos** (5.9 R) Not often climbed. If you fall—you're dog meat! Begin below intermittent cracks. Runout climbing up the cracks leads to the right side of a cave feature. Finish up a wide crack out the right side of the cave to the top of a pillar and the summit. 120'. **Descent:** Walk off. **Rack:** Stoppers, RPs, TCUs, and Friends.

59. **Windsong** (5.10-) Good but somewhat runout face climbing. Begin just right of *Dog Meat Tacos*. Face climb up banded rock past 3 bolts, pull a small roof, and follow incipient cracks to a long roof. Pull the right side (5.9+) or the left (5.10-) and face climb to another bolt. Finish up easier rock to the top of the fin. **Descent:** Walk off. **Rack:** Mostly small gear.

STOVE PIPE

This 70-foot-high pinnacle sits immediately west of the New Wave Wall/Ribbit Wall fin. Approach it by following directions to Indigo Tower or New Wave Wall. The Stove Pipe formation is obvious. Routes, located on both the north and south faces, are described from the right side of the north face. **Descent:** There are summit anchors for a rappel descent on the south side.

MOUNT LEMMON
STOVE PIPE

chains
XX

chains
XX

61

61
62

63

60

60. **Stove Pipe Pinnacle** (5.7) The easiest route on the tower gets you to its airy summit. Begin on the right side of the north face. Climb an easy crack onto a ledge and head up the west ridge to the top.

61. **Tangent** (5.11d) Sport. Begin below a short crack on the right side of the north face. Excellent face climbing follows a line of 8 bolts up the right margin of the face, just left of a lower-angle ridge, to a 2-bolt chain anchor just below the summit. **Descent:** Rap or lower 65'.

62. **Sine Wave** (5.12c) A sport direttissima up the center of the north face. Begin same as *Tangent*, only veer up left after the 3rd bolt. Finish at a 2-bolt chain anchor. 8 bolts. 65'. **Descent:** Rap or lower 65'.

63. **Flyboy** (5.12b) Sport. Spread your wings and get ready to soar! Begin on the left side of the north face. Steep edging leads up left to a blunt arête. End at a 2-bolt chain anchor on the left shoulder of the tower, well below the summit. 6 bolts. **Descent:** Rap or lower 40'.

From the north face, drop down around the overhanging east side of the tower, past a couple of projects, to the south face. The next two routes are located on the left side of the south face, left of an obvious chimney. No topos.

64. **Footnotes** (5.11d) Sport. Steep, thin face climbing past 9 bolts to a 2-bolt anchor. **Descent:** Rap or lower 60'.

65. **Dial A Muffin** (5.11d) Sport. Left of *Footnotes* on the left side of the face. Face climb past 7 bolts to a 2-bolt anchor. **Descent:** Rap or lower 60'.

SPECTRE ROCK

This blocky tower/fin is just west of Stove Pipe and immediately south of Wind Wall. All the described routes are on the south face. Access by following directions to Indigo Tower or New Wave Wall. Descend between Stove Pipe and New Wave Wall and turn right under Stove Pipe's south face. Follow a trail through thick brush to the base of Spectre Rock's south face. Routes are listed right to left. **Descent:** For all routes, rappel from a 2-bolt chain anchor above a deep chimney on the north side of the rock.

66. **Sibling Revivalry** (5.10+) Up the right side of the south face. Start from a flat boulder. Step left to the 1st bolt on the shoulder. Continue up the face past 2 more bolts to a ledge. Climb the face above on blunt edges (2 more bolts) to the top. 90'. 5 bolts.

67. **If** (5.9) Above a tree, work up a chimney behind a thick flake. Then face climb up left to a wide crack. Continue past a tree to the summit. 100'. **Rack:** Medium to large cams.

68. **If Direct** (5.10) Begin down left from *If* below a small arch. Face climb over the arch to a bolt. Thin face moves past 3 more bolts lead to the right-angling *If* crack system. Follow the *If* crack to the top. **Rack:** A variety of medium to large cams for upper cracks.

69. **Home Sweet Home** (5.9 R) Just right of a deep chimney. Climb an easy crack past the right side of a roof. Move left above the roof, then up 20' to a bolt. Easier rock above leads to the top. **Rack:** Tricky pro placements with wires, Aliens, and TCUs.

70. **Bertha Butt** (5.6) Climb the deep, see-through chimney—back and foot to squeeze up high. 90'.

71. **Road Bimbos** (5.9) Begin in the obvious chimney and climb to a horizontal break and a fixed pin and bolt on the left. Face climb straight up good edges on the face left of the chimney past 3 bolts to a break. Continue on easier rock above. 90' to top.

72. **Bonsai** (5.10) The left side of the face. Begin left of the chimney. Steep face climbing protected by 2 bolts leads to a horizontal overlap. Move left over the overlap to another bolt. Continue up past 2 more bolts to easier climbing and the summit. 90'.

BIG PINE TOWERS

These blocky, side-by-side towers offer a good selection of short, mostly moderate routes on their west faces and long, hard lines up their east faces. The towers are named for a huge pine tree that grows in a corridor between the south end of the towers and Rupley Tower A.

Approach Big Pine Towers from the second pullout east of the Windy Point parking lot. There is room for a couple of cars at this pullout. The access trail begins on the left (east) side of the pullout by a guardrail. Descend the steep trail through a scree/boulder field. The towers are to the left. Northwest side routes are on the left side of the formation. Southeast side routes are reached via the corridor with the big pine on the right. Route descriptions begin on the west end of the towers. North face routes are listed right to left, while south side routes are left to right.

MOUNT LEMMON
NORTHWEST SIDE OF BIG PINE TOWERS

no bolts shown   75   74   73

NORTHWEST SIDE

73. **Recovery Room** (5.9+) Sport. Quality face climbing. Scramble through trees to the northwest corner of the first tower. Climb excellent granite flakes up the edge of the buttress. 6 bolts to 2-bolt chain anchor. 50'.

74. **The Sloth** (5.11c) Sport route. Begin just left of Route 73 and right of a chimney. Climb the narrow face. 5 bolts to 2-bolt anchor. 45'.

75. **Malpractice** (5.10) Sport. Start 15' left of a chimney. Edge up great flakes on the steep, slabby wall. Finish left of the chimney. 6 bolts to 2-bolt anchor. 50'.

76. **The Trench** (5.8) No topo. Begin up left of Route 75 on boulders. Move up a thin crack 10' to a bolt. Continue up cracks to a right-facing corner. Finish at *Malpractice's* anchors. 1 bolt to 2-bolt anchor. 45'. **Rack:** Mostly small gear-RPs, wires, and TCUs.

77. **Splat** (5.10 R) No topo. Begin 5' left of Route 76. Follow a left-angling crack to a bolt 20' up. Follow a left-angling crack to the top. 1 bolt. 40'. **Descent:** Rap from boulders.

78. **Wicked Indecency** (5.8+) No topo. Fun jamming! Go uphill to the next small formation. An obvious crack splits the face. Jam the finger crack through bulges and corners to summit anchors. 45'. **Rack:** Small to medium gear.

SOUTHEAST SIDE

These routes, mostly hard sport climbs, are reached by hiking through the corridor with the huge pine tree. Routes are listed left to right. No topos.

79. **Coronary Bypass** (5.11b) Sport. This route ascends a steep face between 2 chimneys left of the big pine tree. Face climb past 4 bolts to a narrow stance below a yellow face. Clip the bolt on the ledge and climb left up the edge of a blunt arête to another bolt. Step right and finish up an overhanging headwall to summit anchors. 5 bolts.

80. **Pine in the Ass** (5.12b) Sport. Located on an overhanging wall directly across from the pine tree. Begin by stepping up left to a small stance just right of the deep chimney. Follow the line of bolts up the steep, banded face above. 9 bolts to 2-bolt anchor. 60'.

81. **Pins and Needles** (5.12a) Begin 10' right from the pine tree. Hard moves up thin seams to the 1st bolt. Continue up steep rock past 2 bolts to a steep finger crack that leads to the top of the rock. 75'. **Rack:** Lots of small gear.

82. **Honker** (5.12c) Sport. Well-protected, quality, and recommended. If you do the moves straight up to the 1st bolt, it's 5.12d. Same start as

Route 81. Climb thin seam to 3 bolts. Work up the crack above until it's possible to step left 5' to a bolt. Follow the line of big "honker" bolts up the steep, flaked wall. 8 bolts to bolted anchor. 75'.

83. **Lemmon Arête** (5.12d) Sport. Begin below a wide chimney. Climb groove in the chimney until you can move left to a bolt on an arête. Climb the yellow-and-black streaked arête left of the chimney to anchors. 7 bolts to 2-bolt anchor. 70'.

84. **Crashing by Design** (5.12c) Same start as Route 83 at chimney. Work up the steep yellow arête right of the chimney. 8 bolts to 2-bolt anchor. 75'.

85. **Cat in the Hat** (5.12a) A fun, airy sport route. Begin at an alcove/slot below a chimney. Climb a thin crack up white rock left of an arête (hard to protect) to a bolt on the right side of the arête. You can also reach this bolt from the right or stick-clip it. Continue over the right side of a roof on the arête and follow to anchors. 7 bolts to 2-bolt anchor. 60'.

86. **Catclaw** (5.11d) Sport. Start 10' right of a chimney/slot. Climb broken ledges for 25' to a bolt. Steep face climbing right of the chimney leads to anchors and slings. 6 bolts to 2-bolt anchor. 50'.

87. **Prowess** (5.12a) Good, short, and sport. Walk 75' right of Route 86 and boulder onto a ledge, or traverse onto it from farther right. Climb the excellent, southeast-facing wall just left of a sharp arête. 4 bolts to 2-bolt anchor. 40'.

RUPLEY TOWERS

These towers are directly below the second pullout east of Windy Point and offer some of Mount Lemmon's classic, well-traveled routes. Routes are on the tall, southeast faces and the shorter, northwest walls that face the highway.

Approach by scrambling down a rough climber's trail that begins from the left side of the second pullout by the guardrail. Keep left on the trail to reach a corridor between the Big Pine Towers on the left and the Rupley Towers on the right. Southeast side routes are reached by going through the corridor below Big Pine Towers. Past the big pine, look for a trail that drops down right and follows the cliff's base. Routes are listed right to left. The routes on the northwest faces are reached by walking right from the corridor along the base of the cliffs. These routes are listed left to right.

SOUTHEAST SIDE

88. **Litigation** (5.9-) On the south face of Tower A. Begin below the right side of the south face just left of an oak. Climb a seam for 15' to a

small roof. Clip a fixed piton in a groove above. Climb the low-angle groove above the roof to a thin crack in a right-facing corner. Follow a crack/seam up a wall with a fixed pin to the easy but somewhat runout slab climbing to the base of a headwall split by a crack that leads to a belay ledge. 75'.

89. **Capitol Punishment** (5.11d) Use the same start as Route 88. At the first fixed piton, use a long runner and keep left of a left-arching crack to a bolt. Climb up and left above a large roof past 2 bolts. Stay left to a right-facing corner. Jam and lieback up the corner to a slab to a finishing crack. 3 bolts. 75'.

90. **War Zone** (5.10+) A classic 2-pitch route. This strenuous route ascends a crack system up the right-hand face of Tower B. **Pitch 1:** Jam a right-angling hand and fist crack to a small ledge 25' up and belay. **Pitch 2:** Climb up rotten cracks and past a loose bulge into a good, right-facing dihedral. Lieback up the slabby dihedral until it's possible to move into a right-angling crack system.

91. **Whodunit** (5.11) Begin just left of Route 90. Face climb 20' to a bolt, then up right on flakes 20' to another bolt. Thin edges lead to the 3rd bolt. Above, climb good flakes up left and join *Sheer Energy*. 3 bolts. **Descent:** Rappel off the backside from bolt anchors. **Rack:** Small gear.

92. **Sheer Energy** (5.9) On the south face of Tower B. Start just left of the right corner of the face. Climb a thin crack up through a slot. Follow the crack into a right-facing corner below a large roof. Face climb left of the roof on good holds and move up a slab above to another crack, which leads to lower-angle, black rock. Finish up thin cracks in the headwall above. 140'. **Rack:** Generous selection including wires, TCUs, and Friends.

93. **R-1** (5.8+) 2 pitches. A recommended Rupley trad classic up Tower B first done in the 1960s. **Pitch 1:** Begin below a large flake. Swing up the left side of the flake for 10'. Traverse right 10' across top of the flake into a left-facing corner. Jam and lieback up the corner and over a small roof to a bolt. Traverse left around an overhanging, blocky corner to a belay ledge with 2 bolts right of a tree. **Pitch 2:** Stem up a left-facing corner with a wide crack to a small tree. Step left and work up a wide crack past a couple small roofs. Finesse up the thin crack above to incipient cracks and white bands to a summit belay. **Descent:** Rappel off the backside from anchors. **Rack:** A large selection including Stoppers, TCUs, and Friends.

MOUNT LEMMON
RUPLEY TOWERS

rap anchors
on back

Tower B

Tower A

Big Pine Towers

walk off

X X

X

94

X

93

92

91

90

91

89 88

FP

X

X X XP

X

X

94. **R-2** (5.6+) Route climbs a long chimney between Towers B and C. Start just left of Route 93 below a chimney. Boulder up a groove (5.6) into a squeeze chimney, which widens to a chimney, to the notch left of Tower B. **Descent:** Walk off from the back side. **Rack:** Medium to large cams and runners.

95. **R-3** (5.8) 2 pitches up Tower C. Another moderate classic. Begin on the right side of the southeast face. **Pitch 1:** Follow a left-angling ramp to a bolt. Sweet face climbing up excellent flakes and cracks past 3 bolts, then easy left to a large ledge with a 3-bolt anchor. **Pitch 2:** Up the left-facing corner above, then face climbing up right to an obvious, wide crack. Squeeze up the chimney to the summit. **Descent:** Rappel off the back side anchors. **Rack:** Generous assortment of gear from Stoppers to large cams.

96. **Bop 'Til You Drop** (5.10a) 2 pitches. The 1st pitch is popular and fun. Reach toprope anchors from behind. **Pitch 1:** Finesse up a steep slab with 3 bolts to cracks, then on to a large belay ledge with a 3-bolt anchor. **Pitch 2:** Airy and good. Pull up roofs to the large roof on the left edge. Fire over to a bolt and bop up the face just right of the left

MOUNT LEMMON
RUPLEY TOWER D

To rap anchors on backside

Tower D →

hands

100

99

98

97

edge past 1 more bolt to the top of Tower C. **Descent:** Rappel (single rope) from anchors on the backside of the tower to the ground. **Rack:** Small and medium gear.

97. **R-4 (5.9)** 1 long pitch to the summit of Tower D. Quality route! Start from the right side of Tower D's southeast face. Edge 20' up thin edges to a bolt. Move over small ledges past a hanging block. Continue up right on easier climbing to a stance before working back left under a long, obvious roof. Jam a hand crack over the roof and follow the crack to a plated headwall and the summit. **Descent:** Rappel off the backside from anchors on top. **Rack:** Stoppers to hand-sized cams.

98. **Moving Over Stone (5.11a)** Sport route with a short crux. Begin 10' left of R-4 where a right-angling ramp meets the ground. Face climb up left to a bolt, continue up flakes past 2 bolts and a bulge, and follow 3 bolts over more bulges to the left side of a juggy roof. Fire over roof on good holds and continue up excellent flakes to the top. 10 bolts. 155'. **Descent:** Rappel off the backside from anchors on top. **Rack:** Quickdraws.

99. **R-5 (5.8+ R)** 2 pitches. Begin on the left side of the face below a water groove. **Pitch 1:** Up the groove 60' to a belay ledge with a tree. **Pitch 2:** Traverse right from ledge and follow vertical cracks up right to a headwall. Here join route 98, and at the top, traverse lower-angle rock to the right of the summit block. **Descent:** Rappel off Tower D's backside from anchors. **Rack:** Stoppers and Friends.

100. **Trouble in Paradise (5.8+)** An exposed alternate 2nd pitch for *R-5*. Start from *R-5's* belay ledge. Climb above the tree on the ledge and follow 4 bolts up the blunt arête above to the summit.

NORTHWEST SIDE

The northwest side of Rupley Towers, facing the highway above, offers some fine, single-pitch routes. These climbs are shaded on warm mornings and are reached by descending the rough trail down the scree/boulder field from the second pullout east of Windy Point. Before reaching the big pine, go right on a trail along the base of Rupley Towers. There are no routes on the back side of Tower A. Routes are listed left to right. No topos.

101. **Summer Offensive (5.11a)** This route and Route 102 are on the abrupt left face of Tower B. Expect thin, exposed cranking. Carefully scramble down the loose gully below the wall and set up a belay. Step across to the main wall at a right-facing, arching flake and clip a bolt. Climb up and left on flakes and edges to a short, left-angling crack with yellow lichen. Work up the crack to a bolt and head straight up past 2 more

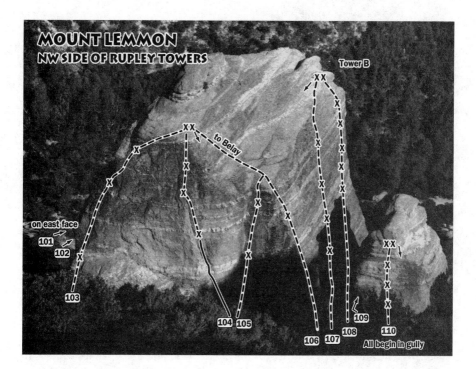

bolts. Above, step right onto a narrow ledge with a 2-bolt chain anchor. 5 bolts. 65'.

102. **Pocket of Resistance** (5.12a) The right-hand route on the left face of Tower B. Same gully start as Route 101. Clip a bolt and lieback a flake corner up right. Reach another bolt up left from the uppermost lieback and crimp thin edges to a narrow ledge and 2-bolt chain anchor. 4 bolts. 65'. **Rack:** Quickdraws, wires, and small cams.

103. **Backside** (5.6 R) Begin at the left corner of Tower B's north face. Climb knobby rock past a bolt to a ledge. Easy moves lead past 2 more bolts to the flat summit. 3 bolts. **Descent:** Single-rope rappel from chain anchors right of the route finish.

104. **Crash and Burnham** (5.10) Watch out! Has had some serious groundfalls. Begin left of a deep chimney by the northwest corner of Tower B. Lieback and jam up a left-facing corner for 30' to a bolt. Above the crack, the line becomes a seam. Climb past 2 bolts to 2 cold-shut summit anchors. 3 bolts. 45'. **Rack:** Small gear.

105. Trauma Center (5.11b) Same start as Route 104, but where the corner angles left, step right below a shallow right-facing corner to a bolt. Climb corner to a bolt at the top and mantle onto the summit. Belay from Route 104's anchors. 2 bolts. 45'. **Rack:** Small stuff.

106. Ground Zero (5.10 R) Serious. Scramble into a gully on the west side of Tower B, just right and below Route 105. Stiff climbing up a left-angling, left-facing corner to the left-side exit past a large roof. Continue up a thin crack in the corner to undercling/lieback moves out an arch. Don't fall through this section—you'll hit the corner below. Thin edges lead to a bolt, then more thin moves followed by jugs. 1 bolt. **Rack:** Small and medium gear.

107. Cerebral Jig (5.11d) Start from boulders in the gully below the right-hand face of Tower B. Jam and lieback a left-arching crack. Make a long reach at the end of the arch and clip a bolt. Thin face climbing leads up the steep, banded face past 4 bolts to the summit and a 2-bolt chain anchor. 5 bolts. 70'. **Rack:** Small and medium gear.

108. Border Patrol (5.10a) A modern classic! Start from boulders in the gully (same as Route 107). Climb a short crack to a narrow shelf for your hands. Work right to a good lieback crack and pro. Climb up right and follow a line of bolts up the excellent, steep slab. 5 bolts to 2-bolt chain anchor. 70'. **Rack:** Small and medium gear.

109. Out on Bail (5.9+) No topo. Sport. This climb and Route 110 are on a small, blocky pinnacle immediately right of Tower B. Begin in the gully between Tower B and the pinnacle. This line climbs the left wall of the pinnacle. Flakes, liebacks, finger jams, and underclings lead past 4 bolts to a 2 cold-shut anchor. 6 bolts. 40'.

110. Kick the Bottle (5.10) Sport and short. 3-bolt face climb to 2-bolt anchor on north side of pinnacle. 30'.

TRI-LEVEL SPIRE

This narrow, blocky spire, standing more or less by itself, sits southwest of Rupley Towers. Approach via the Rupley Towers southeast side approach. From the base of Tower D, follow a trail down and left to the base of the southeast face of Tri-Level Spire. These routes are listed from right to left. The northwest side routes are reached by continuing along the base of Rupley Towers. These routes are listed from left to right.

MOUNT LEMMON
TRI-LEVEL SPIRE
NW FACE

NORTHWEST FACE

111. **Afternooner** (5.11b) Sport. A must-do Lemmon neo-classic! This route ascends the highest tower. Climb superb flakes and edges up the face to anchors just below the summit. 7 bolts to 2-bolt anchor. 75'.

The following two routes are on the west side of the farthest west buttress on Tri-Level Spire. Follow the trail downhill from *Afternooner* to the base of these routes. No topos.

112. **Cliptomania** (5.12a) Sport. Crucial holds have broken off, so it probably doesn't go anymore. Start on the far right (west) side of the northwest face. Thin, technical moves past 6 bolts to a 2-bolt chain anchor. 60'.

113. **Prancer** (5.11b) Sport. Begin just downhill from Route 112 on the northwest corner of the buttress at an obvious hole in the rock. Move out right to a bolt and edge onto the narrow, west face. Climb abundant flakes up the superb yellow-lichen face to a bolted summit belay. 7 bolts. 70'.

SOUTHEAST FACE

114. **Slip Knot** (5.11) Sport. Scramble left onto a large ledge that splits the face. Climb directly up the center of the middle tower to the spire's summit. 9 bolts to 2-bolt chain anchor.

115. **Help on the Way** (5.10+) Begin on a large ledge behind a large, semiattached boulder. Move up right onto a right-angling ramp. Work into a left-facing flake/crack (handle the thin flake with care!). Jam and lieback the crack to an alcove under a large roof. Jam a thin crack through the roof to the summit of the left shoulder. 1 bolt.

116. **Unknown** (5.11b) Sport. Start left of the large boulder on the ledge. Face climb up flakes along incipient cracks to a short arête. Pull onto a shoulder and finish up a yellow wall to a 2-bolt chain anchor on the lip. 6 bolts.

117. **Pumping Philosophy** (5.9 R) This climb and the following routes are on the lower tier below the large ledge. This is a good toprope route. Begin below a right-angling seam/crack. Clip a bolt and climb up right along seams (dicey pro) to a high bolt. Climb onto a stance below the block boulder and swing up its edge past another bolt to a belay atop the flat block. 3 bolts. 60'. **Rack:** RPs, wires, and TCUs.

118. **Dr. Sniff and the Tuna Boaters** (5.10a) Sport. A quality face and good toprope route. Begin at the same place as Route 117. Step up left to a

MOUNT LEMMON
TRI-LEVEL SPIRE, SE FACE

116

114

115

walk off →

MOUNT LEMMON
TRI-LEVEL SPIRE, SE FACE

var.

walk off ledge

118

117

119

bolt, and climb great flakes and edges to the large ledge and belay. 6 bolts. 50'. **Descent:** Walk off right on the ledge.

119. **Sweet Surrender** (5.11d) Sport. A long, sustained pitch. Begin below an obvious slot/cave feature on the far left side of the south face. Follow a right-angling crack, then face climb to a bolt (30'). Edge up right past 3 bolts to a beautiful, black-and-yellow, right-facing corner. Stem and face climb the corner past a bolt to the final bolted headwall. An easier alternative finishes left up cracks at the top of the corner. Belay atop the buttress. 7 bolts. 140'.

ANDURIEL TOWER

Anduriel Tower is a tall, slender fin about 150 feet northeast of Big Pine Towers. Approach it by hiking along the base of Big Pine Towers to the base of the tower's overhanging prow. Another choice is to park at the third pullout east of Windy Point. Hike down a steep trail over boulders to the base of the tower. Routes are listed left to right on the southwest face.

120. **Leapin' Lizards** (5.12d) A crimp nightmare! Thin crimping leads up the slightly overhanging face. 6 bolts to 2-bolt chain anchor. 40'.

121. **Arkshelly** (5.9) Climb the left side of a large, left-facing flake. Above, work right and mantle into a water groove. Go through a notch to the 2-bolt chain anchors on a ledge on the opposite side. **Descent:** Rappel from chains on the opposite side of the tower. **Rack:** A selection of small to large gear.

122. **Bubblenutz** (5.11b) Sport. Great face climbing. Scramble down a gully to a 2-bolt chain belay on a slab. Climb over thin overlaps to a narrow roof, then pull out the left side of the roof. Continue up excellent edges to 2-bolt chain anchors below the lip of the right-hand summit. 7 bolts. **Rack:** Some wires give extra pro.

123. **Birthday Girl** (5.10b) Sport classic. Begin from the same slab belay as Route 122. Step right onto the face and move up right over small roofs to an immaculate slab. Edge into a thin, right-facing corner before exiting (exposure) left onto the upper wall. Finish up good edges to 2-bolt chain anchors below the lip. 7 bolts.

124. **Arizona Flighways** (5.11d) Sport. Excellent, 3-star route up the overhanging prow. Getting harder because holds are breaking. Easiest approach is from the northeast side of the tower. Scramble down bouldery slopes to the base of the prow. Follow the line of 9 bolts to a 2-bolt chain anchor.

125. **Miss Adventure** (5.10b) Good route on the right side of Route 124's prow. No topo.

Eric Scully on the overhanging sport route *Arizona Flighways* (5.11d), Anduriel Tower.

MIDDLE EARTH

Middle Earth is a 300-foot-high, northwest-facing wall hidden on the east side of Willow Canyon. Over 20 sport routes, put up by Scott Ayers and friends, lace this climber-friendly wall. The crag, lying at 7,000 feet, is a good summer area, especially in the morning when the wall is in the shade. All of the described routes are well protected, with lots of beefy 3/8-inch bolts and lowering/rappel stations. **Rack:** 20 quickdraws and two ropes are needed. A 200-foot (60-meter) rope is useful on some routes.

Finding the crag: The crag is obscure, but not hard to find. Drive past Windy Point to milepost 15 and park at a pullout on the right (east) side of the highway 0.4 mile past the mile marker. Walk up the shoulder of the highway a short distance to a drainage on the left (west) that is just south of a blocky rock formation with an arch. Follow a rough trail up the drainage to the ridgeline above and locate a better trail that contours north through forest on the west side of the ridge. Continue down this slowly descending trail to the slabby top

of Middle Earth. Follow the trail north above the slabs to an obvious path that descends loose boulders and gravel on the north edge of the slabs. Below the slabs, the path cuts left and follows the base of the slabs to the base of the cliff. Allow 20 to 30 minutes to approach. Routes are listed left to right from the left side of the cliff.

126. **Project** (5.13+) Still unclimbed in 1998. 7 bolts to 2-bolt chain anchor.

127. **Delirious** (5.12a) Recommended pump. Scramble onto a ledge. Follow bolts up and left. 2 bolts to 2-bolt chain anchor. 80'.

128. **Irresistible** (5.12c) Good and continuous. Go up right after the 4th bolt of *Delirious*. Finish up an excellent corner. 13 bolts to 2-bolt chain anchor. 85'.

MOUNT LEMMON
MIDDLE EARTH

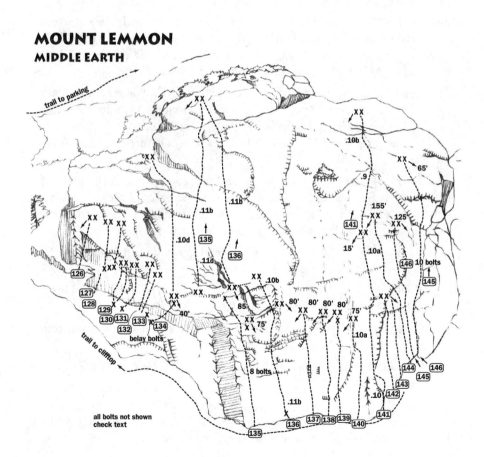

129. **The Gift** (5.12d) A fine route until the top-out because some of the holds are falling apart. Class 3 onto a ledge below a cave to begin. 7 bolts to 2-bolt anchor. 55'.

130. **The Bump** (5.12d) Belay from a bolt on a ledge. Pull the big roof, then finesse it. A hold broke and it hasn't been climbed since then. 6 bolts to 2-bolt anchor (same as *The Gift*). 55'.

131. **The Breeze** (5.11b) A classic and easiest line on the left side. Belay from a bolt on a ledge to start. Expect underclings and long moves between big jugs. Follow buckets out the big overhang. At the top, go right onto a ledge, then straight up to anchors. 8 bolts to 2-bolt anchor. 55'.

132. **Fireball** (5.12b) Belay from a bolt on a ledge. Long reaches between decent crimps. Watch the bouldery crux. 5 bolts to 2-bolt anchor. 45'.

133. **Red Hot** (5.12b) A superb sport line. Belay from the bolt on the ledge. 7 bolts to 2-bolt anchor. 45'.

134. **The Roof of the Homeless Yuppie** (5.11d) 2 pitches. Maybe the worst route on the wall. Begin on the far right side of a ledge at a belay bolt under a 10-foot roof. **Pitch 1:** Climb the roof (5.11d). 6 bolts to 2-bolt anchor. 40'. **Pitch 2:** 5.10d. 11 bolts to 2-bolt anchor.

135. **The War of the Worlds** (5.12a) 2 pitches. Pitch 1 is recommended. Some of the bolts seem a little suspect. **Pitch 1:** 16 bolts to 2-bolt anchor on the left side of a ledge. Pitch 1 variation goes up right to 2-bolt anchor.Lower 75'. **Pitch 2:** 18 bolts to 2-bolt anchor on top. Walk off.

136. **The Planet Eater** (5.11b) 2 pitches. A long, good route, but gets sort of monotonous on the 2nd pitch. **Pitch 1:** 14 bolts to 2-bolt anchor on a ledge. Convenient 1st pitch anchor at 80'. **Pitch 2:** 16 bolts to 2-bolt anchor on top. **Descent:** Rappel the route with 2 ropes.

137. **Premonition** (5.12a) Very good. Underclings and shallow corners. 10 bolts to 2-bolt anchor. 80'.

138. **Hobbit in a Blender** (5.12a) Thin edging, technical moves, and multiple cruxes. 10 bolts to 2-bolt anchor. 85'.

139. **S'Blended** (5.11b) Just right of Route 138. Edges, crimps, and thin moves. 10 bolts to 2-bolt anchor. 85'.

140. **Grand Opening** (5.11a) High crux. 9 bolts to 2-bolt anchor. 75'.

141. **Silmarillion** (5.10b) 2 pitches. Sustained 5.10 face moves up the 1st pitch. **Pitch 1:** 15 bolts to 2-bolt anchor on a ledge. 155'. **Pitch 2:** Face climbing to jugs over a big roof. 8 bolts to 2-bolt anchor on top. **Descent:** Walk off or rappel the route with 2 ropes.

142. **You Betcha It's Sketchy** (5.10d) Low cruxes. 8 bolts to 2-bolt anchor. 75'.

143. **Middle Earth** (5.10a) A long, slab pitch. Step right at the 8th bolt to Route 144's anchors for a shorter 5.9 pitch. 14 bolts to 2-bolt anchor. 155'. **Descent:** Rappel the route with 2 ropes.

144. **Earth Angel** (5.9) Easiest route on Middle Earth. Good warm-up with lots of bolts. 9 bolts to 2-bolt anchor. 70'.

145. **Centennial** (5.11b R) A long, sustained face route up the right edge of the wall. Runout and scary in places. 19 bolts to 2-bolt anchor. 165'. **Descent:** Rappel the route with 2 ropes.

146. **Pull Me Up** (5.10d) Begin just left of the deep chimney on the right side of the face. Go left across *Centennial* at 5th bolt. 14 bolts to 2-bolt anchor. 125'.

RIDGELINE

This is a superb cliff for moderate leaders, with a selection of well-protected sport routes. It's also a good summer crag, with cool temperatures and afternoon shade. All the routes are bolted. **Rack:** Quickdraws only.

Finding the crag: Drive up the Mount Lemmon Highway to mile 18.4 and park in one of the pullouts by the obvious, huge slide area of jumbled boulders, just before Sollers Point Road. Hike up a trail just left (west) of the rocky drainage on the west side of the slide. As the trail flattens out, it follows the draw up right to a saddle in the ridgeline. Turn left (west) and follow a dirt trail marked by a cairn to a fork just past some fallen trees. A group of broken cliffs is visible through the trees to the right just before the fork. Ridgeline is the obvious, good-looking wall on the left. Take the right fork and hike up to the base of the crag. Allow 15 to 20 minutes to reach the cliff. Routes are described left to right.

147. **Unknown** (5.10a) Start by the left-most of three pines at the base. A slabby start to an overhang at the 4th bolt. Then cruise easy rock. 6 bolts (brown hangers) to 2-bolt chain anchor. 60'.

148. **Firezone** (5.9) Begin just right of a tall, thick pine tree at the cliff's base. Climb up a slab right of a right-facing corner, then up overlaps. 4 bolts with brown hangers to 2 large cold shuts. 50'.

149. **Sudden Impact** (5.7) A bouldery slab start to a juggy overhang. 4 bolts to *Firezone*'s anchors. 50'.

150. **Never To Be the Same** (5.6) A slab start to an easy overhang. Finish up excellent rock to high anchors. 7 bolts to 2-bolt chain anchors. 100'.

151. **Wind of Change** (5.7+) Begin 10' right of Route 150. Fun climbing up great rock. 7 bolts to 2-bolt chain anchors. 85'.

152. **Two Birds With One Stone** (5.7) Just left of the lone pine at the cliff's base. Boulder up a groove behind the pine, then step left to the 1st bolt. Grab good edges to anchors. 6 bolts to 1 large cold shut anchor. 75'.

153. **Glowing in the Distance** (5.9-) Same start as Route 152. Expect some thin, delicate face moves. 6 bolts to 2 large cold shut anchors (same as Route 152). 75'.

154. **Unknown** (5.8) Good, but a little run-out. 4 bolts to 2-bolt anchor.

155. **Grid-Locked** (5.10b/c) Perfect stone, perfect edges. The far right-hand route up a smooth, steep, green wall above a short gully. 5 bolts to 2-bolt chain anchors.

SUMMIT CRAGS

Mount Lemmon's summit area offers a selection of excellent crags. Due to space considerations, however, they are not covered in this guide. These cliffs are cool in the summer when heat envelops the lower elevation crags.

Rappel Rock, a large and popular cliff, offers a superb selection of multi-pitch classic routes. There are lots of link-ups that create three-star routes. Some of the best lines to do include *Black Quaker* (5.7), *Chiboni* (5.9+), *Voodoo Child* (5.11a), *Black Magic Woman* (5.10d), and *The Corner* (5.8+).

Nearby are The Murray Wall, The Fortress, and The Ravelin. Lots of bolted sport routes are found on these awesome crags. The Murray Wall, on the backside of The Ravens, yields some pumpy and bouldery 5.11 and 5.12 routes up to 50 feet long. The Fortress is a large, knobby wall with a spectacular assortment of both sport and traditional routes from 5.7 to 5.11. The Ravelin's southeast face offers stunning views and a handful of great bolted routes characterized by small knobs and edges. Must-do lines here are *Fern Roof* (5.10c), *Crystal Roof* (5.11b), and *Crystal Ball* (5.11c).

Information on these and other cliffs, including The Reef of Rocks on the north side of Mount Lemmon, are found in the guidebook *Squeezing the Lemmon*. Information and topos to the newer sport routes are found in *Climbing Magazine* #144 and a stapled sport climbing guide available at Tucson mountain shops.

LEVIATHAN DOME

OVERVIEW

The north slope of Pusch Ridge, a long, jagged ridge on the west slope of the Santa Catalina Mountains, is studded with immense cliffs and domes. Dramatic views of the ridge unfold from suburbs and shopping centers along Arizona Highway 77 north of Tucson. This remote but visible area is protected in Coronado National Forest's 56,933-acre Pusch Ridge Wilderness Area. The wilderness is a rugged sanctuary that offers a stunning diversity of plant communities and wildlife near the edge of Tucson, Arizona's second largest city.

Climbers find many excellent rock climbs on Pusch Ridge's numerous backcountry crags. One of the best and most popular cliffs is Leviathan Dome, a 1,000-foot-high wall of north-facing, metamorphosed granite. The dome, perched above deep Alamo Canyon, is flanked on the west by Solitude Dome, while Wilderness Dome looms above. The ten-pitch *North Face,* one of Arizona's best long routes, offers a variety of crack, face, and traversing pitches. The steep, streaked wall right of *North Face* yields Jim Waugh's sustained and difficult seven-pitch route *Over the Rainbow.*

Leviathan Dome, despite its proximity to Tucson, gives a true wilderness climbing experience. It begins with a heinous bushwhack, typical of Arizona approaches, from Catalina State Park, which includes three hours of boulder-hopping up a usually dry creek bed and thrashing through thickets of underbrush to the base of the dome. The routes themselves are straightforward enough, but climbers should be competent and fast. Many parties, especially those already familiar with the lines, are able to ascend the routes car-to-car in a day. Others opt to hike in the night before and camp in the canyon below the wall. Jim Waugh advises that if you want to do *North Face* in a day, "Get an early start, be really fast, and carry a headlamp."

Climbing history: The first ascent of Leviathan's *North Face* route was a five-year project that began with Merle Wheeler and Joanna McComb's 1972 attempt at the featureless-appearing wall. The pair pushed the route two pitches up the initial slab before bailing. Wheeler returned with Dave Baker and extended the line to the base of the upper headwall before failure. A couple of years later, Baker returned to the project with Gary Hervert and the talented Rich Thompson, who was killed in a fall on Mount Lemmon in 1977. The trio found the key to the route—a long 5.7 traverse to the right that gained a long corner system and led to the summit. Their attempt, however, was aborted high on the wall. A week later, Hervert and Brett Oxbury snagged the first complete ascent of the face, aiding a few critical sections. In 1977, Dave Baker and Fig climbed the route all free.

Over the Rainbow, a difficult free route up the streaked west face of Leviathan Dome, was conceived and executed by Phoenix hardman Jim Waugh. Waugh

LEVIATHAN DOME

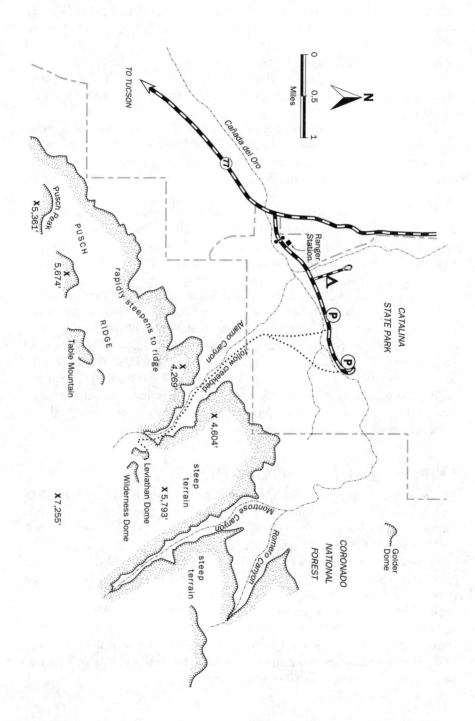

coupled with Ray Ringle to first establish the route in 1981 as *West Face.* The following spring he came back with Jim Zahn and freed this intricate and demanding line. It has seen few repeats. A third route on Leviathan, *User Friendly,* was established in 1989 by local guidebook author Bob Kerry and Jeff Mayhew.

Since its first ascent, Leviathan Dome's *North Face* has become one of Arizona's best classic long routes. Despite its popularity, you'll rarely encounter another party on this wilderness dome. The routefinding on the cliff is sometimes intricate, but it's hard to get off route. **Descent:** A two-rope rappel, then scrambling down the east flank of the dome.

The best climbing season on Leviathan Dome is from October through December. The cliff is mostly north facing, so it does get shade on hot autumn days. Likewise, it can be chilly on cool days. The other good season is springtime, but the dome is closed to climbing from January 1 through April 30 for bighorn sheep lambing.

Besides the two described routes in this chapter, there are a couple of other good lines on Leviathan Dome. *User Friendly* (III 5.9) is a good seven-pitch route up the slabby wall left of the *North Face.* This climb is less committing and much easier than *North Face,* with only a couple of 5.9 sections. Another good route is *3-D Witch Hunt,* a three-pitch variation to *North Face.* This line works up the shallow dihedrals left of *North Face*'s upper crack system before joining its last two pitches. *Backcountry Rockclimbing in Southern Arizona* has topos and descriptions of both routes. Lots of other great routes are found on Pusch Ridge, including *Solitude* (III 5.10 A2) and *The Deep* (III 5.9) on Solitude Dome, *Rivendell* (III 5.10 R) on Wilderness Dome, and the classic *Cherry Jam* (III 5.8+) and *Crescent Crack* (III 5.9) on Table Mountain. Golder Dome, northeast of Catalina State Park, has some fine shorter lines and a relatively easy approach. Again, consult the comprehensive guide for route information.

TRIP PLANNING INFORMATION

General description: A couple of excellent, multipitch routes up a 1,000-foot dome on the north flank of Pusch Ridge on the west end of the Santa Catalina Mountains.

Location: Southern Arizona, north of Tucson.

Camping: Public camping is found at Catalina State Park off Arizona 77.

Climbing season: October through December is the prime season because the dome is currently closed to access in springtime.

Restrictions and access issues: The dome is in Pusch Ridge Wilderness Area in Coronado National Forest. The west part of the wilderness area is currently closed annually from January 1 through April 30 for bighorn sheep lambing. Travel during these months is restricted to established trails. Hikers and climbers may not venture more than 400 feet off the trails.

scramble to summit

LEVIATHAN DOME

1

2

Guidebooks: *Backcountry Rockclimbing in Southern Arizona* by Bob Kerry, Backcountry Books of Arizona, 1997, has descriptions and topos to Leviathan Dome, as well as many other fine routes on Pusch Ridge.

Nearby mountain shops, guide services, and gyms: The Summit Hut and Bumjo's Climbing Shop in Tuscon. Rocks & Ropes is the Tucson gym.

Services: All services are found in Tucson, including great Mexican restaurants. Cheap showers are available at Kino Veterans Memorial Center on the south side of Tucson.

Emergency services: Call 911. Kino Community Hospital, 2800 East Ajo Way, Tucson, AZ 85713, 520-294-4471 and Tucson General Hospital, 3838 North Campbell Avenue, Tucson, AZ 85719, 520-318-6300.

Nearby climbing areas: Lots of excellent routes on other domes and crags on Pusch Ridge. These include *Cherry Jam* (5.8+) and *Crescent Crack* (5.9) on Table Mountain; Jim Waugh's route *Rivendell* (5.10 R) on Wilderness Dome behind Leviathan; and finally, routes on the 400-foot-high Golder Dome east of Catalina State Park. For directions and topos to other quality backcountry crags on Mount Lemmon, check the comprehensive guidebook, *Backcountry Rockclimbing in Southern Arizona*.

Other Tucson climbing areas include all the crags along the Mount Lemmon Highway (Green Slabs, Chimney Rock, Windy Point, Middle Earth, etc.), Milagrosa Canyon (sport routes below Mount Lemmon), Sabino Canyon, and Esperero Spires. Farther afield are Baboquivari Peak and crags on Kitt Peak.

Nearby attractions: Saguaro National Park, Sabino Canyon, Colossal Cave, Tucson attractions; Tucson Mountain Park, Old Tucson, Arizona-Sonora Desert Museum, Catalina State Park, Fort Lowell Museum, San Xavier del Bac Mission, Madera Canyon, Santa Rita Mountains.

Finding the dome: Drive north from Tucson on Oracle Road/Arizona 77 to Catalina State Park. Turn right into the park and drive to the visitor center. Pay the daily entrance fee and drive 1.5 miles to a parking area and trailhead at the end of the road. From the trailhead, follow Romero Canyon Trail across wide Sutherland Wash to a trail junction on its far side. Go right on Birding Trail. Follow the trail to a Y-junction and go left. After the trail climbs a series of steps made of railroad ties, look for a bench on the left in front of an abandoned, overgrown road. Go left up this road, which quickly becomes a trail heading southwest up a broad bench. The trail reaches the bottom of Alamo Canyon after about 1 mile.

This point can also be reached by a good trail that begins from the picnic area. Park at the trailhead for Romero Ruin. Cross the road and follow Romero Ruin Interpretative Trail across Sutherland Wash to its far side. Where the trail goes left at a trail sign, take an unmarked right fork that climbs east onto a bench below a hill and then gently ascends to Alamo Canyon.

From the edge of the canyon, follow a trail left above the canyon. After a

2-rope rappel from
slings on trees off back
to saddle

To summit

chimney
.6

.9

X Bad pin
.10

.7

.10a

.9

.7R

.7

.9

.8+

.10c

SLAB X X

.8+

LEVIATHAN DOME
NORTH FACE

1

2

short distance, it dips into the dry streambed. A faint path also traverses the scrubby, saguaro-covered slopes left of the creekbed, but it is bushy and hard to find. Hike up the streambed for a couple of miles. This involves lots of boulder hopping, occasional bushwhacking, and routefinding through flash flood debris. Eventually you reach a canyon fork directly below Leviathan Dome, where there are some good bivouac spots. Finally, scramble uphill to the base of the dome. The *North Face* route begins at the toe of the buttress. Reach *Over the Rainbow* by hiking right (south) up along the base of the wall. Allow three hours of hiking from the parking lot to the base of the dome.

1. **North Face** (III 5.10c R) 10 pitches. This route ascends the almost 1,000-foot northwest face of Leviathan Dome. Most parties bivouac below the dome, climb the route, and descend to the parking lot the next day. Parties familiar with the approach, route, and descent have done car-to-car in a day. Carry a headlamp and leave bivy gear with your packs. Begin the route at the toe of the buttress. **Pitches 1 and 2:** Work up cracks and slabs to an obvious, bushy belay ledge. **Pitches 3 and 4:** Climb cracks and corners to a ledge. **Pitch 5:** A long, horizontal, traversing lead (5.7 R) with scant protection. **Pitches 6 through 10:** Climb the long, obvious crack and dihedral system to the obvious tree at the top of the dome. **Descent:** Scramble northeast down the back side to a tree with rappel slings. Make a 2-rope rappel from the tree to a small saddle. Scramble down and around the north side of the dome to your packs at the base of the route. **Rack:** A generous rack with sets of wired nuts and TCUs, plus double sets of Friends and 2 ropes.

2. **Over the Rainbow** (III 5.12a) 7 pitches. A serious, demanding, and aesthetic route put up by Jim Waugh and Ray Ringle in 1981 and free climbed by Waugh and Jim Zahn in 1982. It's possible that it has not had a second free ascent. Begin 200 feet or so up right of the toe of the buttress and the start of *North Face,* right of the striped wall. **Pitch 1:** Face climb (5.7) to a Class 4 section with loose blocks to a ledge system. 100'. **Pitch 2:** Begin on the right side of the ledge. Climb a left-facing dihedral (5.9) until you're 15' below a left-angling roof system. An off-route bolt is below the roof. Committing face moves go out left to a hanging belay below the roof. **Pitch 3:** Climb out left below the roof past a fixed pin and a bolt to crux moves with your hands on the lip of the roof (5.11+). Work into a left-facing corner left of the roof (5.10) to a thin crack/seam. Crux tips liebacking (5.12a) leads up the crack system until it's possible to exit left and face climb to a 2-bolt belay. The knifeblade protecting the crux may be missing. **Pitch 4:** Traverse right to a left-facing corner. Climb (5.10) to a semi-hanging

scramble
to rappel

2-rope rappel from
trees off back
to saddle

.7

.9

X 10+
X
X FP

.9

X
X X .10
.11 X
X X SB

X X .10
SB
tips LB
.12

.11+
use lip
of roof
X X SB

X off route!
.9

.9

LEVIATHAN DOME
OVER THE RAINBOW

4th
loose

.7

belay stance. **Pitch 5:** A serious and intricate traversing pitch. Climb up and left past 4 bolts (5.10) to a stance. Traverse out left (5.11) and up to a bolt and stance. Continue up left to a hanging belay. **Pitch 6:** Jam a crack (5.9) to a thin section with 1 fixed piton and 3 bolts (5.10+) to a belay stance left of the eyebrow-shaped roofs. **Pitch 7:** Follow the obvious crack up the openbook to a high belay ledge. Above, scramble to the dome summit. **Descent:** Scramble northeast down the back side to a tree with rappel slings. Make a 2-rope rappel from the tree to a small saddle. Scramble down and around the north side of the dome to your packs at the route's base. **Rack:** Should emphasize the small stuff-2 sets of RPs, a set of TCUs, a selection of mostly small and medium wired nuts, 2 sets of Friends, and 2 ropes.

BABOQUIVARI PEAK

OVERVIEW

Baboquivari Peak towers above the southern Arizona desert 60 miles southwest of Tucson. The distinctive 7,734-foot-high granite monolith is one of the few mountains in Arizona that requires technical climbing to reach its lofty summit, while its sheer east face harbors most of the state's Grade VI routes.

The peak, the high point of the 30-mile-long Baboquivari Range, is a sacred site to the Tohono O'odham or Papago Indians. The mountain and the range are the home to the deity I'itoi, or Elder Brother. This not-always benevolent desert god resides in a cave that he enters through a maze of corridors on the flank of the peak. Legend says I'itoi came to this world from a world on the other side and led his people, whom he had turned into ants, up here through an ant hole. He then changed them back to the Tohono O'odham and helped them with his magic. I'itoi often appears in basketry as a male figure above a maze pattern, creating a daily reminder to his people that they must find their way through the maze of life and overcome all kinds of obstacles.

Rock climbers also overcome many obstacles along their chosen vertical paths up the holy peak. The easiest way up Babo is via *Standard Route,* a hike with a bit of Class 4 scrambling near the summit, on the peak's west flank. The other easy way is *Forbes-Montoya Route* up the opposite side of the mountain. This mostly hiking route has two climbing pitches, one of which is the famous Cliff Hanger or Ladder Pitch. A metal and wood suspended stairway once ascended this rock slab. Now the climber ascends the face, tying off old ladder anchors for protection. An unprotected 5.6 move is the route's crux. Baboquivari's East Face, flanked by the classic *Southeast Arête* on the left and *Humungous Woosey* on the right, is Arizona's "big wall." Some hard aid routes, including the *Spring Route, Dreams of I'itoi, Cradle of Stone,* and *Harvest Moon,* ascend the 1,500-foot-high wall.

BABOQUIVARI PEAK

Climbing history: The first ascent of Baboquivari was undoubtedly made by Indians, although no trace or record remains of their passage. Spanish Captain Juan Mateo Manje first noted the peak in 1699. He wrote in his diary of "a high square rock that . . . looks like a high castle." He called it Noah's Ark. The first recorded ascent of the great peak was by University of Arizona professor Dr. R. H. Forbes and Jesus Montoya. Beginning in 1894, Forbes attempted the peak four times before finally succeeding on the north side on July 12, 1898. The key was a "grappling hook" that allowed him to extend his reach to positive holds on a blank rock section. The pair built a huge bonfire, seen as far as 100 miles away, atop the mountain to signal their success to friends below. Forbes made his sixth ascent of Babo on his 82nd birthday in 1949.

Baboquivari's first real technical route was *Southeast Arête*. Five Arizona climbers, Dave Ganci, Rick Tedrick, Tom Wale, Don Morris, and Joanna McComb, ascended the airy ridge route in 11 pitches on March 31, 1957. The route became an instant classic and remains the most popular technical route up Babo.

The peak's imposing and overhanging east face remained unclimbed until 1968. Gary Garbert first showed Bill Forrest the wall in 1966. The pair scoped the face and thought they detected a thin crack system up the center of the wall that would offer a direct route. After humping loads to Lion's Ledge, a slashing ledge system they named for a cougar they saw on it, they started up the first pitch. After nailing 75 feet in five hours, they decided they weren't up for the task yet and retreated. Another attempt later that year again resulted in failure, this time due to uncooperative weather. In 1968, Forrest recruited George Hurley, and in April the duo began the route. They climbed four pitches the first day, finding thin nailing in discontinuous and rotten crack systems. Tied-off angle pitons were hammered into shallow holes to avoid bolt placements. After three more days of hard aid, Forrest and Hurley stood on the summit atop what they called The *Spring Route.* Forrest later wrote, "We felt a pulsating sense of accomplishment and elation—the route, once improbable, was now a reality . . . we could not have been more thankful for life, for once again it was unquestionably ours."

More hard and serious aid lines have gone up the East Face. These include *Cradle of Stone* (V/VI 5.11- A4) by Jim Waugh and Steve Grossman, *Harvest Moon* (IV 5.11R A0) by Waugh and Eric Johnson, Universal Traveler (VI 5.10 A4) by John Steiger and Fig, *Dreams of I'itoi* (V/VI 5.10 A4) by Steiger and Fig, and *The Fellowship* (VI 5.10+ A4). *Harvest Moon,* a mostly free line beginning in Cougar Cave, is highly recommended. The other routes all offer devious and difficult aid climbing. Topos are available in *Backcountry Rockclimbing in Southern Arizona* or by asking at Tucson climbing shops.

Spring and fall are the best seasons for climbing Baboquivari Peak. Bad weather can occur, including high winds and rain. Winter days can also be good. Snow and ice, however, make the descent off the top of the peak treacherous. Many climbers bivouac at the saddle below the face to maximize climbing time on the short winter days. Summer days are usually too hot, although cool spells can occur. Carry plenty of water.

Watch for loose rock, particularly on *Southeast Arête.* It's a good idea to wear a helmet. The approach to the cliff can be time consuming. Plan to hike for a couple of hours. Tote a headlamp or flashlight in case you get stuck on the descent route after dark. Carry sufficient water, particularly during hot weather. A gallon per day per person would not be too much. Drink often. If you're getting thirsty, you're already dehydrated.

TRIP PLANNING INFORMATION

General description: A classic ridge route up the granite monolith of Baboquivari Peak, a sacred mountain to the Papago Indians.

Location: Southern Arizona, southwest of Tucson.

Camping: Primitive camping is available near the road's end before the ranch.

Consider hiking up to the saddle east of the peak and bivouacking there so you get an early morning start.

Climbing season: October through April are the best months. Winter days can be cold and the descent route is sometimes snow-covered and treacherous. Summer is usually just too hot.

Restrictions and access issues: The area is in Baboquivari Peak Wilderness Area and subject to wilderness regulations. Treat the land around the ranch with respect because it is private property with a public access easement. Treat the mountain with respect, also, because it is a sacred place to the Tohono O'odham Indians.

Guidebooks: *Backcountry Rockclimbing in Southern Arizona* by Bob Kerry, Backcountry Books of Arizona,1997, has topos and/or descriptions for many of Babo's routes, including the Grade VIs.

Nearby mountain shops, guide services, and gyms: The Summit Hut and Bumjo's Climbing Shop in Tuscon. Rocks & Ropes is the Tucson gym.

Services: All services are found in Tucson, including great Mexican restaurants. Cheap showers are available at Kino Veterans Memorial Center on the south side of Tucson.

Emergency services: Call 911. In Tucson are Kino Community Hospital, 2800 East Ajo Way, Tucson, AZ 85713, 520-294-4471 and Tucson General Hospital, 3838 North Campbell Avenue, Tucson, AZ 85719, 520-318-6300.

Nearby climbing areas: Santa Catalina Mountain crags and domes, Mount Lemmon crags, Elephant Head (Santa Rita Mountains), Mendoza Canyon and the Coyote Domes, and Kitt Peak crags (Aquagomy and 10-4 Wall). Details and descriptions for these and other areas are in *Backcountry Rockclimbing in Southern Arizona*.

Nearby attractions: Kitt Peak National Observatory, Coyote Mountains Wilderness Area, Tohono O'odham Indian Reservation, Buenos Aires National Wildlife Refuge, Nogales, Tubac Presidio State Historical Park, Tucson attractions.

Finding the mountain: There are two approaches to Baboquivari. The best one, described here, is the eastern approach. Drive west on Arizona Highway 86 (from Tucson and Interstate 10 or 19) to Three Points (Robles Junction). Turn left (south) on Arizona 286 and drive 28 miles to a right (west) turn just past (0.3 mile) milepost 16. Follow this unpaved road for 2.8 miles to an intersection. Go right on another dirt road and continue up Thomas Canyon until you reach a ranch gate at 6.4 miles. Park along the road here before the locked gate.

Go through the gate and walk up the road for about 0.5 mile. Follow signs around the ranch buildings to the mountain access trail up Thomas Canyon. The ranch is private property, but the trail is open to hikers. Respect the privilege of crossing the ranch. The trail works up the east side of Thomas Canyon below

Babo's east face for almost 2 miles, then switchbacks up the loose upper canyon slopes to a 6,380-foot-high saddle on the mountain's north flank. Allow at least two to three hours of hiking time with a pack to the saddle. This spot makes a good bivouac spot for an early morning start. Leave your packs here and rack up for the climb.

To reach the base of the route, you need to follow Lion's Ledge, a prominent, tree-covered ledge system that angles south below Babo's intimidating East Face. To reach the ledge from the saddle, descend a short distance back down the main trail and look for a trail that goes left, marked by a cairn. Follow this obvious path up and across some gullies and through brush. Some routefinding is required. Eventually you will reach the north end of Lion's Ledge. Bushwhack south along the ledge through dense underbrush to the route's start below *Southeast Arête* and just left of an immense boulder below the wall. In most years, a spring drips water into strategically placed buckets at Spring Cave midway across the ledge. Don't camp here and disturb this unique environment.

1. **Southeast Arête** (III 5.6) 6 to 8 pitches. The described pitches might vary from your experience. Some pitches can be combined together with different belay stances and there are various ways each pitch can be climbed. Follow the path of least resistance and you'll be all right. Start below a short, right-facing corner beside a huge boulder. **Pitch 1:** Climb a crack for 30' to a bulge. Pull over (5.5) and climb easier rock

Photo by Jim Waugh.

past a brushy ledge to another ledge covered with prickly pear cacti. Belay here. **Pitch 2:** Move up right into a steep corner. Stem and face climb up the corner to a small tree. Continue up a Class 4 chimney to a belay at a notch. **Pitch 3:** Work up a steep, exposed arête to a brushy ledge. Move up left on loose rock and stem up a corner with a tree to more broken rock. Belay on a boulder ledge below a short headwall. **Pitch 4:** Lieback and face climb (5.6 crux) up the headwall to easier rock and a ledge with a juniper and pine tree. 120'. **Pitch 5:** Traverse left about 25' to a 2-bolt belay ledge. **Pitch 6:** Fun climbing (5.3) leads up a left-facing dihedral above the belay. Atop the dihedral, climb up right on broken, vegetated rock and belay where convenient. After the second climber reaches the belay, scramble up brushy Class 3 slopes to a deep notch. Keep left at the notch for an easier downclimb to a belay tree in the notch. **Pitch 7:** Climb loose, stacked blocks above the notch (5.6) to easier climbing. Belay from a tree. Above, scramble up easy ground to the summit of the peak. **Descent:** The best way off is to make 5 rappels down the route with 2 ropes, using trees for anchors. Otherwise you can descend the *Forbes-Montoya Route* on the north side of the peak. It may take some routefinding to locate the rappels and descent line if you haven't been on this route before. Allow ample time for getting lost. If you get off the trails the underbrush is very thick. **To rappel the route:** Scramble back down the ridge to the belay tree atop Pitch 7. Rappel 1: 60' from the tree to a ledge in notch. Scramble out of the notch and downclimb to the belay tree atop pitch 6. Rappel 2: Rap 130' from the tree to a 2-bolt anchor on a ledge. Traverse right 25' around corner to the juniper and pine tree ledge. Rappel 3: Rap 150' from the juniper tree to the tree in the corner on pitch 3. Hard pulling the ropes here. Rappel 4: Rap 130' from the tree to a ledge with bushes on pitch 2. Rappel 5: Rap 165' from the bushes to the base of the route. Bring some extra webbing for rappel slings. **To downclimb:** Go down a path on the north side and scramble down right to the top of the Ladder Pitch. Make a double-rope rappel 150' down the pitch. At the base of the pitch, scramble left along the cliff's base to some slabs. Downclimb right to a 2-bolt anchor and rappel. Go left (north) from the base of this rappel to a notch. Rappel or downclimb a chimney below and follow a trail back to the saddle above Thomas Canyon.

OTHER TUCSON AREAS

OVERVIEW

There are many other climbing areas in the Tucson area, including lots of backcountry adventures and some sport climbing crags. Some of the areas, like La Milagrosa Canyon, are not included in this guide because of access issues or wildlife closures. Others, while offering excellent climbing, are just so off-the-beaten-track that they are seldom climbed. And don't forget the typically heinous, three-hour Arizona approaches to the bases of these remote areas through forests of catclaw acacia, manzanita, cactus, and yucca. For more information, consult *Backcountry Rockclimbing in Southern Arizona* or ask at Tucson mountain shops.

PUSCH RIDGE

Pusch Ridge is a long, craggy ridge that drops west from the crest of the Santa Catalina Mountains to, Oracle Road on the north side of Tucson. The many domes and cliffs on the ridge's north flank offer excellent wilderness routes. Table Mountain, a huge, flat-topped rock wall, has some awesome routes. *Cherry Jam* (III 5.8+), the best of the lot, is a superlative six-pitch line up the central buttress. *Crescent Crack* (III 5.9), following crack systems right of *Cherry Jam*, is also worth doing. Solitude Pinnacle, right of Leviathan Dome, has a couple of good routes—*Solitude* (III 5.10 A2) and *The Deep* (III 5.9). *Rivendell* (III 5.10), a good six-pitch line up a remote 600-foot-high face, ascends Wilderness Dome behind Leviathan. Golder Dome, while not on Pusch Ridge proper, is a 400-foot-high, north-facing cliff east of Catalina State Park. Some fun moderate, multipitch routes climb the slabby wall.

SABINO CANYON

Sabino Canyon is a 4-mile-long canyon that drains southwest out of the Santa Catalina Mountains to Tucson. Some good climbing is found on gneiss cliffs in the lower part of the canyon. The Acropolis, a 500-foot-high, northwest-facing cliff on the right side of the lower canyon, offers some of the best routes. The routes are up to four pitches long. Watch for bad rock sections. Suggested routes are *Moira* (5.11a), *Colorado Crush* (5.10a), and *Sisyphus* (5.11b/c). The Kor Wall, a flying buttress on the left side of the Whipple Wall farther up the canyon, is ascended by the *Kor Route* (5.8). This popular line, put up by Layton Kor and George Hurley in 1969, yields five pitches of interesting climbing with occasional 5.7 runouts. The Fruitstand, a short hike up Hutch's Pool Trail from the shuttle road's end, is a good moderate crag. There are nine routes from 5.4 to 5.9 lacing the slab.

LA MILAGROSA CANYON

La Milagrosa Canyon, lying along the south base of the Santa Catalina Mountains, is a sport climbing area with almost 100 bolted routes. The cliffs, composed of banded metamorphic rock, offer excellent climbing during the winter. Both sun and shade can be found on the north- and south-facing cliffs. Some private property between the parking area and the canyon has created access problems. Ask at one of the local shops for current access information as well as topos to the cliffs. The area is reached via the Catalina Highway and Synder Road, southeast of the Mount Lemmon Highway.

THE DRY

The Dry is a developing limestone area above Dry Canyon on the east side of the Whetstone Mountains southeast of Tucson. Jon Winsley and Eric Scully established most of the described routes in 1998.

Finding the crag: Drive east on Interstate 10 from Tucson to Exit 302. Exit and turn south on Arizona Highway 90. Drive south for about 12.5 miles to a dirt road. Turn right (west) and drive to a T-intersection. Go right. Take the first left and follow the road west up Dry Canyon. Eventually, a long limestone band appears high on the ridge to the right. Take the first right (north) toward the cliff band. Car type determines how close you can drive to the cliffs; a four-wheel-drive vehicle is best. Hike down through a gully and cut left past a water tank. Approach is easiest at the far left end of the band. The approach time from the parking area to the left side of the cliff is 15 minutes, and it takes another 15 minutes along the band to the biggest cave. Routes are listed left to right along the cliff's base.

1. **Procrastination Proclamation** (5.12c)
2. **Way to Dry** (5.12a)
3. **Swallow Crack** (5.10a) Up an obvious dihedral. 4 bolts to anchors.
4. **Lord of the Bees** (Project) The white wall beneath an overhang.

The next two routes are on the edge of the large cave with the flat roof.

5. **The Spark** (5.13c/d) A project to the second set of anchors.
6. **Wailing Baby** (Project)

Routes on the right side of the cave.

7. **Renaissance** (5.13b) The recommended route. First line bolted at The Dry.
8. **Butterfly Hiccup** (5.11c)

MENDOZA CANYON

Several large, granite domes are found in Mendoza Canyon in the Coyote Mountains southwest of Tucson. The range is protected in the Bureau of Land Management's Coyote Mountains Wilderness Area. A lot of routes have been done here, but most are not climbed much. Expect a long approach hike, variable rock quality, and some scare factor on some routes. Mendoza Canyon is a good winter area, with lots of sun.

The big, south-facing domes in lower Mendoza Canyon have some great backcountry routes up their big, slabby walls. Recommended routes on Elephant Dome include The *Elephant's Trunk* (II 5.7), a fun, four-pitch line, and *Elephantiasis* (III 5.10c), six pitches up the center of the wall. Table Dome has popular *Wily Javelina* (III 5.9), *Table for Two* (III 5.10a), and *Beggar's Banquet* (III 5.9).

KITT PEAK

The Kitt Peak National Observatory, the world's largest solar telescope, crowns Kitt Peak, southwest of Tucson and the Coyote Mountains. Some good slab climbing is found at Aquagomy and the 10-4 Wall along the road to the observatory. Aquagomy is a bright white slab between mileposts 5 and 6. A handful of friction routes, protected by both bolts and natural gear, ascends the 500-foot-high cliff. The 10-4 Wall is just up the road.

SOUTHEAST ARIZONA

COCHISE STRONGHOLD

OVERVIEW

Southeastern Arizona is a rumpled land punctuated by mountain ranges that loom over broad, sediment-filled basins. One of the most beautiful ranges is the north-south trending Dragoon Mountains, a rugged sierra dividing San Pedro Valley on the west from Sulphur Springs Valley on the east. The Dragoons, crossed by Spanish soldiers in 1695, were first dubbed the "Sierra muy Penascosa" or the Very Rugged Mountains. Later the range received a new name from the Dragoons, mounted soldiers armed with rifles, who were sent against the warring Apaches in the 1860s.

The central part of the Dragoons, a fantastic maze of cliff-lined canyons and ridges studded with domes and cliffs, is called Cochise Stronghold after Cochise, a respected Apache chief. His band of Apaches, called the Chokonen or "Tall Cliffs People," used the central Dragoons as a natural fortress. The rocky area was a superb bastion against attack, with numerous secret hideouts and sweeping views of the surrounding countryside.

Through the 1860s, Cochise and his band engaged in a prolonged war with the American government over white settlement in southeastern Arizona. With the mindset that "100 white men should die for every Apache killed," the Chokonen Apache caused hundreds of deaths and thousands of dollars in property damage before a satisfactory truce was reached in 1872. Cochise died, presumably of cancer, in 1874 at his beloved camp in the East Cochise Stronghold. His white friend Thomas Jeffords visited Cochise the day before his death, then participated in his burial at a remote sepulchre in the heart of the Stronghold. The chief's body was decorated with warpaint and mounted on a favorite horse. His family and tribe marched the horse 12 miles to a remote site and buried Cochise in a walled-up grave filled with stones and dirt. Jeffords reported, "His favorite horse was shot within 200 yards of his grave, another horse was killed about one mile away, and a third animal was shot about two miles distant. This was done with the idea that he will find a horse when he needs it in the spirit land." Legend says that Cochise was buried with a treasure in gold, silver, and turquoise, but the grave has continued to elude fortune seekers.

Treasure of a different sort awaits visitors to the Cochise Stronghold's labyrinthine fastness. For rock climbers, the treasure is a marvelous and magical sanctuary of granite domes and cliffs that invites vertical exploration. The Stronghold, for many Arizona climbers, is simply the best climbing area in the state. It's a wild and somewhat remote place that offers superb, multipitch routes up chickenhead-festooned faces, as well as some marvelous crack climbs. No one is quite sure how many routes have been ascended in the Stronghold, but some locals say that more than 500 routes have been established so far. Many area climbers want only basic information divulged about this fabulous playground. Out of deference to these wishes, this guide documents a selection of the best classic routes found in the Stronghold. For more information, you should consult the comprehensive guide *Backcountry Rockclimbing in Southern Arizona* or ask around in Tucson for topos and details on many of the area's newer routes.

Cochise Stronghold is divided into two main areas—the East Stronghold and the West Stronghold. The East Stronghold, the first area to be developed by climbers, is split by Stronghold Canyon. Several deep side canyons drain east into this wide canyon. Numerous domes stud their steep, brushy slopes, including Entrance Dome, Out-of-Towners Dome, and Stronghold Dome. Many excellent face routes up to 700 feet long ascend these cliffs. The Rockfellow Domes, named for early settler John A. Rockfellow, perch atop a ridge above Stronghold Canyon. This group of bullet-shaped domes, reminiscent of The Needles in California, harbors a selection of three-star crack and face routes. Cochise Dome, ascended by the mega-classic route *What's My Line*, sits in a hidden canyon east of the Rockfellow Domes. Be advised that some of the crags in the East Stronghold are closed to climbing during the spring months due to raptor nesting.

The West Stronghold, lying at the eastern terminus of Stronghold Canyon West, is composed of several deep canyons lined with domes and cliffs. This area yields some superb, multipitch slab routes up Westworld and Whale domes, as well as short routes on smaller crags. South of the West Stronghold on the western flank of the Dragoon Mountains is the sport climbing area Isle of You and the Sheepshead area, also called the Southwest Stronghold. Several immense, west-facing domes are laced with routes up to 900 feet long.

The Dragoon Mountains is a fault-block range lifted above the flanking valleys along fault lines. The Cochise Stronghold, in the range's midsection, is formed by the 73-million-year-old Stronghold Granite. This huge intrusion of pale granite has weathered along joints and fractures into today's craggy topography. The granite is ideal for climbing—a rough, abrasive surface dotted with numerous flakes, edges, and large handholds called "chickenheads." These chickenheads are one of the Stronghold's most distinctive climbing features, forming large "Thank God" holds. Some routes, like *What's My Line*, wander

COCHISE STRONGHOLD

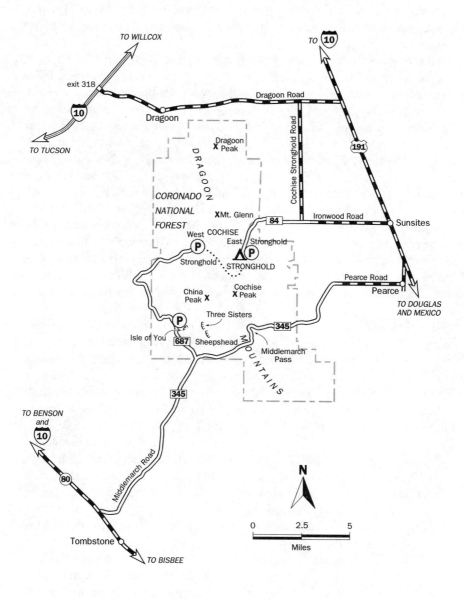

up faces literally covered with chickenheads, where the leader ties them off for protection or slots nuts between them. Chickenheads are often dioritic pods that resist erosion better than the surrounding field granite. Erosion by water breaches the erosion-resistant surface and attacks the softer granite underneath.

Climbing history: The first climbers here were undoubtedly the Apaches, who used the cliffs as lookouts for game or intruding enemies. The first technical climbers came in the 1960s, quietly doing a few routes but leaving few records. Beginning in 1970, Mark Axen and Merle Wheeler were the first to really start climbing at the Stronghold. The 1970s was the golden age for climbing at the Stronghold. During this decade, Tucson climbers, including Mike McEwen, Dave Baker, Mark Axen, Steve Grossman, Merle Wheeler, and Rich Thompson, began frequenting the area. Most of today's classics were put up during that clean climbing era with an emphasis on style and boldness. Landmark ascents were *What's My Line* by Baker, Larry Seligman, and Peter DePagter in 1971; *Days of Future Passed* by Grossman, Thompson, and Baker in 1973; *Abracadaver* by McEwen, Baker, and Grossman in 1975 (McEwen led the corner, a flawless on-sight); and *As the Wind Cries* on Chay Desa Tsay by Grossman, John Steiger, and Paul Davidson in 1979. McEwen, by all accounts, was a brilliant free climber and undoubtedly one of the best in the early 1970s for his routes here and around Tucson.

The 1980s brought consolidation. All the obvious, classic routes had been done, so climbers began venturing onto the steeper, seemingly blank faces. In 1979, a couple of Brits, Pat Littlejohn and John Motherseal, ventured onto the forbidding Entrance Dome and put *Echoes* up the wall's right side. Karl Rickson and Mark Pey established *The Wasteland* to the left of Entrance Dome, creating an instant classic up the chickenhead-strewn face. On the Rockfellow Domes, Ray Ringle and Chip Chase climbed the difficult *Uncarved Block*, *Sound of One Hand Thrashing*, and *Sensory Desuetude*. In 1981, Ringle and Jim Waugh added *Jabberwock*, a beautiful corner that yielded the area's first 5.12 lead. As the 1980s closed, area climbers began exploration of the West Stronghold. In 1989, Eric Fazio-Rhicard and Bob Kerry, who later wrote the Stronghold's comprehensive guidebook, established *Warpaint*, an excellent, five-pitch slab route up Westworld Dome. They later came back and added many of the bolts on this neoclassic route. Kerry and Josh Tofield did the first ascent of the moderate classic *Moby Dick* on Whale Rock.

The 1990s saw further exploration and controversy, with new crags developed and new routes established by a variety of tactics. Because all the good cracks had been ascended, climbers sought out lines on blank faces that required bolt protection, creating a turf war in this area that previously had a staunch ground-up ethic. Traditional Stronghold climbers sought to keep new activists from drilling everything in sight. The result was the squeezing of lines on many formations. Activisits included Scott Ayers, Mike Colby and Mike Strassman.

Cochise Stronghold is in Coronado National Forest. The only climbing regulation currently in effect is cliff closures for nesting peregrine falcons from February 15 to June 30. The area closed includes Rockfellow Domes and Cochise Dome. Check with the Forest Service or at the campground for updated closure areas and dates. The ban could be lifted in the future. Climbers should minimize their impact on the rock and the surrounding topography to help preserve this fragile area. Follow existing trails to the cliffs whenever possible. Carry out all your trash, including cigarette butts, Mylar wrappers, and wads of tape. Remember that this is not a convenience bolting area. Don't add bolts to existing routes and if you're in search of new routes, use bolts sparingly. Many existing routes were climbed without bolts. Ask around before you jump on that stellar-looking line and sew it up with drilled anchors.

Rack: Gear information is given for many of the routes. Keep in mind that this is only a suggestion. What you may or may not actually need on the rock is up to you. Take a close look at your proposed line and determine what you need to safely climb it. A general rack should include sets of RPs and Stoppers, two sets of Friends or equivalent camming units, and at least a half-dozen, 2-foot runners. Some crack routes might require a large crack piece like a #6 Camalot for an off-width. Other routes require many slings for tying off chickenheads for protection and belay anchors. A standard 165-foot rope is fine, although a 200-foot (60-meter) rope is useful for running pitches together. Two ropes are necessary for rappelling off many crags, including End Dome, Rockfellow Dome, and The Whale. You might need extra webbing to reinforce or replace old slings at rappel points on some routes.

TRIP PLANNING INFORMATION

General description: A maze of domes and cliffs in the East Cochise Stronghold and the West Cochise Stronghold of the Dragoon Mountains, with superb single and multipitch crack and face routes up excellent granite.

Location: Southeastern Arizona, east of Tucson.

Camping: For the East Stronghold, Cochise Campground, a Coronado National Forest recreation site, sits at the road's end. This fee area offers water, restrooms, and picnic tables. Otherwise, primitive campsites are found along the rough road just northwest of the canyon's entrance. Take the first right past the cattleguard at the forest boundary and pick a site along the road. For the West Stronghold, many excellent, shaded campsites are at the end of the road into the area. Pack out your trash, disperse fire rings, and dispose of human waste properly.

Climbing season: Year-round. Spring (March and April) and fall (October and November) are the best times for warm, sunny days. Winter also offers great climbing weather, with mostly sunny but cool days. Snowfall is generally infrequent and short-lived. Expect cold nights. It can also be too cold in the shade for pleasant climbing. Summer days are usually too hot, except in the morning, although shaded cliffs can be found.

Restrictions and access issues: Cochise Stronghold is in Coronado National Forest. The Rockfellow Domes and the surrounding area, including Cochise Dome, Waterfall Dome, Squaretop, and Lower Squaretop, are closed for peregrine falcon nesting from February 15 to June 30. Dates may vary from year to year. Call the ranger station at 520-364-3468 for closure updates. No other restrictions currently exist. Climbers, however, should use discretion when adding new bolted routes to cliffs in order to avoid any future conflict with the Forest Service.

Guidebooks: *Backcountry Rockclimbing in Southern Arizona* by Bob Kerry, Backcountry Books of Arizona, 1997, offers more details, routes, and topos to lots of other cliffs, including the Sheepshead area.

Nearby mountain shops, guide services, and gyms: The Summit Hut and Bumjo's Climbing Shop in Tucson. Rocks & Ropes is the Tucson gym.

Services: Limited services are in Sunsites, 7 miles east of the Stronghold. Complete services, including gas, groceries, and cheap motels, arein Willcox and Tombstone.

Emergency services: Call 911. Sierra Vista Community Hospital, 300 El Camino Real, Sierra Vista, AZ 85635, 800-880-0088 or 502-458-4641; and Northern Cochise Community Hospital, 901 West Rex Allen Drive, Willcox, AZ 856734, 502-384-3541.

Nearby climbing areas: Sheepshead area, offering some superb, multipitch routes, including *Absinthe of Mallet* (5.9+), *Stampede* (5.11a), and *Sheep Thrills* (5.11). Nearby crags include Muttonhead Dome, Mt. Chaktar, and The Watchtower. Kerry's book has detailed information and topos. Other areas of interest include Isle of You (sport routes), Klondyker Wall (excellent granite), Santa Teresa Mountains (wilderness rock adventures), Pinaleño Mountains, and Chiricahua Mountains. Climbing is not allowed in Chiricahua National Monument.

Nearby attractions: Chiricahua National Monument, Chiricahua Wilderness Area, Fort Bowie National Historic Site, Tombstone.

EAST STRONGHOLD

The East Stronghold, on the ragged east side of the Dragoon Mountains, is a complicated section of the range—steep slopes studded with towering granite walls and domes, and sliced by deep canyons. This is the location of the most famous of the Cochise Stronghold crags, including the Rockfellow Domes, Cochise Dome, and the mega-classic route *What's My Line*. Expect steep

EAST COCHISE STRONGHOLD

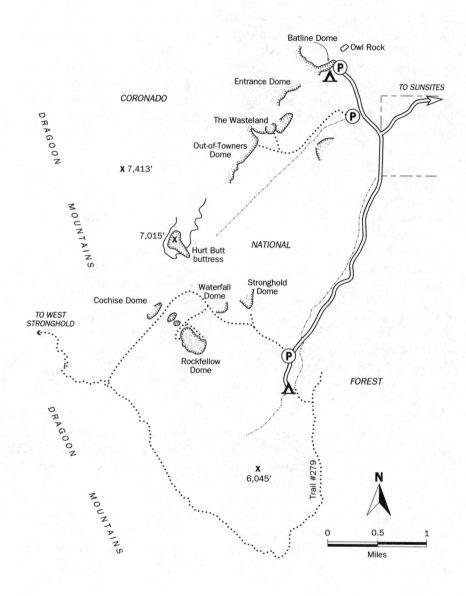

Batline Dome

Owl Rock

Entrance Dome

CORONADO

TO SUNSITES

The Wasteland

Out-of-Towners Dome

X 7,413'

NATIONAL

7,015'

X

Hurt Butt buttress

Waterfall Dome

Stronghold Dome

Cochise Dome

TO WEST STRONGHOLD

Rockfellow Dome

FOREST

DRAGOON

MOUNTAINS

DRAGOON

MOUNTAINS

X
6,045'

Trail #279

N

0   0.5   1

Miles

approaches with dense thickets of manzanita, the occasional endangered Dragoon rattlesnake, and routefinding difficulties. It's a large complex area that requires some looking around and getting lost to find the crags and the routes. Have fun. Crags are described beginning with the ones northwest of the access road and ending with the Rockfellow Domes and Cochise Dome atop the range. Many more cliffs and routes are described in *Backcountry Rockclimbing in Southern Arizona.*

Finding the crags: There are two ways to get into the East Stronghold. From Tucson, travel east on Interstate 10 and take Exit 318. Follow the paved Dragoon Road east to Cochise Stronghold Road. Turn right (south) and follow this paved/gravel road south until it deadends at Ironwood Road. Turn right (west) and follow Ironwood into the East Stronghold. The drive is 19 miles from I-10 to the Cochise Campground.

From Willcox, travel west on I-10 and take Exit 331. Drive south 17 miles on US Highway 191 to Ironwood Road in Sunsites. Turn right (west) onto Ironwood at the sign marked "Cochise Stronghold." The pavement ends after 3.7 miles. Continue to the national forest boundary (7 miles from US 191) at a cattleguard.

The first domes, including Batline Dome, Entrance Dome, and Out-of-Towners Dome, are in the canyon to the right. The parking area is reached by taking the first right at the cattleguard. Drive a short distance and park under oaks on a spur road to the left. The trail into the canyon begins here. To reach Batline Dome and Owl Rock, drive up the rough road for 0.6 mile to the base of Batline. Otherwise, continue another 1.5 miles to the large boulder in the road near the campground entrance. The trail to Stronghold Dome, Rockfellow Domes, and Cochise Dome begins here.

BATLINE DOME AND OWL ROCK

Batline Dome is a 200-foot-high, south-facing dome on the right side of Kerwin Canyon's entrance and east of the entrance to the main canyon. Several good single-pitch routes ascend the dome and offer a good introduction to Dragoon climbing without the longer approach of the bigger crags. Owl Rock is north of the road's end on a bench above a deep wash.

Finding the crags: Take the right turn just past the cattleguard at the national forest boundary. Follow this rough road for 0.6 mile to a parking area immediately south of the obvious dome. A four-wheel-drive vehicle is preferred for the last half of the road. Batline Dome is directly above. The routes on Batline are listed right to left. The trail to Owl Rock, a small spire north and across the wash from Batline, begins at the end of the road. Follow the 0.2-mile trail along the west side of a deep wash and up the opposite side to the base of the rock.

BATLINE DOME

1. **Unknown** (5.9) On the right side of the face above the parking area. Work up a chunky right-facing corner (crux is first 20') onto excellent plated rock. Finish at a 2-bolt chain anchor. Pro is devious. 80'. **Rack:** Wires, small cams, and slings.

2. **Batline** (5.9) Begin at the second ramp left of Route 1, up left from a tree. Climb good holds straight up to the top of the right-hand ramp. Clip a bolt on the face up right and pull past a jug onto a steep, plated slab. Edge to a 2-bolt chain anchor at 70'. Lower here or continue up another 30' of juggy rock to a 2-bolt anchor on a large ledge. **Descent:** Rappel 100' with 2 ropes. **Rack:** Wires and slings.

3. **Unknown** (5.9) Begin left of *Batline* below an obvious crack right of a tree. Stem and face climb the steep crack/groove to a 2-bolt chain anchor on a ledge. 65'. **Rack:** Medium to large cams.

4. **Dikohe** (5.8) 2 pitches. On the far left side of the cliff. **Pitch 1:** A short, easy lead up a blocky corner to a big ledge. **Pitch 2:** Jam a hand crack to a roof slot, then step left and mantle onto a small stance. Work up right to a seam, then face climb up left past 2 bolts to a 2-bolt belay/rappel anchor atop the cliff. **Descent:** Rappel 165' with 2 ropes. **Rack:** Wires, cams, quickdraws, and 2 ropes.

OWL ROCK

5. **Nightstalker** (5.9) An excellent route up the south face of the spire. Begin at the base of the face by a large boulder. Stem up between the boulder and the main face, and then step onto the face to a bolt. Follow a groove up right to a sloping ledge. Traverse left to the 2nd bolt, climb past a wide crack, and pull straight up on big chickenheads (tie off). Above a ramp, keep left on more chickenheads to the 3rd bolt. A thin move leads to alligator plates and a 2-bolt anchor on the summit. **Descent:** Rappel 80'. **Rack:** Slings and quickdraws.

6. **Naked Prey** (5.12a) A sport route that climbs loose cracks to a line of 7 bolts up the overhanging, southwest corner of the rock.

THE WASTELAND

The Wasteland is a spectacular, wandering line up the 600-foot-high face of an immense, semi-detached pinnacle hidden between Entrance Dome and Out-of-Towners Dome. The route, first ascended by Karl Rickson and Mark Pey, explores an intimidating face that was later described by Rickson as "a sea of chickenheads."

Finding the crag: Take the right turn just past the cattleguard at the national forest boundary. Follow this dirt road a few hundred feet to an obvious left turn. Turn and park under some trees at the road's end. A trail begins here and heads north, then southwest up the canyon floor. Follow it until you reach a dry, rocky drainage that drops down from The Wasteland. Hike up this drainage and then up right to the base of the face.

7. **The Wasteland** (5.8) 6 pitches. The route is somewhat wandering and alternative belay stances are found in addition to those described here. Begin up right from the toe of the south buttress and below a right-angling groove system. **Pitch 1:** Climb up left and then right up a right-angling seam (5.7) left of the groove to a short headwall (5.6). Move right on a spacious ledge and belay. **Pitch 2:** Traverse right on easy rock to the groove/crack. Surmount a short, steep section (5.8) and climb alongside the groove to another steeper step. Jam a short crack (5.8) and belay on a good ledge below a right-facing chimney. **Pitch 3:** Climb the easy chimney until it's possible to make an exposed step onto the main wall. Climb chickenheads and plates (5.8) up the right side of an open book and past a short headwall to a belay from tied-off chickenheads on the slab below a long, arching roof. **Pitch 4:** Make a long traverse below the roof to the right side the slab. Belay at a stance here or pull over a small roof (5.8) and belay on the slab above the big roof. **Pitch 5:** Make a spectacular, exposed traverse left above the roof (bit of 5.8) to the far left side of the upper headwall. Climb

COCHISE
STRONGHOLD
THE WASTELAND

descent

.8

.8

alternate
belay

.8

.7+

chimney

.8

.6

.7

7

past a small roof and up chickenheads on the right side of a blunt rib, and belay on a good ledge. Use extra runners to minimize rope drag. **Pitch 6:** A short lead. Climb directly above (5.8) or work out left and then back right to the summit (5.6). **Descent:** 6 rappels and downclimbing on the west side of the dome. Rappel off the northwest side and scramble down a gully. Make 5 single-rope rappels from trees down the west flank with some scrambling between rappel points until it's possible to drop back to your packs at the cliff's base. **Rack:** Sets of Stoppers and Friends, a handful of 2-foot slings, and a single rope.

ENTRANCE DOME AND OUT-OF-TOWNERS DOME

These two large, south-facing domes, flanking the sides of The Wasteland pinnacle, are perched high atop the ridge on the northwest side of the canyon. Both domes are reached by trails that begin off the road to Batline Dome and wind up the steep slopes below the domes. Some great multipitch lines ascend the complex Entrance Dome, including *Whores of Babylon* (5.10a/b), *Echoes* (5.9), *Full Circle* (5.10b/c), and *Falconlore* (5.10d). The last two routes are mostly bolted, making routefinding a cinch. The Out-of-Towners Dome is the big, slabby cliff left of The Wasteland. It offers some superb edge and friction routes including the classic multipitch lines *Arribas Amoebas* (5.10c) and *The Out-of-Towners* (5.10b). The area guidebook *Backcountry Rockclimbing in Southern Arizona* has route descriptions, topos, and photo topos to both cliffs.

STRONGHOLD DOME

An excellent east- and south-facing, 300-foot-high dome lies on the right side of the canyon northwest of the campground and the parking area with the boulder in the middle. The dome, one of the most accessible and most popular crags in the East Stronghold, offers a great selection of classic face and crack routes.

Finding the dome: Park by the large boulder that splits the road just north of the campground entrance. Look for the start of a good trail directly west of the boulder. The trail follows the slopes south of the bouldery creekbed for about half a mile before dropping into the creekbed. Look for a faint trail here, which heads directly north and uphill to the base of the dome. Total approach time is about 20 minutes. Routes are listed left to right.

SOUTH FACE

8. **End Chimney Left** (5.7) Locate twin chimney cracks left and uphill of the obvious, right-facing dihedral. This route ascends the left-hand crack. Chimney and off-width up the crack to a 2-bolt anchor on the left. **Descent:** Rappel the route with double ropes. **Rack:** Big Friends and big Camalots.

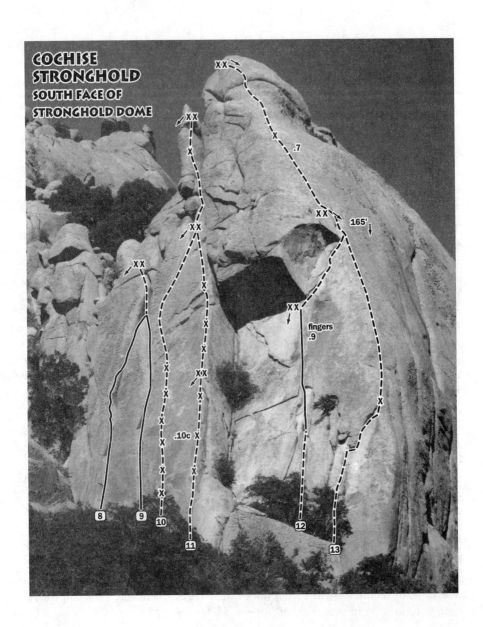

COCHISE
STRONGHOLD
SOUTH FACE OF
STRONGHOLD DOME

.7

165'

fingers
.9

.10c

8   9   10

11

12   13

Noah Hannawalt climbing the Cochise classic *Beeline* (5.9 R) on Stronghold Dome.

9. **End Chimney Right** (5.7) First ascent by Mike McEwen and Dave Baker in 1970. Follow the right-hand chimney crack to the 2-bolt anchor. **Descent:** Rappel the route with double ropes. **Rack:** Big Friends and big Camalots.

10. **Stage Fright** (5.11d) Begin just right of *End Chimney Right*. Climb a short crack, then friction and edge up the steep, smooth slab past 6 bolts. Work up left past a small stance, then straight up plated rock and a water streak to a 2-bolt chain anchor. **Descent:** Rappel the route. **Rack:** Stoppers, runners, and quickdraws.

11. **Big Time** (5.10c) 2 pitches. Start below an arête that forms the outside edge of a large, right-facing dihedral. **Pitch 1:** Work up the outside edge of the arête (5.10c) past 3 bolts to a 2-bolt anchor with slings. Continue up the arête (3 bolts) and left of the big roof to a 2-bolt chain anchor. **Pitch 2:** Climb the face left of a left-facing corner, then up a blunt arête (5.8) past 1 bolt to a 2-bolt anchor. **Descent:** Make 2 double-rope rappels down the route.

12. **Beeline** (5.9 R) 2 pitches. First ascent by Merle Wheeler and Mark Axen in 1970. Classic route with excellent, well-protected climbing. Scramble up to a ledge atop a huge boulder below a crack and directly below the right side of the large, square roof. **Pitch 1:** Work up the stunning finger crack (5.9) to the right side of the roof. A 2-bolt chain anchor allows you to lower from here, but you'll miss some great climbing! Lieback up exposed flakes right of the roof to a blunt prow. Easier moves lead up to a 2-bolt belay anchor. 165'. **Pitch 2:** Continue up and left on run-out face climbing (5.7) with chickenheads and flakes past 1 bolt to a horizontal crack. Pull past and belay on the dome summit. **Descent:** Most parties prefer to rappel with double ropes from the bolt anchors atop pitch 1. From the summit, walk off northward, then down the west side and around the north end of the dome to the base of the east face. **Rack:** Stoppers, small to medium cams, and a few runners.

13. **Reen's 'Rête** (5.8 R) 2 pitches. Another Cochise must-do classic named for 1974 first ascensionist Reen Thompson. This fun route ascends the slabby prow between the south and east faces. Start from the right side of the ledge on top of the boulder below *Beeline*. **Pitch 1:** Work up a short crack that arches up right to a bolt at its right end. Face climb past rappel slings and follow the prow above (pro is tied-off chickenheads) to the 2-bolt belay/rappel anchor on *Beeline*. Rap from here or climb pitch 2 of *Beeline* to the dome summit. **Descent:** Most parties prefer to rappel with double ropes from the bolt anchors atop pitch 1. From the dome summit, walk off northward, then down the west side and around the north end of the dome to the base of the east face. **Rack:** Stoppers, small to medium cams, and runners.

EAST FACE

14. **Greasy Gizzards** (5.10 R) 3 pitches. First ascent by Dave Baker, Mike McEwen, and Kem Johnson in 1979. Locate a prominent, right-leaning, right-facing dihedral capped with a roof on the left side of the east face. This route follows the second crack left of the dihedral. Scramble left onto a large terrace below the corner and the right-angling cracks. Set up a belay on the left side of the terrace. **Pitch 1:** Face climb up left to the base of the crack. Jam the hand and fist crack (5.9) up right to a sloped belay stance. **Pitch 2:** Continue up the thinning crack until it ends. Traverse up right along a dike to a water streak (5.10) and climb to a belay stance with tied-off chickenheads. **Pitch 3:** Easier climbing leads up the water streak to a ledge. Climb up right to a summit belay. **Descent:** From the dome summit, walk off northward, then down the west side and around the north end of the dome back to the base of the east face. **Rack:** A full rack with wires and small to large cams, plus tie-off runners. Some large Camalots are useful on pitch 1.

15. **Shake 'n' Bake** (5.9+) 3 pitches. Classic crack and face route done by Dave Baker and Mike McEwen in 1973. This line ascends the obvious right-angling crack on the east face. Begin below the crack on the large ledge. **Pitch 1:** Jam the awkward off-width and fist crack (5.9+) in a cramped corner up right and over a final bulge to a fine belay ledge. **Pitch 2:** Continue up the crack until it begins to flatten right.

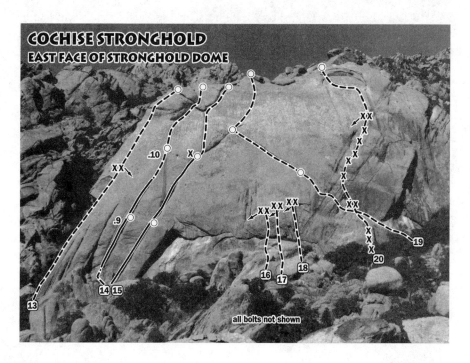

COCHISE STRONGHOLD
EAST FACE OF STRONGHOLD DOME

all bolts not shown

Face climb to a bolt and chickenhead belay. **Pitch 3:** Climb easy Class 5 rock near a water streak to the top of the cliff. **Descent:** From the dome summit, walk off northward, then down the west side and around the north flank of the dome back to the base of the east face. **Rack:** A generous selection of cams including multiple 2" to 4" pieces, some extra-large Camalots, and runners.

16. **Come and Get It** (5.11c) The left-hand sport route on the right side of the overlap, right of the arching dihedral by *Shake 'n' Bake*. Start in oak trees at the cliff's base, below a right-angling crack system. Climb a steep face with 5 bolts over flaky bulges to a long 2-foot-wide roof. Pull over the roof to a bolt, then up a gorgeous alligator-skin face to a 2-bolt chain anchor. 11 bolts. An unfinished 2-bolt sport route begins just left.

17. **The Stand** (5.11d) Sport route that begins 20' right of Route 16 between boulders. Edge up a steep, vertical face with 4 bolts, then up left in corners and over roofs to a vertical face finish. Lower from a 2-bolt chain anchor. 10 bolts.

18. **The Bounty** (5.11b) Just right of *The Stand*. Scramble right, up a crack ramp to a tree. Step out left with hands in a crack on a narrow ramp past 2 bolts. Stem and edge up a steep, right-facing corner capped by a roof. Thin face moves lead left above the roof to a 2-bolt chain anchor. 10 bolts.

19. **Wishbone** (5.8 R) 3 pitches. First ascent by Pat Littlejohn and John Motherseal in 1979. A left-traversing route that begins on the right side of the east face. Begin below a right-angling dihedral. Climb an easy ramp up left and belay from 2 bolts or from gear at the upper end. **Pitch 1:** Face climb left around a corner and into a short, right-facing corner. Work up and left across the face (5.8) to a prominent, left-slanting crack and follow it to a belay stance with chickenheads and gear. **Pitch 2:** Follow the crack up left until it peters out, then traverse left to a belay from chickenheads by the *Shake 'n' Bake* crack. **Pitch 3:** Move up right in the crack and then face climb up easier but unprotected slab to the top of the cliff. **Descent:** From the dome summit, walk off northward, then down the west side and around the north flank of the dome back to the base of the east face. **Rack:** Wires, small to large Friends, and extra runners.

20. **Unknown** (5.11) 3 pitches. A mostly bolted route up the right side of the dome. **Pitch 1:** Climb a thin, right-facing corner with 3 bolts to a wide ramp. Scramble up left to a 2-bolt belay at the base of a large right-facing dihedral. **Pitch 2:** Climb a groove in the dihedral. Above, follow a line of 6 bolts along a dike/seam to a 2-bolt belay anchor.

Pitch 3: Face climb up a maze of chickenheads to the summit. **Descent:** From the dome summit, walk off northward, then down the west side and around the north flank of the dome back to the base of the east face. **Rack:** A small rack with wires, a set of Friends, a few 2-foot runners, and quickdraws.

ROCKFELLOW DOMES

The Rockfellow Domes, named for pioneer settler John A. Rockfellow, perches atop the crest of the Dragoon range between the East and West Strongholds. The multisummited group, composed of End Pinnacle, Chay Desa Tsay, Rockfellow Dome, Bastion Towers, and Hawk Pinnacle, offers a stunning selection of classic face and crack routes. Most of the routes ascend the shady north sides of the towers, except for the south face of End Pinnacle. Most of the routes are all-day affairs, particularly during the short days of late autumn and winter. Bring a headlamp and pay attention to the trail on the way up to avoid unnecessary descent epics. The Rockfellows are closed to climbing from February 15 through June 30 for nesting raptors. Check at the campground to confirm closure dates.

Finding the crags: The Rockfellow Domes can be accessed from both the East and West Strongholds. The east approach is shorter but steeper, while the west approach offers more gradual grades on a better trail, but a slightly longer walk.

The East Stronghold trail to the Rockfellow Domes begins at the same place as the trail to Stronghold Dome. Start from the huge boulder that splits the road just north of the campground. Locate the access trail directly west of the boulder. Hike up the trail as it meanders along the south slopes above a dry drainage. It is a little hard to follow at times, but side trails eventually link up with the main path as it climbs to a dry, slabby waterfall below and south of Waterfall Dome. Scramble along slickrock above the dry falls and into a shallow canyon. Continue along the dry creek bed past the north flank of the domes to an obvious side drainage that comes in from the left. A cairn may mark this drainage. Turn left here and follow this streambed to some large boulders that choke it. Exit right around the boulders and follow the path to a saddle north-west of the Rockfellow Domes and a subsidiary pinnacle on the right. The trail continues east along the base of the cliff to the north face of End Pinnacle and Rockfellow Dome, which includes the routes *Cap'n Pissgums* and *Abracadaver*. Follow the base of the cliff south around the west side of End Pinnacle to the south face routes. Allow about one hour of hiking time from car to cliff.

The West Stronghold approach to the domes is also easily accessed from the end of the road and camping area in the West Stronghold. Follow the marked Cochise Trail (Forest Service Trail 279) east from the parking area. It ascends the south side of a canyon and then contours eastward. After 1 mile, drop north into Dome Valley, an obvious, long canyon to the northeast flanked by Cochise

Dome on the left and the Rockfellow Domes on the right. Hike up this drainage past Cochise Dome. The trail, which is hard to follow through here, works over a low ridge and into another drainage. Eventually, you reach the dry streambed that is northwest of End Pinnacle. Follow a trail up the streambed to the base of the face. Again, allow about an hour of hiking from car to cliff.

END PINNACLE

End Pinnacle is the westernmost formation in the Rockfellow Domes. Several excellent routes ascend its shady north face and its sunny south face. Routes are listed right to left on both faces. **Descent:** 3 rappels. Problematic and complicated. Move east and slightly south below the summit area and locate a small pine tree with rappel slings. Rappel 150' with 2 ropes to a set of bolts. Make another 2-rope rappel into a dark chimney. Scramble north along the chimney to a hole by a chockstone. Squeeze through the hole onto a ledge where the third set of rappel slings is wrapped around a wedged chockstone. Make a last rappel to the ground on the east and north side of the pinnacle.

SOUTH FACE

Reach this face by following a rough trail around the vertical west face to thick forest below the south face. A huge chimney system splits the face in half.

21. **Magnas Veritas** (III 5.11b R) 3 pitches. Pitch 1 is worth doing, then rappel or traverse left to *Days of Future Passed*. **Pitch 1:** Climb superb alligator-skin rock (wires and slings for pro) to a small overhang with a big thread. Pull over and face climb past 5 bolts (5.10a) to a long runout that leads to a 2-bolt anchor. Rap with 2 ropes from here and traverse left to *Days*, or prepare for the crux pitch 2. **Pitch 2:** Thin face climb (5.11b) leads to a long 5.9 runout to a spacious ledge with a 2-bolt anchor. **Pitch 3:** More face moves (5.8 R) past 2 bolts to the summit. A fall onto the belay ledge would be devastating! Use caution. **Descent:** 3 rappels. See previous description. **Rack:** Wires, slings, quickdraws, and 2 ropes.

22. **Days of Future Passed** (III 5.10) 4 pitches. A highly recommended classic route. The difficulty drops to 5.8+ or 5.9- if you do the starting pendulum. Jim Waugh warns, however, "The 5.8 climber will work hard on this route—got to have it together to lead because there is injury potential on some pitches." The line follows the lone crack system on the right side of the pinnacle's south face. **Pitch 1:** Climb a short crack/groove system to a bolt. Pendulum right (A0) or face climb right (5.10c) to the prominent crack. A new, alternative start face climbs a ramp (a couple 5.10 moves) right of the crack to a bolt and into the main crack system. Above, jam, off-width, and chimney up the wide

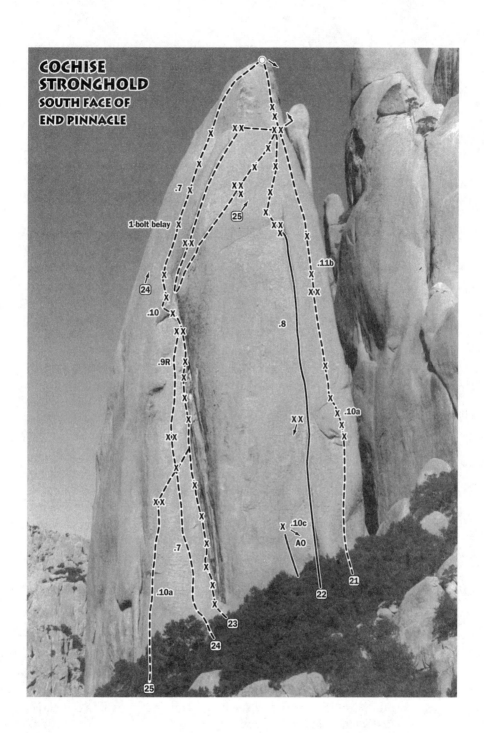

COCHISE
STRONGHOLD
SOUTH FACE OF
END PINNACLE

1-bolt belay

.7

25

24

.10

.9R

.11b

.8

.10a

.10c

AO

.7

.10a

21

22

23

24

25

crack (5.8) and belay at a 2-bolt anchor after 160'. **Pitch 2:** Hand and fist jams lead up the long crack (5.8 and 5.9) to a 3-bolt belay stance at the top of the crack. **Pitch 3:** Traverse left from the belay to a chickenhead. Face climb up right (5.8) past 3 bolts to a good belay ledge. **Pitch 4:** Face climb (5.8 R) past 2 bolts, then up easier slabby rock to the summit. Don't fall on this pitch—you'll hit the ledge. A safer alternative finish traverses around the east side and climbs a bolted face to the summit. **Descent:** 3 rappels. See previous description. **Rack:** A generous rack with an emphasis on medium and large cams for the long crack, and extra slings.

23. **Welcome to the Machine** (III 5.10c/d) 4 or 5 pitches. Great, well-protected climbing. Route ascends the rib left of the deep chimney on the left side of the south face. Begin below a chimney formed by a vertical, pancake-shaped flake beneath a large boulder. **Pitch 1:** Work up the easy chimney to a bolt on the left wall. Follow the long rib left of the chimney past 9 bolts to a 2-bolt belay on an alcove ledge at the top of the chimney. This 200' pitch can be broken into 2 shorter ones. **Pitch 2:** Work up the exposed, bolted crack system above past two hard 5.10 cruxes to a corner that leads up right to a 2-bolt belay stance. **Pitch 3:** Continue past bolts along a seam in the corner (5.10a) that leads up right to a large ledge with a 2-bolt anchor. **Pitch 4:** Climb past 2 bolts (5.8) and then run it to the summit. **Descent:** 3 rappels. See previous description. **Rack:** Sets of Stoppers and Friends to #4, quickdraws, and 2 ropes.

24. **Poetry in Motion** (III 5.10b/c R) 4 pitches. A Stronghold classic. Excellent face route with superb position and interesting moves. Ascends the face left of the deep chimney system. Carefully scramble under a large boulder on the left side of the face and set up a belay. **Pitch 1:** Climb a long unprotected slab (5.7 R) to a bolt. Work up left to a 2-bolt belay stance (hard to see from the ground). **Pitch 2:** Follow an incipient crack system up a steeper face (5.9 R) with delicate face moves. Get pro by placing nuts between chickenheads. Belay from gear under an obvious bulge on a small ledge atop the chimney. It's also possible to move right and belay from the 2-bolt alcove on *Welcome*. **Pitch 3:** Climb the exposed bulge/flake above (5.10) past 2 bolts, then traverse left about 20' to a bolt. Continue straight up to a 1-bolt belay. Routefinding is tricky on this pitch. Use lots of runners to avoid rope drag. **Pitch 4:** Wander up the face (5.7) above past 3 bolts to the top. **Descent:** 3 rappels. See previous description. **Rack:** Mostly small and medium pro—Stoppers and small to medium cams with a few larger pieces—slings, and quickdraws.

25. **Endgame** (5.10a) 5 pitches. A wild, airy line that starts on the left side

of End Pinnacle's south face. Begin down left from *Poetry in Motion* below a huge boulder. **Pitch 1:** Work up a steep bolted face (5.10a) to a crescent-shaped ledge, then up right to a 2-bolt belay stance on the left edge of a steep south-facing slab. **Pitch 2:** Face climb to a bolt (bolt on pitch 1 of Route 24) and then work up right (5.8 R) to the bolted rib left of the deep chimney. Follow these bolts on *Welcome* to the 2-bolt alcove belay. **Pitch 3:** Climb up right along an airy, bolted seam (5.10a) to a 3-bolt belay stance on the upper face. **Pitch 4:** Move up the steep slab past two bolts to the large upper belay ledge with a 2-bolt anchor on its left side. **Pitch 5:** Move the belay to the bolted stance on the right side of the ledge. Traverse right from the ledge and climb the steep slab above past a few bolts to the summit. **Descent:** 3 rappels. See previous description. **Rack:** Wires, TCUs, small to medium Friends, slings, quickdraws, and 2 ropes.

NORTH FACE

The north face of End Pinnacle is split by a deep chimney system ascended by *Cap'n Pissgums*. Reach the face by hiking up from the saddle to the northwest along the cliff's base. Routes are listed right to left.

26. **Be All End All** (5.11d) No topo. This route lies on the northwest corner of End Pinnacle. The first pitch is definitely worth doing. The rest is just all right. Begin on the northwest side of the pinnacle and right of *Cap'n Pissgums* below a prominent, left-facing corner system. **Pitch 1:** Face climb up the corner past 2 bolts, then lieback and stem a seam/groove (5.11d) up the corner past another bolt to a 2-bolt belay stance. 80'. The rest of the route climbs the crack system for 3 more pitches to the summit. **Descent:** Rap the route with 2 ropes. **Rack:** Small and medium cams and Stoppers.

27. **Cap'n Pissgums** (III 5.11a R) 6 pitches. Classic jamming but with some hair factor. Dave Baker and Mark Axen put up this superb route, one of the first on the Rockfellow Domes. The line ascends the obvious, deep crack and chimney system that splits the north face of End Pinnacle. Begin by scrambling atop boulders below the right-hand chimney. **Pitch 1:** A short pitch. Stem or body stem (depending on your height) up the wide chimney (5.11a) past 3 bolts above the boulders with some deep pits below them to a belay alcove below a prow. **Pitch 2:** Traverse right around the corner (5.9) and climb up grooves below the main chimney. Belay at a 2-bolt stance at the chimney's base. **Pitch 3:** Work up a long, unprotected squeeze chimney (5.7 R) to a single-bolt belay stance at a wedged block. **Pitch 4:** Jam a steep, strenuous hand and fist crack (5.11a) up a tight, overhanging

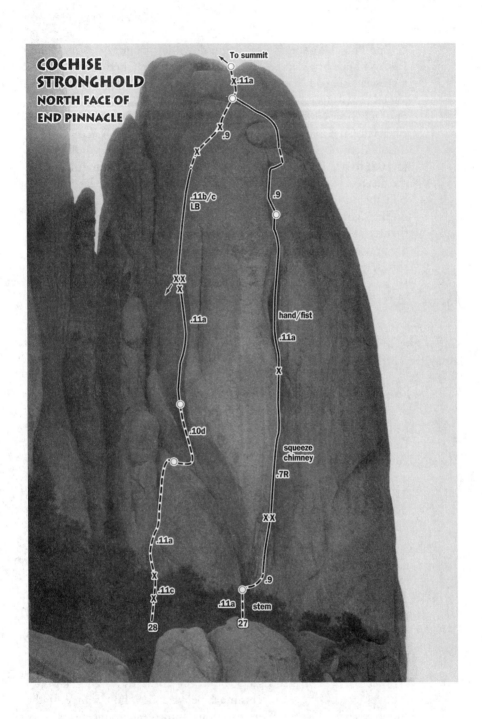

COCHISE
STRONGHOLD
NORTH FACE OF
END PINNACLE

To summit

X .11a

X .9

.9

.11b/c
LB

X X
X

.11a

hand/fist

.11a

X

.10d

squeeze
chimney

.7R

X X

.11a

.9

X

.11c

.11a   stem

28   27

corner (5.11a) for about 30'. The difficulty and angle eases above. Jam to a chickenhead belay. **Pitch 5:** Continue up the crack (5.9) until it bends right. Work up left over bulges to a crack/ledge that leads left to a good belay ledge below the final headwall. **Pitch 6:** Pull a thin face move (5.11a) over a bulge with a bolt to easy climbing up the summit slab. Avoid the 2 aid bolts up left of the ledge. Belay atop the pinnacle in a water basin or from cracks. **Descent:** 3 rappels. See previous description. **Rack:** A full rack with an emphasis on medium to large cams.

28. **Uncarved Block** (III 5.11c R/X) 5 pitches. There have been only a few complete ascents of this very run-out, scary route put up by Chip Chase and Ray Ringle. It's worth doing the first 3 pitches and rappelling off if you're not up to the killer 4th pitch. Route ascends the east side of the north face. Begin left of *Cap'n Pissgums* chimney and on the right side of a deep gully that leads to a skyline notch. **Pitch 1:** Face climb up thin cracks and seams (5.11c and lots of lichen) past 2 bolts to a thin crack (5.11a) in a groove. Above, make an easy face traverse right to a good belay ledge under the uncarved block, a large flake split away from the main wall. **Pitch 2:** A short lead. Make a weird lieback move up an off-width (stiff 5.10d) on the bottom right side of the block. Belay up left on the block. **Pitch 3:** Jam a hands to thin fingers crack (5.11a) with good pro to a 3-bolt semihanging belay. Make 2 raps from here to the ground. **Pitch 4:** The business part of the route! Scary to lead and dangerous for the belayer. Work up a very run-out seam/groove in a left-facing corner system by liebacking up the rounded edge (5.11b/c). If you fall, you'll cream your belayer. Jim Waugh tied off a rounded chickenhead 20' up and cinched it tight with a 9mm rope to the anchor below to keep it from coming off—gulp! Above the groove, face climb out right to a bolt. Continue up the face above past 1 more bolt (5.9) to a spacious belay ledge. **Pitch 5:** Face moves up right past a bolt over a rounded bulge (5.11a), then easy climbing up the summit slab. **Descent:** 3 rappels. See previous description. **Rack:** Full rack from Stoppers to large cams.

28A. **Interiors** (5.7) No topo. A unique, novelty route that traverses the entire formation from north to south in a deep chimney between Rockfellow Dome and Chay Desa Tay. Most folks forego a rope and 3rd class solo up the chimney. Most of the route is easy Class 5 chimneying. Begin by scrambling up an easy ramp into the deep chimney and enter the darkness. Worm your way through with chimneying and scrambling to the south side. Bring headlamps and kneepads.

ROCKFELLOW DOME

Rockfellow Dome is the highest formation in the Rockfellow Domes. While the south face is somewhat nondescript, the north face is a towering sweep of granite split by vertical crack systems. Some of the best routes in the East Stronghold are found here, including the classic *Abracadaver*. This dome is part of the peregrine falcon closure area in springtime. Reach the face by hiking up to the low saddle immediately northwest of End Pinnacle and then following a good climber's trail along the base of the north face. Routes are listed right to left or west to east. **Descent:** 3 double-rope rappels down *Abracadaver*. **Rappel 1:** 2-rope rappel from 2-piton anchor 15' below the summit to a 3-bolt anchor on the face below and left of Friendly Flake, 130'. **Rappel 2:** 2-rope rappel to a set of 2-bolt anchors either at the top of pitch 3 on *Abracadaver* or at the top of pitch 2 on *Jabberwock*. **Rappel 3:** 2-rope rappel to cliff's base.

NORTH FACE

29. **Knead Me** (III 5.10a A0) 5 pitches. A good line up the right-hand crack system on the north face. Begin below the right-angling chimney. **Pitch 1:** Work up the mostly unprotected chimney (5.7 R) to a 2-bolt belay stance on a flake. **Pitch 2:** Continue up the chimney, which narrows to a strenuous off-width crack (5.9), pass right of a large roof, and end at an exposed 2-bolt belay atop a flake. **Pitch 3:** Thin face moves edge up left to a bolt with a fixed carabiner. Clip, lower, and pendulum below the roof or tension traverse left to a crack system and belay ledge. **Pitch 4:** The route joins *Abracadaver* here. Jam the left crack (5.8) to thin, precarious Friendly Flake and jam the right side to a good belay atop the flake. **Pitch 5:** A couple of finishes. The usual way is to climb a short crack to a bolt on the face above and pendulum left to a crack, or downclimb and traverse left (5.9) along a quartz seam to the crack. Jam the hand crack (5.8) to the summit. Or climb directly up the summit face (5.11a) past 2 bolts to the top of the cliff. **Descent:** 3 rappels. See above description. **Rack:** Full rack with an emphasis on medium to large cams. A couple of big pieces will protect the off-width section.

30. **Abracadaver** (III 5.11a) 5 pitches. The Stronghold's super classic, must-do route—sustained and airy with varied cracks from finger to off-width and a hard face pitch. First ascended by Mike McEwen, Steve Grossman, and Dave Baker in 1975 and rated 5.9! Route ascends the central crack system up the north face. Begin below the left of two prominent cracks. **Pitch 1:** Work up a right-angling, off-width groove (5.10a) past a bolt and belay at a 2-bolt anchor below an obvious dihedral. **Pitch 2:** Grunt up an awkward off-width crack and squeeze chimney (5.9 and left side in) past 1 bolt and a fixed copperhead to a

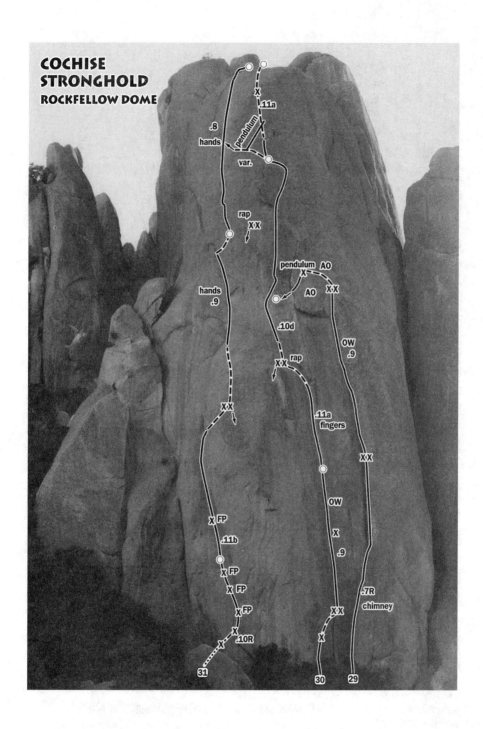

COCHISE
STRONGHOLD
ROCKFELLOW DOME

.11a

pendulum

.8
hands

var.

rap
X X

pendulum   AO
X
hands   AO   X·X
.9

.10d

OW
.9

X X   rap

X·X   .11a
fingers

X X

X FP

.11b

X FP

X FP

OW

X FP

X   X   .10R

X
.9

.7R
chimney

X·X

X

31   30   29

John Groth stems up the superb *Abracadaver* (III 5.11a) on Rockfellow Dome.

belay stance where the crack narrows. Use careful rope management here to keep the rope from getting stuck in the crack below. **Pitch 3:** 3-star pitch! Lieback, jam, and stem up the thin finger crack (5.11a) in the dihedral to a roof. Traverse left below the roof and exit onto a spacious, sloping ledge with a 2-bolt anchor. **Pitch 4:** Jam a thin, disjointed crack (5.10d) that leads up right to a good hand crack. Follow to Friendly Flake, a large, semidetached flake, and jam the right side to a belay stance on the flake. **Pitch 5:** Climb a short, left-facing corner and then edge up the exposed final face (5.11a) past 2 bolts to the rounded summit. **Descent:** 3 rappels. See previous description. **Rack:** Full rack with Stoppers, TCUs, and Friends, plus quickdraws, slings, and 2 ropes.

31. **Jabberwock** (III 5.12a) 4 pitches. Jim Waugh and Ray Ringle's 1981 testpiece is a stunning line with one of the best hard pitches in the Stronghold. Scramble left from the base of *Abracadaver* and squeeze between some boulders and the main wall to the base of a slab and a bright yellow face. The route begins atop the pointed boulder below the slab. **Pitch 1:** A superb, hard pitch. Step from the boulder onto the face and clip a bolt. Edge up to a hole and then delicately traverse right (5.10 R) across the lichen-covered slab to an old bolt below a thin, left-facing corner. Don't fall—you'll probably hit the boulder! Lieback up the steep, fingertip crack past 3 fixed pitons to a small belay stance atop a chickenhead below a left-facing dihedral. **Pitch 2:** Another good one. Stem and jam up the corner (5.11b) past a fixed piton until it trends left. Make an airy chickenhead traverse up right to a 2-bolt belay/rappel anchor on a ledge. **Pitch 3:** Climb a slab up right and follow a hand crack (5.9) until it bends left. Make a traverse up right along a dike to a belay stance below a crack system. **Pitch 4:** Jam a fun hand crack (5.8) to the summit. **Descent:** 3 rappels. See previous description. **Rack:** Full rack with Stoppers, TCUs, and Friends, plus quickdraws, slings, and 2 ropes.

BASTION TOWER

The easternmost tower in the Rockfellow Domes. Scramble east on the trail along the cliff's base from Rockfellow Dome to the base of the tower's north side.

32. **Forest Lawn/Pair A Grins** (II 5.9, 5.10c) 2 pitches. A classic, must-do route. Ascends the northeast corner of the tower. Begin on a boulder below a perfect, left-facing dihedral. **Pitch 1:** This is the 1st pitch of *Forest Lawn*. Lieback and jam up the dihedral (5.9) to a rest stance at 50'. Continue another 35' to a small belay ledge beneath an overhang. **Pitch 2:** *Pair A Grins* finish. Traverse right from the belay and follow bolts up an airy, exciting buttress for a full rope length to the top of the pinnacle. **Descent:** Find a ramp that leads down to a 2-bolt anchor. Make a 2-rope

COCHISE
STRONGHOLD
BASTION TOWER

X X

2-rope rappel
down chimney

.9
LB

32

all bolts not shown

rappel down a chimney slot. **Rack:** A good selection of small to large cams, with extra medium sizes, some Stoppers, and quickdraws.

COCHISE DOME

This excellent, chickenhead-festooned dome, also called What's My Line Dome, sits northwest and across the canyon from the Rockfellow Domes. Its southeast-facing slab offers *What's My Line*, one of Arizona's must-do, all-time classic routes. The crackless face appears intimidating, but closer inspection reveals a line of huge chickenhead holds up the wall. This dome is closed to climbing from February 15 through June 30 for nesting raptors. Check at the campground to confirm closure dates.

Finding the dome: Reach the dome by hiking up the canyon bottom below the Rockfellow Domes. From a good vantage point, study the topography below the dome to figure out the best approach to the cliff's base. For *What's My Line*, scramble up Class 3 rock to a large ledge on the left side of the face. It's important to pick the right crack system to reach the ledge. Leave your packs at the cliff's base below to avoid scrambling back up for them.

33. **What's My Line** (5.6 A0 or 5.10c) 3 pitches. First climbed by Dave Baker, Larry Seligman, and Peter Depagter in 1971. First free ascent was by Steve Grossman. This is Arizona's best moderate route, but not easy for beginner leaders. Double ropes are helpful to alleviate rope drag. Scramble up Class 3 ramps and gullies on the south side of the dome to a large ledge about halfway up the left side of the face. Start at a 2-bolt anchor on the right side of the ledge. **Pitch 1:** Climb up right from the belay to a single bolt. Clip, lower, and pendulum right (A0) to a sea of chickenhead holds. Instead of a pendulum, it's possible to face climb right (5.10c) to the jugs. Follow chickenheads up right to a belay from chickenheads or at a 3-bolt belay near the bottom of a brown water streak. **Pitch 2:** Climb up and right for a full pitch along chickenheads, following the path of least resistance, to a belay from chickenhead anchors on the upper right side of the face. **Pitch 3:** Work up a short headwall, then traverse straight left along a sloped ramp/ledge system past a bolt to a right-facing dihedral that leads to a good belay ledge. Scramble to the summit from here. Two other exit pitches exist—the arête directly above *Double Jeopardy* (5.7 R and grainy) and the scoop 15' left (5.7 R). **Descent:** Locate a 2-bolt rappel anchor on the summit and make 2 single-rope rappels north into a gully. Scramble down the north flank of the dome to the cliff's base. **Rack:** A moderate-sized rack with a selection of Friends and medium to large Stoppers, plus 16 to 20 2-foot runners for girth-hitching and tying off chickenheads.

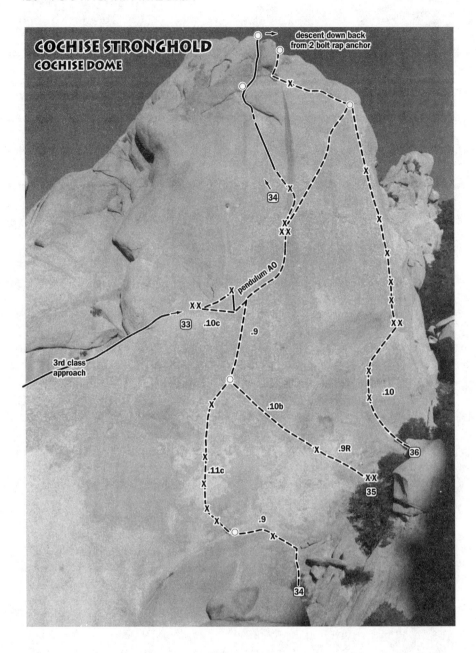

34. **Let's Make a Deal** (5.11c) 5 pitches. A direct line up the face. This is not a great route. Hike up a rough path from the canyon bottom to the right side of the face. Begin by some boulders at the cliff's base. **Pitch 1:** A short pitch. Face climb out left to a bolt and do some thin moves (5.9) to a narrow ledge. Belay at a small tree on the ledge's left side. **Pitch 2:** Hard climbing leads straight up (5.11c) past 4 bolts to a black knob. Run it out above to another bolt, then angle up right to a belay from chickenheads. **Pitch 3:** A thin face section above (5.9) leads to chickenhead buckets. Yard up jugs to a 3-bolt belay near the base of a prominent brown streak. **Pitch 4:** Work up right about 25' on knobs, then traverse left (5.11a) to a bolt on the streak. Climb up left to a left-angling crack system. Above, face climb alligator-skin rock to a left-angling roof/overlap. Move left below the overlap and belay below a shallow, right-facing corner. **Pitch 5:** Climb the corner (5.9) past a tree to a chimney finish on the summit blocks. **Descent:** Locate a 2-bolt rappel anchor on the summit and make 2 single-rope rappels north into a gully. Scramble down the north flank of the dome to the cliff's base. **Rack:** A moderate-sized rack with cams and Stoppers, runners, and quickdraws.

35. **What's My Line Direct** (5.10b R) 2 pitches. A more direct, 2-pitch start to *What's My Line*. Start up right from Route 34 at a 2-bolt anchor on a small flake left of some trees. **Pitch 1:** Face climb (5.9+ R) up to a bolt (old 1/4"), or traverse in from the right (5.7). Continue left (5.10b) to a bolt (new 3/8") just right of a narrow, right-facing corner. Continue left over the corner to a belay off chickenheads. **Pitch 2:** Climb straight up above the belay through a thin face section (5.9) and join *What's My Line*'s 1st pitch. Continue up *What's My Line*.

36. **Double Jeopardy** (5.10c/d R) 3 pitches. First ascent by Steve Grossman and Steve Ampter in 1986. Up the right-hand side of the face. Begin atop boulders. **Pitch 1:** Climb a left-slanting ramp (left of a tree) that gets steeper and turns into a crack. Face climb past 2 bolts (5.10) to a ramp (chickenhead pro) that trends up right to a 2-bolt belay stance below a prow. 75'. **Pitch 2:** Follow the obvious, blunt arête up the right side of the face past 5 bolts and 3 chickenheads to a chickenhead belay at the top of *What's My Line*'s pitch 2. **Pitch 3:** Climb a short headwall, then traverse left to an obvious chimney up a huge, right-facing dihedral that leads to the dome summit. **Descent:** Locate a 2-bolt rappel anchor on the summit and make 2 single-rope rappels north into a gully. Scramble down the north flank of the dome to the cliff's base. **Rack:** A moderate-sized rack with cams and Stoppers, runners, and quickdraws.

WEST STRONGHOLD

The West Stronghold is a beautiful canyon area on the west flank of the Dragoon Mountains. Several deep canyons, lined with towering granite domes and cliffs, drain west from the crest of the range to a wide valley. Much climbing has been done in this area, but many cliffs still await an ascent. Hiking approaches to many of the crags are shorter and easier than those to the crags in the East Stronghold. Great camping is found in the oak groves at the end of the dirt road.

Finding the crags: The best approach is from Interstate 10 at Exit 303 (Tombstone/Bisbee) in Benson. Drive south on Arizona Highway 80 toward Tombstone for 23 miles. Look for a good gravel road marked "Middlemarch Road" that is just before Tombstone. Turn left (east) and follow this road for almost 10 miles to a Forest Service sign that marks a left (north) turn onto Forest Service Road 687. You can also reach this turnoff from the east and the East Stronghold by following FR 345 for 16 miles over Middlemarch Pass from Pearce and US Highway 191.

Follow FR 687, a rough dirt road, northward to its end at 9.8 miles. The narrow road is usually passable to passenger cars, but take your time on a few rocky spots. You will pass the turnoff for The Isle of You at 2 miles. At 7.1 miles, be sure to keep right before a ranch gate and fenceline. The rough road heads east up Stronghold Canyon West. At the end of the road there is a parking area and trailhead. Good camping is found in the forest here.

Cochise Trail, which heads east to the forest campground in the East Stronghold, begins here. It offers access to the Rockfellow Domes and Cochise Dome. The described domes in the West Stronghold are all in an unnamed canyon that trends north to south. Walk about 100 feet on Cochise Trail from the parking area into a creek bed. Take the left-hand dry creek fork with a huge alligator juniper on its west bank. Follow the rough trail up the drainage for about 1 mile to the domes. Total hiking time to the various domes is 30 to 45 minutes. These approaches are shorter and easier than those in the East Stronghold. Specific hiking access is described for each dome.

WESTWORLD DOME

Westworld Dome dominates the east flank of the canyon north of the parking area. The 600-foot-high, west-facing dome is a complex formation of slabs; long, diagonal crack systems; and big dihedrals. Several routes ascend the dome, the best being *Warpaint*. This mega-classic route, one of the most-climbed lines at Cochise Stronghold, offers excellent, well-protected climbing on flawless granite. The west-facing dome receives morning shade and afternoon sun.

Finding the dome: Hike up the trail from the parking area for about 30 minutes to a tall Arizona cypress tree, the tallest in the south part of the drainage, with down-pointing dead branches. A trail marked with a cairn begins here and scrambles up the slope to the east to the base of the dome.

WEST COCHISE STRONGHOLD

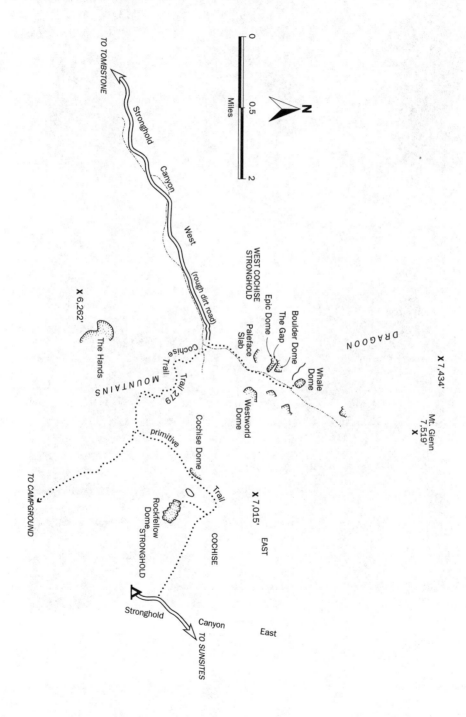

TO TOMBSTONE

Stronghold

Canyon

West

(rough dirt road)

0

0.5

2

Miles

N

X 6,262'

The Hands

Cochise

Trail

MOUNTAINS

Trail 279

primitive

TO CAMPGROUND

WEST COCHISE
STRONGHOLD

Epic Dome

The Gap

Boulder Dome

Paleface
Slab

Whale
Dome

Westword
Dome

DRAGOON

X 7,434'

Mt. Glenn
7,519'
X

Cochise Dome

Rockfellow
Dome STRONGHOLD

X 7,015'

Trail

COCHISE

EAST

Stronghold

Canyon

TO SUNSITES

East

131

COCHISE
STRONGHOLD
WESTWORLD DOME

X·X
.10
.10
X·X
.10
X·X
.8
.10c
bolts not shown
38
37

37. **Warpaint** (III 5.10c) 5 pitches. Great route! This popular classic was put up by Eric Fazio-Rhicard and Bob Kerry in 1989. Most of the pitches are primarily bolt-protected and all belay/rappel stations are bolted. Begin in the middle of the dome below a slab and right of a dark dihedral system. **Pitch 1:** Edge up the slabby, outside buttress of a large pillar past 9 bolts (5.10c) to a spacious belay ledge with tree anchors. **Pitch 2:** A short pitch. To start, move the belay left atop some blocks. Climb a crack up a corner (5.8) to a 2-bolt belay stance. **Pitch 3:** Follow a finger-tip seam up left to its end (5.10), then edge up a perfect, steep slab to a 2-bolt belay stance. 9 bolts. **Pitch 4:** Move across the slab to the right to a left-facing corner. Climb the corner until it's possible to reach up right and pull over excellent plated rock (5.10) to chickenheads and a lower-angle slab. Move up left to the right side of a steep arête and climb to a 2-bolt belay. 7 bolts. **Pitch 5:** Steep climbing up right leads to a final headwall with crystal-filled finger pockets. Finish up the slab left of a huge, left-facing dihedral to a bolt anchor. 7 bolts. **Descent:** 4 double-rope rappels down the route from bolt anchors with chains. **Rack:** Small and medium wires, small to medium cams (#0.5, #1, #1.5, #2, #3 Friends), 12 to 14 quickdraws/runners, and 2 ropes.

38. **Coatimundi Corner** (5.11a) No topo. A fun, pumpy lieback route. Hike south from the base of *Warpaint* to the base of a left-arching dihedral. Tips liebacking and stemming lead up the colorful corner to surprising exit moves onto a 2-bolt belay stance. 3 bolts. **Descent:** Rappel the route. **Rack:** Wires, TCUs, and small cams.

BOULDER DOME

South-facing Boulder Dome towers above the right side of a deep slash called The Gap on the west side of the canyon. Several good bolted and traditional routes ascend the slabby face of the dome.

Finding the dome: Hike up the canyon floor trail for about 1 mile to the obvious gap to the left. Scramble up polished slabs into the canyon. Routes are listed right to left.

39. **Pony Express** (5.11b/c) 2 pitches. Recommended route. Many parties do only the 1st pitch (5.10) and rappel from the anchors. The line begins 20' left of a left-facing corner and just left of a tree on a small ledge. **Pitch 1:** Edge up a steep face past 2 bolts to a thin overlap. Delicate moves head up a steep slab (5.10) with 3 bolts to easier rock and chickenheads. Belay from 2 bolts. **Pitch 2:** (No Topo) Climb up right on a slab to a steep wall with a water streak. Thin face climbing past 4 bolts left of the streak goes to a left-angling thin crack. Work up the crack to large blocks. Belay above from a bolt and a large tied-off chickenhead. **Descent:** 2 double-rope rappels down the route. **Rack:**

COCHISE
STRONGHOLD
BOULDER DOME

41

40

39

routes start in gully

all bolts not shown

Selection of wires and Friends, runners for tying off chickenheads, quickdraws, and 2 ropes.

40. **Desert Ice** (5.10) A dicey, bolted pitch that ends at *Pony Express*'s first anchors. Start 40' left of *Pony Express*. Climb slick, water-polished rock past 4 bolts to thin, sticky face climbing up a steep slab with 2 bolts to an overhanging tongue. Go up the right side of the tongue to a bolt over a bulge. Climb chickenheads to the *Pony Express* 2-bolt belay stance. **Descent:** 2-rope rappel to the base. **Rack:** Wires, small and medium cams, quickdraws, and 2 ropes.

41. **Max Headwall** (5.10) 2 pitches. Scramble up the gully from *Desert Ice* to the base of a steeper pour-off. **Pitch 1:** Work up an easy, water-polished groove to the base of an arête. Climb the arête past 5 bolts to a headwall. Angle up right on the headwall past 2 more bolts and continue up easier slabs to a 2-bolt belay stance. **Pitch 2:** Thin edging and friction up the left side of a steep, smooth face with several bolts lead to an obvious chickenhead on the skyline. Swing above to a tied-off chickenhead and 1-bolt belay/rap station. **Descent:** 2 double-rope rappels down *Pony Express*. **Rack:** Wires and small to medium cams, quickdraws, and 2 ropes.

WHALE DOME

This big dome, which looks like a whale from a distance, towers above the west side of the canyon. There are several classic routes on the dome, the best being *Moby Dick*. *Dem Bones* (5.10) is also good. Check Kerry's book for a description.

Finding the dome: Hike up the canyon for 30 to 45 minutes until you're below an obvious gully that descends to the canyon floor on the south side of the slabby dome.

42. **Moby Dick** (III 5.8) 6 pitches. Highly recommended. An excellent, classic route with mostly easy climbing. Scramble up the steep, brushy, boulder-choked gully to a flat area at the base of an arching, double-crack system. Rope up here. **Pitch 1:** Climb the right-hand crack for 25' to where it splits. Go up the left fork via a thin, left-facing corner with a bolt (5.8). Continue up left to a small ledge with a 2-bolt belay anchor left of a wide, left-facing crack. **Pitch 2:** Step left to a blunt prow and edge up it for 10' (5.7), then face climb left of a wide crack to chickenheads. Continue up the face left of the crack to a good ledge with two small trees. **Pitch 3:** Swing up the moderate face with chickenheads (5.6) left of the wide crack in a corner for a rope length to a belay from chickenheads. Look for a bolt where the corner narrows and jogs right. **Pitch 4:** Continue up the crack system for 40' to an obvious right traverse out of the corner at a bolt. Face climb past

COCHISE
STRONGHOLD
WHALE DOME

2-rope rappel from anchors to
saddle on west side

.8

.6

.7

.8

39

Start hidden

another bolt, then up right to a 2-bolt belay stance on a dike below a steep face dotted with chickenheads. **Pitch 5:** Fun climbing up the steep face (5.8) past 2 bolts to a belay stance where the climb slabs off. **Pitch 6:** Class 4 climbing to the summit. **Descent:** Locate a 2-bolt chain anchor on the west side of the summit and make a mostly free, 2-rope rappel to a saddle on the west side. Scramble south and east down the brushy gully to the base of the route. **Rack:** Sets of Stoppers and cams, runners for tying-off chickenheads, quickdraws, and 2 ropes. A big piece helps protect the wide crack section.

THE ISLE OF YOU

OVERVIEW

The Isle of You is an excellent sport climbing area nestled against the west side of the Dragoon Mountains between the West Stronghold and the Sheepshead area. Numerous ribs, fins, buttresses, and faces are scattered across the craggy

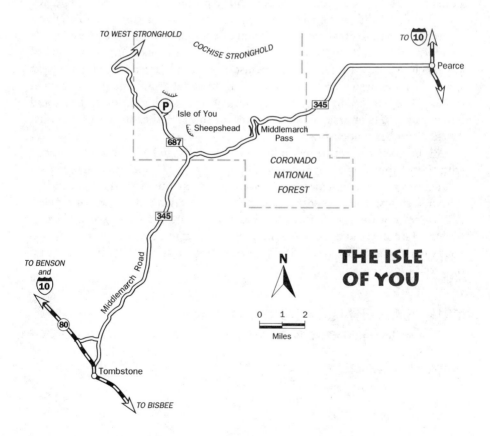

escarpment, offering a wealth of route possibilities for the exploring climber. The main developed area is comprised of three granite cliffs—Trad Rock, Rad Rock, and Glad Rock—that offer a selection of fun, bolted face climbs ranging from 5.6 to 5.11. All of the routes are single-pitch and well-protected with closely-spaced bolts, allowing even the timid leader to safely go for it. This is a good place to spend a couple of days camping under the spreading oaks, climbing the splendid clip-up routes, and discovering hidden canyons, cliffs, and amphitheaters tucked into the mountain's flank.

The area, lying at the relatively high elevation of 5,000 feet, is a good year-round climbing choice. Trad Rock and Rad Rock, facing northwest, are shaded almost all morning, even in summer, while Glad Rock gets afternoon shade. Expect dry and sunny conditions most of the year. In winter it can be too cold for comfort until the sun comes around and warms the crags.

Climbing history: Most of the routes at The Isle of You were put up by Tucson activists Mike Strassman, Elizabeth Ayers, and Scott Ayers in the early 1990s. Strassman humorously describes the initial development in a 1994 *Rock & Ice* article. After putting up the area's first route, *The Isle of You*, in the traditional ground-up mandate of the Dragoon Mountains, Strassman recounts a dream he had: "I was tied to a stake while Apache braves danced around me. Then I realized they were climbers well known for their traditionalist ethics: Robbins, Bachar, Croft—even Ken Nichols. Eventually ol' Cochise himself made an appearance. His face grew contorted, showing a range of emotions, and as I looked closer, I saw that it wasn't Cochise at all, but Warren Harding. He took a swig of some firewater and commanded, 'Just make sure you put up a good route.'" The trio of climbers quickly took Warren's admonition to heart and bolted this excellent array of sport routes for the 1993 Beanfest, a semiannual Arizona climber rendezvous.

All the described routes are bolted with camouflaged hangers and equipped with beefy rappel/lowering anchors. Clip quickdraws or locking carabiners on to anchors for toproping to avoid wearing them out. Use the hangers for descending only. **Rack:** A sport rack with 20 quickdraws and 2 ropes for rappels. A 200-foot cord is also handy on a lot of the routes. Use the existing access trails to the cliffs to avoid creating needless social trails. And, of course, pick up your own and anyone else's trash, pop cans, and cigarette butts from the base of the cliffs.

TRIP PLANNING INFORMATION

General description: Excellent and fun single-pitch, bolted routes on granite fins along the west side of the Dragoon Mountains between Sheepshead and the West Stronghold.

Location: Southeastern Arizona, southeast of Tucson near Tombstone.

Camping: Great free campsites are found in the shady oak grove at the parking area below the cliffs. No water or latrines. Pack your trash out and dispose of human waste properly.

Climbing season: October to May. Winters can be chilly, particularly in the morning because the crags all face west. Summer is usually too hot. Try early morning when the cliffs are in the shade.

Restrictions and access issues: None currently. The area is in Coronado National Forest.

Guidebooks: A mini-guide appeared in *Rock & Ice* #59. Also, there are topos in *Backcountry Rockclimbing in Southern Arizona* by Bob Kerry, Backcountry Books of Arizona, 1997.

Nearby mountain shops, guide services, and gyms: The Summit Hut and Bumjo's Climbing Shop in Tucson. Rocks & Ropes is the Tucson gym.

Services: Nearest services are in Tombstone, about 15 miles away.

Emergency services: Call 911. Sierra Vista Community Hospital, 300 El Camino Real, Sierra Vista, AZ 85635, 800-880-0088 or 502-458-2300; and Northern Cochise Community Hospital, 901 West Rex Allen Drive, Willcox, AZ 85643, 502-384-3541.

Nearby climbing areas: West Stronghold (Warpath Dome, The Tombstone, Westworld Dome, The Gap, Epic Dome, Whale Dome), Sheepshead, Big Sister and Little Sister Domes, Watchtower, Texas Canyon bouldering, The Dry.

Nearby attractions: Tombstone, Cochise Stronghold, ghost towns, San Pedro Riparian National Conservation Area, Kartchner Caverns State Park, Willcox Playa, Chiricahua National Monument.

Finding the crags: The Isle of You is about 75 miles and one-and-a-half hours from Tucson. Best approach is the drive out Interstate 10 to Exit 303 (Tombstone/Bisbee). Drive through Benson and south on Arizona Highway 80 toward Tombstone for 23 miles. Look for a left (east) turn just before Tombstone that is marked "Middlemarch Road." Follow this good gravel road for almost 10 miles to a Forest Service sign that marks a left (north) turn on Forest Service Road 687 to the West Stronghold. You can also reach this turnoff from the east side of the Dragoon Mountains by following FR 345 for 16 miles over Middlemarch Pass west from Pearce and US Highway 191. Follow this narrow, rougher road north for 2 miles to a cattleguard. Just past the guard, make a right (east) turn on FR 687E and drive east for 0.2 mile, down a slight hill, to the camping area in an oak grove at the road's end. The cliffs are a five-minute walk up a climber's trail northeast from the parking area.

Rad Rock

Trad Rock

trail

to Glad Rock

to camping

TRAD ROCK

This is the obvious northwest-facing cliff northeast of the circular parking/camping area. Access it by walking five minutes uphill on the climber's trail from the end of the parking area. Routes are listed from right to left.

1. **Baby Jr. Gets Spanked** (5.6) The first route on the right side of the wall. Easy climbing up edges and flakes leads up the obvious, black water streak. 7 bolts to 2-bolt chain anchor.

2. **Baby Jr.** (5.8+) Begin up left of Route 1 on a ledge. Fun face climbing past 7 bolts to 2-bolt anchor.

3. **Stone Woman** (5.10a) Start just left of *Baby Jr.* An early crux above the 1st bolt, then cruise. 8 bolts to 2-bolt anchor.

4. **The Chosen One** (5.11a) Begin just left of small oaks. Boulder to the high 1st bolt, then begin thin face climbing (5.11a). Continue up past three 5.10 cruxes to anchors just below the top. 17 bolts to 2-bolt anchor. 165'. **Descent:** Rap with double ropes.

5. **Isle of You** (5.9) The area's first route, put in ground-up and on lead, gave the crag its name. Begin atop a gravel terrace beside a solitary

ISLE OF YOU CRAGS

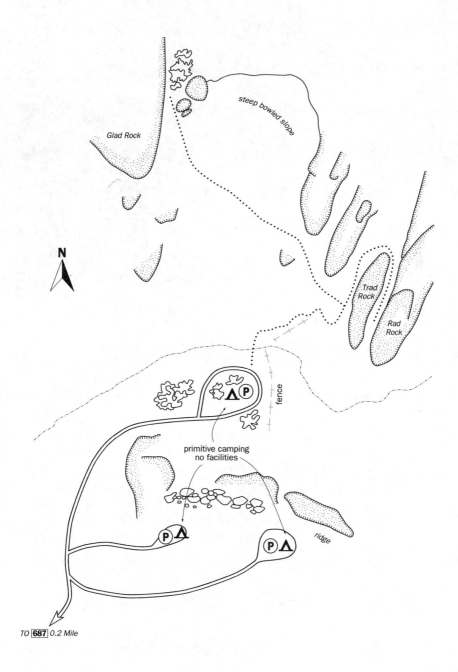

Glad Rock

steep bowled slope

N

Trad Rock

Rad Rock

fence

primitive camping
no facilities

P △

P △

ridge

TO 687 0.2 Mile

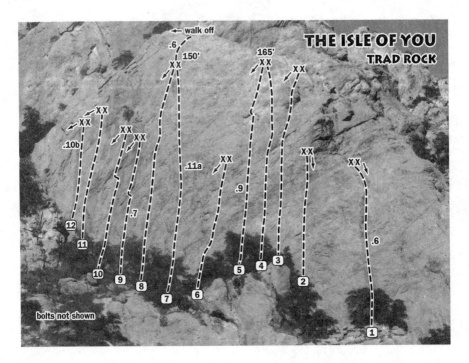

oak. Edge up right 15' to the 1st bolt. Continue up right to a shallow scoop and the 2nd bolt. Climb straight up the wall on great edges to the top. 14 bolts to 2-bolt anchor (same anchor as Route 4). 165'. **Descent:** Rappel with double ropes.

6. **Jizzneyland** (5.10c) Begin right of 2 large boulders and a right-slanting, left-facing corner. Thin crux edging to the 1st bolt. Continue up right to a small ledge. Climb the headwall above past two 5.10 cruxes to anchors. 8 bolts to 2-bolt anchor. Lower off.

7. **Ass Over Teacup** (5.11a) Begin 20' left of a right-angling ramp. Excellent, well-protected face climbing up thin edges and slopers to anchors on a high stance. 14 bolts to 2-bolt anchor. 150'. **Descent:** Rappel with 2 ropes or do a short, runout 5.6 pitch to the summit and walk off.

8. **Hell in a Handbasket** (5.11a) Begin 10' left of Route 7. Follow lots of bolts to a final 5.11a crux bulge, or step left for the weenie 5.10c finish. 13 bolts to 2-bolt anchor. 150'. **Descent:** Rappel with 2 ropes or do a short, runout 5.6 pitch to the summit and walk off.

9. **OK Corral** (5.7) A stellar, moderate route that looks way harder! Start up left from Route 8 at some boulders. Lots of great edges lead up a brown streak to anchors. 9 bolts to 2-bolt anchor.

Ian Spencer-Green on *Jizzneyland* (5.10c) at Trad Rock.

10. **Now It's My Turn** (5.10b) Just left of Route 9. Work up to thin face moves (5.10b) below a small roof, then pull over onto a sloping ledge. Thin edging above (5.10a) to anchors below a prominent oak tree on a ledge. 8 bolts to 2-bolt anchor.

11. **Rise and Shine Cupcake** (5.10c) Begin 20' left of Route 10. Steep, continuous face climbing. 10 bolts to 2-bolt anchor.

12. **Cochise Toecheese** (5.10b) Farthest route to the left. Climb edges up excellent rock on a brown water streak to anchors on a sloping ramp. 7 bolts to 2-bolt anchor.

RAD ROCK

The cliff is directly behind Trad Rock. Only the top half can be seen from the parking area; the bottom is in a wide corridor. Access the cliff from Trad Rock by hiking uphill on a fairly steep trail and turning right into the corridor. Routes are listed left to right.

13. **The Blister** (5.11b) Start in the trees on the left side of the cliff. Climb lichen-covered rock past 2 bolts. Continue up right of a yellow, right-facing flake to a beautiful headwall to anchors. Note the chickenhead that looks like a blister to the left of the anchors. 9 bolts to 2-bolt anchor. 80'.

14. **Hothead** (5.11b) Step on to the trees and pull up on good holds to start. From the narrow ledge, move up the left side of a brown streak. Step right at the last bolt for a slightly easier finish. 7 bolts to 2-bolt anchor. 85'.

15. **Hairs on Fire** (5.10b) Quality climbing. Same start as Route 14. It's kind of high to the 1st bolt, so use care. Jugs to ledge and 1st bolt to the right. Head straight up excellent rock to anchors at the base of an alcove/scoop. 6 bolts to 2-bolt anchor.

16. **Gringo en Quema** (5.11b) Climb a thin, right-facing corner and work up right to the base of a long, narrow right-facing corner. Follow the arching corner to a pull (5.11b) over a small roof and a headwall finish. Anchors set back right of the alcove. 10 bolts to 2-bolt anchor.

17. **Fire in the Hole** (5.10b) Classic. Begin right of a thin, right-facing corner and a yucca. Thin face climbing up immaculate gray rock leads to a right-angling roof. Fire past the hole under the roof (5.10b) and continue up excellent rock to anchors. 10 bolts to 2-bolt anchor.

18. **Liquor and Porn** (5.11a) Start left of a narrow, right-facing corner. Climb up and over the corner and head up the steep wall above to

THE ISLE OF YOU
RAD ROCK

The Hole

13 14 15 16 17 18 19 20 21

15

a right-angling seam. The anchors are above a bulge. 10 bolts to 2-bolt anchor.

19. **Caught in the Crotch Fire** (5.11d) Begin right of the right-facing corner. Climb up the line of bolts on steep rock. 11 bolts to 2-bolt anchor.

20. **Hotter Than a Three Peckered Goat** (5.11b) Superb face climbing with good position and great protection. Begin immediately left of a small oak clump. Climb along a brown streak to a bulge. Pull onto a narrow stance. Thin face moves lead left over a final bulge, then back right to anchors. 11 bolts to 2-bolt anchor.

21. **Burning Beer Time** (5.10d) Right-most route on the wall. Swing up good edges to anchors, then back to camp for brews. 7 bolts to 2-bolt anchor.

GLAD ROCK

This southeast-facing wall lies northwest from Trad Rock. A rough trail begins at The Isle of You and crosses the slope to the cliff. Routes are listed left to right.

22. **Platos de Plata** (5.10c) No topo. The left-most route on the cliff. Begin left of a right-angling, left-facing corner system. Work over a bulge and climb up right on good edges over plated rock to anchors. 6 bolts to 2-bolt anchor.

23. **Curva Peligrosa** (5.11c) Begin on the left side of a large clump of trees and right of a chossy, angling system of roofs. Climb straight up an overlap past 3 bolts, then move up left on flakes above the roofs before angling back right to anchors on top of the cliff. 10 bolts to 2-bolt anchor.

24. **Desemboque** (5.11a) Same start as Route 23 but continue above the 3rd bolt to anchors. 10 bolts to 2-bolt anchor.

25. **Clown's Teeth** (5.11c) Pull up and over jagged "clown's teeth" overlaps (5.11c) to another crux above the 5th bolt. Motor up good rock above and finish up Route 22 to anchors on top of the cliff. 10 bolts to 2-bolt anchor.

26. **Choy Chi** (5.10d) Start at the obvious, partially denuded pine tree at the wall's base. Climb the pine and bridge across to the 1st bolt, or climb directly up (5.11b) overhanging stone. Climb up and left across dikes. After the 7th bolt, reach a right-angling ramp and finish straight up. 11 bolts to 2-bolt anchor.

27. **Bunny** (5.11a) Just right of the pine tree. Climb up to bolt 1, then follow excellent dike handholds up left. After 4 bolts, continue straight up plated rock. 10 bolts to 2-bolt anchor.

PHOENIX AREA

CAMELBACK MOUNTAIN

OVERVIEW

Camelback Mountain, looming above eastern Phoenix and Scottsdale, is a well-known landmark visible from anywhere in the Valley of the Sun. It's an easily accessible, unique, and old climbing area that offers a quick getaway to hone your skills on the mountain's cliffs and boulders. Out on the mountain, it's easy to feel far from the teeming Phoenix freeways and crowded shopping malls.

Camelback is a two-summited mountain that looks like a kneeling camel to the imaginative eye. The eastern summit, rising to 2,704 feet, forms the camel's hump, while the lower summit to the west is the camel's head. Most of the climbing is found on the north-facing cliffs below the head.

The camel's hump and mountain summit is composed of granite, while the head is what geologists call the Camel's Head Formation, which is divided into four distinctive members. Most of the routes are on the thick Echo Canyon member and the Papago Park member. The Papago Park member is a reddish sandstone deposited by streams on a broad alluvial fan. The rock is alternately layered with coarse beds of cobbles, pebbles, sand, and silt. Many popular areas, including the Praying Monk and the Gargoyle Wall, are composed of this sandstone. Climbing holds are usually flakes, cobbles, and pebbles. Cracks are usually intermittent and sandy.

Camelback has a climber's reputation for rotten rock and indeed, there are many routes with bad sections. All the described routes, however, are generally sound because they have seen numerous ascents and all the loose stuff has been cleaned off. Remember when climbing here, as at any soft rock area, to pull down and not out on the holds. Never trust a single-bolt anchor, unless it's one of the large glued-in eyebolts.

Climbing history: Camelback Mountain was not only one of the first technical climbing areas in Arizona, but also in the United States. It was also one of the first areas to see placement of expansion bolts to protect blank faces. The earliest routes were put up in the 1940s by a group of Boy Scouts dubbed The Kachinas, who wore hiking boots and used hemp ropes and soft iron pitons. The group was organized after World War II by Ray Garner, an ex-Teton guide. The members, including Ed George and Ben Pedrick, put up many Camelback classics like *Pedrick's Chimney*, *Hart Route*, and *George Route*. Another notable ascent was the first pitch of *Suicide*, put up by traveling climbers Herb and Jan Conn. The Praying Monk was first summited by Gary Driggs in 1951 and protected by funky pitons that were later replaced with bolts. Bill Forrest, a college student in the 1960s, pushed local standards by finishing *Suicide* and

CAMELBACK MOUNTAIN

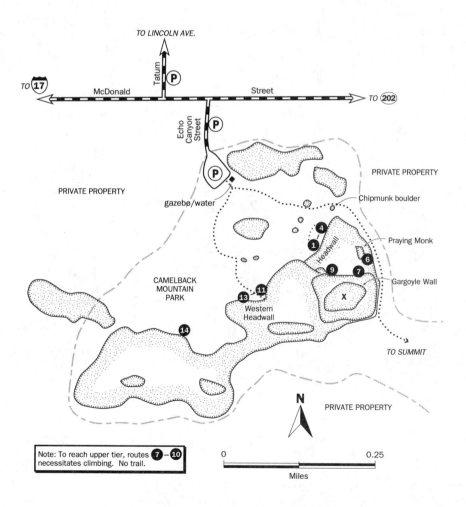

OTHER PHOENIX AREAS

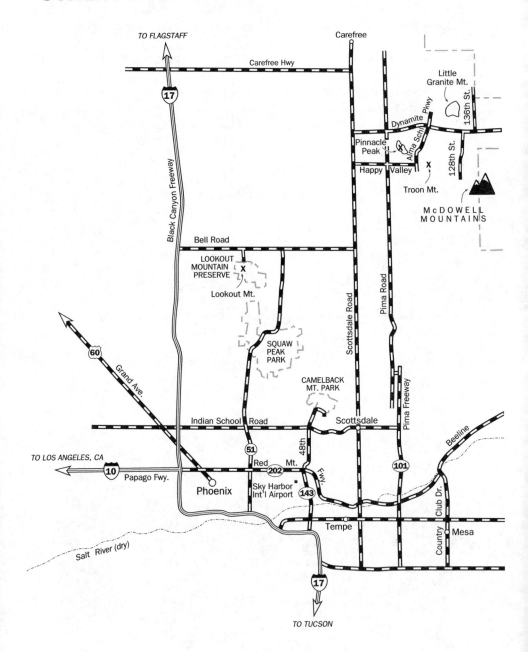

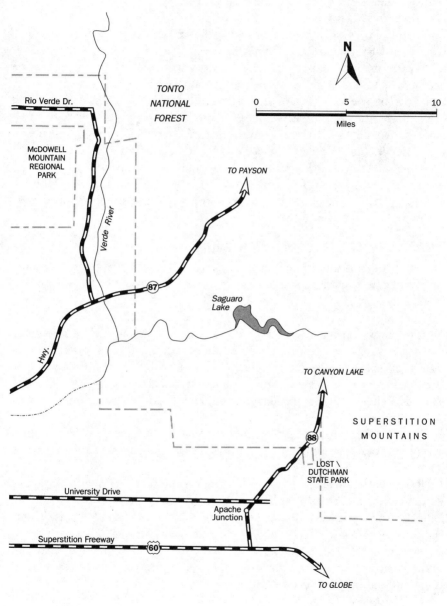

N

0   5   10
Miles

TONTO
NATIONAL
FOREST

Rio Verde Dr.

McDOWELL
MOUNTAIN
REGIONAL
PARK

Verde River

TO PAYSON

87

Saguaro
Lake

Hwy.

TO CANYON LAKE

SUPERSTITION
MOUNTAINS

88

LOST \
DUTCHMAN
STATE PARK

University Drive

Apache
Junction

Superstition Freeway

60

TO GLOBE

Dromedary Peak

doing a direct start on Praying Monk. *Suicide Direct* was free-climbed in the 1960s by the brother team of Lance and Dane Daugherty. A couple more recent routes bolted in the 1990s include *Black Direct* by Manny Rangle and *3-Star Nightmare* by Marty Karabin.

There are currently no climbing regulations at Camelback Mountain, which is a Phoenix Mountain Park. Climbers, however, need to follow existing trails to the cliff base. The parks department is doing trail work to minimize erosion and to keep hikers on the paths, lessening damage to the park's desert ecosystem. Keep off the rock after rain; the soft sandstone is more friable and subject to breakage after precipitation. Some of the bolts are suspect. Back them up whenever possible and never rely on a single anchor for toproping or rappelling. Loose handholds and rubble on ledges make it a good idea to wear a helmet at Camelback. **Descent:** Descend off routes by rappelling from large, glued-in eyebolts or by walking off. Descent routes can be complicated. **Rack:** The usual rack is a set of Friends, medium to large Stoppers, a few hexentric nuts, extra slings, and quickdraws.

TRIP PLANNING INFORMATION

General description: Fun urban cragging and bouldering on coarse sandstone and granite cliffs up to 200 feet high, that are surrounded by Phoenix and its suburbs.

Location: Central Arizona, in the metropolis of Phoenix.

Camping: None nearby. McDowell Mountain Regional Park, off Fountain Hills Boulevard, is the nearest public campground. The fee area offers RV sites with hook-ups, water, and restrooms. Call 602-471-0173 for information. Lost Dutchman State Park, east of Apache Junction, is a great camping choice, with showers, water, great scenery, and good enough security to leave your tent there during the day.

Climbing season: The best months are October through April. The summer is way too hot, although climbing happens on early mornings before the smothering midday heat.

Restrictions and access issues: Camelback Mountain is a Phoenix Mountain Park. There are currently no restrictions. Parking is often problematic at the Echo Canyon Trailhead because of the popularity of the summit trail—not enough spaces and too many cars. Try to time your visit so you can park before the evening joggers visit. The parking lot is closed from 5:30 P.M. to 6:30 A.M. during the cool weather months. Additional parking spaces are found on Echo Canyon Road off McDonald Road.

Guidebooks: *Phoenix Rock II* by Greg Opland, Falcon Publishing/Chockstone Press, 1996, is the complete guide to Camelback and the rest of the Phoenix area crags. Marty Karabin publishes *Camelback Mountain*, a fold-out topo to routes, with a good overview of the area's bouldering.

Nearby mountain shops, guide services, and gyms: Desert Mountain Sports (Phoenix), REI (Paradise Valley and Tempe), Trailhead Sports (Scottsdale), The Wilderness (Phoenix); Phoenix Rock Gym (Phoenix), Climbmax Climbing Center (Tempe).

Services: All services are found in Phoenix and Scottsdale.

Emergency services: Call 911. Humana Hospital, 1947 East Thomas Road, Phoenix, AZ 85016, 602-241-7600; Scottsdale Memorial Hospital, 7400 East Osburn Road, Scottsdale, AZ 85025, 602-994-9616.

Nearby climbing areas: Pinnacle Peak, Troon Mountain, Little Granite Mountain, Cholla Mountain, Lookout Mountain, McDowell Mountains, Superstition Mountains.

Nearby attractions: Squaw Peak, Phoenix Zoo, Desert Botanical Garden, Papago Park, Phoenix Art Museum, Heard Museum, Pueblo Grande Ruin and Museum, Hoo-Hoogam Ki Museum, Museo Chicano, Usury Mountains, Lost Dutchman State Park, Superstition Mountains, Apache Trail.

Finding the crags: Camelback Mountain, with its cliffs and summit hiking trail, is accessed from the parking lot on Echo Canyon Street on the northwest corner of the mountain park. Reach the lot by driving east on McDonald Street from 44th Street or west on McDonald from Scottsdale Road, or any other major north-south street in Scottsdale. Just east of the intersection of McDonald and Tatum is Echo Canyon Street. Turn south on this road and drive a few blocks to the parking area. Parking can be a problem on busy days. Additional parking is on the east side of the street. Park only in designated areas. Police will ticket all parking offenders.

To reach most of the described routes, hike up the summit trail to a saddle north of the cliffs. A short climber's path ascends the hill to the south and leads to the base of The Headwall. The Western Headwall is reached by a trail that goes south from the parking area. Pick an existing climber trail up the slopes to the cliff's base.

THE HEADWALL

The Headwall is a northwest-facing cliff band that lies south of a large boulder where the summit trail reaches a saddle. Hike up a climber's path to the base of the cliff. Four easy routes on the wall allow access to the upper terrace routes, including the routes on Praying Monk. Routes are listed left to right. **Descent:** Descend from the upper terrace by downclimbing *Class 3 Gully* or preferably by making a single-rope rappel from a large eyebolt atop *Rappel Gully*. The bolt is hard to find initially because it hides below a large boulder above the gully and can't be seen from above. It's wise to clip into the bolt while setting up the rappel rope.

CAMELBACK MOUNTAIN
THE HEADWALL AND PRAYING MONK

Praying Monk

to routes
5 6

X X

X X

4 bolts

3

4

2

1

1. **Class 3 Gully** (Class 3) Easy but still risky. Rope up if you're unsure of your own and your partner's abilities. Climb an easy gully or ridge on the left side of the wall. Cross behind a small, detached pillar and scramble up another gully to the upper terrace.

2. **The Walk-Up** (Class 4) Not exactly walking. Climb easy rock up a gully 70' right of Route 1 and scramble to the upper terrace.

3. **Rappel Gully** (5.4 R) Climb a recessed gully with hard-to-find pro to a ledge with an eyebolt below a large boulder. This is the rappel bolt from the upper terrace.

4. **Headwall Route** (5.4) A good pitch to access the upper terrace. Climb a shallow water groove past 4 bolts to a 2-bolt anchor. Scramble up a gully onto the terrace.

PRAYING MONK

This 80-foot-high tower, perched on the east side of the upper terrace, is a Phoenix landmark that looks like a kneeling monk. The best and only route to do on the tower is the *East Face* with the *Southeast Corner* start. It's protected with old bolts. Try to avoid falling! The rounded summit offers a superlative view that includes Squaw Peak, the McDowell Mountains, Pinnacle Peak, Four Peaks, and the western escarpment of the Superstition Mountains.

5. **East Face** (5.4) The must-do Phoenix classic. Traditionally rated 5.2. Begin at the southeast corner of the spire below a huge boulder leaning against the corner. Climb up left into a shallow cave formed by the boulder and the main face. Traverse out right around a corner to the left side of the east face and follow 5 bolts to the summit anchors—a rappel eyebolt and 2 belay bolts. 120'. **Descent:** A single-rope, mostly free rappel from the large eyebolt on the south side of the summit. **Rack:** Quickdraws and a rope.

6. **Southeast Corner** (5.6) A direct start to Route 5 that makes it a better route. Begin below the southeast corner of the tower. Face climb up right (5.6) to the 1st bolt, pull onto a stance above to the 2nd bolt, step right around the corner onto the east face, and climb cobbles to the summit anchors—a rappel eyebolt and 2 belay bolts. 7 bolts. 120'. **Descent:** A single-rope, mostly free rappel from the large eyebolt on the south side of the summit. **Rack:** Quickdraws and a rope.

GARGOYLE WALL

This high wall south and west of Praying Monk offers some of Camelback Mountain's best routes. Most of the routes have been climbed a lot, so they are clean and free of loose rock. Access the cliff by climbing one of the Headwall routes and following a climber's path up the upper terrace to the cliff base. Routes are listed left to right.

7. **Pedrick's Chimney** (5.1) The obvious chimney on the left side of the cliff. Scramble up to the highest point of the talus field. Climb an easy open book to the base of the chimney. Work up the chimney past a bolt to a large rappel eyebolt and belay. The summit of the camel's head is easily reached from here by scrambling south and west up gullies to the top. **Descent:** Rappel 90' from the eyebolt. This is the standard descent for many of the routes that reach the summit of the camel.

CAMELBACK MOUNTAIN
GARGOYLE WALL

8. **Misgivings** (5.8) 4 pitches. Ascends the blank wall 140' right of Route 7. **Pitch 1:** Work up right along a thin crack on an easy ramp to a bolt. Climb up left past two old bolts and surmount a steeper headwall (5.8) to a 2-bolt belay on a ledge. **Pitch 2:** Traverse left about 25' and then up to a belay ledge. **Pitch 3:** Climb up right to a huge ledge that runs across the face. **Pitch 4:** Traverse left across the big ledge and then downclimb to the top of *Pedrick's Chimney*. **Descent:** Rappel 90' from eyebolt anchor.

9. **Hart Route** (5.2) 4 pitches. An easy old classic. Start on the left side of a large buttress in the middle of the face. **Pitch 1:** Climb an easy gully up right past a bolt to a 2-bolt anchor on a ledge. **Pitch 2:** Continue up the gully/groove, passing an overhang on the left, to a chimney and a good belay ledge. **Pitch 3:** Move the belay by scrambling up right in a short gully to the base of a slab. Friction 60' up the slab to a 2-bolt belay anchor. **Pitch 4:** Climb an easy face past a couple of bolts to the top. **Descent:** Scramble south and east along gullies and ledges to the top of *Pedrick's Chimney* (Route 7). Rappel 90' from an eyebolt. **Rack:** An assortment of nuts and Friends.

10. **Hard Times** (5.7) 2 pitches. Start west of Route 9 below two large holes. Start below the right-hand hole. **Pitch 1:** Climb easy rock for

25' to the right hole. Duck through the archway into the left hole and belay from a bolt. **Pitch 2:** Climb up the rib between holes to a bolt. Continue up the face above (5.7) past 3 more bolts to a 2-bolt belay stance atop a boulder inclusion. Most parties rap here. The route continues another pitch by working straight up past a bolt to a ramp system that leads up right to ledges. **Descent:** 2-rope rappel from 2-bolt anchor atop pitch 2.

WESTERN HEADWALL

These routes ascend the walls of a cul-de-sac on the northwest side of the Camelback Mountain massif. To reach the wall, hike up the summit trail to the large boulder on the left. Just past the boulder, look for a trail that heads southwest into an arroyo. Follow it down and up the other side past some large boulders. A path continues up steep slopes to the base of the walls.

11. **Suicide** (5.5) 3 pitches. A classic line that's had a few serious falls. Watch out for general looseness. Start below a deep groove in the back of a wide alcove. **Pitch 1:** Stem up the groove past 2 bolts (5.5) to a hole. Traverse up right on easy rock to a good ledge belay with bolt anchors. (For a variation to pitch 1, climb a steep, 5.9 R face right of the groove with 3 bolts to the ledge belay. It's hard getting to the 2nd bolt and you might ground if you fall. This pitch is actually the 1st pitch of a different route.) **Pitch 2:** Easy climbing leads up left along a ramp with 2 bolts to a vertical hole. Clip a bolt left of the hole and pull up to a stance with another bolt. Traverse up left from here (5.5) to a 2-bolt belay at a protruding boulder. **Pitch 3:** The traditional finish is to traverse left to a gully and a 2-bolt belay/rap anchor. Rap 140' here or climb this Class 4 gully to its top and a belay. The preferred finish is to climb straight up to a stance with a fixed piton. Traverse up right along a ramp system past 2 bolts to a ledge, then scramble down right to a 4-bolt belay/rappel anchor atop Route 12. **Descent:** If you do the preferred finish, make 2 double-rope rappels to the ground. To get off the traditional finish, rap from the 2-bolt anchor 140' to the ground. Or do the adventure descent—scramble east into August Canyon and continue to the summit, or scramble around the south side of the summit to a ledge that leads north to rappel anchors on the left side of Gargoyle Wall above Praying Monk. Rappel single line from here. Scramble north to anchors atop The Headwall and make another single-rope rappel to the cliff's base. **Rack:** Some medium to large wires, a few TCUs, and a set of Friends.

12. **Black Direct** (5.10c) 2 pitches. A good line up solid rock established by Manny Rangle. **Pitch 1:** Climb good rock (Class 4) to a ledge below a right-facing cave formed by a flake. Continue up right of the flake to a large, boulder-strewn ledge and belay. **Pitch 2:** Work up from the ledge to a face left of a black water streak. Face climb up solid rock (5.10c) past 6 bolts. All the cruxes are well-protected. Above, angle up right to a ledge with a 4-bolt anchor near a paloverde tree. **Descent:** 2 double-rope rappels down the route. The first rap is 110' from 4 bolts to the ledge, and the second rap is 90' from 2 bolts to the ground.

13. **Suicide Direct** (5.8) 2 pitches. Airy, direct route up the steep wall right of *Black Direct* that was put up in 1949 and later freed by Lance and Dane Daugherty. Begin right of the deep groove below a slabby face. **Pitch 1:** Same as Route 12—climb good rock (Class 4) to a ledge below a right-facing cave formed by a flake. Continue up right of the flake to a large, boulder-strewn ledge and belay from 2 bolts. **Pitch 2:** Work up from the ledge to the base of a black water streak. Face moves lead up the streak past 3 bolts. The crux is a bulge (5.8). Higher up, the streak becomes a groove. Follow it up to a large terrace and belay from 4 bolts. The pitch is a bit runout, but easy climbing leads to the well-protected crux. **Descent:** Make 2 double-rope rappels down the route. **Rack:** A small selection of wires, TCUs, Friends, and quickdraws.

14. **3-Star Nightmare** (5.8) No topo. A long pitch. This face route established by Marty Karabin. Definitely not for the 5.8 leader. This route ascends a steep, granite wall on the right (west) side of Boulder Canyon, the deep canyon around the buttress right (west) of *Suicide*. Look for a line of bolts on a face right of a ramp/slab below the Camel's Foot. Scamble up left to a belay bolt on a ramp. Follow the left side of a black water streak up the 150-foot-high face past 11 bolts to a small cave with a 4-bolt chain belay/rappel anchor. **Descent:** A double-rope rappel 150' to the ground.

LITTLE GRANITE MOUNTAIN

OVERVIEW

Little Granite Mountain, called Granite Mountain on the USGS topographic maps, was renamed by climbers in deference to the more famous Granite Mountain outside Prescott. This isolated 3,526-foot-high mountain rises above a sloped plain north of the McDowell Mountains. Numerous small granite crags and boulders are strewn across the mountain, offering rock climbers a quiet and fairly remote getaway close to the Phoenix megalopolis. The mountain's

Martha Morris belays Jim Waugh on *3-Star Nightmare* (5.8), Camelback Mountain.

LITTLE GRANITE MOUNTAIN

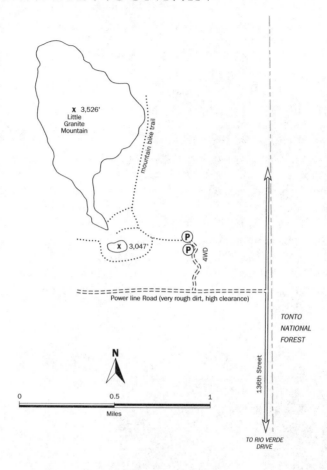

pristine Sonoran desert ecosystem, with towering saguaro cacti and other typical desert plants, makes for an unusual climbing experience for Arizona visitors.

Climbers should expect short, single-pitch routes up bolt-protected faces and slabs, along with the occasional crack line. Some excellent bouldering is found at the Morning Glory Boulders around the parking area. The granite here is generally abrasive and knobby with lots of flakes and edges, as well as more xenoliths than other area granites. Xenoliths, Greek for "strange rocks," are inclusions that are usually black and finer grained than the surrounding granite. They are weather resistant and often form excellent "Thank God" type holds amidst a sea of small granite edges. Xenoliths form when chunks of surrounding rock break off into liquid magma and are not melted.

All the described crags are found on the south end of the mountain and are reached by a short, pleasant hike through the desert. Trails lead to all the cliffs, but they are sometimes hard to locate initially. It's best to pick the easiest route to a crag and you will eventually run into a trail. Try to follow existing trails and washes as much as possible to avoid damaging plants and causing erosion. Other good crags are found farther north on the mountain. Use the comprehensive guidebook *Phoenix Rock II* for information on accessing and climbing these more remote outcrops.

Little Granite Mountain has so far avoided the access problems that plague other Phoenix-area crags. The mountain lies just inside the Scottsdale city limits, so it is possible in the future that the area west of the mountain could be developed. Perhaps the city fathers will be far-sighted enough to preserve this unique desert ecosystem and its recreational opportunities, which include not only climbing, but hiking and mountain biking, as a mountain preserve.

Climbing history: Climbing at Little Granite Mountain, along with nearby Cholla Mountain, Troon Mountain, and the McDowell Mountains, mainly developed in the 1980s. John Ficker was one of the area's first activists, putting up some of the mountain's classic routes, including *Sweet Surprise* on The Loaf and *Spectrum* on Lost Bandanna Wall in 1981. Most of the mountain crags were discovered and climbed in the late 1980s by many locals, including Steve Smelser, Chuck Hill, Jim Waugh, Jan Holdeman, Jim Zahn, Doug Fletcher, and Mike Covington.

LITTLE GRANITE MOUNTAIN
VIEW FROM PARKING LOT
Lost Bandanna Wall
Bobcat Boulder
The Loaf

TRIP PLANNING INFORMATION

General description: Lots of small granite crags with sport and crack routes, scattered across the slopes of Little Granite Mountain north of the McDowell Mountains.

Location: Central Arizona, northeast of Phoenix.

Camping: Excellent primitive camping is available off the road at the parking area. Keep a low profile and pack out all your trash. McDowell Mountain Regional Park, off Fountain Hills Boulevard, is the nearest public campground. The fee area offers RV sites with hook-ups, water, and restrooms. Call 602-471-0173 for information. Lost Dutchman State Park, east of Apache Junction, makes a good climber's base camp for climbing in the Phoenix area.

Climbing season: Best months are October through April. Summers are very hot, but early morning can be cool enough for a few pitches in the shade.

Restrictions and access issues: There are currently no restrictions, but that could change in the future as development encroaches on the area. Ask at Desert Mountain Sports or one of the local rock gyms for access updates.

Guidebooks: *Phoenix Rock II* by Greg Opland, Falcon Publishing/Chockstone Press, 1996, is the complete guide to Little Granite Mountain and the rest of the Phoenix area ranges.

Nearby mountain shops, guide services, and gyms: Desert Mountain Sports (Phoenix), REI (Paradise Valley and Tempe), Trailhead Sports (Scottsdale), The Wilderness (Phoenix); Phoenix Rock Gym (Phoenix), Climbmax Climbing Center (Tempe).

Services: All services are found in Phoenix and Scottsdale.

Emergency services: Call 911. Phoenix General Hospital, 19829 North 27th Avenue, Phoenix, AZ 85027, 602-879-5353; Scottsdale Memorial Hospital North, 10450 North 92nd Street, Scottsdale, AZ 85260, 602-860-3000; Humana Hospital 3929 East Bell Road, Phoenix, AZ 85032, 602-867-1881.

Nearby climbing areas: Pinnacle Peak, Troon Mountain, McDowell Mountains, Cholla Mountain, Lookout Mountain, Camelback Mountain, Superstition Mountains.

Nearby attractions: Phoenix attractions (Phoenix Zoo, Desert Botanical Garden, Heard Museum, Phoenix Art Museum), Apache Trail, Superstition Mountains, Lost Dutchman State Park, Casa Grande Ruins National Monument, Pioneer Arizona Museum.

Finding the crags: The best access is from Scottsdale Road or Pima Road, major north-south streets in Scottsdale, east of Phoenix. Drive north on Scottsdale Road to Pinnacle Peak Road. Turn right (east) on Pinnacle Peak Road and drive a few miles to Pima Road. Turn left (north) on Pima, drive to Dynamite Road, and turn right (east). Follow Dynamite Road to 136th Street (past the McDowell Mountain turnoff) and turn left (north) on this dirt road. Drive north 1.9 miles to Power Line Road. This unmarked road is right under the obvious power lines. Turn left on Power Line Road, go through a gate (remember to close it),

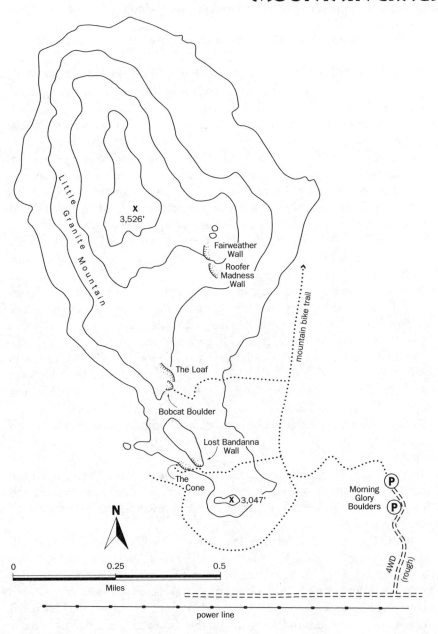

Little Granite Mountain

X
3,526'

Fairweather
Wall

Roofer
Madness
Wall

mountain bike trail

The Loaf

Bobcat Boulder

Lost Bandanna
Wall

The
Cone

X 3,047'

Morning
Glory
Boulders

P

P

4WD
(rough)

N

| 0 | 0.25 | 0.5 |

Miles

power line

and drive 0.4 mile to a right turn, which leads 0.2 mile to a parking area among boulders on the southeast side of the mountain. Power Line Road and the access road to the parking area are very rough roads; high-clearance or four-wheel-drive vehicles are needed. Otherwise, park where you feel comfortable and walk into the parking area.

Trails to the crags begin from the parking area at the end of the road near the first group of boulders. None of the trails is obvious. It's best to pick the easiest line toward the crags and you will eventually reach one of the trails. A climber's trail works up to the saddle southeast of Lost Bandanna Wall, while another trail follows a wash up to The Loaf.

LOST BANDANNA WALL

This south-facing wall sits just west of the first low saddle on the far south end of the mountain. Its craggy top is visible from the parking area. Walk west to the saddle and contour west to the base of the wall. All the described routes are

on the left side of the cliff and are listed right to left. **Descent:** The easiest descent is to walk off (either right or left) from the ledge system where the routes end. It is also possible to rappel from a 2-bolt anchor in the middle of the ledge.

1. **Loosy Loose** (5.11b) Begin just left of two large boulders at the cliff's base. Follow 5 bolts up the steep, flaky face to a 2-bolt anchor on a ledge.

2. **Lawless and Free** (5.9+) A good face route. Begin left of Route 1. Climb good edges up to the 1st bolt, pull up right to a bulging protuberance and the 2nd bolt, and continue up a short headwall to easier climbing and the 3rd bolt. Belay from a 2-bolt anchor on a ledge.

3. **Spectrum** (5.7) A fun crack. Start just left of Route 2 below a right-facing corner. Climb a broken crack system up the corner to a 2-bolt anchor on a ledge (same as Route 2). **Rack:** Selection of wires, TCUs, and small to medium cams.

4. **Graceland** (5.10d) Edge up thin flakes just left of a prow past 3 bolts to a high, rusty bolt on *Limbo*. Continue up easier rock to a belay ledge. 4 bolts.

5. **Limbo** (5.6) 2 pitches. Easier than it looks. **Pitch 1:** Work up a right-angling crack system and onto the face above (5.6) to a bolt. Climb up to a belay ledge. Walk off west or climb **Pitch 2:** Climb a short, left-facing corner (5.6) to the summit. **Rack:** Wires and a small selection of cams.

6. **Climb at First Sting** (5.11b) Start just left of Route 5. Steep face climbing past 3 bolts leads to a thin crack. Belay above on a spacious ledge.

7. **Slot** (5.6) On the far left side of the wall. Jam the obvious crack up a left-facing dihedral to a good belay ledge. **Rack:** Mostly medium and large cams.

THE CONE

This slabby, south-facing wall sits down and west from Lost Bandanna Wall. Follow a path down to the crag from the west end of Lost Bandanna Wall. Routes are listed right to left. **Descent:** Walk off all routes down the east side of the crag.

8. **Three Dopes on a Rope** (5.4) A good beginner route up the crag's right-hand slab. Edge past two bolts to a thin crack. Follow onto an easy slab split by a horizontal crack. Belay up top by a skyline tree. **Rack:** Wires and small cams.

9. **Sideshow** (5.6) Climb the buttress just left of a prominent, bushy crack past 2 bolts to a belay on top of the cliff.

10. **Kate's Fault** (5.9) Work up the slabby apron in the middle of the left wall to a bolt below a dark xenolith. Climb thin face moves on flakes that lead to the 2nd bolt, then run it out to the top of the cliff.

11. **Unknown** (5.10-) On the far left margin of the crag. Climb a slab to a bolt, then up a groove to the cliff summit.

BOBCAT BOULDER AND THE LOAF

These two crags lie on the southeast side of the mountain just north of the second obvious saddle from the south. Find the crags by hiking northwest from the parking area and the boulders along a mountain bike trail. When you are directly east of the cliffs, look for a well-traveled path that heads west along a wash and climbs to the base of the cliffs. Approach time is 15 to 20 minutes.

LITTLE GRANITE MOUNTAIN
BOBCAT BOULDER

BOBCAT BOULDER

Bobcat Boulder is the small, broken crag down and left of The Loaf, which is the prominent slab. Some good, single-pitch routes are found on the crag's east face. Routes are listed left to right. **Descent:** Scramble down the back side and then down the gully between Bobcat and The Loaf.

12. **Grin and Bear It** (5.7) Bobcat's best route. Start at the junction of the south and east faces on the far left side of the cliff. Face climb past 2 bolts to a roof, pull past on the right to the 3rd bolt, and cruise to the top.

13. **Crystalline Grin** (5.10c) Thin face moves past 2 bolts on the lower slab to a horizontal crack. Above, move right into a crack system and end on a bushy belay ledge.

14. **Snakes are Poodles Too** (5.8) Work up an incipient crack system (5.8) to a stance at a horizontal crack. Continue face climbing up cracks to a high bolt, move up a slab to a break, and finish up a final headwall (5.8) with a bolt. Belay atop the formation.

15. **Missing Lynx** (5.8) Begin just right of Route 14. Climb a seam to a crack to a ledge on the far right side of the face. Step left and do some fun face moves past 2 bolts up the face and right-side arête to the rock summit.

THE LOAF

The Loaf, one of Little Granite Mountain's best and tallest crags, offers a good selection of 5.7 to 5.10 slab and face routes. The east-facing outcrop gets afternoon shade. Routes are listed left to right, beginning from the toe of the buttress. **Descent:** Scramble down either side of the formation from the summit. The north-side descent is better for reaching packs along the uphill side of the cliff's base.

16. **Wimpy** (5.8 R) The start will leave you whimpering! Start at the base of the buttress on a boulder left of a deep chimney. Make thin face moves (5.8 and no pro) up crystals and edges for 20' to a horizontal seam. Climb a thin crack above to a slab with a bolt and then run it out, keeping left of a right-angling crack, to a large belay ledge. **Rack:** Wires and small to medium cams.

17. **Young Monkeys** (5.7) A fun moderate up a low-angle prow. Begin right of the obvious chimney at the toe of the buttress. Face climb up a seam to the 1st bolt. Continue past 2 more bolts, then left into a crack system. Follow the crack to a final headwall with a bolt to a belay ledge. 4 bolts. **Rack:** Wires and small to medium cams.

LITTLE GRANITE MOUNTAIN
THE LOAF

Scott Korey leads *Sweet Surprise* (5.7) on The Loaf at Little Granite Mountain.

18. **Blow Fly's Last Ride** (5.10c) A classic, long pitch that will keep you on your toes. Start 30' right and uphill from Route 17 by a left-angling crack. Hand traverse left along the crack (small cam pro) to a prow. Work up right on thin face moves (5.10c) below the ridgeline past 4 bolts. These are entertaining, thought-provoking moves that are a little scary at times. At the 4th bolt, traverse right to the 5th bolt, then up and right on easier rock past 2 bolts to a spacious belay ledge. **Descent:** Scramble off right.

19. **"A" Crack** (5.10c R) A variation start to Route 18. Begin uphill to the right. Climb a thin crack with a piton to a bolt. Delicate moves (5.10c) lead up left to Route 18's 3rd bolt, then finish up it. Don't fall off the traversing moves or you'll take a nasty, swinging fall into the gully.

20. **Dike Walk** (5.10b R) Begin off a boulder up the gully from Route 19. Face climb over dikes past 2 bolts. Move left along a dike just above the 2nd bolt until it's possible to stand up on a good hold. Face climb straight up on easier but runout rock to Route 18's last bolt, then cruise to the belay ledge.

21. **Sweet Surprise** (5.7) Sweet jams up the prominent crack on the crag's right side. Pull up the left side of a large, triangular flake. Jam a thin hand crack that pinches to fingers at a Y-junction. Belay on the ledge above. **Rack:** Wires, TCUs, and small to medium cams.

22. **Lose Yer Stance, Shitcher Pants** (5.10c/d) Start just right of the crack. Hard face climbing past 4 bolts to a belay ledge. The top 2 bolts are currently chopped, so until they're replaced, it's a toprope.

McDOWELL MOUNTAINS

OVERVIEW

The McDowell Mountains, towering more than 2,000 feet above the surrounding valleys, forms a ragged skyline of 3,000- and 4,000-foot-high peaks across northeastern Phoenix. The northwest-trending range, pinched by encroaching suburban growth, offers, along with neighboring Pinnacle Peak, Phoenix's best climbing opportunities. The granite crags, scattered across the north slopes of the McDowells, yield some excellent face and slab routes on Gardener's Wall and Sven Slab. In contrast, the bulky and striking monolith of Tom's Thumb boasts a superb selection of crack climbs.

The McDowell Mountains, named for General Irwin McDowell, was long a desolate and arid wilderness, inhabited first by the Hohokam and later the Yavapai Indians. Prospectors found little gold here, preferring to concentrate

McDOWELL MOUNTAINS

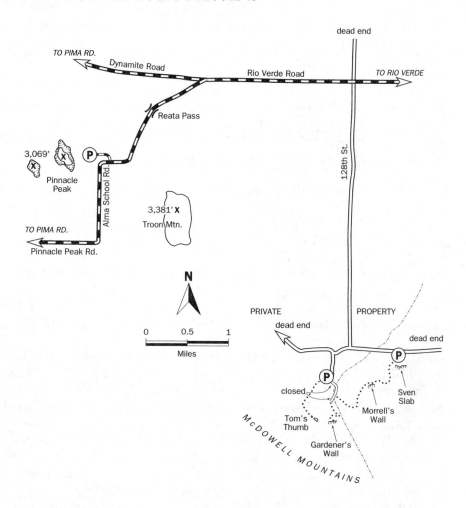

their efforts on the richer promises held by the Superstition and Bradshaw mountains. For years, cowboys frequented the rocky McDowell slopes, where each head of cattle required 350 acres a year of desert scrub.

Climbing history: After the cowboys came the climbers and hikers. The first climbers, members of the Arizona Mountaineering Club, began venturing out here in the 1960s. Notable early ascents included the classic *Hanging Gardens* (5.5) on Gardener's Wall by brothers Lance and Dane Daugherty, Larry Treiber, and Joe Theobald in 1965, and *Treiber's Deception* (5.7) on Tom's Thumb by Larry and Beck Treiber, Bill Sewrey, and Tom Kreuser. Tom's Thumb, named for Kreuser's opposable appendage, was climbed in 1948 via the Class 4 *West Corner* route. The 1970s was the golden age of McDowell climbing. Most of the classic testpiece cracks were jammed, including *Deep Freeze* (5.11a) on Tom's Thumb. Jim Waugh, who did the first free ascent with Stan Mish in 1978, calls it "One of the best climbs in Phoenix!" In his Phoenix rock climbing guidebook, Waugh recalls the 1978 first ascent of *Ubangy Lips* on the Thumb. "On the first ascent bolt hangers were forgotten. The leader had to tie-off the bolt driver to finish the lead. Gulp!!!!!!"

Few new routes have been done on the slabs and faces at the McDowells recently. Instead, the suburbs are slowly creeping up the broad aprons below the mountains, snatching up pristine desert lands and turning them into roads, shopping centers, and golf courses. On July 1, 1995, a large fire, set by a lightning bolt, ran amok across the McDowell Mountains, scorching over 20,000 acres, which included most of the climbing crags. The rock, however, was undamaged and the range's ecosystems are making a slow comeback. Access has been the climbing issue for the 1990s in the McDowells. Most of the range is private property. In 1995, the citizens of Scottsdale approved a ballot measure to purchase and preserve most of the range from further development. The measure, passed by a 2 to 1 margin, will raise over $8 million a year for land acquisition. Exactly what portions are purchased for the mountain park remains to be seen, but climber groups, including The Access Fund and Arizona Mountaineering Club, are pushing for the climbing areas and their trailheads to be included in the park. At the time of this writing, the traditional access to the McDowell crags is closed because of a landowner dispute. Scottsdale is working to create and fund a new access point with a parking area, restrooms, and trailhead. Check at the local rock gyms and climbing shops for current access information.

The main climbing crags in the McDowell Mountains lie on the north slopes of the range. Tom's Thumb is the obvious 160-foot-high monolith perched atop the west ridge, while Gardener's Wall sprawls on the west side of a boulder-strewn ravine. Morrell's Wall and Sven Slab both are prominent, slabby domes eroded out of the northeast side of the range. The crags are composed of a pale, abrasive granite that has weathered into steep slabs studded with edges, knobs, and thin flakes and sharp walls split by vertical crack systems.

Climbers should remember that climbing here is a privilege, not a right; especially because so much of the range remains in private hands. Climb, as always, at your own risk and take responsibility for your actions. Demonstrate to other users, including hikers and mountain bikers, that climbers are a polite, friendly, and responsible user group. Pick up all your trash, cigarette butts, and tape, as well as anyone else's litter. There are no restrooms at the parking areas. Dispose of human waste properly by burying it and burning your toilet paper. Follow existing climber's trails to the cliffs. These paths are sometimes hard to follow, so take your time initially to find the right trail. Carry plenty of water, particularly in hot weather, and wear a hat. Keep a watchful eye out for rattle-snakes among the boulders and bushes.

Rack: Most of the crack routes require 1 to 2 sets of Friends, a set of TCUs, a set of Stoppers, and quickdraws. Sets of RPs and a large Camalot are useful on some routes. Bring two 165-foot (50-meter) ropes for climbing and rappelling. A 200-foot (60 meter) rope is also useful.

TRIP PLANNING INFORMATION

General description: Many crack and face routes, some of the best in the Phoenix area, on granite domes and crags in the northern end of the McDowell Mountains. Includes Tom's Thumb and Gardener's Wall.

Location: Central Arizona, just northeast of Phoenix.

Camping: McDowell Mountain Regional Park, off Fountain Hills Boulevard, is the nearest public campground. The fee area offers RV sites with hook-ups, water, and restrooms. Call 602-471-0173 for information.

Climbing season: Best months are October through April. Summers are very hot, but early mornings can be cool enough for a few pitches in the shade.

Restrictions and access issues: Most of the McDowell Mountains are still private property, although the city of Scottsdale will be purchasing much of the range for a mountain park. There are currently no restrictions, but that could change in the future.

Guidebooks: *Phoenix Rock II* by Greg Opland, Falcon Publishing/ Chockstone Press, 1996, is the complete guide to the McDowells and the rest of the Phoenix-area ranges.

Nearby mountain shops, guide services, and gyms: Desert Mountain Sports (Phoenix), REI (Paradise Valley and Tempe), Trailhead Sports (Scottsdale), The Wilderness (Phoenix); Phoenix Rock Gym (Phoenix), Climbmax Climbing Center (Tempe).

Services: All services are found in Phoenix and Scottsdale.

Emergency services: Call 911. Phoenix General Hospital, 19829 North 27th Avenue, Phoenix, AZ 85027, 602-879-5353; Scottsdale Memorial Hospital North, 10450 North 92nd Street, Scottsdale, AZ 85260, 602-860-3000; Humana Hospital, 3929 East Bell Road, Phoenix, AZ 85032, 602-867-1881.

Nearby climbing areas: Pinnacle Peak, Troon Mountain, Little Granite Mountain, Cholla Mountain, Lookout Mountain, Camelback Mountain, Superstition Mountains.

Nearby attractions: Phoenix attractions (Phoenix Zoo, Desert Botanical Garden, Heard Museum, Phoenix Art Museum), Apache Trail, Superstition Mountains, Lost Dutchman State Park, Casa Grande Ruins National Monument, Pioneer Arizona Museum.

Finding the crags: Keep in mind that the described access points will probably change in the future. Contact local gyms and shops for access updates and information.

The easiest access is from Scottsdale Road and Pima Road, both major north-south streets in Scottsdale, east of Phoenix. Drive north on Scottsdale Road or Pima Road to Dynamite Road and turn right (east). Follow Dynamite Road several miles to 128th Street and turn right (south) on this dirt road (may eventually be paved). The McDowell Mountains are directly south.

Drive south on 128th Street for 3.3 miles (the road gets progressively rougher as you go south) until it deadends at a dirt road that runs east-west. To reach Sven Slab and the current parking area for the other crags, take a left (east) turn at the T-junction and drive about half a mile to a track that goes right to a parking area below the slab. Park here. Sven Slab is directly south and is reached by a five-minute walk. To reach Gardener's Wall and Tom's Thumb, hike for 20 minutes along public property on the north flank of the McDowells to the obvious canyon where the crags are located. See the crag descriptions for detailed information about reaching Gardener's Wall and Tom's Thumb.

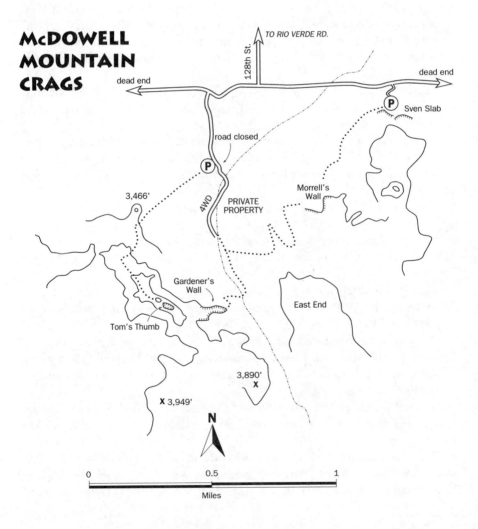

The traditional access route is described here in hopes that it will be reopened. From the T-junction, turn right (west) and drive about a half-mile to an obvious left turn. This rough track passes a house on the left. Low-clearance, two-wheel-drive cars should look for a parking spot past the house. Beyond, there is a parcel of private property posted "No Trespassing." And the trailhead for Gardener's Wall and Tom's Thumb. Hike west onto the mountain slopes along a rough trail. To reach the Thumb, hike onto the ridge north of the formation and west of the parking area, and follow it southeast. To reach Gardener's Wall, contour along the mountain slope until it's possible to scramble up to the cliff's base.

GARDENER'S WALL

This excellent, northeast-facing wall offers a selection of mostly moderate face and crack routes on its wide, slabby wall. The 300-foot-high cliff is sometimes too cold in winter for comfortable climbing, but it offers shade and indirect sun in spring and fall.

Finding the crag: Reach the crag by hiking up a rough trail on the left side of the boulder-strewn wash. Look for the trail just before large boulders block the wash, and follow it above the wash until more boulders block the wash. Look for a climber's path that more or less ascends directly up the hillside below the cliff, or hike farther up the canyon before cutting uphill and contouring to the cliff's base from the side. Routes are described left to right.

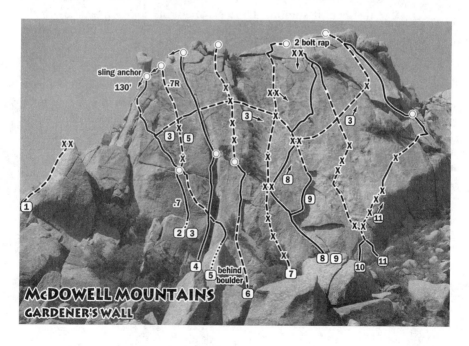

1. **Southeast Arête** (5.10b) This short route ascends the left, slabby faces of two large blocks on the far left side of the wall. Climb to a bolt, continue up easier rock, and finish up a blunt arête with 2 bolts. Descent: Scramble off left.

2. **The Phantom** (5.7) 2 pitches. Begin off large boulders below the left side of the wall and to the left of the deep chimney. **Pitch 1:** Climb a finger crack (5.7) that trends up left to a good belay ledge. **Pitch 2:** Move up left along a low-angle crack above a tree. Follow flakes and cracks up left to a skyline belay stance. **Descent:** Rappel to the ground 135' with 2 ropes from a sling over a flake, or traverse the summit ridge and do 2 double-rope rappels down *Hanging Gardens*.

3. **Gobs of Knobs** (5.8) 5 short pitches for someone who's climbed everything else here. This girdle traverse of the face from left to right yields "gobs of knobs" for your hands. Variations are possible. Begin on boulders at the start of Route 2. **Pitch 1:** Jam *The Phantom*'s 1st pitch crack (5.7) to a good belay ledge. **Pitch 2:** Climb easy cracks up left to a right-angling crack. Traverse up right to crack's end. Edge (5.8) over to another thin, horizontal crack. Belay in the wide crack (*Kreuser's Chimney*). **Pitch 3:** Traverse right to *Renaissance*'s 3rd bolt. Continue right across a brushy gully crack to a slab (*Fearless Leader*'s 5th bolt) and downclimb right on slab to *Hanging Garden*'s 2-bolt belay. **Pitch 4:** Traverse right (5.6) past 2 bolts to a tree-covered ledge. Belay above the ledge. **Pitch 5:** Swing over the left side of a roof and slab climb (5.6) to the cliff summit. **Descent:** 2 double-rope rappels down the wall's center. **Rack:** Carry a selection of Stoppers, small to medium Friends, and quickdraws.

4. **Kreuser's Chimney Direct** (5.3) 2 pitches. Begin below the obvious chimney. **Pitch 1:** Thrutch up the wide chimney to a hole. Squeeze through to a belay ledge on the right. **Pitch 2:** Step left into the chimney. Follow the squeeze chimney, then an off-width crack to the summit ridge. **Descent:** A double-rope rappel from a slung horn on Route 2, or 2 double-rope rappels down the center of the wall.

5. **Phantom of the Opera** (5.10a R) 2 pitches. The "R" rating comes from a 5.7 runout on pitch 2. Begin right of the chimney, between a boulder and the main wall. **Pitch 1:** Engaging face moves lead up a thin crack (5.10a) to a bush. Move out left and step across the chimney to a horizontal crack. Traverse left a few feet and climb a thin finger crack for 20' to a belay ledge. **Pitch 2:** Edge directly up the slab past 2 bolts to a slashing crack. Run it out above (5.7 R) to the summit ridge. **Descent:** A double-rope rappel from a slung horn on Route 2, or 2 double-rope rappels down the center of the wall.

Superb liebacking characterizes the first pitch of *Hanging Gardens* (5.5) on Gardener's Wall.

6. **Renaissance Direct** (5.7) 2 pitches. Superb and well-protected face climbing make this a must-do route for the moderate leader. Local guidebook author Marty Karabin calls this the "best route in the McDowells!" Begin right of Route 4 behind boulders. **Pitch 1:** Crisp face moves (5.7) past 2 bolts lead to a small stance below a thin, right-facing corner. Jam the corner (5.6) to a roof, then pull over and continue up diagonal cracks to a spacious belay ledge with trees. **Pitch 2:** A great pitch with fun moves! Climb straight up past 4 bolts to a summit belay. **Descent:** 2 double-rope rappels from 2-bolt station at top.

7. **Fearless Leader** (5.10a R) 2 pitches. Start below a steep slab beneath the left side of the hanging flake. **Pitch 1:** Thin face climbing (5.10a) past 2 bolts, then up left to a flake and the 3rd bolt (kind of run-out here). Continue up to the crack intersection on *Hanging Gardens* but climb straight up slab above past 2 more bolts to a 2-bolt belay stance. 130'. **Pitch 2:** Move up slab (5.6) past another bolt to a summit belay. **Descent:** 2 double-rope rappels down *Hanging Gardens*.

8. **Hanging Gardens** (5.5) 2 pitches. Arizona's best 5.5 route? You decide! Classic beginner route with plentiful pro, fun moves, and enough exposure to keep it interesting. Begin below the large, right-leaning flake in the middle of the wall. **Pitch 1:** Scramble up an easy, left-angling ramp/crack to the base of the flake. Insert pro and climb diagonally up left with hands in a crack to a small stance. Continue up right in a right-angling crack to a 2-bolt belay/rappel station. **Pitch 2:** Diagonal up right in a crack to a bolt and steeper hand crack that leads to a hanging tree. Keep left via easy cracks and face to a belay on top of the cliff. **Descent:** 2 double-rope rappels from bolted belay stations to the cliff's base. **Rack:** A generous selection of medium to large cams.

9. **Bruisin' and Cruisin'** (5.8) 2 pitches. It's "bruisin'" to off-width up the flake or "cruisin'" if you lieback up it. Same start as Route 8. **Pitch 1:** Off-width or lieback up the obvious right-leaning flake. Pro's harder to get if you do the lieback moves. At the top of the flake traverse up left to Route 8 and finish 20' higher at the bolted belay. **Pitch 2:** Face climb directly above the belay past 1 bolt for 110' to a summit belay. **Descent:** 2 double-rope rappels from bolted belay stations to the cliff's base. **Rack:** A selection of medium to large cams.

10. **Lackey Split** (5.7 R) 2 pitches. A bold, somewhat run-out slab route. Start 25' right of Route 9 below a narrow, right-leaning arch or atop a flake just right. **Pitch 1:** Lieback the arch or stand atop the pointed flake, then move up left and stand on a left-angling crack. Clip a bolt and traverse left along crack above an overlap. Face climb straight up

(hard to get pro—mostly psychological!) for 25' to a 1-bolt belay in a shallow scoop. **Pitch 2:** Edge up to a bolt, then angle up right to a bolt at the base of an obvious water groove. Climb the groove (5.7 R, no pro) to a bushy crack. Keep left of the trees and finish up top. **Descent:** 2 double-rope rappels from bolted belay stations to the cliff's base. **Rack:** Stoppers, TCUs, and small to medium Friends.

11. **For Crying Out Loud** (5.10d) 2 pitches. Kind of hard and serious. Same start as Route 10. **Pitch 1:** Stand on the pointed flake, step up left into the horizontal crack, clip the bolt, and edge up 15' to another bolt. Angle right to a small stance and bolt. Move along the right edge of the slab above a steep wall for 15' to the 4th bolt. Traverse up right to a vegetated crack. Follow the angling crack to another bolt. Then climb up and right below a large block to a gully and belay. Avoid belaying on the tree-covered ledge because it's a nesting site for owls. **Pitch 2:** Climb up left below a roof. Step over the roof on its left edge and face climb up the slab to the summit. **Descent:** 2 double-rope rappels from bolted belay stations to the cliff's base. **Rack:** RPs, Stoppers, and small to medium cams.

TOM'S THUMB

Tom's Thumb, at 3,800 feet, is the obvious blocky, thumb-shaped tower perched high atop a ridge in the northern McDowell Mountains. The Thumb, named for climber Tom Kreuser's thumb, offers a great selection of classic crack and face routes, as well as marvelous views of the surrounding valleys, ranges, and subdivisions.

Finding the crag: Access the crag by parking at the canyon entrance below. Follow a faint trail west from the posted road closure and work onto the ridge northwest of the crag. Follow the ridge to the formation. Approach time is about 30 minutes. Other approaches are from farther up the canyon below Gardener's Wall. A trail ascends the boulder-strewn, brushy slopes directly below the crag. It may be hard to locate at first. An alternative and easier route follows the trail on the left side of the wash left of Gardener's Wall. Once past the wall, look for a side trail that crosses large boulders in the draw and ascends a short, steep slope into a valley behind Gardener's Wall. A good path works up behind Gardener's and follows a ridge to the Thumb. Routes are described counterclockwise on the free-standing formation, starting with *Treiber's Deception* on the southeast corner.

EAST FACE

12. **Treiber's Deception** (5.7) A 140' pitch. A superb, classic line. Begin on the left (south) side of the East Face beside a boulder and below an obvious crack system. Chimney up between the boulder and the main wall until it's possible to pull into a flake crack about 15' off the ground. Follow the broken crack (a fixed piton may be present) above to a small ledge with a large block. Climb easy cracks up left onto the skyline. Clip a bolt and edge up the face above to the base of a wide crack. Work up the crack past another bolt to another wide crack. Waltz up it to summit. **Descent:** Traverse west across the summit to a 3-bolt anchor. Rappel 140' with double ropes to the ground. **Rack:** Stoppers and a generous selection of Friends.

13. **Hot Line** (5.10b) A sustained and exposed pitch. The left crack of an obvious, left-angling crack system. Start 25' right of Route 12 on boulders below the crack. Jam the awkward, left-hand finger crack (5.9) to a small alcove. Continue up left along crack to the left side of a wedged block. Jam steep, flared crack past a fingery section to a large flake. An airy traverse right 10' leads to a flared hand/fist crack finish. **Descent:** Traverse west across the summit to a 3-bolt anchor. Rappel 140' with double ropes to the ground. **Rack:** A good assortment of Friends, mostly medium to large sizes.

14. **Hard Drivin'** (5.10b or 5.11a) 2 pitches. The 1st pitch (5.10b) is popular by itself. Begin below a large pointed boulder on the outside face of a large pillar on the right (north) side of the East Face. **Pitch 1:** Edge up the pointed boulder for 30' (5.10a start and no pro) to its top. Reach across the gap and clip a bolt. Face climb (5.10b) up and left on the pillar past 3 more bolts to a spacious belay ledge with a 2-bolt anchor. Bring a #1.5 Friend or medium nut for a hidden crack between the 1st and 2nd bolts. Rap from here or climb **Pitch 2:** Start on the right side of the ledge. Climb over horizontal overlaps to a bolt. Hard face moves (5.11a) above lead to a horizontal crack. Follow it up and right onto the summit and a belay bolt. **Descent:** Traverse the summit to its west end and rappel 140' with 2 ropes from 3 bolts. Or rappel 70' from a 2-bolt anchor atop pitch 1 to the ground. **Rack:** Quickdraws, Stoppers, and small to medium cams.

McDOWELL MOUNTAINS
EAST FACE OF TOM'S THUMB

Peter Takeda climbing the two-pitch route *Hard Drivin'* (5.10b or 5.11a) on Tom's Thumb.

15. **Ubangy Lips** (5.10c) A 150' pitch. The 1978 first ascent party of Jim Waugh and Dave Black forgot a bolt hanger, so the drill was tied off for pro! Scramble through a tunnel in boulders right of Route 14 to the base of an obvious crack with a pod. Chimney up between boulders and the cliff until it's possible to climb flakes (5.9) up to the crack. Jam a good crack to a flare and into the "Ubangy Lips" pod. Exit the pod via a thin, discontinuous crack to face holds (5.10c) and a single bolt. Above, face climb a thin crack to a wide crack finish. **Descent:** Traverse the summit to its west end and rappel 140' with 2 ropes from 3 bolts. **Rack:** Selection of Stoppers and small to medium cams.

16. **Pretty Girls Make Graves** (5.12a) A 150' pitch. Brilliant sustained climbing that requires edging technique and mind control. Don't fall— it's a long way between bolts! Start just right of Route 15 at the base of a blunt arête. Face climb up the arête with small flakes and edges past 4 bolts. Work up left above the 4th bolt to the bolt on *Ubangy Lips*. Clip it and continue to a thin, horizontal seam, then move right past a bird shit streak. Climb straight up over a small roof right of the obvious crack system to another bolt and the summit. **Descent:** Traverse west across the summit to a 3-bolt anchor. Rappel 140' with double ropes to the ground. **Rack:** Quickdraws, RPs, Stoppers, TCUs, and a few Friends.

17. **Sacred Datura Direct** (5.9) A 150' pitch. Another good route with superb rock and thin climbing. Begin 10' right of Route 16 below a shallow, left-facing corner. Climb the small corner with a thin crack until you can face climb flakes to the right to a bolt (5.9) 30' up—pro is hard to find. Step right into a vertical crack system broken by large pockets. Climb the crack past a fixed pin into a scoop alcove. Follow a thinning crack (5.9) above to a hand crack and a bolt. Continue up right along thin seams and face climbing (5.8) to the summit ridge. **Descent:** Traverse west across the summit to a 3-bolt anchor. Rappel 140' with double ropes to the ground. **Rack:** Stoppers and small to medium Friends.

18. **Succubus** (5.10a) A 155' pitch. Many parties do the first 45' and rap from a single bolt. The initial crack is classic. Start right and around a corner 15' from Route 17 and below a dark, right-facing corner. Jam awkward hands up the black corner 20' to a V-shaped roof. Thin liebacks and fingerlocks lead up right in the thin crack to a small stance with a bolt. Jam the flared fist and off-width crack above to the top. **Descent:** Traverse west across the summit to a 3-bolt anchor. Rappel

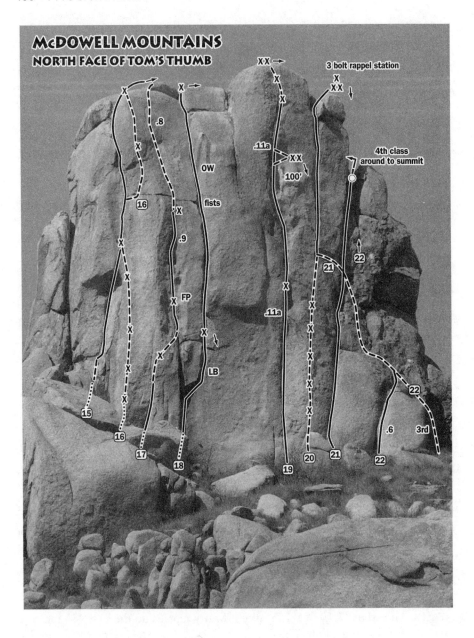

McDOWELL MOUNTAINS
NORTH FACE OF TOM'S THUMB

140' with double ropes to the ground. **Rack:** Stoppers and small to large Friends. A big Camalot will work up high.

19. **Deep Freeze** (5.11a) 2 pitches. Jim Waugh calls this "One of the best climbs in Phoenix!" Start 25' right of Route 18 below an obvious crack system and right of a smooth face. **Pitch 1:** Face climb a thin, discontinuous crack (5.10) or stand atop a boulder and step left into the crack system. Jam a good hand crack up a shallow, left-facing corner. The crack thins to fingers and ascends a difficult bulge. Continue up a narrow, right-facing corner to a bolt. Work past the bolt (5.11a) to discontinuous cracks on yellow-lichened granite with pockets. Belay from 2 bolts on a ledge up right by a streak of bird shit. **Pitch 2:** Climb past a final bulge (5.11a) onto the final face with 2 bolts. Move left to the uppermost summit. **Descent:** Traverse west across the summit to a 3-bolt anchor. Rappel 140' with double ropes to the ground. Or rappel 100' from the anchors atop pitch 1 back to the route base. **Rack:** A generous selection of Stoppers and Friends.

20. **Pinto Bean a.k.a. Garbanzo Bean Direct** (5.10d) A 150' pitch. Excellent face climbing on flakes. Start 3' right of Route 19. Edge up flakes on a rounded buttress past 5 bolts to a right-leaning crack. Continue up the wide crack to a bolted belay on blocks. **Descent:** Rappel 140' west to the ground with double ropes. **Rack:** Quickdraws and medium to large Friends.

21. **Garbanzo Bean** (5.7) 2 pitches or 1 long pitch. A 1973 classic. Start 5' right of Route 20. **Pitch 1:** Jam a flared hand crack (5.7) to a broken chimney, then climb the broken chimney to a belay stance. **Pitch 2:** At the obvious break, traverse left on the face to a wide crack. Jam the crack to a bolted belay on boulders atop the Thumb. **Descent:** Rappel 140' west to the ground with double ropes. **Rack:** Medium to large Friends.

22. **Kreuser's Route** (5.4) 2 pitches. A mountaineering adventure, named for Tom Kreuser, that climbs up the northwest corner of the north face. Begin up right from Route 21 on a ledge reached by scrambling. A variation to the start jams a 5.6 crack right of *Garbanzo*'s start. **Pitch 1:** Work up left on ramps and cracks to a deep chimney. Climb past a fixed piton and belay on a large ledge at a notch. **Pitch 2:** Class 4. Climb up right to an overhang. Skirt it on the right and head to the top. **Descent:** Rappel 140' with double ropes to the ground. **Rack:** Mostly medium and large cams.

140' 2 rope rappel

4th class

X

.9R

X

X

24

25

4th

23

24 25

26

McDOWELL MOUNTAINS
WEST FACE OF TOM'S THUMB

WEST FACE

23. **The Settlement** (5.7) 2 pitches. A good line up the west wall. Begin off a boulder at the base of the face. **Pitch 1:** Climb up a large pointed flake and face climb straight up to a bolt below an overlap. Traverse right below the overlap crack past another bolt to a left-angling corner system. Pull an overhang (5.7) and follow the corner up left to a belay ledge. **Pitch 2:** Class 4. Climb cracks to a blocky ledge. Face climb up and right around a roof to the summit. **Descent:** Rappel 140' with double ropes to the ground. **Rack:** Selection of Friends.

24. **West Corner** (Class 4) 2 pitches. A classic, easy summit route. Start 20' right of Route 23 at trees. **Pitch 1:** Scramble up a crack/ramp to a ledge with trees. **Pitch 2:** Work up wide cracks to a ledge with boulders. Traverse out right below a roof and face climb to the top. **Descent:** Rappel 140' with double ropes to the ground. **Rack:** Medium and large Friends.

25. **Face First** (5.9 R) Same start as *West Corner,* only scramble up ramp to a belay below a steep slab. Edge up the slab to a thin overlap. Climb above to a bolt to easier climbing that leads to Route 23's belay. Continue up Route 23 to top. **Descent:** Rappel 140' with double ropes to the ground. **Rack:** Small and medium gear.

SOUTH FACE

26. **Experiment in Terror** (5.11c) 3 pitches. Most climbers only do pitch 1. Rating is height-dependent. Start on the left side of the south face. **Pitch 1:** Follow thin, discontinuous seams to a fixed piton. Jam a fingery crack (5.11c) past a bush to a belay ledge. 40'. **Pitch 2:** Kind of wandering. Traverse right across horizontal cracks on the south face until you reach a short vertical crack. Follow to another horizontal crack. Step right and face climb to a ledge below the summit. **Pitch 3:** Jam a finger and hand crack (5.8) to top. **Descent:** Rappel 140' with double ropes to the ground. After pitch 1, scramble left down a ramp to the ground. **Rack:** RPs, Stoppers, TCUs, and small to medium Friends.

27. **Waughbo** (5.11a) Begin right of Route 26 below a thin left-leaning arch. Undercling up the arch, reach up right to a bolt, and step up right onto a narrow ledge. Undercling out a flake crack to a bolt. Face climb flakes to a belay ledge. 50'. **Descent:** Scramble off left down a ramp. **Rack:** TCUs and small Friends.

28. **West Face Direct** (5.11d) 2 pitches. Excellent but stiff edging chal-

McDOWELL MOUNTAINS
SOUTH FACE OF TOM'S THUMB

X 140' rap
XX
.8 hand
.9R
28
25
walk off
.11c
fingers
X
X
X
X
fixed
piton
X
26
27 28

190

lenge. Same start as Route 27. **Pitch 1:** Undercling up the arch, reach up right to a bolt, and step onto a narrow ledge below a flake crack. Undercling right to a bolt and then face climb straight up past 2 more bolts onto a ramplike ledge and horizontal crack. Traverse left along horizontal cracks to a vertical crack. Climb crack to another horizontal crack. Face climb to belay ledge. **Pitch 2:** Climb the 3rd pitch of Route 26. **Descent:** Rappel 140' with double ropes to the ground. **Rack:** RPs, Stoppers, TCUs, and small to medium Friends.

SVEN SLAB

This excellent, north-facing slab offers a selection of easily accessible and mostly bolted routes. The crag was named for a Sven saw used by the first climbing party to hack a trail through dense vegetation to the cliff's base.

Finding the crag: Follow directions to 128th Street. Turn south on 128th and drive 3.3 miles to a T-junction. Turn left (east) and follow a very rough road for 0.6 mile to an obvious right turn just north of the cliff. Park here unless you have a four-wheel-drive vehicle, in which case you can drive another 100 yards to a turnaround below the cliff. A trail leads up right to the lower area near *Nit Nat* and then up left along the base of Sven Slab. Routes are listed right to left.

29. **Hippity Hop** (5.6 R) Begin on the far right side of the face that harbors *Nit Nat* in a crevice between boulders and a huge flake. Stem up an obvious flared slot/crack to a boulder-filled chimney. Traverse left onto the face of the pillar and climb past a bolt to a 2-bolt anchor with slings at the top. (A variation to the start begins off boulders on the outside, left face of the flake. Climb crystals to a bolt 15' up. Continue up right on thin 5.10d R face moves and follow the easier ridge to the anchors.) **Descent:** Rappel or lower from anchors.

30. **Nit Nat** (5.10a) Begin just left of a prominent squeeze chimney. Climb 10' to a flake, then pull over the flake and climb to a bolt 25' up. Work out left 15' to the 2nd bolt then edge up the steeper headwall past another bolt to a runout slab finish. 3 bolts. **Descent:** Walk off. **Rack:** Small and medium cams.

31. **Changes in Latitude** (5.10b) Begin on the left side of the main block. Climb a delicate, run-out slab for 25' to the first bolt. Continue past another bolt to thin headwall to a runout slab. **Descent:** Walk off.

32. **Peaches and Cream** (5.7) The obvious crack between the big blocks. Climb a fist crack to a large chockstone in a chimney (sling it for pro). Stem past an overhanging, off-width section and thrutch up the off-width to the top.

McDOWELL MOUNTAINS
SVEN SLAB

beehive

OW

Fist

XX

To Sven Slab
34 - 39

33

32

31

30

29

33. **Dark Passage** (5.10c) The bolted route on the left block, left of a tree. Thin face climbing past 3 bolts to a horizontal break. Watch for a possible beehive here! Pull over break and cruise an easy slab. **Descent:** Walk off left.

34. **Quaker Oats** (5.5) Fun route and fine beginner lead. The right-hand bolt line on the right side of Sven Slab. Begin on the right side of the steep, white slab. Scramble right onto boulders and belay. Climb up left on a ramp to the 1st bolt. Continue straight up on excellent rock with great holds to an eyebolt belay on a ledge with trees. 5 bolts. **Descent:** Rappel 110' with 2 ropes. A 200' rope will reach the ledge to the right with rope stretch.

35. **Colorado Crosscut** (5.6) A great, left-traversing route. Begin on the right side of the slab at the *Quaker Oats* belay boulders (cams in crack for anchor). Traverse up left on the ramp to the 1st bolt on *Quaker Oats*. Continue up left past the 2nd bolt on *Sinkso*, then left to a large

flake (gear) and the 3rd bolt on *Cakewalk*. Work up left on thinner edges to another bolt. Move left to edge moves (5.6) that lead to a wide, right-angling crack (#3 Camalot). Follow crack up right to eyebolt belay. 4 bolts. **Descent:** Rappel 110' with 2 ropes. A 200' rope will reach the ledge to the right with rope stretch.

36. **Sinkso** (5.8 R) Tricky below and above 1st bolt. Begin at cliff's base left of a large boulder. Delicately climb (5.8) up 15' to the 1st bolt. Continue up left (5.8) above the bolt with groundfall potential below the 2nd bolt. Above, angle right to another bolt and motor up the easier slab to the eyebolt belay, or angle left to the top bolt of Route 37 and up. 3 bolts. **Descent:** Rappel 110' with 2 ropes. A 200' rope will reach the ledge to the right with rope stretch.

37. **Ego Trip** (5.7 R) Old, black hangers on bolts and a little run-out. Begin on a boulder near a small tree. Edge up (5.7) for 15' to the 1st bolt. Continue up right another 15' to the 2nd bolt (possible groundfall), then up good edges to an inverted flake (small Friend). Face climb straight up on good edges past another bolt and to the eyebolt belay. 3 bolts. **Descent:** Rappel 110' with 2 ropes. A 200' rope will reach the ledge to the right with rope stretch.

38. **Cakewalk** (5.8) Begin off a large boulder 15' left of Route 37. Thin face climbing (5.7) on good edges to the 1st bolt. Entertaining and continuous moves for the next 15' to bolt 2 at a horizontal break. Climb up right on good edges to the 3rd bolt, then up easier rock past another bolt to the eyebolt ledge belay. 4 bolts. **Descent:** Rappel 110' with 2 ropes. A 200' rope will reach the ledge to the right with rope stretch.

39. **Black Death** (5.8) Begin by a triangular flake at the base of the face left of Route 38. Climb 10' to the top of the flake. Put pro in a right-leaning crack and make delicate face moves up left to the 1st bolt. Climb a left-facing, lieback flake to bolt 2 and then directly up easier rock to a right-angling crack that leads to the eyebolt belay. 2 bolts. **Descent:** Rappel 110' with 2 ropes. A 200' rope will reach the ledge to the right with rope stretch. **Rack:** Medium Stoppers and small to medium cams.

More routes are found on the upper left side of Sven Slab. These include the excellent moderate crack route *One For The Road* (5.6). Check *Phoenix Rock II* for descriptions and topos.

OTHER MCDOWELL CRAGS

The McDowell Mountains are sprinkled with some other good crags. Check out *Phoenix Rock II* for the beta on these cliffs and routes. Glass Dome, south of Gardener's Wall, has a few good routes, including *Feminine Protection* (5.10). The Lost Wall is down the ridge northwest of Tom's Thumb and offers some good moderates from 5.5 to 5.8. Morrell's Wall, a slabby cliff east of the access road, is less popular and has a fine assortment of classic crack and face routes, but the approach is more brushy. Classics are *Space Cadets* (5.10a), *Beat Feet* (5.7), *Epacondilitis* (5.8), and *Jeff* (5.10a).

SUPERSTITION MOUNTAINS

OVERVIEW

The Superstition Mountains sprawl across central Arizona east of Phoenix like a rumpled Indian blanket. It's a tangled tapestry of precipitous canyons, sharp volcanic peaks, soaring tawny cliffs, undulating mesas, and stately forests of saguaro cacti. Most of this austere and beautiful range is protected in the 160,200-acre Superstition Wilderness Area, the wild centerpiece of 2.9-million-acre Tonto National Forest, one of the nation's largest national forests.

The haunting Superstitions, now nicknamed the Supes, were first called *Sierra de la Spuma* ("Mountains of Foam") by the Spanish and figure prominently in Arizona mythology as the site of the infamous Lost Dutchman Mine. The search for the mine began in 1892 when an old German prospector, Jacob Walz, died of pneumonia in Phoenix. On his deathbed, the old man supposedly revealed a cryptic description of his mine. He said, "There's a great stone face looking up at my mine. If you pass three red hills you've gone too far. The rays of the setting sun shine on my gold. Climb above the mine and you can see Weavers Needle." A few handed-down facts led to a lot of speculation, interpretation, fantasy, and fiction. Fortune-seekers have searched tirelessly for the lost gold, and over 50 people have died or been killed looking for the fabulous lode.

The location of the mine and its supposed treasures has eluded everyone, and geologists say no gold exists in the Superstition's volcanic dust and ashes. Many historians believe the lost mine is a hidden cache of Spanish gold possibly deposited in the 1840s by Don Miguel Peralta and his men after being attacked by Apaches. Another theory says Walz concocted his Superstition mine story to cover a gold-laundering operation for high-graders at Wickenburg's Vulture Mine. Who knows? So the search for the fabled Lost Dutchman Mine goes on.

The Superstitions rise more than 3,000 feet above the surrounding plains to the south and west, reaching heights of 6,000 feet. Towering rock ramparts surround the western perimeter of the range, creating a formidable barrier. The range is rough country broken by ragged ridges, a few lofty peaks, and deep canyons. This harsh environment is home to a diverse assortment of plants and animals from saguaro cacti to ponderosa pines, and from rattlesnakes to mule deer. Life here, as in all deserts, depends on water or its relative scarcity.

The Superstition Mountains were forged by fiery volcanism between 15 and 24 million years ago. Most of the climbing occurs on two types of rock—intrusive, igneous dikes and necks, like Weavers Needle and The Hand, and ash flow tuff canyon walls, like Bark Canyon Wall. The tuff, deposited as layers of volcanic ash, is generally very soft. The surface, however, is often case-hardened and forms a sturdy surface for climbing. Vertical crack systems were formed by fractures in the hardening rock, while softer pumice eroded away into pockets and other handholds.

Rock climbers look for another kind of treasure here—a spectacular assortment of climbing routes up towers, buttes, buttresses, and cliffs in a remote wilderness setting. Hundreds of technical routes, both sport and traditional lines, ascend many of the range's crags. The Supes offer an excellent concentration of middle-grade, multipitch adventures that are among the best that Arizona offers. The climbing opportunities are little known, and the routes are seldom climbed outside of the southern Arizona cadre of climbers.

Climbing history: The 4,553-foot-high Weavers Needle, a soaring landmark spire, was the first technical climb established in the Supes. Apache or Pima Indians, undoubtedly clad in 5.10 Moccasyms, probably scrambled to the lofty summit of the "Finger of God" centuries ago, although no trace or legend of the ascent is found. Most early explorers looked at the peak as a landmark or as the point to begin their search for the lost gold. No one knows exactly who did the first ascent, although one account pins it to some time in the 1950s. Now Weavers Needle, named for pioneer trapper and mountain man Pauline Weaver, is the single most popular climb in the range, with several hundred people lining up each year to ascend the popular *West Chimney* (5.0) to the summit.

In the 1960s, a group of Arizona Mountaineering Club members, including the legendary desert climber Bill Forrest, began pioneering routes on the towers and cliffs. Notable ascents include *Razor's Edge* (5.6) on The Hand by Bill Forrest, Key Punches, and Gary Garbert in 1965; *Regular Route* (5.5) on The Crying Dinosaur by Forrest and Garbert in 1966; and *The Glory Road* (5.7) on Bark Canyon Wall by Larry Treiber, Dave Olson, and Bill Sewery. During the late 1960s and 1970s, the prolific Treiber began pushing standards and establishing numerous routes on new crags all over The Supes. The 1980s brought sport climbing and controversy to the range. This golden age saw many new areas developed, including Zonerland, Land of Nod, and The Labyrinth, as well as the elimination of aid on many older routes. Jim Waugh was one of the prime movers, bringing 5.12 to the Supes. Other activists were Rick Percival, Scott Heinz, John Ficker, and Todd Swain. Controversy between climbers who rap-bolt and climbers who take the ground-up approach surfaced during the late 1980s, but the two factions reached a peaceful coexistence by developing their own areas.

Tonto National Forest, however, became alarmed by the placement of fixed anchors in the Superstition Wilderness Area and posted signs in 1988 that banned the placement of bolts. This occurred after a photographer complained to the forest service about chalk and bolts in Zonerland, a remote group of pinnacles about half an hour off the Peralta Trail. This is supposedly the only known instance in which a nonclimber has complained to the Forest Service about bolts. The outright ban on bolting led to the general demise of new routes in the Superstitions in the 1990s.

The Superstitions was designated a national wilderness area by Congress in 1964. The range was originally protected as a forest reserve in 1908 and a primitive area in 1940. Tonto National Forest manages the wilderness area, an area roughly 12 miles north to south and 24 miles east to west. The Forest Service maintains several management objectives that include keeping the area's primitive character, perpetuating the natural ecosystems, and providing public enjoyment of the resource. The area is closely managed because of the close proximity to Phoenix and Tucson and the accompanying potential for human use and abuse.

There are several wilderness regulations in place. Permanent structures are prohibited, including buildings and antennas (some Forest Service employees are considering bolts "permanent structures"). Trail size is maintained and hiking parties are limited to 15 persons. Hunting, trapping, and fishing are managed; guides and outfitters are regulated; and livestock is restricted. The use of motorized equipment and mechanical transport, including power drills, mountain bikes, generators, and motorcycles, is prohibited. No permits are required for hiking, backpacking, or climbing in the Superstition Wilderness Area.

When visiting and climbing here, keep some other wilderness rules in mind. Keep all dogs on leashes. Pack out all your trash, as well as any left by inconsiderate users. This includes tape and cigarette butts. Try to use a stove for cooking. Fires are allowed, but wood is scarce. Dispose of all human waste at least 300 feet from all water sources, including dry washes. It's best to carry out your toilet paper in a plastic baggie. If that is not possible, then burn it rather than burying it under a rock because it will never decompose. Try to follow existing trails and paths whenever possible. All of the described crags have at least faint trails to their bases. Take the time to find and use them to avoid damaging fragile desert plants. If you do have to hike cross-country, try to follow drainages or slickrock areas. Lastly, let Tonto National Forest know that climbers are responsible wilderness users. Let them, as well as the legislators and bureaucrats, know that fixed protection is basic to the safe climbing experience and that it has long been part of climbing in wilderness areas.

The best climbing months in the Supes are March, April, October, and

SUPERSTITION MOUNTAINS

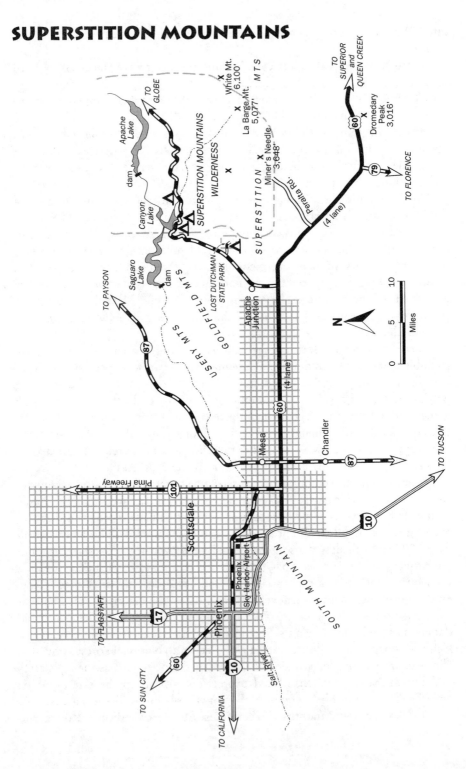

November, with daily highs between 60 and 100 degrees. The winter months are excellent, but periods of rain and cooler weather can occur. Summer is just too darned hot. Daily highs are usually above 100 degrees, even in the higher elevations. Temperatures in the lower elevations can exceed 120 degrees. Because of the extreme heat and lack of water, dehydration and heat exhaustion are real possibilities. Always carry plenty of water. Consider a minimum of a gallon a day per person. Gatorade and other sport drinks are also good for replenishing electrolytes and salt. Drink often. If you're getting thirsty, you're already dehydrated.

Many objective dangers are found in the Superstitions. Loose sections of rock are found on most long routes. Bring and wear a helmet to protect yourself from falling rocks when climbing and belaying. Approaches to the cliffs can be time-consuming. Leave with ample time, plan for routefinding delays along the trails, and allow at least an hour to walk to most of the cliffs. Tote a headlamp or flashlight, particularly during the winter months, in case the route and descent take more time than daylight allows. Descents can be hazardous, with loose rock, cacti, and hazardous drop-offs. Some descents are by rappel. Carry extra webbing to replace worn, weakened, and desiccated rappel slings. Know self-rescue techniques—help is a long way off.

Rack: A basic Supes rack should include sets of cams, TCUs, and Stoppers. Longer routes might require more cams or specialized gear like slider nuts or Aliens. Sometimes hexcentric nuts fit the cracks better than cams. You make the call. Two ropes are needed for most rappel routes. Climbers here should be able to competently place gear on routes and set up equalized, solid belay anchors. Gear placements are tricky on many Supes routes, with gear wedged in incipient cracks, runners over flakes, and Friends cammed in pockets.

TRIP PLANNING INFORMATION

General description: Excellent traditional and sport routes on pinnacles, crags, and cliffs in the spectacular and rugged Superstition Mountains.

Location: Central Arizona, east of Phoenix.

Camping: Lost Dutchman State Park, on the west side of the Superstition range, makes an excellent base camp for climbing here. The park, 8 miles north of US Highway 60 off Arizona Highway 88, has a 35-site campground with water, restrooms, showers, and tables. The fee area ($10 per night) is open year-round. Campsites might be hard to come by in the cooler months. Primitive camping is found along the spur road to Carney Springs Trailhead on the south side of the range.

Climbing season: October through April offers the best climbing weather. Expect some hot days in spring and fall. Summers are just too hot for comfortable climbing, even in the shade. Stay out of the sun on hot days, wear a hat, and carry plenty of water—a gallon per person is not too much. Drink Gatorade

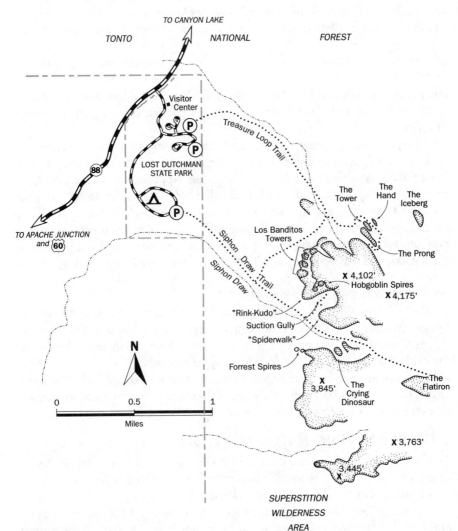

**WEST
SUPERSTITION
MOUNTAINS**

The Iceberg
The Prong
Los Banditos Towers
"Grandfather Hobgoblin"
"Rink-Kudo"
North Buttress
Hobgoblin Spires
Siphon Draw
The Tower
The Hand

WEST SUPERSTITION MOUNTAINS

or other sports drinks to keep electrolytes and other essentials replenished.

Restrictions and access issues: Most of the Supes are in Tonto National Forest's Superstition Wilderness Area. No permits are required for climbing, hiking, or camping. Wilderness rules and regulations include: no new bolts, no motorized drills or other mechanized equipment, no vehicles including mountain bikes, groups limited to 15 people, pets on leashes at all times, and no wood gathering for fires (use a stove). In addition, you should pack out all trash, including anyone else's you encounter on the trail or at the cliff. Bury human waste and keep it at least 300 feet from all water sources, burn or carry out toilet tissue, and try to follow existing trails and paths whenever possible. If you do walk cross-country, try to follow drainages or rock-hop to avoid damaging fragile vegetation.

Guidebooks: *Superstitions Select* by Greg Opland, Steel Monkey Publishing, 1998. A good guide for other routes is Jim Waugh's out-of-print classic *Phoenix Rock*, 1987.

Nearby mountain shops, guide services, and gyms: Desert Mountain Sports (Phoenix), REI (Paradise Valley and Tempe), Trailhead Sports (Scottsdale), The Wilderness (Phoenix); Phoenix Rock Gym (Phoenix), Climbmax Climbing Center (Tempe).

Services: All services are in Phoenix and its suburbs, including Apache Junction just west of the range.

Emergency services: Call 911. For a rescue, contact the Pinal County Sheriffs Department, 575 North Idaho Road, Apache Junction, AZ 85219, 602-982-2241 or 800-352-3796. Nearby hospitals include Phoenix General Hospital, 19829 North 27th Avenue, Phoenix, AZ 85027, 602-879-5353;

Scottsdale Memorial Hospital North, 10450 North 92nd Street, Scottsdale, AZ 85260, 602-860-3000; and Humana Hospital, 3929 East Bell Road, Phoenix, AZ 85032, 602-867-1881.

Nearby climbing areas: Queen Creek Canyon, Upper and Lower Devil's Canyon, Apache Leap, Oak Flat bouldering, Dromedary Peak, Camelback Mountain, Lookout Mountain, McDowell Mountains, Pinnacle Peak, Troon Mountain, Little Granite Mountain, Jacuzzi Spires.

Nearby attractions: Apache Trail Scenic Drive, Phoenix attractions (Phoenix Zoo, Desert Botanical Garden, Heard Museum, Phoenix Art Museum), Lost Dutchman State Park, Casa Grande Ruins National Monument, Pioneer Arizona Museum, Boyce Thompson Arboretum.

NORTHWEST PINNACLES

This spectacular collection of towers sits on the northwest side of the immense escarpment that forms the west end of the Superstition Mountains. The Hand, also called The Praying Hands, is a prominent, free-standing spire that stands by itself to the left of the main cliffs. The Tower and The Prong are between The Hand and the main cliffs, while The Iceberg sits on a ridge on the north side of the cliffs and east of The Hand.

Finding the pinnacles: Drive a few miles northeast on Arizona Highway 88 from Apache Junction to the marked right turn for Lost Dutchman State Park. Turn here and enter the park. Although this is a fee area ($4), you are better off parking here because your car will be safer and the trails through the park are easy to find and follow. From the ranger station, take the first left turn and follow the road to the Cholla Day Use Area. Restrooms, water, and picnic tables are located next to the parking lot.

Hike east up Treasure Loop Trail (Trail 56) on the sloping bajada on the west side of the Superstitions. The spires are visible as you're hiking. Follow the wide, main trail just over 1 mile to a rest bench. A climber's path leaves the main trail just past the bench and climbs northeast across slopes to a saddle right of a dome-like crag. Contour northeast on the trail to the base of The Hand. The Tower and The Prong are reached by following a subsidiary trail up the slopes.

NORTHWEST PINNACLES

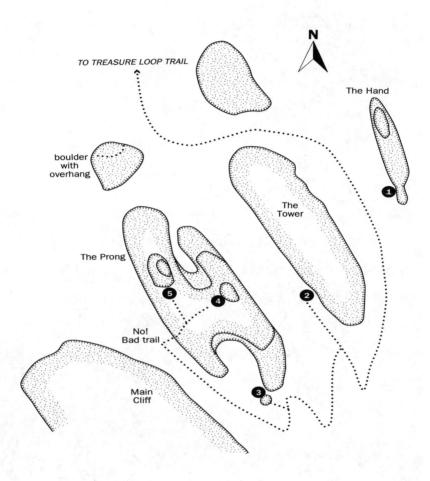

TO TREASURE LOOP TRAIL

N

The Hand

boulder
with
overhang

The
Tower

The Prong

No!
Bad trail

Main
Cliff

THE HAND

This 150-foot-high pinnacle offers one of the best and most popular spire routes in the Superstitions. Large parties are not recommended on this route.

1. **Razor's Edge** (5.6) 3 pitches. Begin below a gully on the southeast side of the spire. **Pitch 1:** Climb the gully (Class 4) to a skyline notch between The Hand and The Thumb (the smaller pinnacle to the east). **Pitch 2:** Work up the left side of the ridge past a fixed piton and 3 bolts to a 2-bolt belay on Chicken Ledge. **Pitch 3:** Continue up the airy ridge (5.6) past 4 bolts and 2 fixed pins to the summit anchors. **Descent:** Make a 2-rope rappel from summit bolts 150' down the south face to the ground. **Rack:** A selection of medium and large Friends and nuts, plus 2 ropes.

THE TOWER

This tall, spectacular pinnacle/fin lies immediately south of The Hand.

2. **The Tower** (5.8 R) 2 pitches. This route, with some serious, unprotected climbing, accesses an excellent, airy summit. Begin on the right side of the south face below a small notch. **Pitch 1:** Face climb up unprotected, overhanging rock (5.8 R) for 25' to a ledge. Step left and work up a steep trough to a ledge with a 2-bolt belay anchor. **Pitch 2:** Climb up the loose arête above (5.7 R) past 3 bolts for 90' to a fixed piton at a hollow horn. Climb down right 10' from the piton and traverse right into a gully. Follow the gully to the summit. A 5.8 variation on the finish moves left from the piton and face climbs over two bulges to the summit. **Descent:** Make a 2-rope rappel 165' down the south face to a saddle between The Tower and The Prong. **Rack:** A selection of Friends and Stoppers, plus 2 ropes.

THE PRONG COMPLEX

The Prong is the highest and westernmost spire in a group of pinnacles south of The Tower. Two other smaller spires—The Periscope and The Pickle—also have good routes. To find these three routes, hike southeast about 100 yards from The Tower to The Pickle, a small pinnacle at the end of The Prong complex. The Pickle is on the south side. To reach The Periscope and The Prong, walk south and southwest around The Pickle to a bushy gully that heads southwest to a saddle between The Prong complex and the main headwall. No topos.

3. **The Pickle** (5.4) This pitch, on a squat, pickle-shaped spire, is easier than it looks. Begin on the south side of the pinnacle and follow the

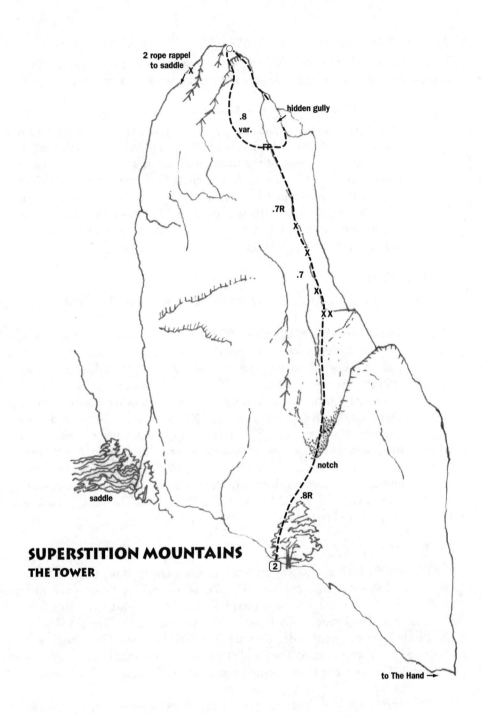

2 rope rappel
to saddle

hidden gully

.8
var.

FP

.7R

.7

notch

.8R

2

saddle

SUPERSTITION MOUNTAINS
THE TOWER

to The Hand →

line of least resistance to the summit and a belay/rappel bolt. **Rack:** Medium to large Friends and nuts.

4. **The Periscope** (5.4 R) Another pitch on a small pinnacle. From the saddle between The Prong complex and the main wall, scramble northwest up Class 3 rock to a small col just below The Prong. This is the small pinnacle northeast of the saddle. Climb the southwest face to the summit.

5. **The Prong** (5.6) From the saddle between the Prong complex and the main wall, scramble northwest up Class 3 rock to a small col just below The Prong (same approach as *The Periscope*). From the saddle, climb northwest across a low-angle face (Class 4) to a spacious ledge on the north face of The Prong. Climb a short, wide crack (5.6) up the north face to another ledge. Scramble southeast to the lofty summit. **Descent:** Downclimb to a tree anchor above the wide crack. Make a single-rope rappel back to the ledge. Downclimb back to col. **Rack:** Medium and large Friends and nuts.

THE ICEBERG

The Iceberg is a massive fin 0.25 mile northeast of The Hand. The first ascent was done on a cold day, hence the name. All three described routes are on the southwest face.

The easiest way from Lost Dutchman State Park to this distant crag is to hike to The Hand and then contour out across the basin to the northeast to the obvious, blocky tower. Allow about 1 hour from the parking area. The Iceberg can also be accessed from Massacre Grounds Trailhead off Forest Service Road 78, which takes off right just past Lost Dutchman State Park. Locate the tower to the south and pick your own hiking route. Routes are described left to right.

6. **The Snake** (5.5) 2 pitches. Route is named for a rattlesnake that was encountered here. Start on the left side of the south face below a west-facing chimney. **Pitch 1:** Work up the chimney to a ridgeline belay. **Pitch 2:** Easy face climbing (Class 4) leads up the west ridge to a surprise move onto the summit. **Descent:** 2-rope rappel from a 2-bolt summit anchor 130' down the south face to the talus. **Rack:** Medium to large Friends and nuts, plus 2 ropes.

7. **Withered Witch** (5.8) 3 pitches. Begin 10' right of Route 6 below a steep trough. **Pitch 1:** Climb the trough to a belay stance. **Pitch 2:** Continue up a double crack system (5.8) to a belay ledge. Watch for loose rock. **Pitch 3:** Traverse up left to the west ridge and follow it (Class 4) to a surprising finish at the summit. **Descent:** 2-rope rappel from a 2-bolt summit anchor 130' down the south face to the talus. **Rack:** Medium to large Friends and nuts, plus 2 ropes.

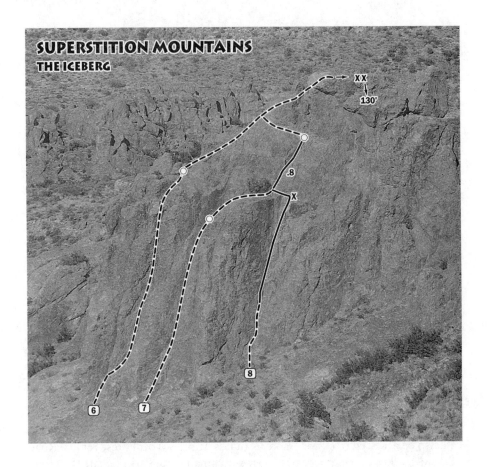

8. **Tinkerbell** (5.7) 2 pitches. Start 20' right of Route 7 below the middle of the south face. **Pitch 1:** Climb up a shallow groove and crack system (5.7) to a belay ledge up right of a tree. **Pitch 2:** Follow a ledge system out left to the west ridge. Climb east up the ridge (Class 4) to interesting finishing moves and the summit. **Descent:** 2-rope rappel from a 2-bolt summit anchor 130' down the south face to the talus. **Rack:** A selection of Friends and nuts, plus 2 ropes.

HOBGOBLIN SPIRES

The Hobgoblin Spires is a bewitching, multisummited complex of pinnacles that dominates the north wall of Suction Gully, the first side canyon left of Siphon Draw's obvious canyon. The spires are inconspicuous from many directions and blend into the high wall behind them. They are best seen from the amphitheater at the top of Suction Gully.

downclimb east
to rappel

.7R

loose
rock

chimney

hole

.7

9

SUPERSTITION MOUNTAINS
HOBGOBLIN SPIRES

Finding the crags: Reach the pinnacles by starting from Siphon Draw Trailhead on the loop road in the campground (Lost Dutchman State Park). Hike up Siphon Draw Trail (Trail 53) until you're southwest of Suction Gully, the abrupt, cliff-lined canyon up left (north). Hike past an old road that goes left to the now reclaimed site of Palmer Mine. Past the road, look for a rocky draw flanked by small gravel ridges. A climber's trail ascends the right side of this shallow draw. Hike up the steep path to the gully entrance. *Rink-Kudo* is left of the entrance and *Spider Walk* ascends the high buttress on the right. The Hobgoblin Spires line the upper left side of the gully. Reach them by scrambling up the steep, boulder-filled gully into an immense amphitheater. The spires form the north (left) wall. Allow about 1 hour from car to cliff.

9. **Rink-Kudo** (II 5.7) 4 pitches. A 450' route up the west side of the Hobgoblin Spires. The route ascends crack systems on the wall just left of the entrance to Suction Gully. Watch for loose rock and wear helmets. Begin on the right side of the face at a left-angling crack system near a paloverde tree. **Pitch 1:** Work up double cracks until it's possible to step left (5.7) into the left-hand crack. Follow the crack up left to a narrow ledge 25' up. Continue up the crack in a thin, right-facing corner and behind a finger to a belay ledge. **Pitch 2:** From the middle of the ledge, climb a left-leaning crack system past a white spot. Squeeze through a hole at the top of the crack and move left to a tied-off belay boulder on a ledge beneath a chimney. **Pitch 3:** Work left and climb into the chimney for 80' to a belay stance at an obvious traverse to the left. **Pitch 4:** Traverse left on loose rock around a corner and follow cracks and corners (5.7) up good rock to a false summit. Scramble east to a bouldering move onto the summit. 150'. Pro is sparse and hard to find on this pitch. **Descent:** Downclimb south and east from the summit to a notch between a small pinnacle and the main wall. Use a belay on this exposed downclimb. Locate a tree with rap slings and make a 2-rope rappel down a chimney to a niche. Find another set of rap slings on a chockstone below the niche and make another 2-rope rappel down a gully to the ground. **Rack:** Wires, small to large Friends, nuts, and 2 ropes.

10. **Mish Monster (via Dan's Birthday Route)** (III 5.10a) 3 pitches. Scramble up to the top of the gully into a large amphitheater. Locate Grandfather Hobgoblin, the highest spire, on the left (north) side. Mish Monster is the subsidiary summit to the left. Locate a notch on the right side of the spire (2nd notch left of Grandfather Hobgoblin). An obvious trough/gully system descends to the ground from the notch. Begin below the left gully. **Pitch 1:** Climb a steep ramp up a left-facing corner to a belay ledge in the trough. **Pitch 2:** Work up the loose trough to the notch and belay/rappel anchors. **Pitch 3:** Move up right of an

arête and climb a shallow corner system to a small roof (watch for loose rock). Traverse left (5.10a) under the roof and around the arête to easy climbing that leads to a 2-bolt belay stance. For an easier variation on the start, climb the first 2 pitches of Grandfather Hobgoblin and traverse left to the 2nd notch from just below the 1st notch. **Descent:** 2 rappels. For the 1st rap, do a single-rope rappel from the upper anchors back to the notch. For the 2nd rap, do a 2-rope rappel from a 2-bolt anchor down the trough to the ground. **Rack:** A selection of Stoppers, nuts, Friends, and 2 ropes.

11. **Grandfather Hobgoblin** (III 5.9) 4 pitches. One of the best spire routes in the Supes. Scramble up to the top of the gully and start 30' right of Route 10, below the right trough/gully system on the south side of Grandfather Hobgoblin, the tallest pinnacle. **Pitch 1:** Climb a short, left-facing corner (5.6) that starts behind a small sticker tree. Follow cracks and ledges above to a 1-bolt belay ledge. 85'. **Pitch 2:** Move up left in a ramp and trough system to a skyline notch with a bolt belay. **Pitch 3:** The pinnacle looms to the northeast above the notch. Traverse 25' left to a ledge below an easy gully/chimney. Climb the chimney past a ledge to a 2-bolt belay. **Pitch 4:** Move left from the belay ledge and climb a short crack to a good stance with a funky bolt. Climb up right onto a sloping ledge and another bolt. Continue up left (stiff 5.9) to the 3rd bolt. Climb obvious rock above to the summit and two sets of belay anchors. **Descent:** 3 rappels. For rap 1, do a 2-rope rappel past pitch 4's belay (20' below) to anchors in an east-facing gully/ramp. For rap 2, do a 2-rope rappel to a bolt anchor atop pitch 1. For rap 3, rappel to the base. **Rack:** A good selection of Stoppers, nuts, and Friends, plus 2 ropes.

12. **Totgoblin** (III 5.6) 3 pitches. The smallest of the Hobgoblins and hidden from the ground. Totgoblin is directly behind the notch between Grandfather Hobgoblin and Mish Monster. The start and first 2 pitches are the same as Route 11. **Pitch 1:** Climb a short, left-facing corner (5.6) that starts behind a sticker tree. Follow cracks and ledges above to a 1-bolt belay stance. 85'. **Pitch 2:** Move up left in the ramp and trough system to a notch with bolt belay. **Pitch 3:** Climb the hidden spire behind the notch via the easiest route (5.4). **Descent:** Downclimb pitch 3 back to the notch. Make a 2-rope rappel back to the ground from a 2-bolt belay in the notch, or climb left and then downclimb to the 2-bolt anchor at the bottom of Route 10's pitch 3. Make a 2-rope rappel to the ground from double anchors. **Rack:** A selection of Stoppers, nuts, and Friends, plus 2 ropes.

SUPERSTITION
MOUNTAINS
NORTH BUTTRESS

The Eye

.6

.7

chimney

.6

Siphon Draw

Suction Gully

13

4th class

NORTH BUTTRESS

The North Buttress is the prominent buttress on the left (north) flank of Siphon Draw after the trail enters the main canyon. Follow the hiking directions from the main canyon to Suction Gully. The route is on the right side of the prominent buttress on the right side at the gully entrance. The route is easily seen during the approach hike, as it ascends the outside of the buttress.

13. **Spider Walk** (III 5.6) 4 pitches. Locate an obvious boulder perched on the ridgeline up right (south) of the entrance to Suction Gully. Start the route by scrambling up right (Class 4) across a slab to a large boulder on a ridge. Belay from the south side of the boulder. **Pitch 1:** Face climb up right around an overhang. Work up a steep headwall with 2 old bolts into a pour-off trough. Follow the trough up and right to a 2-bolt belay in an obvious notch on the North Buttress proper. 160'. **Pitch 2:** Careful routefinding is needed on this pitch. Run-out face moves lead up right to a bolt. Continue up right to another bolt on a blunt prow. Work up the face above just left of an indistinct prow (5.6), then past another bolt to a sloping ledge with a 2-bolt anchor left of a large chimney. 150'. **Pitch 3:** Step right into the chimney and work up right in the chimney and a crack system (5.6) to a high ledge with a 2-bolt belay anchor atop a perched boulder. 160'. **Pitch 4:** The loose "Spider Walk" pitch. Make an exposed traverse by stepping left onto the wall, moving right past the crack up a rotten rib, and then going back left into the crack above. Jam the crack (5.6) to belay below "The Eye." Scramble through The Eye and up to the exposed summit of North Buttress for a spectacular view. For a better variation on pitch 4, work directly up the crack (5.7) above the belay ledge. The rock on this variation is more solid. **Descent:** Make 4 double-rope rappels down the route using the 2-bolt belay/rappel anchors at each stance. The rappel from The Eye is from a tied-off block. **Rack:** Stoppers, medium to large Friends and nuts, plus runners and 2 165-foot ropes. A 200-foot rope is useful.

THE CRYING DINOSAUR

The Crying Dinosaur is a 200-foot-high tower/fin high on the south side of Siphon Draw next to the main cliff. Siphon Draw is the deep canyon that slices through the western escarpment of the Superstition Mountains. Suction Gully and the towering North Buttress guard the left (north) side of the canyon's entrance, while the South Buttress and Forrest Spires flank the right (south) side. The tower, which resembles a dinosaur with an open mouth from the trailhead, is hard to identify from a distance because it blends into the canyon walls. Before you leave the main trail, take some time to locate the formation and scope out the surrounding terrain. The route, put up by Bill Forrest and Gary Garbert in 1966, ascends the north face and is visible from the trail. The line is often shaded, particularly in the cooler months, and the sun rarely touches the tower's north face.

Park on the loop road of the campground (Lost Dutchman State Park) at the trailhead for Siphon Draw Trail. Hike southeast on Siphon Draw Trail (Trail 53) across a wide bajada and into the wide canyon mouth. Continue up the good trail past an isolated rock outcrop on the right, where the trail begins climbing more steeply. Locate The Crying Dinosaur to the right and find the route on the north face. Leave the main trail wherever it looks good, descend across the canyon floor, and hike up steep, brushy slopes past the west side of the tower to the base of a slope between it and the main wall to the south. Rack up and stash your packs here because the rappel ends on this side of the tower. Scramble around the east side of the tower to the base of the north face.

SUPERSTITION MOUNTAINS
THE CRYING DINOSAUR

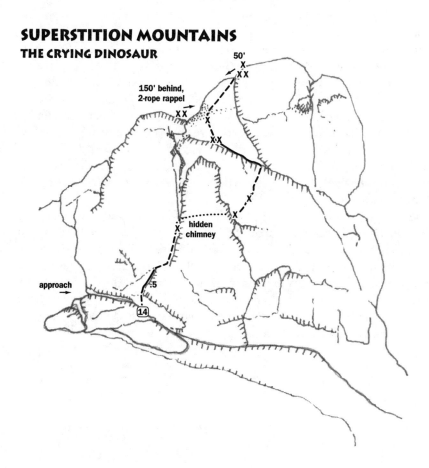

14. **Regular Route** (5.5) 3 pitches. Start near the middle of the north face below a crack system that leads up right to a huge flake pillar. **Pitch 1:** Work up a short groove and face (5.5) to an easy ramp. Follow the ramp up right to a bolt, then climb a chimney behind the flake pillar to an exposed 1-bolt belay stance on its right side. **Pitch 2:** Climb directly up to a hidden bolt and continue to a ledge/crack. Move up left along this crack to a 2-bolt belay stance. **Pitch 3:** Go up past a bolt and reach easier rock. Scamper to the summit and a 3-bolt belay anchor. The high point is just to the west. **Descent:** Rappel 50' south from the 3-bolt summit anchor to an alcove ledge with anchors and a saguaro. Make a mostly free, double-rope rappel 150' down the south side of the formation to your packs. **Rack:** A selection of medium to large cams and nuts, plus 2 ropes.

OTHER SIPHON DRAW CRAGS

On the western escarpment of the range east of Apache Junction, there are lots of towers not included in this guide. Los Banditos Towers, north of Siphon Draw, is a group of strangely shaped spires first climbed by The Banditos in the late 1970s and early 1980s. One of the best routes is *Monster Mash* (II 5.5).

The Forrest Spires, named for early rock pioneer Bill Forrest, is a group of pinnacles on the south side of Siphon Draw's mouth. On the north side of Siphon Draw, opposite The Crying Dinosaur, are several spires that were climbed by Bill Forrest. The Three Old Maids are three prominent pinnacles. The west pinnacle is 5.4, the middle pinnacle is Class 3, and the east pinnacle is climbed via a Tyrolean traverse from the middle. Don Quixote is a pinnacle east of The Three Maids. The Papoose is a spire on the north side of Siphon Draw, opposite The Flatiron.

The Flatiron is an immense rock wedge perched high above Siphon Draw on the range's west crest. A couple of Class 5 routes ascend the buttress, but most of the cliff is loose and rotten. Above The Flatiron is an impressive group of pinnacles that is reached by an arduous trek up Siphon Draw. Spire routes include *Begging Dog* (5.5), which resembles its namesake; *The Cobra* (5.8), the prominent, thin pinnacle seen from the draw atop The Flatiron; and *The Killer Whale* (A4), another small pinnacle atop The Flatiron. Forrest notes, "It requires imagination to climb difficult and dangerous aid to the summit."

SUPERSTITION MOUNTAINS
THE MIRAGE

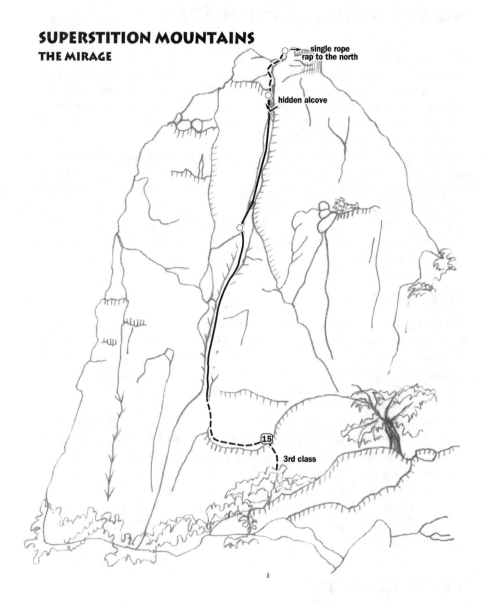

single rope
rap to the north

hidden alcove

15

3rd class

HIEROGLYPHIC CANYON AREA

OVERVIEW

Hieroglyphic Canyon is a steep canyon that drains south from the crest of the Superstition Mountains to the broad basin south of the range between Siphon Draw and the trailhead for Carney Springs. The deep canyon is easily seen from US Highway 60. Two good pinnacles—The Mirage and Vertigo Spire—are located in the high cliffs east of the canyon.

Finding the crags: Approach via Kings Ranch Road from US 60 a few miles east of Apache Junction. Follow a network of roads until you're below Hieroglyphic Canyon, the deep, obvious canyon sliced into the escarpment. Hike north on an old road 1 mile or so until it climbs left onto a ridge. Head northeast here and hike along the cliff bands to the spires. The Mirage is to the left, while Vertigo Spire is on the west side of the first canyon east of Hieroglyphic Canyon. Allow at least one hour to make the approach.

THE MIRAGE

The Mirage is a 180-foot-high spire located high on the ridge separating Hieroglyphic Canyon from the unnamed draw to the east. The spire is a "mirage" because it is very difficult to see on the approach and it merges into the cliffs behind. Hike up west-facing slopes to a saddle. Scramble up left over steep slopes and cliff bands to the base of the spire.

15. **Spectre** (5.6) 3 pitches. Up the south side of The Mirage. Wear helmets—the groove is loose. **Pitch 1:** Traverse left along a ledge system to the base of a groove/dihedral. Follow the right-hand crack system up right to a small belay ledge. **Pitch 2:** Continue up the crack and groove in a large, left-facing dihedral past loose blocks to a large, hidden alcove. **Pitch 3:** Scramble up confusing terrain to the summit. **Descent:** Go east from the summit to broken blocks and make a single-rope rappel north.

VERTIGO SPIRE

Vertigo Spire is a prominent, 180-foot-high pinnacle perched high on the west side of the first canyon east of Hieroglyphic Canyon. This is a worthy climb and the airy summit will give you a distinct feeling of "vertigo." The pinnacle is visible from US 60 and the approach road. However, it disappears into the cliffs behind on the hike.

SUPERSTITION MOUNTAINS
VERTIGO SPIRE

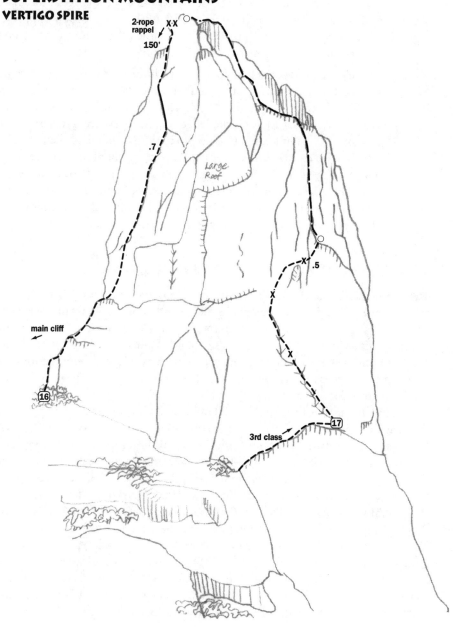

2-rope rappel
X X
150'

.7

Large Roof

.5
X
X

X

main cliff

16

X

17

3rd class

16. **The Last Fandango** (5.7) A long pitch up the narrow, 150' west face. Begin by scrambling up to the notch between the spire and the main cliff to the west. Face climb up the vertical face to the summit. **Descent:** Make a 2-rope rappel 150' back down the route from a 2-bolt summit anchor. **Rack:** A selection of Stoppers and Friends.

17. **The Grope** (5.5) 2 pitches. An easy but improbable looking route up the south face put up by Larry Treiber, Bruce Grubbs, and Bill Betcher in 1972. Locate a ledge that begins at the gully on the left side of the face. Traverse out right on the ledge to a belay stance. **Pitch 1:** Climb rotten rock up left to a bolt. Move up to the 2nd bolt and then traverse out right on exposed, steep rock (5.5) past another bolt to better rock and a belay ledge. **Pitch 2:** Climb straight up good rock above the ledge to an overhang. Go left around the roof and on to the summit. **Descent:** Make a 2-rope rappel west 150' from a 2-bolt summit anchor. **Rack:** A selection of Stoppers and Friends.

SOUTHERN SUPERSTITION CLIFFS

The southern cliffs of the Superstitions, including Bark Canyon Wall, The Fortress, Weavers Needle, and Miners Needle, are all approached from the Peralta Trailhead on the south side of the mountains. Lots of other climbing areas are found in this section of the range. These include Zonerland, Land of Nod, and The Labyrinth. There are many sport routes on these cliffs. Brief directions are given to locate these areas, but for the most part, they are left as adventure climbing areas for you to find and explore.

Finding the trailhead: The Peralta Trailhead is the jumping-off point for all the crags in the southern Supes. From Phoenix, drive east on four-lane US Highway 60, also called The Superstition Freeway. From Apache Junction, drive another 8 miles on US 60 to a well-marked left (north) turn onto Peralta Road (Forest Service Road 77) between mileposts 204 and 205. Follow this dirt road for 8 miles to a dead end at the trailhead. Plenty of parking is found here.

Several trails begin at Peralta Trailhead. Peralta Trail (Trail 102) goes up Peralta Canyon and over Fremont Saddle to the west side of Weavers Needle. This extremely popular hiking trail accesses Weavers Needle, Zonerland, and Land of Nod. Bluff Springs Trail (Trail 235) climbs over ridges into Bark Canyon and accesses Bark Canyon Wall and Wild Horse Wall. Cave Trail (Trail 233) splits off Bluff Spring Trail and climbs north to The Fortress and The Labyrinth. Dutchman's Trail (Trail 104) heads northeast to Miner's Needle.

SOUTHERN SUPERSTITION CLIFFS

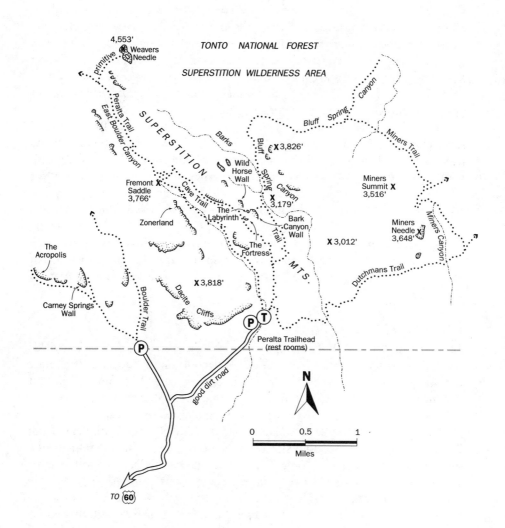

THE ACROPOLIS AND CARNEY SPRINGS WALL

These two walls are among the largest and most impressive cliffs in the Superstition Mountains. The south-facing walls loom above West Boulder Trail and Carney Springs Trailhead west of Peralta Trailhead. Some excellent multipitch, all-day, adventure routes ascend the walls and offer a true wilderness climbing experience. Both cliffs are reached by rigorous, uphill hiking and bushwhacking. The climbing, on generally good rock, is interesting, fun, and worthwhile. Expect a long day to approach and climb a route. A headlamp is a good idea for descents. Consult *Superstitions Select* or Jim Waugh's out-of-print *Phoenix Rock* for approach information and route descriptions.

To reach the Carney Springs Trailhead, turn left off Peralta Road about 6 miles from US 60 and follow this rough road to the wilderness boundary and trailhead. The Acropolis is the westernmost wall of a trio of cliffs to the northwest. *The Odyssey* (III 5.8) is a three-star, five-pitch route up the left side of the wall. Expect some good crack climbing. Two other good routes are the six-pitch *South Face* (III 5.11b) and the seven-pitch *Southeast Ridge* (III 5.7).

The east-facing Carney Springs Wall, the right-hand cliff, offers *DeGrazia* (III 5.7), one of the best long routes in the Phoenix area. This excellent six-pitch route ascends cracks and corners up the left side of the wall. The route was first ascended by John Annerino and Ben Lane in 1973 and named for famed Arizona artist Ted DeGrazia.

BARK CANYON WALL

Bark Canyon Wall, a 300-foot-high cliff on the west rim of Bark Canyon, yields some of the best long routes in the Supes. Guidebook author and Arizona climber Jim Waugh calls this "the best wall for climbing in the Superstitions." The cliff is peaceful and fairly remote, considering that Peralta Canyon to the west is traversed by one of central Arizona's most popular hiking trails.

The northeast-facing wall is reached via the Bluff Springs Trail. Begin from Peralta Trailhead on the south side of the Superstitions. Follow Peralta Trail a short distance to the Bluff Springs Trail. Turn right on this trail and follow it for about 1.5 miles as it climbs over a ridgeline and drops into Bark Canyon. The wall, dominating the west side of the canyon, is directly west of the point where the trail crosses the wash toward the east. Look for a climber's path that winds up the brushy slope to the cliff's base. For an alternative approach that doesn't lose the elevation into the canyon, hike northwest up the ridgeline before the trail drops into the canyon. When you reach a saddle left of a large buttress and south of the wall, contour north along a faint trail to the base of the cliff. As always, watch for rattlesnakes in the warmer months. Routes are described left to right on the cliff.

SUPERSTITION MOUNTAINS
BARK CANYON WALL
LEFT SIDE

all summit routes descend 65'
via rappel bolts behind wall

X X

wide
chimney

.9

.7

20

X X

22

squeeze

23

X X

21

X

.8

.9

.10

.7

20

FP

21

X

.23

X

.116

22

X X

.7

X

.6

2FP

X

chimney

X

18

19

X no hanger

20 21

23

22

all bolts not shown

18. **The Long Lead** (III 5.8) 4 pitches. A must-do Supes moderate classic—definitely 3 stars! The route ascends the left side of the wall via cracks, corners, and chimneys. **Pitch 1:** Squeeze up a chimney. Continue above up a chimney and crack (5.7) to a small belay stance. **Pitch 2:** The 140' Long Lead pitch. Move up right around a corner into a dihedral. Climb the dihedral (5.8) to a sloping ledge. Continue above for 20' past an overhang to a squeeze chimney. Belay on a spacious ledge with 2 bolts. **Pitch 3:** Work up left into a wide chimney. Bridge up the chimney past a wedged chockstone for 40' to a belay atop a large chockstone (5.7). **Pitch 4:** Continue up the chimney past more chockstones to a final squeeze hole up right to a belay ledge. **Descent:** Downclimb north to the top of *The Glory Road* (use a belay), locate anchors, and make a single-rope rappel 65' west. Walk west, then scramble south and east to the base of the cliff. **Rack:** Generous selection of Stoppers, nuts, and Friends.

19. **Big Bruno** (III 5.9) 4 pitches. Start below a large, left-facing dihedral right of *The Long Lead*. **Pitch 1:** Climb the dihedral (5.8) to a small belay ledge. **Pitch 2:** Jam cracks to a steep corner. Continue up the corner (5.9) to a short traverse left to *The Long Lead*'s pitch 2. Chimney up to a belay ledge with 2 bolts. **Pitches 3 & 4:** Climb the last 2 pitches of *The Long Lead*. **Descent:** From *The Glory Road* at the top of the wall, locate anchors and make a single rope rappel 65' west. Walk west and then scramble south and east to the base of the cliff. **Rack:** Selection of Stoppers, nuts, and Friends.

20. **Stroke It Gently** (III 5.10a) 4 pitches. Recommended route put up by Larry Treiber and Frank Hill in 1975. Begin just right of *Big Bruno* below a shallow open corner. Right of this is a smooth, blank wall. **Pitch 1:** Climb the open book (5.6) past 2 fixed pitons to a belay ledge with a bolt. 70'. **Pitch 2:** Move up right to the base of a left-arching crack. Jam this strenuous crack (5.10a) to a small roof. Exit left to a 2-bolt, semihanging belay stance. **Pitch 3:** Traverse left, climb up, and move back right. Face climb past a bolt to a large ledge with a 2-bolt belay (same ledge as *The Long Lead*). **Pitch 4:** Climb an indistinct rib (5.7) past a bolt to a large roof. Follow a horizontal crack up right to the top. **Descent:** From *The Glory Road* at the top of the wall, locate anchors and make a single-rope rappel 65' west. Walk west, then scramble south and east to the base of the cliff. **Rack:** Selection of Stoppers, TCUs, and Friends.

21. **The Glory Road** (III 5.7) 4 pitches. Excellent moderate climb up the center of the wall. Same start as *Stroke It Gently*. **Pitch 1:** Climb the obvious open book (5.6) past 2 fixed pitons to a belay ledge with a bolt. **Pitch 2:** Traverse right and down into a sharp dihedral topped

with an overhang. Work up the dihedral past a fixed pin, pull the overhang (5.7), face climb up a wide crack and belay above on a good ledge. **Pitch 3:** Traverse right and down across easy rock to ledges. Climb a moderate crack to a large belay ledge. **Pitch 4:** Head up the long, prominent chimney to the summit and a 2-bolt belay/rappel anchor. **Descent:** Make a single-rope rappel 65' west. Walk west, then scramble south and east to the base of the cliff. **Rack:** Selection of wires, TCUs, and Friends.

22. **The Long Road** (III 5.9) 3 pitches. Begin below the open book (same start as *Stroke It Gently*.) **Pitch 1:** Climb the obvious open book (5.6) past 2 fixed pitons to a belay ledge with a bolt. **Pitch 2:** Traverse right and down to a dihedral capped with an overhang. Continue traversing right across the face from the dihedral to the base of an obvious, vertical crack. Jam the crack to a ledge on the right with a belay bolt. **Pitch 3:** Jam the crack above to broken rock. When possible, traverse left into a left-leaning corner and follow (5.9) to the summit. **Descent:** Locate *The Glory Road*'s anchors and make a single-rope rappel 65' west. Walk west, then scramble south and east to the base of the cliff. **Rack:** Selection of wires, TCUs, and Friends.

23. **Bandito Route** (III 5.11b) 3 pitches. Begin about 30' right of *The Long Road*. **Pitch 1:** Climb a slab (5.8) protected by a rivet (bring a wired nut to sling it) to a roof with 2 old bolts and a rivet. Pull the crux roof (5.11b) and face climb up an intermittent, right-angling crack to a slab. Belay from 2 bolts. **Pitch 2:** Face climb to a bolt, then up a "potted" face to smoother rock and a bolt. Climb up right to a left-angling flake system and follow flakes and cracks up left to a large belay ledge. **Pitch 3:** From the ledge's right side, climb a thin crack up a short, bulging wall (cross *The Glory Road* here) and face climb into a left-leaning dihedral. Jam and stem up the dihedral (5.9) to the top (same finish as *The Long Road*). **Descent:** From *The Glory Road* at the top of the wall, locate anchors and make a single-rope rappel 65' west. Walk west, then scramble south and east to the base of the cliff. **Rack:** Selection of wires, TCUs, and Friends.

24. **Erection Direct** (III 5.10b) 3 pitches. This route, on the right side of the wall, ascends the obvious erection pillar. **Pitch 1:** Climb either side of "Erection Pinnacle" (5.8) to a ledge with a bolt. **Pitch 2:** Traverse left (5.10b) to a right-angling crack. Follow the crack up right to a small roof. Jam a vertical crack over the roof and continue to a spacious belay ledge. **Pitch 3:** Step right off the ledge and face climb up past horizontal cracks to the top. **Descent:** Scramble off the back side of the crag. **Rack:** Stoppers, TCUs, and Friends.

scramble off backside

SUPERSTITION MOUNTAINS
BARK CANYON WALL
RIGHT SIDE

X X

.10b
X X

Erection
Pinnacle .8

LB

6 bolts

var.

X   25
24   belay bolt

X X

X

X

X

X

X

X

26

to The Labyrinth

3rd class
onto ledge

not all bolts shown

24

25. **Simmer 'til Done** (5.10a/b) A good face route 20' right of *Erection Direct*. Scramble onto a ledge right of the pillar, then move left to a belay stance with a bolt. Climb the face right of the erection past 6 bolts to a ledge. Move right and follow thin cracks to a 2-bolt belay stance under a small overhang. **Descent:** Rappel.

26. **Fettuccini Afraido** (5.11a/b R) Begin off a ledge 15' right of Route 25 below a bulge. Pull over the crux bulge past two bolts and angle up right past another bolt to a thin crack. Work up the vertical crack to steep face climbing (5.11a R) and a bolt. Follow the crack to the long overhang and step left to a belay bolt. 5 bolts. **Descent:** Rappel. **Rack:** Stoppers and small cams.

WILD HORSE WALL

This rarely visited, east-facing cliff north of Bark Canyon Wall offers some of the best rock in the Superstitions. The 125-foot-high wall has a great selection of excellent, single-pitch face routes. A subsidiary buttress juts out from the wall's northeast corner and also offers some fine climbs.

Use the directions for Bark Canyon Wall from Peralta Trailhead. Hike up the Bluff Springs Trail for about 1.75 miles. The wall, at 3,500 feet, is visible on the west canyon rim north of Bark Canyon Wall. Follow the trail north a few hundred feet after it crosses the dry creekbed in the canyon bottom. Where the canyon bends sharply right, scramble west up steep, rocky slopes from the trail to the cliff's base. You may find a faint climber's path, but don't count on it. And watch for rattlesnakes in warmer weather. An alternative route is to scramble and bushwhack north from Bark Canyon Wall to the base of the cliff. Routes are listed left to right.

27. **Mustang Sally** (5.8 R) Jim Waugh says, "This route yields excellent face climbing on very solid rock." Start below the obvious slab in the middle of the wall. Face climb past 2 bolts to a traverse left that leads to a steep ramp. Follow thin, discontinuous cracks over a bulge (5.8) and face climb up easier rock left to the summit. **Descent:** 1-rope rappel from *Wailing Banshee*'s anchors. **Rack:** Wires, small nuts, and TCUs.

28. **Even Cowgirls Get the Blues** (5.9) Start just right of *Mustang Sally*. Face climb up a slightly overhanging wall (5.9) past a bolt. Face climb above past 4 more bolts and finish up a short crack. 5 bolts. **Descent:** 1-rope rappel from *Wailing Banshee*'s anchors. **Rack:** Medium wires and Friends.

29. **The Bronc** (5.9) Begin in the middle of the wall, right of a prominent slab. Jam a finger crack recessed back in a flared chimney until the crack widens to hands. Continue jamming to an overhang, then move left to another crack that leads to the top. **Descent:** 1-rope rappel from *Wailing Banshee*'s anchors. **Rack:** Wires, TCUs, and Friends.

30. **The Blind Leading the Naked** (5.10d) Start up right from *The Bronc*. Face climb up overhanging rock (5.10d) past 2 bolts to a thin crack. Climb the crack up a right-facing corner to a face below a large, detached flake. Move up the right side of the flake, then right to a belay stance with 2 bolts. **Descent:** Rappel the route. **Rack:** Wires, TCUs, and Friends.

31. **Wailing Banshee** (5.10a) Begin below a slightly overhanging wall. Face climb (5.10a) up past 3 bolts to a headwall. Clip another bolt and work up an unusual groove to a 2-bolt anchor. **Descent:** Rappel the route. **Rack:** Quickdraws.

32. **Ridin' High** (5.5) Start on the right side of the wall below a left-arching dihedral. Jam and lieback up the dihedral to a traverse under an overhang. Finish up *The Bronc*'s final crack. **Descent:** 1-rope rappel from *Wailing Banshee*'s 2-bolt anchor.

The following three routes are on a small crag just northeast of Wild Horse Wall's right side.

33. **High Over Texas** (5.6 R) No topo. Up the southwest face. Climb a flawless corner behind a tree up right to the top. **Descent:** Scramble down west. **Rack:** Stoppers and TCUs.

34. **5.8 Flu** (5.8) No topo. Climb the right-hand crack up the south face. **Descent:** Scramble down west. **Rack:** Medium Stoppers, nuts, and Friends.

35. **Gunfight at Hueco Corral** (5.11b) No topo. On the north face. Face climb up right past 3 bolts and a horizontal crack to a ledge with 1 bolt. **Descent:** Scramble down west. **Rack:** Small Friends.

THE FORTRESS

The Fortress, perched atop the ridge east of Peralta Canyon, is a 150-foot-high, fortress-looking crag that offers an assortment of fine routes on good rock. This remote, rarely visited cliff yields a great wilderness climbing experience in a stunning setting.

To approach The Fortress, hike up Bluff Springs Trail from Peralta Trailhead to Cave Trail. Go left up the steep Cave Trail to the crag, a large, west-facing

outcrop above the trail and about 200 yards south of Geronimo's Cave. The trail is sometimes hard to follow because it winds through boulders and across slickrock. Look for scuff marks and cairns that mark the way. Allow about one hour from the parking area to the crag. Routes are listed right to left on the west face. Rappel from all routes that end on ledges to avoid rope damage by lowering.

36. **South Side** (5.5) No topo. This route begins on the right side of the south face above the trail and right of an overhanging wall. Work out left along a ledge system to the base of an obvious crack. Stem and face climb up the crack to the summit. **Descent:** Scramble off the east side. **Rack:** Medium to large Stoppers and a set of Friends.

37. **Bon-Bons in Space** (5.11a/b) Begin on the right side of the wall at a small alcove below an arête. Pull above the alcove and follow the arête to a ledge. 4 bolts to a 2-bolt rap anchor on the ledge. 70'.

38. **Pocket Full of Rainbows** (5.11a) A classic sport route. Start 10' right of the obvious, left-leaning dihedral. Climb the overhanging face above past 4 bolts, then move right around a corner and finish at anchors on a large ledge. 4 bolts to 2-bolt rap anchor. 70'.

39. **The Linear Accelerator** (5.11b/c) Same start as Route 38. Face climb past the first 2 bolts. Work up left to a crack and past another bolt to a thin vertical crack that ends at a large ledge with anchors. 3 bolts to 2-bolt rap anchor. 70'. **Rack:** Some Stoppers and TCUs.

40. **Bypass** (5.7) Begin below a left-leaning dihedral on the right side of the west face. Climb the dihedral (easier than it looks!) and finish up the left crack to the summit. Watch for loose rock. 125'. **Descent:** Walk off. **Rack:** Stoppers, nuts, and Friends.

41. **Freely Freaking** (5.7) 2 pitches. The first ascent party in 1972 "freely freaked" on the opening moves. Start about 20' left of *Bypass*. **Pitch 1:** Work up an intimidating thin crack (5.7) on a small rib. Continue to a big ledge below a left-facing dihedral. **Pitch 2:** Climb the dihedral. **Descent:** Walk off. **Rack:** Stoppers, nuts, and Friends.

42. **A Fistful of Pockets** (5.10a R) Kind of scary, but fun climbing up pockets. Climb the vertical face left of *Freely Freaking* past 2 bolts to a 2-bolt rap anchor on the left side of a spacious ledge. Find extra pro in pockets. **Rack:** Small gear.

43. **For a Few Pockets More** (5.11a R) Climb a thin crack and blunt arête 10' left of *Fistful* with a single bolt to a 2-bolt rap anchor on a large ledge. To start, either climb to the first bolt on *Stardust* or use a tied-off hook in a pocket for pro like the first ascent party. **Rack:** Small gear.

Ian Spencer-Green and Noah Hannawalt pair up on *Freely Freaking* (5.7) at The Fortress.

44. **Stardust** (5.11b/c) The slightly overhanging face right of a prominent crack system. Begin off boulders. Step up left to a short, shallow crack, climb past it, and continue past 3 bolts to a 2-bolt rap anchor on a large ledge. **Rack:** Small gear.

45. **Bay Tree Belay** (5.7) Locate a wide, overhanging crack on the left side of the wall. Jam and stem up the crack to the crag summit. **Descent:** Scramble down the east side. **Rack:** Large nuts and Friends.

THE LABYRINTH

This north-facing cliff, home to some of the hardest routes in the Supes, hides in a brushy, cliff-lined canyon northwest of Bark Canyon Wall. The cliff is hard to find initially. Follow the access directions carefully, but be advised that some exploration might be necessary in the maze of shallow canyons. Once you're there, expect superb pocket pulling on vertical to overhanging walls, as well as some thin crack lines. Most of the lines are 1980s-style sport routes, with one to four bolts that need to be supplemented with a small rack. You can toprope most of the routes from anchors on top of the cliff. The Labyrinth is a good place to go when it's hot because most of the walls are north-facing and shaded. Most of the routes were established and climbed by Jim Waugh in 1987.

Approach the cliff from above via the Bluff Springs Trail and the Cave Trail. Before the Cave Trail passes The Fortress, scramble north through a broken cliff band and hike north on a cairn-marked path along a broad, rocky ridge until it drops down to the top of a shallow canyon that drains east. The Labyrinth lies just east in this canyon. Bushwhack down a faint trail on the left edge of the canyon to the right-hand cliffs or hike across the rimrock south of the canyon to a rappel station above the Myth Wall. A short rappel puts you on the far right side of the area. Allow forty-five minutes to one hour to reach the cliff from the parking area. An alternative approach exists from Bark Canyon Wall. From the north side of the wall, scramble along a faint trail through brush on the wall's north flank into a shallow canyon. The routes are on the south side of the canyon. A rough trail follows the cliff's base. Routes are described right to left.

MYTH WALL

The following routes are on Myth Wall, a vertical and slightly overhanging north face directly south of Sundeck Boulder, a large, flat-topped boulder. A 2-bolt belay/rappel anchor is atop the cliff on the east.

46. **Deadset** (5.10c) The far right side of the face just left of a black pour-off. Climb a mossy seam, then step left on face past a bolt.

47. **Jet Set** (5.11c/d) A right-leaning crack. Start off an erect boulder. Thin finger crack to a handjam pod. Continue up a narrow, right-facing corner. **Rack:** Wires, TCUs, and small to medium cams.

48. **Daedalus** (5.11b) Start by stepping onto a tree. Work up a thin crack to a bolt 20' up. Continue up before stepping onto the bolted face to the right. 4 bolts to 1-bolt anchor.

49. **Atlas** (5.12b) A thin, left-angling crack with 2 fixed pitons. At top of crack, move right past 2 bolts, then face climb to top. **Rack:** Wires and TCUs.

50. **Icarus** (5.12d) Watch that your wings don't melt in midsummer. Bouldery moves off the deck lead to crimpy sequences. 5 bolts to 2-bolt anchor.

51. **Delilah** (5.11d) Excellent route and rock 8' left of *Icarus*. Crimps and pockets on the middle of the face lead to thin crux moves between the 3rd and 5th bolts. 5 bolts to 2-bolt anchor. A good 5.12a variation launches up right from the 3rd bolt to another bolt, then back up left to Delilah's last bolt.

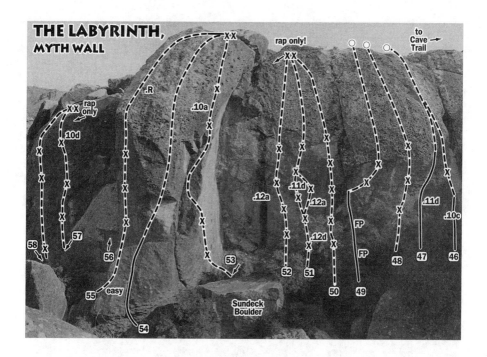

52. **Samson** (5.12a) Great technical climbing up the tan, pocketed face right of a black streak. Superb pocket pulling with some long reaches lead to crimps. 4 bolts to 2-bolt anchor.

53. **Lion's Den** (5.10a) On the right side of a jutting buttress left of Myth Wall. Begin at the left side of Sundeck Boulder. Face climb up left to a blunt prow with 2 bolts. Above, step left into a short, right-facing and leaning corner that leads to a vertical, pocketed 2-bolt face. 4 bolts to 2-bolt anchor. **Rack:** Small and medium cams for the corner crack.

Reach the next routes by downclimbing past a wedged boulder between the east side of the Sundeck Boulder and the wall.

54. **Fluff Boys in Heat** (5.10a R) Start just left of the wedged block and right of a tunnel. Climb an overhanging hand crack to a slab. Pull up past a white spot, then up pocketed rock to a 2-bolt anchor. No bolts— find gear in pockets and thin cracks. **Rack:** Stoppers, TCUs, and small cams.

55. **Christian Arête** (5.8 R) Begin left of a tunnel atop a boulder. Climb an easy slab, then up the right side of a blunt arête past 3 bolts to a 2-bolt anchor. Kind of run-out up high, but easy.

56. **Enga's First** (5.8) Start at the left side of the prominent buttress below

Jim Waugh climbing *Lion's Den* (5.10a) on Myth Wall.

THE LABYRINTH EAST SIDE

an open corner. Climb the steep corner to a left-leaning crack above a slab. Follow the crack to a thin crack to the top and a 2-bolt anchor set back from the edge. **Rack:** Selection of cams.

57. **Electric Raguland** (5.11a) Excellent, sustained, and pumpy. Unique holds up high. Begin below a right-angling groove. Scramble up the groove, then step left to the 1st bolt. Follow edges and pockets up the steep wall. 4 bolts to 2-bolt anchor set back from the edge.

58. **Spaghetti Western** (5.10b/c) Recommended. Begin just left of the groove. Climb to the 1st bolt; pulling straight up is reachy and 5.11a. It's easier to step right to a groove, then back left above a bulge. Pull pockets and edges up the blunt prow. 3 bolts to 2-bolt anchor.

59. **Run-It-Out** (5.10 R) Face climb to a single bolt, then up right on steep rock. Look for pro in pockets and small cracks. A few hard moves, then it gets a lot easier but mostly unprotected.

60. **Unknown** (5.7) Follow right-angling cracks and corners up the left side of the face. **Rack:** Selection of cams.

61. **Unknown** (5.10c) The route is up a slabby face above some boulders in a shallow gully. Face climb past 3 bolts to the anchors set back from the edge.

62. **The Last Fool A-Hammerin'** (5.11) Face climb past 2 bolts to a thin crack to a small roof to a 1-bolt, featured headwall. No Topo.

63. **Never Named It** (5.8) At the far east side of the wall directly west of the backside of Bark Canyon Wall and just around the corner to the left of Route 62. Climb a short crack onto a ledge. Pull pockets past a couple bolts and a horizontal crack. No Topo.

The canyon north of The Labyrinth has five bolted routes on the shaded south canyon walls. Scramble up to the ridge north of Myth Wall, traverse east along the ridge, and downclimb to a notch, then down to the canyon floor. This short canyon can also be reached by easy hiking down the canyon from the west. Routes are listed right to left.

The first three routes are on a good-looking wall near the west end of the canyon. No topos.

64. **Unknown** (5.11d) Kind of sharp—don't save it for the last route of the day. 2 bolts and 1 fixed piton to a 2-bolt anchor. **Descent:** Walk off west on the ridgetop.

65. **Unknown** (5.11b) Sharp edges and pockets left of Route 64. 2 bolts to 2-bolt anchor. **Descent:** Walk off west on the ridgetop.

66. **Unknown Crack** (5.10) Jam and lieback the crack on the left side of the wall. **Rack:** Small and medium cams.

These routes are down left (east) on a north-facing cliff. No topos.

67. **Petite** (5.11b) Face moves past 2 bolts to 2-bolt lowering anchor.

68. **Pandemonium** (5.12c) Thin and sharp with technical moves. 3 bolts to 2-bolt lowering anchor.

This route is farther east near the end of the canyon and right of a chimney. No topo.

69. **Hercules** (5.11d/.12a) Really good climbing over a couple of bulges. Work up an overhanging crack with liebacks past two fixed pitons to a break, then up a pocketed bulge with 2 bolts to anchors on top of the cliff.

The next canyon to the north (two canyons north of Myth Wall) has some good, hard routes on its north-facing cliff at the far east end. The Wild Horse Wall is immediately north of here. Reach the routes by hiking west out of Labyrinth Canyon and then walking north to the second canyon. Hike and scramble down the canyon. Where it begins to narrow and get brushy, traverse out of the canyon floor onto lichen-covered slabs to the right. The following two routes are in a shallow amphitheater. It will take some work to find the cliff, but it's well worth it for the climbing and the views. No topos.

70. **Medusa** (5.12b) An overhanging, technical face route with 4 bolts to a 2-bolt anchor.

71. **Jim's Crack** (5.11 R) A difficult crack and seam right of *Medusa*.

ZONERLAND

Zonerland is a large group of pinnacles off Peralta Trail south of Fremont Saddle. There are many sport routes in this maze of pocket pinnacles and excellent volcanic rock. Approach Zonerland by hiking about three quarters of the way up Peralta Trail to Fremont Saddle from Peralta Trailhead. After a section of slickrock, look for a faint trail that heads up left on the west side of the canyon. Follow this good trail up left to a large group of towers. Look for an alcove on the left. Scarface Crag is a large block southwest of the alcove. When you reach the top of the ridge in Zonerland, the obvious dome is Zonerland Fortress, while the cliff below the ridge is Bovine Wall. Some good routes include *Tone of the Bell* (5.9), 8 bolts up the largest pinnacle just past some slickrock on the approach; *Boomerang* (5.12b); *The Heckler* (5.11b); and *Shreadlocks in Babylon* (5.11c). You're on your own to find routes. Explore and climb whatever looks good.

WEAVERS NEEDLE

Weavers Needle, dominating the Superstition Range, is one of Arizona's most striking and famous landmarks. This 4,553-foot-high peak yields an easy but potentially dangerous ascent to its crumbling summit. Don't underestimate the route or its objective dangers, including heat, lack of water, lack of protection and belay anchors, and other climbers. Try to avoid climbing the needle on weekends in spring and fall—it can be really busy! Elevation gain from the trailhead is 3,400 vertical feet with about 600 feet of climbing terrain. Hiking mileage is 8 miles round trip.

Begin at the Peralta Trailhead and hike northwest for 2.25 miles on the well-used Peralta Trail to 3,766-foot-high Fremont Saddle. The saddle offers an excellent vista of Weavers Needle. Continue on Peralta Trail into East Boulder Canyon to Pinyon Camp. This place makes a good overnight camping spot. One mile north of Pinyon Camp (4 miles from Peralta Trailhead), leave the trail and hike east up steep talus to the base of a steep gully that lies between the higher north summit and the lower south summit. Work left into the gully below the west face of the south summit and climb the gully (Class 3 scrambling over rock steps) to the foot of the 1st pitch, about 150 feet below an obvious chockstone in a notch.

72. **West Chimney** (III 5.0) 4 pitches. The classic Supes route. **Pitch 1:** Climb 60' of Class 4 rock to a small ledge on the left wall of the gully. A pipe hammered into the rock offers some protection. **Pitch 2:** Continue up poorly protected but easy Class 5 rock to the chockstone. Here, the leader has 3 choices. Crawl under the chockstone (5.0), climb left of the chockstone (5.4), or climb right of the chockstone (5.2).

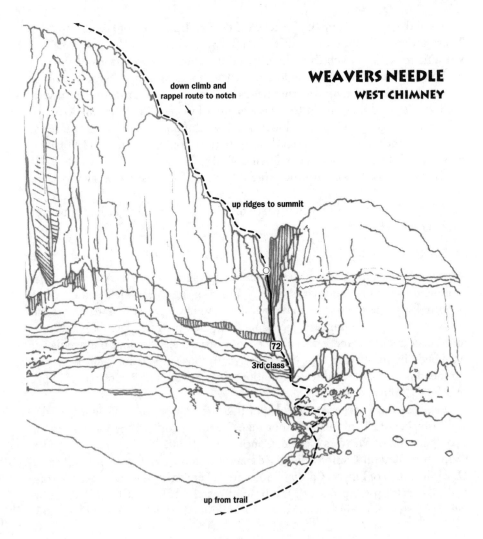

down climb and
rappel route to notch

WEAVERS NEEDLE
WEST CHIMNEY

up ridges to summit

72

3rd class

up from trail

Belay from several rappel bolts atop the chockstone. Pitches 1 and 2 can be combined in a long lead. **Pitch 3:** From the notch, scramble 15' up a step (Class 3) and continue up a gully with easy rock steps above for about 300' to the southwest face of the final summit headwall. **Pitch 4:** Easy but exposed and dangerous climbing. There are no good anchors available at the bottom of the pitch. Use extreme caution. Climb a broken groove (Class 4) up left for 40' and follow a juggy crack to a natural horn for an anchor belay. Scramble onto the summit for marvelous 360-degree views. **Descent:** Scramble back down to bolt anchors south of the top of pitch 4. Rappel back to the gully and downclimb to the notch between the south and north summits. From bolt anchors atop the chockstone in the notch, make a long, 2-rope rappel west to the base of pitch 1. **Rack:** A selection of Stoppers and medium to large nuts and Friends, plus some extra runners, 2 ropes, and a helmet.

MINERS NEEDLE

Miners Needle, a prominent landmark of the southern Superstition Mountains, is a complex mass of pinnacles and walls that yield a surprising number of good climbing routes. The pointed 3,648-foot-high needle, visible to the northeast from Peralta Road, is reached by a lengthy but pleasant desert hike. The longest routes are found on the Lower East Wall, a 250-foot-high, southeast-facing cliff on the east flank of Miners Needle. Other shorter lines are found on the pinnacle groups atop the peak.

Begin at the Peralta Trailhead on the south side of the Supes. From the north end of the parking area, go east on the Dutchman's Trail (Trail 104). The trail works over a ridge and descends into broad Barkley Basin. Miners Needle rises to the northeast. The trail skirts the north edge of the basin along the mountain edge and passes south of the needle before bending north up Miners Canyon. The trail switchbacks onto the east side of the canyon and contours north toward Miners Summit, a saddle north of Miners Needle. The obvious large wall to the west is the Lower East Wall. Resist the urge to hike directly up the slopes to Miners Needle, which are steep, brushy, and much slower going than if you stay on the main trail. When the trail reaches a switchback north of Miners Needle, leave the trail and hike south up slabs and slopes to the cliffs. The Lower East Wall is to the left, while three needle groups form the summit area, Middle Needle being the other one most climbed.

MINERS NEEDLE
LOWER EAST WALL
rappel down backside
window needle
chimney
walk-off
.8
window
.9
.8R
.6
tunnel
74
75 76
73
74
Fixed anchors are not shown

LOWER EAST WALL

This high, east-facing wall offers a selection of great moderate routes in a remote, pristine desert setting. Rack up and stash your pack on the north side of the Needle before hiking to the base of the cliff because the descent route scrambles down the north side. Watch for loose rock. Routes are listed left to right.

73. **Rockabilly** (III 5.8 R) 2 pitches. First ascent was by Jim Waugh and Bill Hatcher in 1986. Start on the left side of the wall at a southeast-facing prow. **Pitch 1:** Work up a crack just right of a roof system to a small roof. Move up left around the roof and step left into a shallow, right-facing corner. Climb the corner to a stance. Avoid the evil-looking crack above by climbing up left on a slightly overhanging face to a ledge. Climb the face above (5.8 R) to another ledge and belay. **Pitch 2:** Climb a crack and face up right to a large, right-facing dihedral. Move out right from the dihedral and face climb to a bulge with a thin crack. Pull over the bulge (5.8) and traverse left and up to a spacious terrace. **Descent:** Scramble north along the terrace and back down brushy slabs to your packs. **Rack:** Wires, TCUs, and a selection of small to large Friends.

74. **Pokey Dance** (III 5.8) 3 pitches. Starts at the same place as *Rockabilly*. **Pitch 1:** Climb a crack just right of a roof system to a small roof. Traverse up right (5.6) to a stance. Continue traversing up right on

flakes to a belay ledge. **Pitch 2:** Follow cracks up left to a bolt at the base of a slab right of the large, right-facing dihedral. Edge right up the slab past a hidden fixed piton to a belay ledge. **Pitch 3:** Work up a short chimney to the wide terrace below the summit. **Descent:** Scramble north along the terrace and back down brushy slabs. **Rack:** Wires and small to large Friends.

75. **Pseudonym** (III 5.9) 3 pitches. First ascent in 1973 by Larry Treiber, and Frank and Fred Hill. This good route is on the right-hand side of the face below Window Needle, the northeast summit pinnacle with a large arch. Note a large, broken column below the window. The route starts below the dihedral on the left side of the column. **Pitch 1:** Climb the dihedral for 90' to a small tunnel. Continue up the left dihedral (5.9) for another 40' to the window. **Pitch 2:** Traverse left 20' past some overhangs and then move up right to the base of an overhanging squeeze chimney and belay. **Pitch 3:** Work up the chimney for 30' to the summit terrace. **Descent:** Scramble southeast from the summit to a 2-bolt rappel station. Make a single-rope rappel down the back (west) side of the needle to the ground. **Rack:** Wires and small to large Friends.

76. **The Anonymous** (III 5.7) 3 pitches. Begin at the same place as *Pseudonym*. **Pitch 1:** Climb the good crack up the left-facing dihedral for 90' to a small tunnel and belay. **Pitch 2:** Squeeze through the tunnel to the right side of the column and work up a series of chimneys for another 110' to a belay at the window. **Pitch 3:** Traverse left along an exposed ledge with a fixed piton to a ledge. Follow a groove to the summit of the pinnacle. **Descent:** Scramble southeast from the summit to a 2-bolt rappel station. Make a single-rope rappel down the back (west) side of the needle to the ground. **Rack:** Mostly medium and large nuts and Friends.

77. **Threading the Needle** (5.0) 2 pitches. No topo. A fun route to the top of Window Needle. The route ascends the west face to the needle and then up the east face to the summit. Scramble up talus to a point directly below the window on the west side. **Pitch 1:** Climb an easy, shallow gully (Class 4) to a broken section. Climb an easy ramp to the window and belay from bolts. **Pitch 2:** Traverse left on an exposed ledge past a fixed piton to another ledge. Climb a groove to the summit. **Descent:** Scramble southeast from the summit to a 2-bolt rappel station. Make a single-rope rappel down the back (west) side of the Needle to the ground. **Rack:** Small rack of medium and large nuts and cams.

MIDDLE NEEDLE

This is a pinnacle complex just west of Window Needle. Most of the routes face north and are visible from Dutchman's Trail. Scramble up slabs to the cliff's base. Routes are listed left to right.

78. **Overeasy** (5.8) Good crack line up the northwest face. Begin at the left side of the face below a thin crack. Jam the thin crack (5.8). Finish up a chimney and face to a 2-bolt belay on top. 75'. **Descent:** 1-rope rappel from bolt anchors back to base. **Rack:** Selection of Stoppers, TCUs, and small to medium Friends.

79. **Schism** (5.9) Begin about 10' right of *Overeasy* beneath an angling crack system. Work up the cracks, using the middle and right cracks as you get higher, to a wide chimney. Above, step left to a 2-bolt belay (same as *Overeasy*). **Descent:** 1-rope rappel from bolt anchors back to base. **Rack:** Selection of Stoppers, TCUs, and small to medium Friends.

SUPERSTITION MOUNTAINS
MIDDLE NEEDLE, NORTHWEST FACE

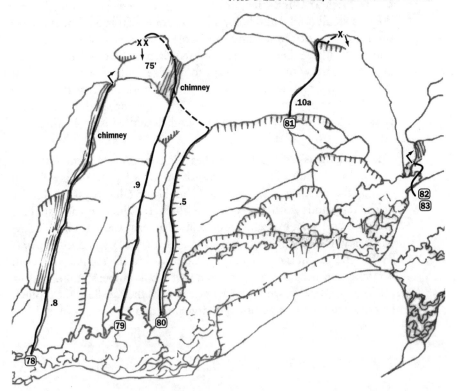

80. **Regular Route** (5.5) Climb a chimney right of *Schism* to a hand crack (5.5) that angles right to a ledge. Face climb left to *Schism's* wide chimney and finish up to the 2-bolt belay anchors. **Descent:** 1-rope rappel from bolt anchors back to base. **Rack:** Selection of Stoppers and medium to large Friends.

81. **Undereasy** (5.10a) Begin 30' up and right from *Regular Route* on a large ledge reached by scrambling. Move up a slightly overhanging, right-leaning crack (5.10a) to a ledge. Step up right onto the summit and a belay bolt. **Descent:** 1-rope rappel back to the ground. **Rack:** Stoppers and small to medium Friends.

82. **Cloudy** (5.7 R) Scramble west from *Undereasy* and through a notch to the south face. Start at the left side of the pocketed south face. Climb directly up to a bolt (5.7 R) and continue to the summit (5.7) and a belay bolt. **Descent:** 1-rope rappel back to the ground. **Rack:** Friends.

83. **Sunshine** (5.2) Begin at the right side of the pocketed south face. Move up and left to *Cloudy's* bolt. Continue up left 10' and then up to another bolt. Continue up left, then back right to the summit and belay bolt. **Descent:** 1-rope rappel back to the ground.

SUPERSTITION MOUNTAINS
MIDDLE NEEDLE, SOUTHEAST FACE

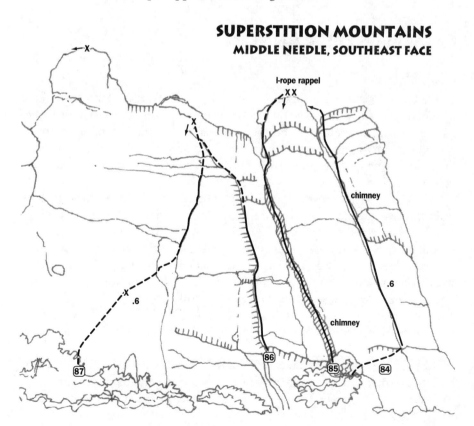

The next four routes are on the southeast face, directly behind the northwest face. Routes are listed right to left.

84. **Too Easy** (5.6) On the right side of the southeast face. Move right and jam a crack (5.6) to a chimney until it's possible to step up left to a 2-bolt belay anchor atop the pillar. **Descent:** 1-rope rappel back to the ground. **Rack:** Medium to large Friends.

85. **Ciphysus** (5.7) Begin below a large chimney. Chimney up and over a large chockstone (5.7). Finish up the wide chimney before stepping right and pulling onto the top of the pillar with a 2-bolt anchor. **Descent:** 1-rope rappel back to the ground. **Rack:** Selection of nuts and Friends.

86. **Senility** (5.8) Start 6' left of *Ciphysus*. Follow a right-facing dihedral up left to a bolt belay. **Descent:** 1-rope rappel back to the ground. **Rack:** Small to large nuts and Friends.

87. **Wham Bam Thank You Ma'am** (5.6) Start 15' left of *Senility*. Begin on a flake and climb the face above past a bolt (5.6). Angle up right to a crack system. Follow the crack to *Senility*'s belay bolt. **Descent:** 1-rope rappel to the ground. **Rack:** Stoppers and Friends.

QUEEN CREEK CANYON

OVERVIEW

Queen Creek Canyon slices sharply through the southeast edge of the Superstition Mountains, a crumpled desert range that forms a transition between the higher Mogollon Rim to the north and the arid basin and range topography to the south. The canyon, carved by Queen Creek and traced by US Highway 60, is lined with compact cliffs, buttresses, pinnacles, and fins composed of pocketed volcanic ash.

The rock offers a great medium for climbers, with sinker pockets, shallow dishes, crisp edges, and positive holds. The rock is a thick formation of ash flow tuff that was deposited between 15 and 24 million years ago by violent volcanic eruptions. It is a soft rock, often soft enough that a fingernail can scratch it, although much of it was hardened and welded by heat and pressure. The weathering of softer chunks of pumice from the main rock formed the myriad pockets found on exposed cliffs. Queen Creek, like so many other welded tuff climbing areas, including Smith Rock in Oregon, Cochiti Mesa in New Mexico, and the nearby cliffs in the western Superstitions, yields inviting, vertical faces for climbers.

The sheer numbers of bolted and traditional routes at Queen Creek Canyon and the surrounding area make this Arizona's premier climbing area. The crags in Queen Creek Canyon, as well as those in nearby canyons and hills, offer more than 700 bolted routes and more than 1,200 boulder problems where climbers can test their skills. The startling amount of rock equals the diversity of climbing experiences, from pocket-studded slabs and vertical crimpfests to overhanging jug hauls and pumpy, technical testpieces. Some fine traditional crack routes are also found. Routes range in difficulty from 5.6 to 5.13, with most falling between 5.9 and 5.11, making Queen Creek an ideal moderate destination. Accessibility is no problem either. In Queen Creek Canyon, the crags line the highway corridor, making most approaches less than ten minutes from car to cliff. Add almost perfect weather, convenient camping, and a desert setting with saguaros, yuccas, cacti, and oak forests and Queen Creek becomes a major destination area.

Climbing history: Arizona climbers first took note of Queen Creek Canyon's cliffs back in the 1970s. One of the first known routes established was *Legal Dihedral* (5.7) on Sunday School Wall in 1973 by Dave Brighton, Doug Rickard, Scott Kronberg, and Larry Treiber. Through the 1970s, a handful of climbers, including Kent Brock, Don O'Kelley, and Pat McMahon, developed all the crack lines on the Little England Wall, Sunday School Wall, Wounded Knee Wall, and South Side Wall.

Jim Waugh's 1987 book *Phoenix Rock* noted, "In the past this area has seen little traffic . . . for the volcanic rock can be quite loose . . .The author feels that if more routes (than just the classics) are climbed, then they too will eventually become cleaned and subsequently worthwhile climbs." In retrospect, this statement proved to be prophetic. The area's amazingly climbable rock became a Bosch driller's paradise in the early 1990s, when the sport climbing revolution came to Arizona. Between 1990 and 1994, literally hundreds of bolted sport routes went in. Most of the climbers hailed from nearby Phoenix and included Craig Keaty, Chris Raypole, Scott Hynes, Mark Trainor, and Marty Karabin, who authored the authoritative, complete guidebook to the Queen Creek area.

The described cliffs lie along US 60 and are among the most accessible and the busiest of Queen Creek's crags. Atlantis, a narrow canyon below the highway, is lined with many moderate routes up to 80 feet long. The shady corridor is a perfect destination on warm days. The Pond, a long cliff band above the highway, has many of the area's harder routes, as well as a generous selection of moderate classics that includes *Pocket Puzzle* (5.10a). Many of the area's best crack routes are found in Queen Creek Canyon on Little England Wall above Atlantis and Sunday School Wall.

After climbing all the described routes in Queen Creek Canyon, pick up a copy of Marty Karabin's guidebook *A Rock Jock's Guide to Queen Creek Canyon*. It provides descriptions and topos to many excellent crags and spires in the backcountry south and east of the main canyon. These areas include The Hook Wall, a tall cliff with several great 5.12s; The Pancake House, with a huge assortment of good, short, moderate clip-and-gos; Upper and Lower Looner Land, with many excellent bolt routes up pinnacles and faces; Upper Devil's

QUEEN CREEK CANYON

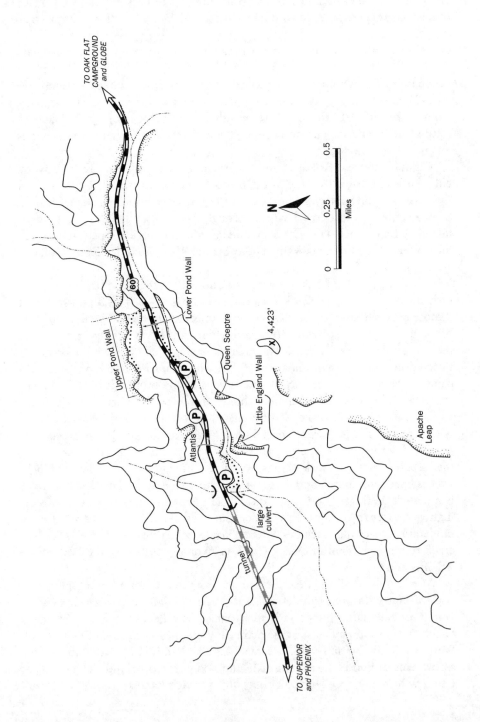

TO OAK FLAT
CAMPGROUND
and GLOBE

N

0.5

0.25

0

Miles

Upper Pond Wall

Lower Pond Wall

60

Queen Sceptre

Little England Wall

X 4,423'

Apache
Leap

Atlantis

P

P

P

large
culvert

tunnel

TO SUPERIOR
and PHOENIX

Canyon's collection of routes on The Beach and Lost Wall; and Lower Devil's Canyon, a wilderness canyon filled with classic sport crags, including the free-standing Totem Pole.

When you're tired of clipping bolts, take a break and explore some of Arizona's best bouldering at Oak Flats, the home of the Phoenix Bouldering Contest. There are thousands of problems of all grades and styles spread out over a 2-square-mile area. Many of the problems have toprope anchors. For problems, ratings, and beta, consult Karabin's comprehensive guide.

Climbing is possible year-round, although summer days are usually too hot, with daily highs reaching into the low 100s. Early summer mornings are best when the temperatures are still cool enough for comfort. Atlantis is one of the coolest summer areas. October through April are the best months for climbing in Queen Creek. Sun or shade can easily be found in the canyon. At an elevation of 3,600 feet, an occasional snowflake might fly from a winter storm, but 60 degrees, clear, and no wind is the norm. Queen Creek is a great winter getaway and an alternative to traditional winter hot spots like Hueco Tanks and Joshua Tree.

Few objective dangers are found here. Watch for the occasional loose flake or block on some routes. Keep an eye out for rattlesnakes in brushy areas or boulder fields. The short routes might make free soloing an enticement, but handholds can and do break. Be careful walking along and crossing the highway. Traffic travels through the canyon pretty fast. Don't climb at any crag right along the highway. The rock is often rough and harsh on the skin, especially in the cracks, and pockets can be painful. Bring lots of tape to mitigate the blood and gore. Trash is a real problem near some crags because of the sheer numbers of people passing through this roadside area. The parking lot at Atlantis and the trail to the crag are particularly bad. Pick up and pack out your trash and anyone else's.

Rack: A rack of 15 quickdraws and a 165-foot rope will do for a day of sport climbing. Crack climbers should plan on sets of cams and Stoppers, along with medium hexes and Tri-Cams for pocket pro. Most routes have cold shut anchors. Use quickdraws for toproping to avoid unnecessary wear to the anchors.

TRIP PLANNING INFORMATION

General description: Arizona's premier sport climbing area, with plentiful bolted sport routes and boulder problems in Queen Creek Canyon and nearby Oak Flat and Devil's Canyon.

Location: Central Arizona, 60 miles east of Phoenix.

Camping: Oak Flat Campground is a free campground in Tonto National Forest on Magma Mine Road, just east of Queen Creek Canyon and south of US 60. A 14-day limit is imposed. Bring water. Free primitive camping is found in Tonto National Forest, including the area south of the campground.

Climbing season: Year-round. The best months are October through April.

Expect sunny days and mostly warm temperatures. Winter highs are usually between 50 and 65 degrees. Summers are usually very hot, although some cool days occur. Best bet is to look for shady cliffs in the morning. Summer temperatures can exceed 100 degrees in the shade.

Restrictions and access issues: Most of the crags along the highway are on public land. Climbing and new routes are not allowed on cliffs alongside US 60 in the canyon. There are several other nearby climbing areas, including Devil's Canyon and Oak Flat, in Tonto National Forest.

Guidebooks: *The Rock Jock's Guide to Queen Creek Canyon* by Marty Karabin Jr., 1996 is very complete guide to the region, including nine climbing areas, lots of boulder problems, and extra information of interest.

Nearby mountain shops, guide services, and gyms: Desert Mountain Sports (Phoenix), REI (Paradise Valley and Tempe), Trailhead Sports (Scottsdale), The Wilderness (Phoenix); Phoenix Rock Gym (Phoenix), Climbmax Climbing Center (Tempe).

Services: All services are found in Superior and Globe.

Emergency services: Call 911. Nearest hospital is Cobra Valley Community Hospital, 1 Hospital Drive, Claypool, AZ 85532, 520-425-3261.

Nearby climbing areas: Many other areas in the immediate vicinity are covered in Karabin's comprehensive guidebook to Queen Creek Canyon, including Upper Devil's Canyon, Lower Devil's Canyon, Oak Flat bouldering, Euro Dog Valley, The Mine Area, and Apache Leap.

Dromedary Peak, with both sport and trad routes, is to the west just south of US 60 by milepost 217. The climbs are on the peak's high cliffs in the middle of beautiful cactus country. Marty Karabin publishes a fold-out climbing guide that is available at Phoenix climbing shops. Some of the towers on Picketpost Mountain west of Superior were climbed years ago but have very rotten rock.

The awesome Superstition Mountains lie to the west. Lots of great climbing is found here, including Bark Canyon Wall, The Fortress, Miners Needle, Weavers Needle, and Zonerland.

Nearby attractions: Superstition Wilderness Area, Boyce Thompson Arboretum, Besh-Ba-Gowah Archeological Park (Globe), Salt River Canyon.

Finding the crags: Queen Creek Canyon lies between Superior and Globe, 60 miles east of Phoenix. US 60 traverses the canyon. From Superior, drive east on US 60 for 4 miles. Just after the tunnel, you'll reach Queen Creek Canyon.

ATLANTIS

Atlantis is a corridor of two cliffs that flank Queen Creek's narrow canyon below the highway just past the tunnel east of Superior. Most of the routes, beginning from the creekbed, are bolted sport climbs up steep walls with lowering anchors. With easy access and over 30 routes, Atlantis is very popular, especially on weekends. Routes range from 5.7 to 5.12b, with most between 5.10

ATLANTIS

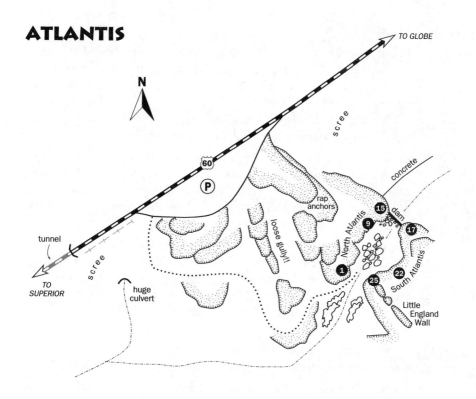

TO GLOBE

scree

concrete

N

rap anchors

loose gully!!

15

9

dam

North Atlantis

17

1

tunnel

scree

25

22

South Atlantis

TO SUPERIOR

scree

huge culvert

Little England Wall

and 5.11. The cliffs are often shaded and cooled by the running creek, making it a good choice on warm days. The base of the cliffs may not be accessible during periods of heavy rain in spring.

Use caution on some of the routes. Some bolts are just above ledges instead of several moves up, which has resulted in several broken ankles suffered by climbers falling from above onto the ledges.

Finding the crags: From the west, drive east from Superior on US Highway 60 for 4 miles. Pass through the tunnel and park in a pullout on the right (south) immediately past the tunnel. Atlantis is south of the pullout in the hidden canyon below. The easiest and best approach is to hike down a rough trail on a steep, scree-covered slope that begins on the right (west) side of the pullout. Scramble down to the left side of the huge culvert and bend left on the rough trail that drops east to the west entrance of the canyon corridor. Avoid the steep gullies directly below the pullout.

An alternative approach begins on the left (east) side of the pullout. Scramble through boulders and locate two rappel bolts on the cliff's edge. Make two single-rope rappels to the canyon floor. Be careful not to knock any rocks down on climbers in the canyon below. Routes are listed from left to right and begin on the left (west) side of the north cliff and the left (east) side of the south cliff.

NORTH ATLANTIS

1. **Brush Your Teeth Before You Kiss Me** (5.9) Begin about 50' in from the corridor's west entrance on the left side of the north canyon beneath a head-high roof. Climb up and over the left side of the 3-foot roof to the 1st bolt. Continue up a slab to a sloping ledge. Angle left up the slab over a bulge to a headwall finish. A small Friend protects a crack over the high bulge. 5 bolts to 2-bolt anchor.

2. **Public Hanging** (5.11c) 20' right of Route 1. Begin 5' right of a long crack system. Face climb 25' to a small ledge; Stoppers down low, otherwise no pro. Continue up the steep face right of the crack over a 3' roof to a short left-facing corner. Pull another corner and continue over bulges to anchors. 8 bolts to 2 cold-shut anchor.

3. **Capital Punishment** (5.11d) 18' right of Route 2. Begin at a blocky, left-facing corner. Edge up a smooth face to the 1st bolt and continue to a sloping ledge, then to another ledge 15' higher. Climb the overhanging wall above and over a roof. Head up easier slabby rock to anchors on a high ledge. 7 bolts to 2 cold-shut anchor.

4. **Armed and Dangerous** (5.11b R) Same start as Route 3. Climb to the second ledge and then climb a steep face to a right-slanting crack. Continue straight up to anchors. 6 bolts to 2 cold-shut anchor.

5. **Feast and Famine** (5.10c) 15' right of Route 3. Begin below a broad, slabby tongue of rock. Climb up left across the tongue to the left side of an overhang. Pull over the well-protected roof. Move up steep rock to a 2-foot roof. Yard over and finish up left on a slab. 7 bolts to 2 cold-shut anchor.

6. **Phantom** (5.12a) Excellent pulling. Same start as Route 5. Head up the rock tongue to a right-slanting, left-facing overhang. Swing up the steep outside wall to a sloped ramp. Climb the left side of a white-mottled, overhanging wall past 2 bolts. Continue over bulges to anchors. 7 bolts to 2 cold-shut anchor.

7. **Fluid Dynamics** (5.12a) Recommended. 15' right of Route 6 on the right side of the tongue. Climb the slabby tongue to a stepped overhang. Above, pull onto a steep diagonal ramp and step right. Pull over the left side of the large roof and climb the right side of the white, overhanging wall. Follow the right side of a steep prow to anchors. 8 bolts to 2 cold-shut anchor.

8. **All the King's Men** (5.12b/c) 10' right of Route 7. Wild climbing over the big roof. Begin below a corner and broken crack system right of the slab tongue. Climb easy, slabby rock and then head left under the 10' roof. Muscle over the roof on good holds (3 bolts) to a strenuous lip. Continue over bulges and steps above to a technical finish up vertical rock. 10 bolts to 2 cold-shut anchor.

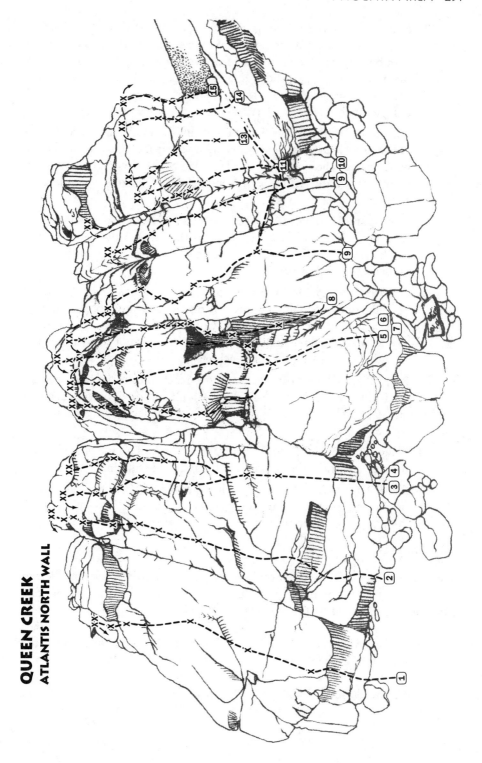

QUEEN CREEK
ATLANTIS NORTH WALL

9. **Neptune** (5.10a) Superb, classic, and fun. Start 15' right of Route 8 and the crack system. Ascend a slabby ramp 20' to the 1st bolt. Move left up juggy, broken rock to a small overhang. Edge up right across a steep slab and enter a short, right-facing dihedral that finishes at anchors on a ledge. A 2nd pitch heads up the steep slab above past 3 bolts to anchors left of a tree. 6 bolts to 2 cold-shut anchor.

10. **Impending Doom** (5.10b) 5' right of Route 9. Good and pumpy. Climb polished rock 15' onto a ledge. Head up a left-facing corner to the 1st bolt. Edge up the steep, sustained face left of the obvious crack system to anchors on the right side of *Neptune*'s ledge. 7 bolts to 2 cold-shut anchor.

11. **Schizophrenic Boulevard** (5.10c) 10' right of Route 10. Boulder up a short, polished wall to a ledge. Climb the blunt prow between two crack systems. Finish right of a triangular roof and obvious prow. 7 bolts to 2 cold-shut anchor.

12. **Smokin' Guns** (5.11c) A quality route. Same start as Route 11. Move up right onto a sloping, chiprock ledge. Climb up and over a large roof right of an overhanging crack. Continue up the vertical wall above to anchors. The flake that is bolted on the roof is not really needed as a hold. 7 bolts to 2 cold-shut anchor.

13. **Project** (5.13?) Start off a sloping ledge reached by scrambling out left from the concrete and rock dam. Climb the obvious overhang to anchors just over the lip. Bring cams for the crack in the roof. 4 bolts to 2-bolt anchor.

14. **Flakes of Wrath** (5.11a) Begin atop the dam. Pull up the bulging overhang to a vertical finish. 45'. 4 bolts to 2 cold-shut anchor.

15. **Shark Attack** (5.12a) Good climbing with big jugs between long moves on this steep overhanging bulge on the far right side of the cliff. 40'. 3 bolts to 2 cold-shut anchor.

SOUTH ATLANTIS

South Atlantis is the cliff on the south side of the creek. Routes are listed left to right (east to west). The first route, Route 16, is 50 feet upstream to the east from the concrete dam on the left side of a boulder-filled gully.

16. **Diaper Rash** (5.10a) No topo. Begin off boulders just above the creekbed on the left side of the obvious gully. Face climb just left of a crack system to a horizontal break/ledge. Continue over a bulge to a headwall finish. 5 bolts to 2-bolt anchor.

17. **U.S. Senators Are Space Aliens** (5.11a) Just east of the top of the dam on the right side of the gully. Climb a blunt prow to a sloping ledge. Move over bulges to anchors. 6 bolts to 2-bolt anchor.

18. **Project** A crack project. Begin from the top of the dam. Climb a finger crack up the overhanging wall and move right to a wide crack finish. **Rack:** A selection of Friends. 2 bolts to 2 cold-shut anchor.

19. **Unknown** (5.12) Start 10' right of the dam base below an overhanging wall. Crank the steep wall with small crimps to a bulge, then out right with lieback flakes to anchors above the lip. 40'. 3 bolts to 2-open cold shut anchor.

QUEEN CREEK CANYON
SOUTH ATLANTIS, LEFT SIDE

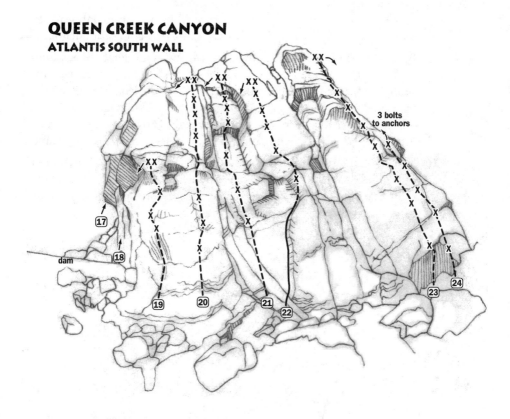

20. **Duck and Cover** (5.11d) Begin just right of Route 19 and left of a broken, double crack system. Move over a bulge to a pocketed face and a sloping rest shelf. Edge up the vertical wall above to anchors under a nose. 6 bolts to 2 cold-shut anchor.

21. **Shoot First, Ask Later** (5.11c) Right of the double crack system. Climb broken rock to a sloping ledge. Head up the pocketed face right of a chimney to a slab finish. 6 bolts to 2 cold-shut anchor.

22. **Grumpy After Eight** (5.10a) Great climbing that will keep you smiling! Begin by moving up a right-angling crack and broken face 20' to a large ledge. Continue up the steep, pocketed face right of a chimney to a final slab. 5 bolts to 2 cold-shut anchor.

23. **KGB** (5.10b) 40' right of Route 22 on the left side of a buttress. Thin face climbing past 4 bolts to a small overhang. Pull onto upper slab and move up right to second roof. Pull roof to bulging endgame. 7 bolts to 2 cold-shut anchor.

24. **Giggling Marlin** (5.9) Laughable entertainment all the way. 8' right of Route 23. Good face moves ascend to a small, left-facing corner. Climb

corner crack to right-facing corner capped by a roof. A slab leads to an upper crack/groove and anchors. 8 bolts to 3-cold shut anchor.

25. **Bunny Slope** (5.8) 15' right of Route 24. A fun moderate line. Climb pockets for 15' to the 1st bolt. Go right into a short crack to a spacious, sloping ledge (old cable hazard!). Step right on the ledge and climb the face and bulges past a couple of breaks to a final bulging prow. At the 4th bolt, move left to cracks, then back right above to keep the grade 5.8; otherwise the face moves are 5.11. 6 bolts to 2 cold-shut anchor.

26. **Sir Charles** (5.10a) Begin on outside (west) face of buttress 20' right of old cables. Climb an easy, broken chimney to a large ledge. Climb the right side of the vertical face above to anchor bolts with slings. 5 bolts to 2-bolt anchor.

QUEEN CREEK CANYON
ATLANTIS SOUTH WALL, FAR RIGHT

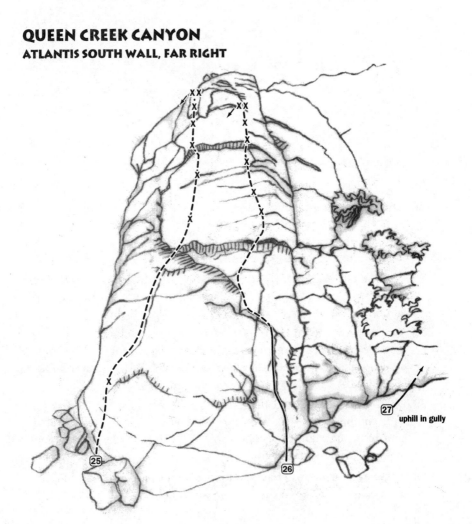

uphill in gully

QUEEN CREEK CANYON
QUEEN SCEPTRE

on south and east sides

30
31

28

29

bolts not shown

27. **Mondo Freako** (5.7) No topo. Scramble up right from Route 26 to the base of a slab left of a gully. Fun pocket moves lead up the left side of the slab. 3 bolts to 1-cold shut anchor.

QUEEN SCEPTRE

This spectacular, semidetached pinnacle is on the slope south of the highway and above the creek. Two excellent routes ascend the obvious, steep west face. Approach Queen Sceptre by parking at the second pullout on the south side of the highway east of the tunnel. Drop down to the creek and scramble up a climber's path to the base of the west face. Routes are listed left to right, or counterclockwise from the west face.

28. **Queen of Hearts** (5.12b/c) A long pitch up the left side of the tiered west face. Work up and over several roofs to anchors just below the top. 120'. 15 bolts to 2 cold-shut belay anchor. **Descent:** Make 2 single-rope rappels down Route 28's 2 sets of anchors.

29. **Queen Sceptre** (5.12a) A 110' sport line up the west face. 15 bolts to 2- cold shut belay anchor. **Descent:** Make 2 single-rope rappels down Route 28's 2 sets of anchors.

30. **King of Fools** (5.11d) No topo. On the north side of the rock. Hard face moves up and over a roof. 10 bolts to 2 cold-shut anchor.

31. **Whistling Idiot** (5.10b) No topo. On the east face. 4 bolts to 2 cold-shut anchor.

THE POND

The Pond, on the hillside north of US Highway 60, is one of the best and most popular sport climbing venues in Queen Creek Canyon, if not in Arizona. Lots of south-facing routes, ranging from 5.6 to 5.13, ascend the cliff bands and make The Pond an ideal winter crag. The Upper Pond, nestled among soaring cliffs and fed by a 50-foot-high waterfall in spring and after rain, is a good swimming hole when it's hot. It's probably best to avoid swimming unless the waterfall and creek are running.

Finding the cliffs: Park at the third pullout on the right past the tunnel east of Superior. The pullout, with picnic tables and trash cans, sits on the south side of a rock island. Walk east along the south side of the highway on a trail that parallels the guardrail. At the bridge, drop down and pass under the bridge to the opposite side of the highway. Try to avoid crossing the highway. Traffic is usually fast and furious, making the crossing a risky maneuver. Lower Pond Wall is the lower cliff band up left from the bridge. Scramble up a rough trail to the routes.

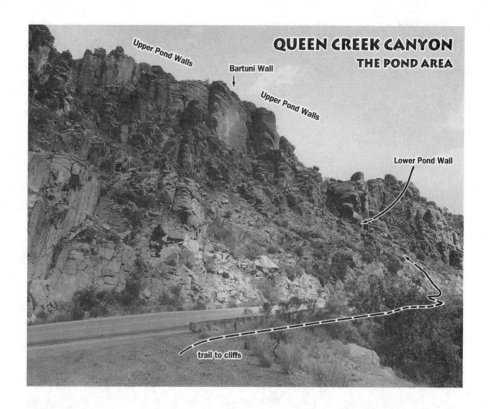

QUEEN CREEK CANYON
THE POND AREA

Upper Pond Walls

Bartuni Wall

Upper Pond Walls

Lower Pond Wall

trail to cliffs

These routes are listed right to left. To reach the upper tier, follow a climbers' trail that threads over water-worn bedrock and then climbs up boulders and grooves right of a tumbling cascade to the upper pond. Upper Pond routes are listed right to left and begin with the cliffs just right of the pond.

LOWER POND WALL

Lower Pond Wall is the lower cliff band up left from the creek and the highway bridge. Hike up a short trail from the creek to the base of the wall. Both routes are uphill and listed right to left.

32. **Liquid Sunshine** (5.10c) Quality route. Begin below some boulders. Climb a boulder with a bolt, then step up left onto a ledge. Climb bulges on the triangular face to anchors on a high ledge. 5 bolts to 2 cold-shut anchor.

33. **Return From the Ultimate Mormon Experience** (5.12b) Uphill from Route 32. Start below a right-angling chimney. Climb the steep wall right of a blunt prow past many bolts to anchors just below the top of the cliff. 9 bolts to 2 open cold-shut anchor.

QUEEN CREEK CANYON
LOWER POND WALL

3rd class

open shut/chain

2cs

34

35

36

37

38
39
2-bolt belay on ledge

THE POND

The low band of cliffs that surround the upper pond composes The Pond area. Routes are listed right to left. Reach the first four routes by scrambling up right from the pond to a short, southeast-facing cliff.

34. **Beer and Dead Animals** (5.9) A good, short, pocketed line on the right side of the wall. 2 bolts to 2 cold-shut anchor.

35. **El Gato Grande D'Amore** (5.12a) Stick-clip the 1st bolt. Up thin holds on the right side of an obvious white streak. Bolt at the lip of a roof at the top. 4 bolts to a 1-open cold shut/1-chain anchor.

36. **Crazy Fingers** (5.11c) Excellent. Climb the left side of the wide white streak to a final roof with a bolt at its lip. 5 bolts to 2-bolt anchor.

37. **Natural Wonder** (5.8) A good hand to off-width crack just left of *Crazy Fingers*. Rappel from Route 34's anchors. **Rack:** Medium and large Friends and some large Camalots.

The next two routes begin on a large ledge overlooking The Pond. Scramble up the right-hand trail and traverse left across the obvious ledge to a 2-bolt belay stance. No topos.

38. **Interloper** (5.11b/c) Belay from bolts on the left side of the ledge. Work up overhanging rock left of the large, angled roof above the belay. Pull pockets up the steep wall, over a bulge, and to a vertical finish. 8 bolts to 2-bolt chain anchor.

39. **Inner Basin** (5.10c) Start from the 2-bolt belay stance for Route 38. Traverse left on the ledge and pull onto a small stance with a bush below a crack system. Climb directly up the vertical face above to anchors. 5 bolts to 2-bolt belay.

There are two routes just left of Route 39 and right of the pour-off groove. *Big Legged Woman* (5.10b) is reached by rapping from the top to anchors, while *Drowning* (5.10a) is missing its hangers.

The following routes are left of The Pond. Follow a trail past the pond to the cliff's base. Routes are listed right to left from The Pond.

40. **Dead Pool** (5.8 R) Scramble up left from The Pond and onto a ledge with a 1-bolt belay anchor. Move up right to a bolt and then up the run-out, rounded prow past 1 more bolt. 2-bolts to 2 cold-shut anchor. No topo.

41. **Unknown** (5.7) Start on the ledge with the bolt anchor (same as Route

40). Fun, well-protected moves climb myriad pockets. 9 bolts to 2 cold-shut anchor. No topo.

42. **Date Rape** (5.7 R) Same start as Route 41. Climb up left from the belay ledge to a bolt below a horizontal break. Continue up the left side of the face. 70'. 4 bolts to 2 cold-shut anchor. No topo.

43. **Mistaken Identity** (5.12b) Begin left of Route 42 on the far right side of the overhanging wall. Climb up right on an easy ramp past 1 bolt to a ledge. Pull up the overhanging face left of a chimney. 7 bolts to 2 cold-shut anchor.

44. **Hot House** (5.12c) Same start as Route 43. From the ledge, climb directly up the steep face. 7 bolts to 2 cold-shut anchor.

45. **Hot Line** (5.12d) Same start as Route 43. From the left side of the ledge, follow bolts up a black streak to a bulge finish. 6 bolts to 2 cold-shut anchor.

46. **Death Row** (5.12d) Classic climbing but a lot of drilled holds. Swing up the overhanging wall left of an angling crack and black streak to anchors on the lip. 6 bolts to 2 cold-shut anchor.

47. **Desert Devil** (5.13a) Good, but some glued and drilled holds. Up the middle of the steep wall with thin gastons and a real hard crux at the last move. 7 bolts to 2 cold-shut anchor.

48. **The Emerald** (5.13b) Follow a line of bolts up left to anchors over the lip. 7 bolts to 2 cold-shut anchor.

49. **Project** (5.13?) Up the left side of the overhanging wall to a steep bulgy finish. 7 bolts to 2 cold-shut anchor.

50. **Out on Parole** (5.10c) Good and pumpy. Start below the far left side of the overhanging wall and right of a crack. Work up the left side of the wall to a pocketed bulge. Finish up an overhanging headwall. 5 bolts to 2 cold-shut anchor.

51. **Pompasfuc** (5.12b) A variation to *Out on Parole*. Move out right at the 3rd bolt and finish with pockets up an overhang. 5 bolts to 2 cold-shut anchor.

52. **Weak Sister** (5.10a) Popular and pleasant. Begin right of a chimney cleft. Climb crux crimps up a slab past 2 bolts to a left-angling crack, or stem up the shallow chimney to the left for an easier start. Stand up high and make a delicate step right to the 3rd bolt. Move left over a bulge and motor up the steep slab to anchors at the upper horizontal break. The cold shut anchor is hard to see from the ground. 6 bolts to 2 cold-shut anchor.

53. **Behind Bars** (5.10a) On the low buttress left of Route 52. "Ugly route!"

Peter Takeda on *Weak Sister* (5.10a) at the Pond.

says guidebook author Marty Karabin. Pockets and edges to anchors right of a yucca on top of the cliff. 25'. 3 bolts to 2 cold-shut anchor.

54. **The Warden** (5.10b) On the flat face left of Route 53. Climb pockets up the vertical face to anchors at the rock's high point. 4 bolts to 2 cold-shut anchor.

UPPER POND WEST

To reach this cliff band, continue hiking uphill along a trail left (west) from The Pond. Past *The Warden*, the trail steps around an airy corner to an upper cliff. Routes are listed right to left above the trail.

55. **Cowboy** (5.10a) On a southeast-facing wall. Begin on boulders around a corner right and above a large juniper at the cliff's base. Climb a pocketed slab to a 3-bolt headwall with a light streak. The 1st bolt is reached by easy but run-out climbing up a ramp slab. 3 bolts to 2-open cold shut anchor.

56. **Pocket Pow-Wow** (5.10b) Recommended and fun. The right route on a steep, southeast-facing cliff around the corner from Route 55. A bouldery start to the 1st bolt, then up pockets and edges to an anchor below a ledge. 5 bolts to 2-bolt anchor.

57. **Pocket Party** (5.10b) 15' left of Route 56. Excellent. Fun and pumpy climbing up the long, pocketed face to anchors at the very top of the cliff. 7 bolts to 2 cold-shut anchor.

58. **Just Can't Get Any** (5.12b) Located on an overhanging, triangular face. Pull up and over the big roof and pump it up to anchors at the lip. Some chipped holds. 3 bolts to 2 cold-shut anchor.

59. **Pocket Puzzle** (5.10a) A load of adjectives for this one—superb, excellent, fun, awesome! Just do it. The west-facing, vertical wall left around the corner from Route 58. Work up the steep, pocketed face to a break and needed rest, then continue over the bulge above to a finishing slab. 70'. 8 bolts to 2 cold-shut anchor.

60. **The Soft Parade** (5.11a) A classic line. The right side of the south-facing wall left of a big, left-facing dihedral and Route 59. Follow a line of cold shuts up and right to anchors above a finishing bulge. 85'. 10 bolts to 2 cold-shut anchor.

QUEEN CREEK CANYON
UPPER POND WEST

Jim Waugh dances up *The Soft Parade* (5.11a), one of the Upper Pond Wall's excellent pocket routes.

61. **Bartuni** (5.11b) 10' left of Route 60. Begin up a thin slab to the 1st bolt. Head up small crimps, edges, and pockets to a tricky, final headwall. 90'. 10 bolts to 2 cold-shut anchor. Use a 200' rope.

62. **Blisters in the Sun** (5.12a) Start 6' left of Route 61. Climb directly up the steep wall to anchors above a slanting break. 10 bolts to 2-bolt anchor.

63. **Mona Lisa** (5.11a) Begin on the left side of the wall below a left-angling crack system. A bouldery start leads to a shallow, open corner that goes up left. Pull a thin, upper bulge with a crack to anchors at a horizontal crack. 9 bolts to 2 cold-shut anchor.

64. **Nothing Lasts Forever** (5.10d) Marty Karabin calls this an "awesome, classic route!" Left and around a corner from Route 63 on the next face past an arête. Begin right of a large boulder. Climb a blunt prow past 3 bolts to a sloping ledge. Step up left and work up a steep, vertical wall to anchors above the last break. 9 bolts to 2-bolt anchor. 200' rope.

65. **Casting Shadows** (5.11b) Recommended. Start left of Route 64 and right of a deep chimney. Climb pockets and thin edges up the vertical face. 7 bolts to 2 cold-shut anchor.

66. **Sappy Love Song** (5.8) Walk left (west) from Route 65 past a broken buttress. Fun pocket pulling up the steep face to anchors on top of the

to other
routes

cliff. 4 bolts to 2 cold-shut anchor.

67. **Fat Boy Goes to the Pond** (5.6) One of the easier offerings here. The route climbs the short buttress left of Route 66. Climb the slabby prow to anchors with rap slings on a small ledge. 2 bolts to 2-bolt anchor.

To reach the following routes, walk left and scramble over boulders to the cliff tier behind and to the north. The first two routes are up the smooth, south-facing wall on the right side. The other routes are to the left.

68. **Endomorph Man** (5.12b) Hard and thin moves on the right side of the wall. Climb shallow pockets and small edges past 4 bolts, and then angle up left to a final slab and anchors just below the top of the cliff. 5 bolts to 2 cold-shut anchor.

69. **Loc-Tite** (5.11d) Great route! 6' left of Route 68. Pockets and edges up the steep wall right of a right-facing dihedral. 6 bolts to 2 cold-shut anchor.

70. **Nothing's Right** (5.7) Walk left and downhill from Route 69 to a pocketed face. Fun climbing up the right side of the steep, well-pocketed slab. 5 bolts to 2-bolt lowering anchor.

71. **Nothing's Left** (5.8) Start 6' left of Route 70. More fun up the left side of the face. 5 bolts to 2-bolt lowering anchor.

72. **Project** (5.12) On the left face of the slab just around the corner to the west and right of a waterfall pour-off. Thin moves up the steep, polished wall. 4 bolts to 2-bolt anchor.

73. **Nothing To It** (5.10c) Scramble west from Route 72 past a small outcrop to the next buttress. Start left of a crack and climb the steep, pocketed face. 5 bolts to 2-bolt anchor.

74. **Next to Nothing** (5.4) Continue west on the trail to the next buttress right of a big dihedral. Fun pockets up the easy slab. 4 bolts to 2-bolt anchor.

75. **Nothing's There** (5.11d) On the right side of a streaked face, left of a diagonal crack, and up a large, right-facing dihedral. Climb past the diagonal crack, then up the steep, edgy wall. 5 bolts to 2-bolt chain anchor below a ledge.

76. **Is Nothing Sacred** (5.11c/d) Directly up the center of the wall with a low crux and good upper pockets. 5 bolts to 2-bolt anchor.

77. **Nothing But Air** (5.11d) The left side of the wall. Pull up a series of angling seams and breaks to anchors. 5 bolts to 2-bolt chain anchor.

OTHER CENTRAL ARIZONA AREAS

OVERVIEW

There are many other climbing areas in central Arizona near Phoenix, ranging from boulder fields and sport routes to multipitch lines in the surrounding mountains. The rock in most of these areas is rough desert granite, featured with crystals and edges and split by crack systems. Other crags are composed of volcanic rock and limestone. The following areas, particularly Pinnacle Peak, are worth a visit, but for various reasons, including access difficulties or limited number of routes, were not given their own separate sections.

PINNACLE PEAK

Pinnacle Peak, a prominent granite spire on the northeast edge of Scottsdale, rises almost 200 feet above a growing sprawl of subdivisions. The peak, along with some smaller satellite crags, boasts a superb selection of quality crack climbs and bolted face routes. The area, easily accessible from Phoenix and its suburbs, has more three-star lines than any other Phoenix crag, making it a worthy destination.

Access, however, has been the big problem at Pinnacle Peak in the 1990s. The encroaching houses in gated communities around the mountain led to the area being fenced off and closed to all recreational use. At the time of this writing, most of the peak has been donated to the city of Scottsdale for a park. Trails are being constructed and a parking area has been designated on the east side of the mountain. The peak is expected to reopen for climbing by mid-2000. Check at local climbing shops and gyms for current information on Pinnacle Peak access.

Finding the peak: The easiest access is via Scottsdale Road, Pima Road, or Arizona Highway 101, which makes a loop north from US Highway 60, the Superstition Freeway. Turn east on Happy Valley Road and drive to Alma School Road. Make a left (north) turn on Alma School Road. Follow it until it bends right past the restaurant Pinnacle Peak Patio. A parking area and trailhead are located on the west side of the road below the east flank of the peak. Good trails ascend the peak and reach the various crags.

AMC BOULDER

This large, east-facing boulder, named for the Arizona Mountaineering Club, sits halfway up the hillside below Pinnacle Peak. Descend off the boulder via a rappel east from an eyebolt. Routes are listed left to right.

PINNACLE PEAK
SATELLITE CRAGS

1. **Reunion** (5.8 TR) A toprope on the left side of the face. Originally had 2 bolts that were chopped. Thin face moves lead up the face left of a crack.

2. **Varicose** (5.6) Climb the left-hand crack.

3. **Rurpture** (5.10b) Thin face moves lead up past a bolt to a right-angling crack. Above, edge past a couple more leaning cracks to the top.

4. **Mickey Mantle** (5.8) Climb a slab up right past a bolt to a blunt arête. Step off a flake, mantle past a bulge and bolt, then cruise.

LOAFER'S CHOICE SLAB

This east-facing slab is just north of the AMC Boulder.

5. **Loafer's Choice** (5.10a R) Climb a short, left-facing corner to a slab with 2 bolts. Belay in a crack or climb the run-out face to the right to a 2-bolt anchor. **Descent:** Walk off.

6. **Dead Meat** (5.7) Right of Route 5. Climb a face with a bolt to a small roof at a horizontal crack. Work up the slab above along the left-hand crack and follow the arête to the top. **Descent:** Walk off.

THE WEDGE

This wedge-shaped, 45-foot-high block sits higher on the slope above the AMC Boulder. **Descent:** For all routes, descend via a one-rope rappel from the two-bolt summit anchor.

7. **Naked Edge** (5.9) Cool route, but watch your rope on the arête. Begin just left of the east arête. Work up a thin crack and corner past two bolts and finish up the arête.

8. **Redemption** (5.9) Start left of Route 7. Face climb up left to the south-west arête. Edge and smear up past 2 bolts to the summit.

9. **Hiliter** (5.7 R) A face route with 1 bolt on the northeast face.

PINNACLE PEAK/EAST FACE

The East Face of Pinnacle Peak, facing toward the parking area, yields some of the area's best routes. Routes 10 through 15 are on the lower east face to the left, while the other lines are on the upper bulging face. Routes are described left to right.

10. **Mr. Creamjeans** (5.10d) Carefully edge up a steep slab with 1 bolt on the left side of the face. Belay atop blocks. **Descent:** Scramble south and downclimb Class 4 rock.

11. **Birthday Party** (5.7) A classic moderate. Work left up an angling, right-facing dihedral to broken boulders. Traverse up right under a long, narrow roof and jam the obvious crack (5.7) over it to a belay ledge. **Descent:** Scramble south and downclimb Class 4 rock. **Rack:** A selection of medium and large cams and nuts.

12. **Pecker Party** (5.10b) Begin at Route 11. Climb up right along a diagonal crack/ramp, then edge past 2 bolts (5.10b) to a roof. Traverse right and finish up an easy crack. **Descent:** Scramble south and downclimb Class 4 rock. **Rack:** A few cams.

13. **Dried Oatmeal** (5.10b R) Start right of Route 12 below a corner capped by a roof. Climb the easy corner to the roof, traverse left, and face climb up a blunt prow (5.10b R) with 2 bolts to an easy right-leaning crack. **Descent:** Scramble south and downclimb Class 4 rock. **Rack:** Stoppers and a few medium and large cams.

14. **Boxer** (5.7) Begin a few feet right of Route 13. Work up a right-angling crack to a stance. Climb an easy slab to a face traverse under a roof, jam over the roof (5.7), and finish up a crack to a belay ledge. **Descent:** Scramble south and downclimb Class 4 rock. **Rack:** Medium and large cams.

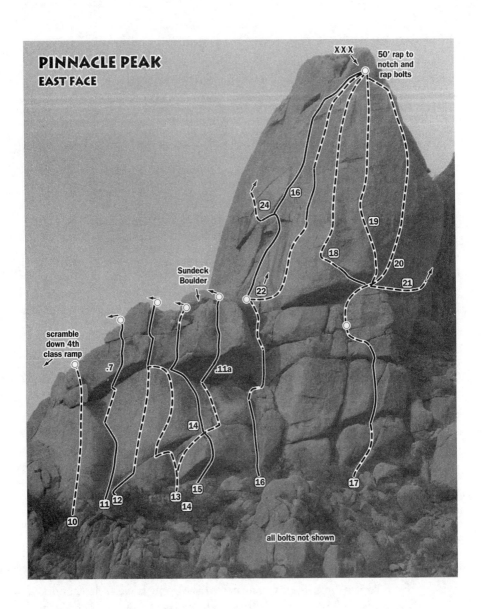

PINNACLE PEAK
EAST FACE

XXX

50' rap to notch and rap bolts

24 16 19 18 20 21 22

Sundeck Boulder

scramble down 4th class ramp

.7 .11a

14 16 17

11 12 13 15 14 10

all bolts not shown

15. **Beegee** (5.11a) A roof problem that was Phoenix's first 5.11 and first flashed by Peter Noebels. Climb right up a flared crack (5.10c) to a ledge. An easy slab leads to a short and stiff, overhanging roof crack (5.11a). Follow a groove above to a belay at the Sundeck Boulder. **Descent:** Scramble south and downclimb Class 4 rock. **Rack:** Medium nuts and cams.

16. **South Crack** (5.3) 2 pitches. A classic beginner route to the peak's summit. Start below a chimney system. **Pitch 1:** Easy climbing (Class 4) leads to the Sundeck Boulder below the south face. **Pitch 2:** Climb over boulders into a chimney system that leads to the east summit. **Descent:** 2 single-rope rappels. For rap 1, rappel 50' from 3 bolts to a notch north of the summit. For rap 2, rappel to the base of the east face from 2 bolts. **Rack:** Medium and large nuts and cams.

17. **Name It** (5.6) This is the easiest access pitch to the base of the upper east face. Begin right of Route 16 below a right-angling crack. Jam and face climb cracks to a belay ledge under a roof and the east face. **Descent:** Scramble south to Sundeck Boulder. **Rack:** Medium to large cams.

18. **Fear of Flying** (5.10c) A face climbing classic. Start at Route 17's belay below the roof. Move up right and then climb left along an angling crack under a small roof (5.10c) to the left edge of the east face. Face climb up the left side of a blunt arête with 3 bolts and past a horizontal crack with a fixed pin (5.10b). Continue up to the summit on more thin moves (5.10b). **Descent:** 2 single-rope rappels. For rap 1, rappel 50' from 3 bolts to a notch north of the summit. For rap 2, rappel to the base of the east face from 2 bolts. **Rack:** Stoppers, TCUs, and a selection of cams.

19. **Powder Puff Direct** (5.11a) Airy, exposed, and excellent. Begin just right of Route 18. Work up a short, right-facing corner right of a roof and step left onto the steep face. Hard face climbing leads past 5 bolts to the summit. **Descent:** 2 single-rope rappels. For rap 1, rappel 50' from 3 bolts to a notch north of the summit. For rap 2, rappel to the base of the east face from 2 bolts. **Rack:** Stoppers and small cams.

20. **Lesson in Discipline** (5.11c) Hard, desperate face climbing on perfect granite—a Phoenix classic. Start at Route 19's belay. Climb a short corner and work down right to a thin crack. Work up the crack (5.11a) to a bolt and then face climb steep rock past 2 more bolts. Above, the angle and difficulty eases. Pass the 4th bolt and follow a crack and face to the summit. **Descent:** 2 single-rope rappels. For rap 1, rappel 50' from 3 bolts to a notch north of the summit. For rap 2, rappel to the base of the east face from 2 bolts. **Rack:** Stoppers and small cams.

21. **Sidewinder** (5.11c) Another face climbing masterpiece. First free ascent was a 1979 flash by Peter Noebels. Begin right of Route 20. Traverse right along a horizontal crack that arches vertically around the right corner of the face. Work up the strenuous crack (5.11a) until you can move right into an off-width crack. Follow to a stance and continue up a face (5.9) to the top. **Descent:** 2 single-rope rappels. For rap 1, rappel 50' from 3 bolts to a notch north of the summit. For rap 2, rappel to the base of the east face from 2 bolts. **Rack:** Stoppers and small to large cams.

PINNACLE PEAK/SOUTH FACE

The airy South Face towers above Sundeck Boulder. Reach the base of the face by climbing one of the East Face routes (10 to 16), or by scrambling up Class 4 rock on the south side of the formation. Routes are listed right to left.

22. **Shalayly Direct** (5.11c) A 3-star classic. Sustained and excellent. Begin on the Sundeck Boulder. Face climb up right past 4 bolts (5.11a) until you can traverse right to a flake crack (5.9). Follow the crack (5.9) and then face climb up thin edges (5.11c) past 3 more bolts to the summit. 8 bolts. **Descent:** 2 single-rope rappels. For rap 1, rappel 50' from 3 bolts to a notch north of the summit. For rap 2, rappel to the base of the east face from 2 bolts. **Rack:** Stoppers, TCUs, and small to medium cams.

23. **Silhouette** (5.8) Begin just left of the Sundeck Boulder. Climb the first 50' of *South Crack*. Step left and face climb past 3 bolts up a rock rib to a horizontal crack. Move up right to the 4th bolt and edge (5.8) to the top. 4 bolts. **Descent:** 2 single-rope rappels. For rap 1, rappel 50' from 3 bolts to a notch north of the summit. For rap 2, rappel to the base of the east face from 2 bolts. **Rack:** Medium and large cams.

24. **Twenty-Eighth Day** (5.9 R) 2 pitches. A recommended route. Begin at Sundeck Boulder. **Pitch 1:** Climb the first few feet of *South Crack* to a ledge out left. Face climb up left to an inverted flake. Climb past the right side of the flake to a small ledge, step left along ledge, and move up the face and corner above past a bolt to a belay ledge. **Pitch 2:** Climb the short face above (5.9) past 2 bolts to the summit. **Descent:** 2 single-rope rappels. For rap 1, rappel 50' from 3 bolts to a notch north of the summit. For rap 2, rappel to the base of the east face from 2 bolts. **Rack:** Selection of Stoppers and small to medium cams.

25. **Never Never Land** (5.11a) An excellent route with sustained, exposed face climbing. Start left of the Sundeck Boulder below a gully chimney (*South Gully*). Climb the gully until you can traverse left along a horizontal crack (5.7) to a small ledge. Thin face climbing (5.11a) heads

PINNACLE PEAK
SOUTH FACE

XXX

50' to notch and rap bolts

.9

23 16

.11c

24 chimney

.11c

.11a

.11a

25 26

16

22

18

19

Sundeck
Boulder

4th class
approach

.10b

.10d

10

12

17

all bolts not shown

up the face above past 4 bolts to the west summit. 4 bolts. **Descent:** 2 single-rope rappels. For rap 1, rappel 50' from 3 bolts to a notch north of the summit. For rap 2, rappel to the base of the east face from 2 bolts. **Rack:** Selection of Stoppers and small to medium cams.

26. **South of Heaven** (5.11c) Begin off a boulder left of the gully. Thin face moves lead past 2 bolts to a horizontal crack. Edge and smear the face above past 8 more bolts to the summit. 10 bolts. **Descent:** 2 single-rope rappels. For rap 1, rappel 50' from 3 bolts to a notch north of the summit. For rap 2, rappel to the base of the east face from 2 bolts.

LOOKOUT MOUNTAIN

Lookout Mountain, the northernmost peak in the Phoenix Mountain Preserve, lies on the north side of Phoenix. The Dead Dobie Wall, a short, west-facing, basalt cliff, is below the mountain's west summit. A selection of sport routes from 5.7 to 5.11d is found on this cliff. Expect good views, privacy, and some loose rock. Most of the routes, however, have cleaned up nicely since they were first bolted in 1993. **Descent:** For all routes, rappel or lower. **Rack:** For all routes, you'll need a single rope and a small rack of quickdraws.

There are several good hiking trails in the area, including the 0.6-mile Summit Trail (Trail 150) and the 2.6-mile Circumference Trail (Trail 308). Marty Karabin publishes a fold-out guide to Lookout Mountain with a map, topos, and route descriptions. The following route information is courtesy of Marty.

Finding the crag: The Dead Dobie Wall and Lookout Mountain Park are south of Greenway Parkway in north Phoenix. Greenway Parkway intersects Interstate 17 to the west. Cave Creek Road and 32nd Street (via Squaw Peak Freeway) runs north from Phoenix to the parkway. Follow Greenway Parkway to 16th Street and turn south toward the mountain. The road deadends at a parking area below the peak. Hike southwest from the lot on Trail 150. When you reach the fourth switchback, look for a large boulder in a ravine to the right. Follow a rough climber's trail that contours up to the cliff on the west side of the west summit. Routes are described left to right.

1. **Loose Lieback** (5.8) Scramble up a loose Class 4 face to a short 2-bolt face. 2 bolts to 2-bolt anchor.

LOOKOUT MOUNTAIN

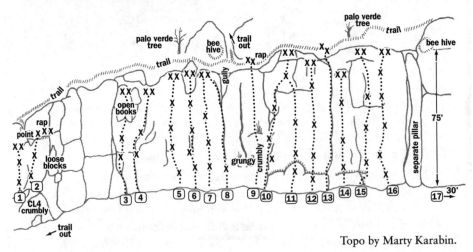

Topo by Marty Karabin.

2. **The Gnome** (5.10a) Scramble up a loose Class 4 face. Climb a short headwall up right. 2 bolts to 2-bolt anchor.

3. **I Love Loosie** (5.9 R) Climb an unprotected crack to a 2-bolt face and a corner. 2 bolts to 2-bolt anchor.

4. **Junkyard Dog** (5.10d) An overhanging crack to a bolted face. 2 bolts to 2-bolt anchor.

5. **Speed Freak** (5.11b) Recommended. 4 bolts to 2-bolt anchor.

6. **When Lester Comes Out to Play** (5.11a) 4 bolts to 2-bolt anchor.

7. **Little Miss Dangerous** (5.10d) Go up right above the 3rd bolt. 3 bolts to 2-bolt anchor.

8. **Too Loose to Goose** (5.9) Climb past a bolt to a crack. Face climb along a crack to Route 7's anchors.

9. **Unnamed** (5.11a) A toprope right of a grungy crack system. 2-bolt toprope anchor.

10. **Falling Stars** (5.11d) A loose start to steep rocks. 4 bolts to 2-bolt anchor.

11. **The Contender** (5.11a) Pull a roof, then face climb good rock. 4 bolts to 2-bolt anchor (same as Route 10).

12. **Double Feature** (5.10c) Double roofs off the ground, then face moves up solid rock. 4 bolts to 2-bolt anchor.

13. **Unknown** (5.9) The cliff's first route. Missing its bolts. Tricky moves to a grungy groove and a 2-bolt anchor.

14. **Devil in Disguise** (5.10b) A strenuous roof start to fun moves up good rock. 3 bolts to 2-bolt anchor.

15. **Totally Trad** (5.8) 3 bolts to 2-bolt anchor.

16. **Unknown** (5.7) Marty Karabin says this is the best route on the crag. Left of a broken pillar. 5 bolts to 2-bolt anchor.

17. **Pushin' Your Luck** (5.9) 30' right of the pillar. 3 bolts to 2-bolt anchor.

BEARDSLEY BOULDER PILE

The Beardsley Boulder Pile is a large group of fine granite boulders on the east flank of a low mountain between Beardsley Road and Deer Valley Road in north Phoenix. This is a fun and easily accessible area for a quick outing. There are over 100 boulder problems that range in difficulty from V0- to V6 scattered along the base of the mountain. On the hillside above the boulders, are several small crags with both bolted and traditional routes. Information on the boulder problems and the routes is found in *Phoenix Rock II* and *Beardsley Boulder Pile*, a fold-out topo guide by Marty Karabin.

Finding the boulders: The area is in north Phoenix, about 5 miles east of Interstate 17. The easiest approach from the interstate is to take the Deer Valley Exit. Drive east on Deer Valley Road to a rough dirt road that heads south on the east side of the mountain. Follow this road south to the northeast flank of the mountain and park. The boulders are scattered along the base. The routes are on the mountainside above. The parking area is also reached via Beardsley Road and 20th Street to the south of the mountain.

DROMEDARY PEAK

Several surprisingly good crags are found on Dromedary Peak, a low, humped mountain south of US Highway 60 and the Superstition Mountains. The area is just south of the highway before you reach Superior and Queen Creek Canyon. The three crags, the East Face, Ivory Tower, and Gray Wall, are composed of a volcanic rhyolite rock. The East Face has an assortment of good crack and sport routes reached by a steep approach. The Ivory Tower, the peak's premier sport climbing area, is a south-facing cliff with some superb bolted lines, as well as a few good cracks. The Gray Wall, facing the highway, has seen the least

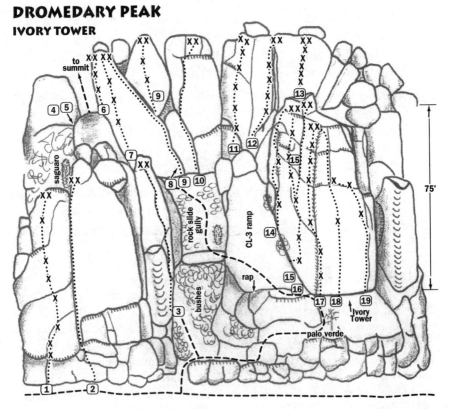

DROMEDARY PEAK
IVORY TOWER

Topo by Marty Karabin.

development because of a large, active beehive. Now that the hive is gone, expect more sport routes here. Most of the routes at Dromedary Peak were put up by Marty Karabin in 1994, and he published *Dromedary Peak Rock Climbing Guide*, a fold-out topo guide with maps and descriptions, which is available at Phoenix shops and gyms. The route information and topo to the Ivory Tower are courtesy of Marty Karabin.

Finding the crag: Drive east from Phoenix on US Highway 60 for about 45 minutes. Dromedary Peak rises south of the highway 5 miles past Florence Junction. At milepost 217, look for a dirt road that goes south from the highway. Turn here and pass through a barbed wire gate. Drive south on this rough road across a wash and up a hill. The first parking on the right can be reached by two-wheel-drive vehicles. High-clearance or four-wheel-drive vehicles can continue south to another parking area. Trails lead from the parking areas up the steep, cactus-covered slopes to the base of the cliffs. The East Face is the obvious crag on the right side, while the Ivory Tower faces south or to the left. Routes are described left to right.

IVORY TOWER

1. **The Eliminator** (5.11c) Karabin calls it a "Fantastic route!" Face climb up a crack and a steep face. 7 bolts to a 2-bolt anchor.

2. **Bowling Pin** (5.7) A vertical crack to a 2-bolt anchor. **Rack:** Small to large cams.

3. **If 6 Was 9** (5.9) On the left side of a brushy gully. Climb a zigzag crack to a 2-bolt anchor. **Rack:** Small to medium gear.

4. **The Floozie** (5.10b) Higher up the left side of the gully. Jam a left-facing dihedral to a ledge to a 1-bolt face to a 2-bolt anchor.

5. **One Move Wonder** (5.10b) Right of Route 4. Climb a 1-bolt face to an overhanging crack and a 2-bolt anchor. **Rack:** Medium cams.

6. **Pierced Olisbo** (5.10a) Right of a gully that leads to the summit. A short, 2-bolt face to a 2-bolt anchor.

7. **Funky Lemon** (5.11a) Another shortie. 3 bolts to 2-bolt anchor.

8. **The Flying Chipmunk** (5.7) A left-angling hand crack to Route 7's anchors. **Rack:** Medium-sized pro.

9. **Loco Visionaires** (5.10a) Jam the first part of Route 8's crack, then climb up a 2-bolt face to a 2-bolt anchor.

10. **Shake and Bake** (5.10d) Jam a crack up left to a ledge. Head up another crack to a 2-bolt anchor.

11. **Winghingdingadee** (5.10d) 3-star sport route. 5-bolt face moves to a 2-bolt anchor.

12. **Singing in the Rain** (5.9) Karabin says, "Looks chunky but it is really pumpy." 4 bolts to 2-bolt anchor.

13. **Balancing Act** (5.11b) Balance up technical moves past 5 bolts to a 2-bolt anchor.

14. **Sunny Delight** (5.9+) On the left side of the Ivory Tower. Climb a face and arête to a ledge. 5 bolts to 2-bolt anchor.

15. **Tempest** (5.11b/c) Highly recommended. Down right of Route 14. Face climbing left of a crack. 6 bolts to 2-bolt anchor.

16. **The Natural** (5.10c) An excellent sport and crack route. Climb *Tempest* for 3 bolts, then up a thin crack to a 2-bolt anchor. **Rack:** Small to medium gear.

17. **Me and My Bulldog** (5.11a) Bulldog Bosch that is. First sport route here. Great route—just do it! Tricky climbing up an exposed arête on the left corner of the tower. 6 bolts to 2-bolt anchor.

18. **Project** (5.12?) A sport route up a smooth face.

19. **The Ivory Line** (5.12a) Work up a vertical crack to a stance. Traverse left and climb past 3 bolts to a crack that leads to Route 17's anchors.

MORE CENTRAL ARIZONA AREAS

Other climbing areas in central Arizona include Jacuzzi Spires, Cholla Mountain, Troon Mountain, White Tank Mountains, The Ice Castles, Four Peaks, Eagletail Mountains, El Capitan Canyon, and Seneca Falls. Farther afield, Jim Waugh reports a secret sport climbing area somewhere north of Yuma, but all guidebook authors are sworn to secrecy to preserve the area's unique environment. Information on some of these areas is found in *Phoenix Rock II* (Falcon Publishing/Chockstone Press) and *Adventuring in Arizona* (Sierra Club Books). Marty Karabin publishes a fold-out topo guide to The Ice Castles.

The Jacuzzi Spires are an off-the-beaten-track area north of Phoenix and east of Exit 238 off Interstate 17. The three blocky towers sit on a ridge high above a creek with "jacuzzi" pools carved in the bedrock. Some good, fun routes are found here, particularly on the First Spire.

Cholla Mountain is a low, hump-backed peak west of Little Granite Mountain and north of the McDowells. Many short routes are found on Cholla's granite outcrops. The east side offers some good, easily accessible crags, while the west side has the longest routes at The Far Side.

Troon Mountain, on the northeast side of Scottsdale, is one of the area's "lost" climbing areas. The mountain is private property and is now surrounded by gated communities, making access to the peak and its crags a serious problem. It is still possible to reach the area from the east. Lots of worthy crack and face routes on granite outcrops and boulders are scattered all over the mountain.

The White Tank Mountains are a rugged range bordering the Phoenix metro area on the west. Much of the range is in White Tank Mountain Regional Park. Routes up to 300 feet long are found on broken and sometimes loose cliffs in a canyon.

The Ice Castles is a bouldering and short-route granite area on the northwest side of Phoenix and west of Interstate 17. Marty Karabin wrote and diagrammed a fold-out topo guide to the area.

The Four Peaks is a distinctive quartet of mountains on the horizon northeast of Phoenix. Brown's Peak, the massif's 7,657-foot high point, offers an interesting mountaineering route up its broken north face. *The Ladybug* (II 5.5) works its way up cracks and corners for four pitches. *Phoenix Rock II* and *Adventuring in Arizona* offer directions and descriptions.

The Eagletail Mountains is a rugged, sawtoothed desert range towering above the Harquahala Plain some 60 miles west of Phoenix. The range, south of Interstate 10, is studded with soaring rock formations that include the free-standing Feathers atop Eagletail Peak, the highest point. The three pinnacles, composed of crumbly volcanic rock, offer a great climbing adventure in the Arizona outback. Technical climbing is required for all three summits. The North Feather has a 90-foot 5.6 route; the Middle Feather, a 50-foot, 5.5 climb; and the South Feather, a 60-foot 5.0 chimney to an airy acme. On the northwest end of the range is Courthouse Rock, a 1,000-foot-high formation that catches every climber's eye when traveling between Phoenix and Joshua Tree. The eight-pitch *Standard Route* (III 5.5) is a fun, easy adventure route up this impressive monolith.

El Capitan Canyon is a developing limestone area in a cliff-lined canyon off Arizona Highway 77 just south of Globe. It's best to ask around in Phoenix for information on the area.

Seneca Falls, on the San Carlos Apache Indian Reservation north of Globe, is a sport climbing area in a north-facing amphitheater of volcanic rock. The area offers about 30 bolted routes ranging from 5.8 to 5.12b and up to 165 feet long. The climbing here was set up for convenience sport climbing with an abundance of closely spaced bolts—some lines have as many as 25 bolts in a rope-length. Be advised that there is a lot of loose, fractured rock on belay ledges and on the routes. Since the climbing was established in 1994, there has been a history of closures and conflicts here. It's best to inquire at mountain shops and gyms in Phoenix for current access information. A guide to Seneca Falls by Diedre Burton appeared in *Rock & Ice* #70. A small guidebook with the same information is also available.

PRESCOTT AREA

GRANITE DELLS

OVERVIEW

The Granite Dells, lying northeast of Prescott, are an amazing and beautiful garden of mini-domes, sharp pinnacles, abrupt cliffs, and shallow canyons. Numerous routes are found at the three main climbing areas—High Rappel Dell, Westside Dells, and Watson Lake Dells. High Rappel Dell, the oldest climbing area, offers lots of easily accessible routes on a maze of cliffs east of Arizona Highway 89. The Westside Dells, lying west of the highway, is a jumbled area of humped domes creased by canyons. This area, not covered here, has access problems and is succumbing to housing developments. The Watson Lake Dells, the newest Dells climbing area, is a lovely, quiet enclave of cliff-walled canyons and low, rocky ridges.

The small crags at the Granite Dells are justifiably popular with local climbers. The cliffs are close to Prescott and its college population, are easy to access with short approaches, and offer a wide variety of grades and styles from sport clip-ups to traditional jam cracks. The Dells' rock is a coarse-grained granite, similar to that found in Joshua Tree National Park and the desert granites in the Phoenix area. Some of the rock is high-quality granite with crystalline edges, friction smears, and vertical cracks. Other sections are brittle, crumbling, and subject to breakage. Pick and choose. Many of the cracks are painful to jam, making tape very useful. Most of the routes are single-pitch, although there are some multipitch lines. Most of the climbs are well protected with a mixture of gear and bolts. The prolific Dells pioneer Rusty Baillie notes that "this area treats beginners like human beings."

Climbing at the Granite Dells, as at so many climbing areas, is a privilege, not a right. Prescott climbers, united as the Prescott Climber's Coalition, have long worked at creating dialogue between climbers and landowners and managers, particularly at Granite Mountain. The Granite Dells are no exception. Baillie notes that back in 1972, when the area was just getting established, climbers could have acquired the land and turned it over to the state as a park. Now the Dells are slowly being developed as exclusive housing subdivisions,

GRANITE DELLS

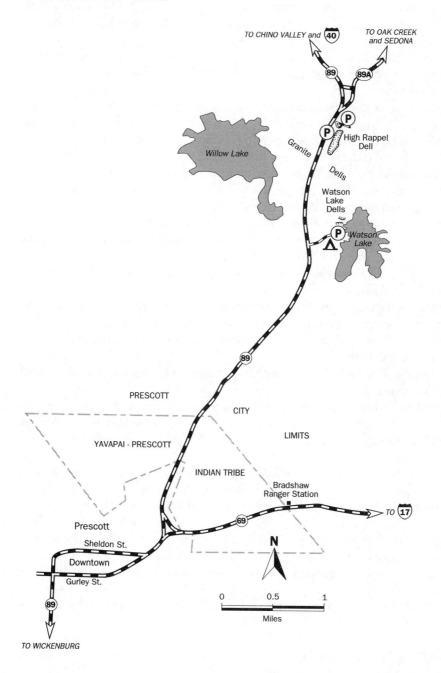

TO CHINO VALLEY and **40**

TO OAK CREEK and SEDONA

89

89A

P

P

High Rappel
Dell

Willow Lake

Granite

Dells

Watson
Lake
Dells

P

Watson
Lake

89

PRESCOTT

CITY

YAVAPAI - PRESCOTT

LIMITS

INDIAN TRIBE

Bradshaw
Ranger Station

TO **17**

Prescott

69

Sheldon St.

N

Downtown

Gurley St.

89

0   0.5   1

Miles

TO WICKENBURG

and only bits and pieces of granite can be saved. An exception is the Watson Lake Dells, which is already a city park around the reservoir. In the meantime, access to High Rappel Dell has come and gone, and the cliff has been opened and closed to climbing. The area is now open to climbers again, thanks to the efforts of Rusty Baillie and the Prescott Climber's Coalition. The Westside Dells across the highway is also open to climbing and the coalition is working with the owner for access.

Climbing history: Technical rock climbing began on High Rappel Dell back in the 1960s. Many of today's classic crack routes were established in the late 1960s and early 1970s, including the flake crack *Guillotine*, the *Crack of Doom* (originally rated 5.7), *Bom Bay*, and *Siege*. Siege, put up in 1971 by Rusty Baillie, Royal Robbins, Scott Baxter, and David Lovejoy, was Prescott's first 5.10 route. An early area guide, costing $.10, noted that the first pitch "is a possible candidate for F.10ness." That was a time when no one was really sure what 5.10 was, but this route was darn harder than 5.9! National exposure to the Dells came in 1972 when the fledgling *Climbing* magazine featured the perfect hand crack atop *Thank God* on its cover.

In the mid-1980s, the Dells saw a resurgence in new route activity after a period of dormancy. Local climbers Leo Henson, Paul Peterson, and Tom Cecil spearheaded a Dells revival with new ethics. The rap-bolted *Non-Dairy Screamer* became an instant classic in 1986 along with *Steal Your Face,* which was bolted off hooks. Throughout the 1990s, climbers have continued to fill in High Rappel Dell with new bolted lines.

Nearby Watson Lake Dells is the newcomer to the area. Until Bill Cramer began exploring and climbing on the crags northwest of Watson Lake in 1994, virtually no routes had been established here. Over the next three years, Cramer climbed over 300 topropes and boulder problems. In the winter of 1996 and 1997, he enlisted the help of Rusty Baillie, and the duo proceeded to bolt and climb over 50 routes.

Ethics are relaxed at the Dells. Remember though, this is not a convenience bolting area. Natural gear placements remain on many bolted routes and fixed belay stations are not found on many routes, particularly at Watson Lake Dells. Here are some general rules to follow when visiting the Dells. Park only in designated areas; pick up broken glass, tape, cigarette butts, and Mylar wrappers; and stay on existing trails whenever possible. If there are no trails, walk on bedrock to avoid trampling vegetation. At Watson Lake Dells, swimming is not permitted in the lake.

Rack: Bring a cragging rack for climbing at the Dells. This should include sets of Stoppers, TCUs, and Friends or equivalent cams, a dozen quickdraws, a few longer slings, and a 165-foot rope. Offset cams also work well in the shallow, flared cracks found here. **Descent:** For all routes, either walk off or rappel. A few routes have lowering anchors.

TRIP PLANNING INFORMATION

General description: A diverse assortment of one- and two-pitch, sport and gear routes on granite crags and faces at Watson Lake Dells and High Rappel Dell.

Location: Central Arizona, northeast of Prescott.

Camping: Watson Lake Park at Watson Lake Dells has a small fee campground with showers, water, and tables. A good base camp for climbing in the Prescott area is Granite Basin Campground, an 18-site Prescott National Forest area. It's open year-round and sits near Granite Basin Lake west of the Granite Dells and northwest of Prescott.

Climbing season: Year-round. Autumn and spring offer the best temperatures. Winters can be cold, but the cliff receives lots of winter sun. January's average high temperature in Prescott is 50.4 degrees. Summers are often too hot for comfortable climbing. Watch for severe afternoon thunderstorms in summer.

Restrictions and access issues: Watson Lake Dells is on city-owned land and currently has no climbing restrictions. A small daily access fee is required to enter the park. High Rappel Dell is open to climbing but is on private land. Negotiations hopefully will keep the area open for public use.

Guidebooks: No published guidebooks are available. Rusty Baillie and Bill Cramer wrote comprehensive mini-guides to the area for *Rock & Ice Magazine* #81, October 1997. Rick Dennison and Alessandro Malfatto published the out-of-print *A Climber's Guide to the Granite Dells of Prescott, AZ* in the late 1980s.

Nearby mountain shops, guide services, and gyms: Base Camp and Granite Mountain Outfitters in Prescott. Both shops have a selection of climbing and camping gear and are good sources for access information.

Services: All services are found in Prescott.

Emergency services: Call 911. Yavapai Regional Medical Center, 1003 Willow Creek Road, Prescott, AZ 520-445-2700.

Nearby climbing areas: Granite Mountain, Lizard Head and other crags in the Granite Mountain Wilderness Area, Thumb Butte, Groom Creek Boulders and Sullivan Canyon along the Verde River to the north, Crown King crags, Sedona sandstone spires and crags.

Nearby attractions: Dead Horse Ranch State Park, Fort Verde State Historic Park, Jerome State Historic Park, Prescott National Forest, Granite Mountain Wilderness Area, Verde River.

WATSON LAKE DELLS

Watson Lake Dells is a collection of short cliffs tucked into shallow canyons above the northwest shore of Watson Lake, a reservoir off Arizona Highway 89 northeast of Prescott. These crags are on land owned by the City of Prescott. Lots of bolted and traditional routes, as well as toprope problems, are found in this compact area. This is not a bolt-convenience area and some routes require a few pieces of gear to supplement bolt protection. Not all belay anchors are fixed. For a more complete guide to the crags at Watson Lake Dells, check out *Rock & Ice* # 81.

Finding the crags: Drive north out of Prescott on Arizona 89. After a few miles, look for a marked turn to Watson Lake on the right side of the highway. Pass through the entrance booth and drive to a fork. Go left toward the boat ramp. A parking area is on the left (north) just before the ramp. Further directions are listed under the described crags.

THOR'S WALL

This shady, northeast-facing wall, tucked in a shallow canyon just north of Watson Lake, offers a high-quality selection of bolted sport routes. It's a good afternoon crag during warm weather, but is sometimes chilly in the colder months. There are rappel and lowering anchors for all the routes, but they are not typical sport anchors.

From the parking area on the northwest side of Watson Lake, walk down the road to the boat ramp and hike northeast along the lakeshore path. The cliff hides on the west side of the second canyon from the parking lot. Scramble up rocky slopes along a drainage to the wooded base of the cliff. The cliff is not obvious from the trail and it may take some work to find it. Routes are described left to right.

1. **Thermocouple** (5.11d) Start below a bolt just left of an inverted flake. Undercling the flake to a horizontal break and the 2nd bolt. Work up left on good holds (small pro in horizontal cracks) to a groove crack and the 3rd bolt left of a crack. Face climb up right to a double bulge or go left around the corner to keep the route rating 5.11a. Pull the crux bulge to a 2-bolt anchor set back from the edge. 4 bolts. **Descent:** Lower only from carabiners on slings, otherwise downclimb chimney behind the route to ledges.

2. **Monarch** (5.10b) Recommended. Begin 5' right of Route 1. Technical sidepulls lead to a high 1st bolt. Work up crux layaways past 2 bolts. Chimney up the final overhanging slot with a hand and fist crack. Finish at Route 1's anchors. 3 bolts. **Descent:** Do not rappel off the bolts; there are no slings or rap rings. Use carabiners or downclimb chimney behind anchors to ledges.

3. **Under a Dark Sky** (5.11) Thrutch up a wide crack on a left-facing, overhanging flake to a big roof. Traverse left under the roof and finish up *Monarch*'s slot to a 2-bolt anchor. **Descent:** Put draws on the anchor bolts to rappel or lower only, downclimb chimney behind anchors to ledges. **Rack:** A good assortment of medium to large cams, including a couple extra-large Friends or #6 Camalots.

4. **Serpentine Fire** (5.12c) Technical moves. Stick-clip 1st bolt. Begin under a small roof at the base of the left-facing flake/crack. Work up right with right foot on flake edge. Power up crisp edges and slopers on the bulging wall. 6 bolts to a 2-bolt anchor on a ledge. A 5.12 variation goes up left after the 3rd bolt past 2 bolts to the same anchors. **Descent:** Rappel or lower from anchors.

5. **Sinister Exaggerator** (5.11d/12a) Recommended. Begin 5' right of Route 4. Climb onto a semi-detached flake. Work up a rib just left of a seam with sidepulls and stems, then angle left past the top bolt to anchors on a ledge. 7 bolts to a 2-bolt anchor on the right side of a short arête. **Descent:** Rappel or lower from anchors.

6. **Totally Hammered** (5.11c/d) Start just right of a gnarled oak tree. Stick-clip 1st bolt then boulder up edges to the bolt, left of a shallow corner. Climb a blunt arête above to the top of the cliff. Belay out left at Route 5's 2-bolt anchor. 6 bolts.

7. **Thor's Handle** (5.10d) Same start as Route 6. Boulder up to 1st bolt on Route 6 or stick-clip it. Climb right and up a right-facing dihedral left of a finger pillar. Above, move left and finish past the top 2 bolts of Route 6. Belay on the top of the cliff or out left at Route 5's anchors on a ledge. **Rack:** Stoppers and small to medium cams.

8. **Feeling a Little Thor** (5.10d) Begin 6' right of Route 7 and below a dark water groove. Edge up 10' to 1st bolt. Step right and climb a seam up the right-side groove to the top of the cliff. 2 bolts. **Rack:** Small and medium cams.

9. **Ice Breaker** (5.10b) A one-move wonder. Begin on a rock rib below the cliff's face. Clip 1st bolt and lieback a seam crack to jugs up left and the 2nd bolt. Face climb up and right to the 3rd bolt, then cruise to anchors. 3 bolts to 2-bolt anchor.

10. **Trench Warfare** (5.11a) Start in the deep gully right of Route 9. Lieback up a flake, then out left along a seam. Pull straight up and angle out left to Route 9's anchors. 4 bolts to 2-bolt anchor. A hard toprope problem begins in the gully farther right of Route 10.

TIME ZONE

This southwest-facing wall, overlooking the lake's rocky shore, has a great selection of moderate routes that are ideal for the beginning leader.

From the parking area on the northwest side of Watson Lake, walk down the road to the boat ramp and hike northeast along the lakeshore path. The cliff lies on the east side of the third canyon from the parking lot. Scramble up rocky slopes to the base of the cliff. The cliff is not obvious from the trail and it may take some work to find it. The cliff is visible from the parking area. Routes are described right to left.

11. **Time Slot** (5.8) On the right side of the cliff. Follow a seam, which overhangs at the start, right of a line of bolts. Climb the seam using the 4 bolts to a 2-bolt lowering anchor.

12. **Nick of Time** (5.9) Begin below a shallow, right-facing corner. Face climb past 4 bolts to a 2-bolt lowering anchor.

13. **Hour of Power** (5.8) Start just left of Route 12. Climb onto a small flake/ledge. Clip a bolt up right. Thin crux moves lead up right into a shallow, right-facing corner. Pull edges to a 2-bolt lowering anchor (same as Route 12). **Rack:** Small to medium cams.

14. **Quartz Movement** (5.7) Follow a broken seam past horizontal gear placements and a large, hollow flake on the right to a high bolt. Edge past a small bulge to another bolt, then to a 2-bolt lowering anchor 10' higher. **Rack:** Stoppers and small to medium cams.

15. **Minute Man** (5.6) Begin off a large boulder left of Route 14. Boulder up to a narrow, right-facing corner and a bolt. Move up left onto a sloping ledge and climb to a bolt in a bulge. Pull onto a ledge with a 2-bolt lowering anchor. **Rack:** Stoppers and small to medium cams.

Bill Ward edges up *Nick of Time* (5.9) on the Time Zone wall at Watson Lake Dells.

16. **Can't Wait Gotta Go** (5.6) Start just right of a dead tree on the left side of the face. Climb a rib of rock past 2 bolts to a sloping ledge. Clip the 3rd bolt above the ledge and step up right to a 2-bolt lowering anchor (same as Route 15). **Rack:** Small cams.

HIGH RAPPEL DELL

High Rappel Dell is a long, west-facing granite wall that towers east of Arizona Highway 89 northeast of Prescott. Over 100 routes line the 150-foot-high cliff. Other routes, not described here, are found on the back side of the cliff and in side canyons to the southeast.

Finding the crag: Drive north from Prescott on Arizona 89 for almost 5 miles. Past the turn to Watson Lake, the highway dips north between rock walls. High Rappel Dell is the obvious cliff to the east above the highway. A roadside parking area is at the north end of the cliff. Park well off the highway. Another parking area is just north of the crag. Make a right turn on a short dirt road and park. Scramble up slabs to the base of the wall.

DESCENT GULLY WALL

This is a deep, wide gully/corridor on the far north side of the wall. A handful of good routes are on the north-facing (right) wall of the gully. Routes are listed left to right from the back of the gully. The routes are easy to find. No topos.

17. **Wugit** (5.6) The far end of the gully. Scramble onto boulders to begin. Climb to a bolt in a left-facing corner, then work up left (5.6) into a crack system. Follow past a fixed piton to a belay on top of the cliff. **Descent:** Scramble down east. **Rack:** Small selection of larger Stoppers and small to medium cams.

18. **Last Word** (5.10a) Sport. Climb past 4 bolts, with a thoughtful crux at the 3rd bolt, to a 2-bolt anchor atop the cliff.

19. **In the Dark** (5.10c) Sport. A continuous face route up a black streak with 3 distinct 5.10 cruxes. 5 bolts to 2-bolt anchor (same as Route 18).

20. **The Empire Strikes Back** (5.10a) Work up the right side of the wall past 2 bolts, then up cracks to the 3rd bolt. Move left and join Route 19 at its 4th bolt. 3 bolts to 2-bolt anchor. **Rack:** Small to medium cams.

21. **Baillie's Blind Spot** (5.9) A good route. Climb to the 1st bolt and an awkward mantle. Continue up the right side of the face to the top bolt, keeping left of ramps. Angle up left to Route 20's anchors. 4 bolts to 2-bolt anchor.

HIGH RAPPEL DELL

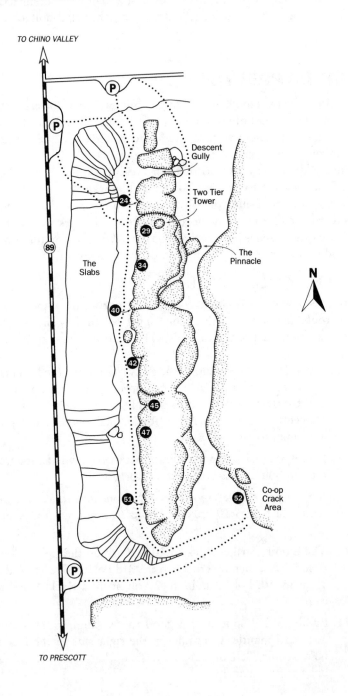

TO CHINO VALLEY

Descent
Gully

Two Tier
Tower

The
Pinnacle

The
Slabs

N

Co-op
Crack
Area

TO PRESCOTT

THE MAIN WALL

The first routes are on the west face of a pillar just south of Descent Gully. The other routes are up the taller formation on the north side of the Main Wall. Routes are from left to right.

22. **Guillotine** (5.8) No topo. A classic route up a huge, guillotine-shaped flake on the northwest side of the pillar and on the west end of the Descent Gully corridor. Climb an obvious off-width crack to an overhanging flake. Lieback and undercling up the flake to the right edge of the buttress. Move up left along an easier crack to a belay atop the pillar. **Descent:** Walk off east. **Rack:** Mostly large cams along with a few medium cams.

23. **David's Climb** (5.11c) Up the blunt prow right of *Guillotine*. Start right of Route 22. Work up and right onto the prow. Thin face climbing leads to the top of the prow. 5 bolts to 2-bolt anchor.

24. **Crack of Doom** (5.9) A classic, off-width, 1968 testpiece up the obvious wide splitter on the far left pillar. Start directly below the crack or traverse up to it from the right. Thrutch and clutch up the finger to hand to fist to off-width to squeeze chimney crack to the top. **Descent:** Walk off east to Descent Gully. **Rack:** Small to large cams with some off-width pro like large Camalots and Big Bros for extra security.

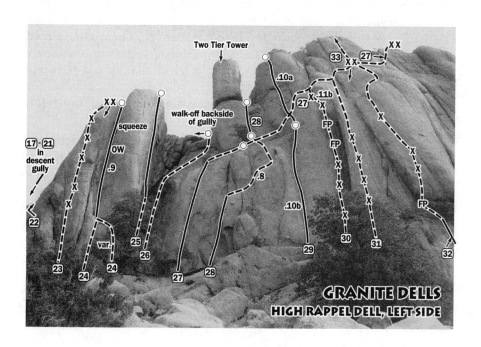

GRANITE DELLS
HIGH RAPPEL DELL, LEFT SIDE

299

25. **Fred** (5.12a) Hidden around the corner right of Route 24 on the left side of the gully. Climb a thin crack system up the slightly overhanging wall. **Rack:** TCUs and small to medium cams.

26. **Organic Farm** (5.4) Climb a groove (5.4) on the right side of the gully to a sloping slab. Continue up a slabby corner (5.4) left of Two Tier Tower past an overlap to a belay. **Descent:** Walk off gully on the back side. **Rack:** Stoppers and cams.

27. **Gambit** (5.10a) 3 pitches. On a wall right of a gully and below the prominent skyline spire. Up an obvious crack system on the left side of the short wall. **Pitch 1:** Climb a wide, flared crack for 35' to a sloping ramp. Follow ramp up right to a belay at a tree. **Pitch 2:** Work up corners and ledges right to a 2-bolt anchor on a ledge. **Pitch 3:** Face climb up right past a bolt and follow a right-angling groove to a 2-bolt anchor. **Descent:** Rappel with double ropes from the anchors, or walk off east and north to Descent Gully. **Rack:** Mostly medium and large cams.

28. **Last Chance** (5.8) 2 pitches. **Pitch 1:** Climb a shallow crack up a left-facing corner. Exit right and work across the top of flakes (5.8) to a ramp. Belay on a ledge at the base of a corner below the right side of Two Tier Tower. **Pitch 2:** Jam a short, pumpy crack up the corner to a good ledge right of the thumb. **Descent:** Walk off east and north to Descent Gully. **Rack:** Selection of wires and small to medium cams.

29. **Siege** (5.10b) 2 pitches. Prescott's first 5.10 lead put up by local legends Rusty Baillie, Scott Baxter, and David Lovejoy with Royal Robbins in 1971. **Pitch 1:** Climb a bottoming, flared groove/crack (5.10b) past two fixed pins to a large, sloping ledge with small trees. **Pitch 2:** Jam an airy but good hand crack (5.10a) up and right on a yellow-lichened wall to a belay atop a pillar. **Descent:** Scramble east and then north to Descent Gully. **Rack:** Good assortment of small to large cams.

30. **Savage Amusement** (5.11d) Scramble up right onto a big ledge below a left-facing dihedral. Climb the steep face (5.11d) left of the dihedral past bolts and 2 fixed pitons. Exit right at the top (5.11b) and climb easy cracks up right to a 2-bolt belay on a ledge. **Descent:** Rappel with 2 ropes or climb *Stairway to Heaven* (Route 33). **Rack:** Quickdraws and a few cams.

31. **Banana Peel** (5.11c) Fun climbing and great position. Scramble onto a big ledge below a left-facing dihedral. Edge up a beautiful, blunt arête past 4 bolts. Above, angle up right in cracks to a ledge with 2-bolt belay/rappel anchors. **Descent:** Rappel with 2 ropes to the base or

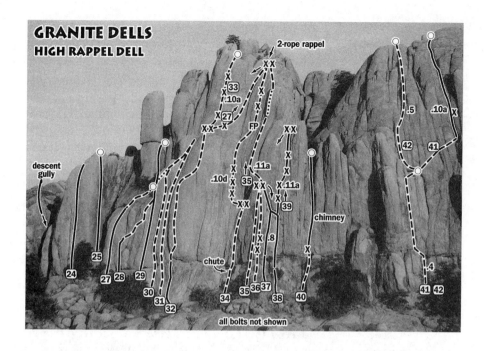

climb *Stairway to Heaven* (Route 33). **Rack:** Quickdraws and a few cams for the upper crack.

32. **Rolling Stone** (5.11c) Begin below a nose by a left-facing corner. Climb a thin crack to the base of the overhanging nose. Move up left to a fixed piton. Work up and make awkward moves out right to a bolt. Climb past 2 more bolts along a thin, left-facing corner. Continue above up easier rock to a 2-bolt belay/rappel anchor on a ledge. **Descent:** Rappel with 2 ropes to the base or climb *Stairway to Heaven* (Route 33). **Rack:** Wires and small to medium cams.

33. **Stairway to Heaven** (5.10a) An excellent and exposed face route to the top of the formation. This is the top pitch for Routes 30 through 32. Move up right from the ledge to a bolt and then work up left to a sloping stance. Edge up the face above (5.10a) past 3 bolts to the summit. **Descent:** Scramble east and north to Descent Gully. **Rack:** Small Stoppers and cams.

34. **Chute** (5.10d) 2 pitches. A recommended route with good pro but thought-provoking moves. **Pitch 1:** Begin at a hollow cave at the base of a squared chute. Work up the overhanging chimney/groove (5.8+) past 2 fixed pitons to a cramped, 2-bolt belay stance in an alcove. **Pitch 2:** Traverse up left to a weird crack and follow 3 bolts up a steep wall (5.10d). Above, work right across the upper slab (5.10a) and

climb (5.9) past a fixed piton and 2 bolts to a 2-bolt anchor on the shoulder. **Descent:** Rappel the route with 2 ropes. **Rack:** Wires and small to medium cams.

35. **Pinnacle** (5.11a) Begin right of *Chute* below a left-facing corner and a finger pillar. Climb the corner (5.9) to the top of the pillar. Climb the headwall above to a bolt, then work left past another bolt (5.11a) into a left-facing corner. Follow to a belay on the shoulder above or continue to a 2-bolt belay/rap anchor. **Descent:** Rappel from 2 bolts. **Rack:** Selection of Stoppers, TCUs, and small to large cams.

36. **Redpoint Mania** (5.10a) Face climb past 2 bolts on the outside of a pillar to a chain anchor.

37. **Left Twin Crack** (5.8) Begin below a finger pillar. Climb edges to the base of a left-hand crack. Jam 20' to a small ledge atop a pillar. **Descent:** Rappel from a chain anchor. **Rack:** Medium and large cams.

38. **Right Twin Crack** (5.9) A good jam. Climb blocks up left to a right-hand crack. Work up the short, pumpy hands to off-width crack. **Descent:** Rappel from a chain anchor. **Rack:** Medium and large cams.

39. **Prescott Grain and Feed** (5.11a) Climb Route 38. Above, move up right along seams past 4 bolts to a 2-bolt anchor. **Descent:** Rappel or lower 80'. **Rack:** Medium and large cams for lower crack, and quickdraws.

40. **Bom Bay** (5.10a) Another classic Baillie and Lovejoy off-width. Begin below an obvious, wide crack system. Climb a groove to the base of an overhanging, bomb bay, off-width crack. Work up off-width, clipping a bolt on the left face for pro (bolt out right is fair game too!). Thrash past and sling a chockstone, then go up an easier chimney to a good belay stance. **Descent:** Scramble up easy rock and downclimb north to Descent Gully. **Rack:** Small and medium cams, plus a runner.

41. **Presidente** (5.10a) 2 pitches. Begin by oak trees at the base of a large, right-facing dihedral. **Pitch 1:** Just right of the dihedral, climb up a thin corner (5.4) to a narrow shelf. Traverse left 10'. Climb up past a flake and move up a bottoming crack to a belay ledge. **Pitch 2:** Climb up right across a slab to the base of a left-facing corner and below a green and yellow pillar. Climb cracks up the corner (5.10a) past a bolt to a summit belay. **Descent:** Scramble off the back side and descend gullies north to Descent Gully. **Rack:** Wide selection of gear including Stoppers, TCUs, and cams to #4.

42. **Debutante** (5.5) 2 pitches. A good beginner route. Start at the same place as Route 41. **Pitch 1:** Climb the thin corner (5.4) right of the big dihedral to a narrow shelf. Traverse left 10' to the dihedral and climb it until a few moves up right (5.5) lead to a small belay ledge. **Pitch 2:**

Follow easy cracks above to the summit. **Descent:** Scramble off the back side and descend gully north to Descent Gully. **Rack:** Stoppers and small to large cams.

43. **Pump Now Pay Later** (5.11d) 3 pitches. Good climbing, good rock. **Pitch 1:** Climb over a small roof and angle up left past 2 bolts (5.11d) to a groove. Work past 3 bolts to a 2-bolt chain belay on a good ledge. **Pitch 2:** Face climb along a seam to a ledge. Step right and work up a left-angling crack with a bolt (5.10a) to a 2-bolt anchor atop a pillar. **Pitch 3:** Face climb up left past 2 bolts to the summit. **Rack:** Stoppers and small cams.

44. **Rip Your Fingers** (5.11d) 2 pitches. Begin just left of an oak tree. **Pitch 1:** Climb over blocky roofs to the 1st bolt. Face climb up a white streak (5.11b) past 2 bolts to a horizontal break. Step left and follow a left-angling seam past 2 bolts to a thin face move up right past a bolt onto a slab. Belay from 2 bolts on a ledge. 6 bolts. **Pitch 2:** Move up right over yellow-lichened rock. Edge up a rib above (5.11b) past 3 bolts to a 2-bolt belay stance. **Descent:** Rappel the route.

45. **Aid Climb** (5.11a) This was a good aid route, but is now a great crack climb. Begin right of a small oak. Bouldery face moves (5.11a) lead past 2 bolts to an excellent finger and thin hand crack. Lieback and jam to a 2-cold shut anchor. **Descent:** Rappel route. **Rack:** Stoppers, TCUs, and cams to a #3 Friend.

46. **Steal Your Face** (5.12a) 2 pitches. Begin 10' right of Route 45. **Pitch 1:** Follow 3 bolts up a water streak to a horizontal crack (5.11c). Move up right over a bulge to a large flake. Belay atop the flake from a 2-bolt chain anchor. **Pitch 2:** Face climb up left along a seam to a bolt, then up past thin cracks and 3 bolts to a 2-bolt chain anchor at a stance. **Descent:** Make 2 single-rope rappels. **Rack:** A few large cams for the flake on pitch 1.

47. **Thank God** (5.11d) In a *Rock & Ice* mini-guide, Rusty Baillie says, "Best TG hold in Arizona!" Also featured on the cover of a 1972 issue of *Climbing Magazine*. Start below the next crack system right of Route 46 and left of a clump of oaks. Climb either the left side (5.8) or the right side (5.9) of a pillar. Work past a horizontal crack and then move up a steep groove (5.11d) past 2 bolts to the flat-edged TG hold and on to a fine hand crack. Belay at a 2-cold shut anchor. **Descent:** Lower or rappel from anchors. **Rack:** A good selection of medium and large Friends.

48. **Stars and Stripes** (5.12b) Sport. Start 15' right of Route 47. Pumpy face climbing past 8 bolts to a 2-bolt chain anchor. **Descent:** Lower off.

49. **Non-Dairy Screamer** (5.11d) Interesting and varied movements. Same start as Route 48. At the 3rd bolt, swing up right past the horizontal break and face climb into a thin, left-facing corner. Above the corner,

work up right along a seam to another flake corner. End on a good stance with 2 bolts. **Descent:** Rappel or lower off.

50. **Ashes, Ashes, All Fall Down** (5.12b) Sport. Begin just left of a large oak. Pull up broken flakes and face climb to a roof above a horizontal crack. Follow a groove seam and crack to a 2-bolt anchor. 10 bolts. **Descent:** Rappel or lower off.

51. **Cerebral Palsy** (5.11c) Also called the *Barber Route* for Henry's bold first ascent lead. Climb 12' to a glued-in bolt. Committing and scary face moves lead to a thin crack (5.11c) and onto a hollow flake. Edge up right along a ramp crack to the 2nd bolt. Continue up a flared hand crack (5.9) to a 2-bolt belay anchor. **Descent:** Rappel or lower off. **Rack:** Stoppers, TCUs, and small to large Friends.

CO-OP CRACK AREA

At the far right side of High Rappel Dell, past Route 46, look east across a shallow canyon to a clean buttress with a large, right-facing dihedral. A few excellent crack routes are found here. Hike and contour across the canyon to the base of the wall.

52. **Co-op Crack** (5.10b) 2 pitches. Superb jamming—one of the Dells' best routes. The line ascends cracks on the pillar left of the large, right-facing dihedral. **Pitch 1:** Climb a face to a crack system and on to a belay at a tree. **Pitch 2:** Move up right and jam the gorgeous hand crack up the pillar to a belay above the crack. **Descent:** Scramble down Class 3 rock to the north. **Rack:** Medium to large Stoppers and small to large Friends.

53. **French Tickler** (5.8+) 2 pitches. A good corner climb. Begin 30' down right from Route 52. **Pitch 1:** Climb an easy ramp up left to a belay below a large, right-facing dihedral. **Pitch 2:** Work up the dihedral to a belay from a tree. **Descent:** Scramble down Class 3 rock to the north. **Rack:** A good selection of gear including Stoppers and cams.

54. **Cling of Pain** (5.10a) Classic! Move up a left-angling finger crack past a bolt to a stance. Step up left and then work back right past a bolt to a 2-bolt anchor on a ledge. 2 bolts. **Descent:** Rappel or lower. **Rack:** Medium Stoppers and small cams.

55. **No Pain No Gain** (5.10a) Begin down right of Route 54. Face climb (5.10a) past a bolt to a left-leaning flake. Jam and lieback up the fingery crack (5.9) to easier rock. End at Route 54's anchors. **Descent:** Rappel or lower from 2 bolts. **Rack:** Stoppers and small to medium cams.

GRANITE DELLS
HIGH RAPPEL DELL, CO-OP CRACK

3rd class
scramble to north

52

XX

X

X

54

53

X

55

GRANITE MOUNTAIN

OVERVIEW

The highlands of central Arizona, a jumble of rugged mountain ranges and small basins, separates the Colorado Plateau to the north from the low, arid cactus country to the south. Prescott, Arizona's old territorial capital, is nestled in the hills on the north flank of the Bradshaw Mountains. Granite Mountain rises northwest of town. This isolated, 7,626-foot-high mountain is studded with boulders, slabs, crags, and an immense, half–mile-long wall that offers some of Arizona's finest climbing adventures. The crag, lying in the Granite Mountain Wilderness Area of Prescott National Forest, has long been one of Arizona's best climbing areas and a guarded bastion of traditional ethics and style.

But with the proliferation of Arizona's clip-and-go sport climbing areas, Granite Mountain, with its staunch ethics and relatively bold routes, has fallen somewhat out of favor with many climbers. The crag's isolation and the steep hike to the cliff's base keep crowds to a minimum. Even on busy weekends, there is seldom a queue for the popular routes, and on weekdays visiting climbers will often have the entire crag to themselves. But those who do make the hike and tick a few of the classics will undoubtedly agree that Granite Mountain, nick-named "Arizona's little big wall," is perhaps the state's finest crag.

The south-facing cliff, simply called Granite Mountain by climbers, yields over 75 routes and variations of all grades on its 150- to 500-foot-high face. Most of the crag's routes follow crack systems with only the occasional bolt for protection or belay anchors. The rock is a coarse granite with a flaky, but generally trustworthy, rough surface that is characteristic of granites that occur in arid, nonglaciated areas. It is not, however, friable like many other desert granites.

Granite Mountain is divided into three wall sections: Swamp Slabs, Middle Section, and Right Section. Swamp Slabs, a relatively low-angled, slabby wall on the southwest side of the cliff, holds a superb selection of beginner and moderate routes. Many of these multipitch routes are between 5.4 and 5.7, with spacious belay ledges between quality face and crack climbs. The south-facing Middle Section encompasses the bulk of the cliff's towering face and its most classic lines. Most of these routes follow crack systems joined by occasional face moves. Expect sustained, intimidating, and varied climbing on this vertical, exposed face. The Right Section lies east of the jutting Flying Buttress and includes some excellent corner, crack, and face routes.

Climbing history: Tom Taber and Bill Ellis established Granite Mountain's first major route, *Chim Chimney* (5.7), in 1966. During the remaining years of the 1960s, a few more lines went up, including the intimidating *Green Savior* in 1969 by Scott Baxter and Tom Taber. The 1970s saw intense development of the crag by an active core of local climbers called El Syndicato Granitica, which included Scott Baxter, Karl Karlstrom, guidebook author David Lovejoy, and

Rusty Baillie, along with Larry Treiber, John Byrd, and Chuck Parker from Phoenix. This cadre of climbers brought a dedication to clean climbing ethics, with boldness, commitment, and the sparing use of fixed pitons and bolts, that continues to this day.

Most of the mountain's moderate free climbs went up in 1970 and 1971. In 1972, Baillie, Baxter, and Karlstrom began Granite's hard free climbing era with the first ascent of *Jump Back Jack Crack*, a classic off-width on the right side of the cliff. Other classic 5.10s that had either first ascents or first free ascents were *Candyland, Reunion, Falling Ross, Thin Slice,* and *Witblitz.* The late 1970s saw the firm establishment of the 5.11 grade when visiting climbers like Ed Webster, John Long, and Lynn Hill climbed *Coatimundi Whiteout* and *Adam's Rib.* The first pitch of *Adam's Rib* (5.11-) was free climbed by Coloradans Chris Reveley and Ajax Greene on a one-week Granite Mountain blitz in 1976. They also freed *Sly's Idea,* the third pitch of *Dream Weaver, Crack and Up,* the *Witblitz* dihedral, and would have done the *Coati* roof but it was too cold that day.

The last of the crag's major routes went up in the 1980s. The prime mover and shaker in this era was Phoenix climber and area guidebook author Jim Waugh. Waugh, coupled with various partners, pushed area standards with the first free ascents of the stunning *Twin Cracks* (5.12-), the excellent *The Good, the Bad, & the Ugly* (5.12), and in 1987, the crag's first 5.13 route, *A Bridge Across Forever.* This spectacular and devious line, one of Arizona's best crack climbs, offers, says Waugh, "contorted positions, intricate sequences, and downright strenuous climbing." The crag's other 5.13 route is *Blowin' in the Wind* on the face above *Sorcerer.* Since then, Granite Mountain has seen few new routes, with most climbers content to repeat the tried and proven classics.

Granite Mountain is easily accessed from Prescott. Although the cliff is 1,600 feet higher than the town, the cliff's sunny, southwest orientation gives it a similar climate to Prescott. Climbing is possible year-round, but the ideal seasons are late September through November and April to mid-June. Expect warm, sunny days with little precipitation, but watch out for Granite Mountain's notoriously fierce winds. The winter months are also good, with the shorter days being the prohibitive factor. Snowfall is generally light and sporadic, usually melting within a day on the south slopes. Winter temperatures are in the 50s and 60s. Nights can be very cold. Summer days are hot in the sun. Plan your outing for early morning or evening, when temperatures are more moderate. Expect daily highs in the 80s and 90s. Watch for severe thunderstorms on July and August afternoons.

The crag is the centerpiece of the 9,799-acre Granite Mountain Wilderness Area in Prescott National Forest. The area is subject to wilderness regulations that are intended to protect and preserve the area's unique geological and ecological resources. The main regulation that affects rock climbing is the closure of the cliff from February 1 to July 15 for raptor nesting. No new bolt anchors are allowed on the cliff, although maintenance of existing fixed anchors is permitted. Power drills are not allowed. Hiking groups are limited to a maximum of 15 people. Dogs must be leashed at all times. Campfires and the collection of firewood are prohibited, although camp stoves are allowed. There is no camping within 200 feet of Granite Mountain Trail (Trail 261.) Other common sense rules apply. Pick up all of your trash, as well as anyone else's along the trail or at the base of the cliff. Do not alter the rock surface by chipping holds or cleaning vegetation from cracks. Follow existing trails whenever possible to avoid damaging easily eroded soils, and dispose of human waste properly.

Objective dangers abound here. The hot, dry climate requires that you carry an adequate water supply. Plan on a minimum of a gallon per person per day in summer. Sports drinks are also good for replenishing essential body nutrients lost through sweating and dehydration. Don't plan on finding any water in the area. The cliff's granite is generally sound and rockfall is rare. You may encounter loose blocks and flakes in cracks or on ledges. Take care not to dislodge any large boulders. A helmet, particularly for the belayer, provides essential cranial protection. Consider fixed pitons and bolts as suspect gear. Always back them up with other pieces for a bombproof anchor. A rescue litter and first-aid kit are stashed at The Front Porch, a large boulder platform at the base of the cliff below The Flying Buttress. Watch for rattlesnakes in the warmer months. Plenty of them live in the dense undergrowth. Keep an open eye for them when following the climber's trail to the cliff and when scrambling up to the cliff's base. Carry a snake stick to probe suspected areas and remember that they don't always sound a warning rattle before striking. Rodents, especially at The Front Porch, will search your packs for food. Use plastic containers to minimize damage.

Granite Mountain ratings are notoriously stiff and conservative because the area developed far from other mainstream climbing areas in the 1970s. Some routes that now carry 5.10 ratings were originally graded 5.8. Some still keep that 5.8 rating, so keep that in mind if you've just traveled here from Jacks Canyon—these are real 5.10s!

Rack: A standard Granite Mountain rack should include a couple of sets of Friends or similar camming devices, a set of TCUs, and a set of wired Stoppers or the equivalent. Carry a few runners for tying off blocks or threading chockstones. Routes with off-width sections require larger gear like Big Bros, Big Dudes, or the larger Camalots. A single 165-foot rope is adequate for most routes, although double ropes are needed if you plan on rappelling. A 200-foot (60-meter) rope allows some pitches to be run together. Use any specific rack information listed under a route description as a guideline only. Scope out your route and decide for yourself what you need for protection. Everyone protects routes differently. The sin is usually not taking too much gear, but not taking enough gear.

GRANITE MOUNTAIN

Swamp Slabs

The Great
Roof

Right
section

Flying
Buttress

Middle section

The Front Porch

trail

TRIP PLANNING INFORMATION

General description: A south-facing, granite cliff with a wide assortment of excellent crack, corner, and face routes from one to five pitches long.

Location: Central Arizona, northwest of Prescott.

Camping: Granite Basin Campground, an 18-site Prescott National Forest area, is open year-round and is located near Granite Basin Lake southeast of the crag.

Climbing season: Year-round. Autumn and spring offer the best temperatures. Winters can be cold, but the cliff receives lots of winter sun. January's average high temperature in Prescott is 50.4 degrees. Summers are often too hot for comfortable climbing. Watch for severe afternoon thunderstorms in late summer. High winds can also occur in any season.

Restrictions and access issues: The cliff is in the Granite Mountain Wilderness Area of Prescott National Forest. For additional information, contact Prescott National Forest, 344 South Cortez Street, Prescott, AZ 66303, 520-445-7253. The cliff is closed because of nesting raptors from February 1 to July 15. Contact the Forest Service for updated information on area closures and current dates. A small day-use fee is charged for parking at the trailhead, but Wednesdays are free. Access and parking are limited to daytime hours.

Guidebooks: *A Topo Guide to Granite Mountain* by Jim Waugh, 1982, is an out-of-print classic. An updated version of the topo guide is in *Rock & Ice* #4. A comprehensive guide by Rick Donnelly is in the works.

Nearby mountain shops, guide services, and gyms: Base Camp and Granite Mountain Outfitters in Prescott. Both shops have a selection of climbing and camping gear and are good sources for access information.

Services: All services are found in Prescott.

Emergency services: Call 911. Yavapai Regional Medical Center, 1003 Willow Creek Road, Prescott AZ, 520-445-2700.

Nearby climbing areas: Lizard Head and other crags in the wilderness area, Thumb Butte, Granite Dells, Groom Creek Boulders and Sullivan Canyon along the Verde River to the north, Crown King crags, Sedona sandstone spires and crags.

Nearby attractions: Dead Horse Ranch State Park, Fort Verde State Historic Park, Jerome State Historic Park, Prescott National Forest, Granite Mountain Wilderness Area, Verde River.

Finding the crag: Granite Mountain lies northwest of Prescott in the Granite Mountain Wilderness Area. Reach the parking area by following Iron Springs Road northwest from town. This road is easily accessed from downtown Prescott (Gurley Street) via Grove Street and Miller Valley Road, or via Montezuma and Whipple streets. Drive northwest up Iron Springs Road a few miles to the marked turnoff to Granite Basin. Turn right (north) and follow this road (Forest Service Road 374) 4 miles to Granite Basin Recreation Area. Yavapai Campground is 2.2 miles up the road. When the road reaches the recreation area, it becomes a one-way loop. Follow the loop to either the Granite Basin Lake parking area or Metate Trailhead parking area. Restrooms and water are at the lake parking lot. A fee is charged for parking at the trailhead.

From either parking area, hike west up gentle grades on Trail 261 for about 1.25 miles to Blair Pass, southwest of the crag. At the saddle, turn north on Trail 261 and hike up the left slopes of Granite Mountain for another 0.25 mile. At the fourth switchback, where the trail bends back west, look for an unmarked climber's trail that heads uphill (northeast) to the cliff. Many climbers mistakenly take the lower second switchback and blunder through some heavy brush before finding the correct trail up higher. The rough trail climbs steep slopes over boulders and through brush to some boulders below The Flying Buttress. A rescue litter is located here. This spot, called The Front Porch, is a good place to stash packs and organize gear for routes on Middle Section and Right Section. Be advised that rodents will search your pack for edibles at The Front Porch and elsewhere. Take appropriate precautions by using plastic food containers. Look for rough trails that leave the main trail and head uphill to Swamp Slabs and the left side of Middle Section. Stay on the trails when possible to avoid bushwhacking through the thick oak brush. Also keep an eye out for rattlesnakes among boulders and bushes.

Descent: The traditional descent off Granite Mountain was a walk off at either the west or east end of the cliffs. Because so many climbers have been rappelling instead and leaving slings all over the crag, a decision was made to establish a single, permanent rappel route down *Coke Bottle* on the right side of The Flying Buttress. Make three rappels from beefy rappel hangers to the ground. The top rappel point is from two bolts halfway between the top of *Beaver Cleaver* and the gully where *High Exposure* ends. Please avoid the temptation to add slings to these hangers because they were not designed to be used with them. The rappels are 102 feet, 90 feet, and 94 feet. Use double ropes or a 200-foot (60-meter) rope, which is mandatory for the first rappel off the top. Note that there is also an extra rap station 30 feet above the ground (on *Coke Bottle*) for anyone with a short (150-foot) rope.

GRANITE MOUNTAIN

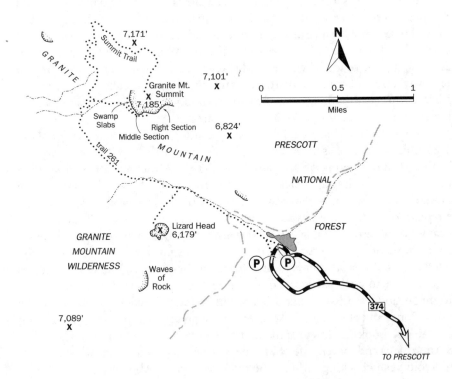

SWAMP SLABS

Swamp Slabs, the southwest-facing slabby wall on the far left side of the crag, offers a stellar selection of beginner and moderate routes. Lots of routes criss-cross the slabs. The described routes are the best, but keep in mind that there are lots of variations and alternative ways to go on this very climbable cliff. The cliff is visible above Blair Pass and the climber's access trail. When the main trail passes below the cliff, look for a path that scrambles up through brush to the cliff's base. Routes are listed left to right.

1. **Beginner** (5.4) 2 pitches. A good beginner route. Scramble along the cliff's base to the far north or left side of the wall. Begin below a left-facing corner. **Pitch 1:** Climb the left-facing corner (5.4) to a large, brushy terrace. Move right and belay beneath a crack. **Pitch 2:** Jam a slabby, left-angling crack and then face climb up right along thin, disjointed cracks to a large belay. **Descent:** Walk off left. **Rack:** Stoppers and small to large cams.

2. **Crawl** (5.7) 2 pitches. Start right 150' from Route 1. **Pitch 1:** Move up left to a right-angling corner. Climb the corner and crack above to a large terrace with trees. **Pitch 2:** Climb a crack up a shallow right-facing corner. At a small roof, move up left and up a right-leaning corner (5.7). Above, work past a roof and finish up a crack. Belay on the large ledge above. A direct finishing pitch edges up the slab above (5.7 R). **Descent:** Walk off left. **Rack:** Stoppers and small to large cams.

3. **Debut** (5.5) 3 pitches. A fun classic. Begin left of a large openbook and right of a black water streak. **Pitch 1:** Climb a crack system up and right past two small roofs. Continue up double cracks to a belay stance. **Pitch 2:** A short lead left of some large blocks atop the big dihedral reach a belay on the right side of the large ledge system. **Pitch 3:** Face climb up right and past the right side of a large, obvious roof. Finish up a right-facing corner (5.5) to a belay ledge right of some trees. **Descent:** Walk off left. **Rack:** Stoppers and small to large cams.

4. **Green Horns** (II 5.6) 4 pitches. Recommended moderate. The route begins on the far left side of Pine Tree Ledge, a spacious terrace that divides the lower cliff. Begin about 60' right of a large tree. **Pitch 1:** Climb a left-facing dihedral (5.6) on the left side of a large, arrow-head-shaped flake to a belay atop the flake. **Pitch 2:** Traverse straight left along a horizontal rock band to a large, left-facing corner. Climb the corner past a fixed pin to a good belay ledge. **Pitch 3:** Traverse right (5.5) 25' along a horizontal crack under some roofs to a belay stance under an open corner. Rick Donnelly describes the traverse as "very British and awkward." **Pitch 4:** Initial hard moves over a bulge

GRANITE MOUNTAIN

SWAMP SLABS

walk-off

.8-

5

6

.6

.3

4

5

Pine Tree Ledge

3rd class

5

6

move belay

.6

7

.10

Ragpicker

6 7

(5.6) lead to easy climbing up the corner to a belay ledge. Class 3 scrambling leads to the walk off from here. **Descent:** Walk off left. **Rack:** Stoppers and small to large cams.

5. **Dislocation Direct** (5.6) 4 pitches. Begin on Pine Tree Ledge about 100' right of the pine tree below a corner capped by a roof. Be advised that previous guides have described a direct start below the ledge—this line is unprotected 5.10. **Pitch 1:** Climb a hand crack right of some roofs (spot of 5.6 high) to a good ledge belay. **Pitch 2:** Follow cracks up left to a belay stance. **Pitch 3:** Climb a tight corner to a small roof. Turn the roof on the right and then face climb to a good ledge with blocks. **Pitch 4:** Cruise the easy groove with two cracks above to the top of the cliff. **Descent:** Walk off left. **Rack:** Stoppers and small to large cams.

6. **Dislocation Buttress** (5.4) 6 short pitches. A brilliant beginner's line. Some pitches can be run together—lots of belay stances on the wall. Begin on the far right side of Swamp Slabs at the toe of the buttress and below an open dihedral. **Pitch 1:** Stem and jam the easy dihedral to the right side of Pine Tree Ledge. Belay by trees. **Pitch 2:** Move the belay left along the ledge to the next clump of trees. Face climb an easy slab up right to a crack that leads up left to a corner. Belay on a good ledge. **Pitch 3:** Follow cracks up left to the left side of a small roof. Traverse right above the roof and clamber onto a spacious ledge and belay. **Pitch 4:** Step left and climb a short, right-facing corner to a horizontal crack. Traverse left and work up a fun, tight corner to some face moves. Belay above on a ledge. **Pitch 5, 6:** Climb an easy groove crack to the summit. **Descent:** Walk off left. **Rack:** Stoppers and small to large cams. (For an extra-credit start, climb the hard 1st pitch, *Ragpicker* (5.10). Begin between Route 5 and Route 6 below a couple of roofs. Climb a left-facing corner that arches left to a roof. Pull over and move to a second roof. Some hard moves (5.10) above lead to another crack system and Pine Tree Ledge.)

7. **Tread Gently** (5.8-) 4 pitches. The first ascent was solo by Rusty Baillie in 1971. A good, mostly easy line up the nose of the buttress. Begin at the same place as Route 6. **Pitch 1:** Climb the easy dihedral to Pine Tree Ledge. **Pitch 2:** Follow a crack up right (5.6) to a diagonal crack. Move left on this crack and follow a crack up left of a large block to a belay ledge. **Pitch 3:** Crack and face climbing leads to a bulge. Jam through via a thin crack (5.8-) and climb up left to broken cracks that lead to a blocky belay ledge. **Pitch 4:** Easy and fun Class 4 climbing up a corner to the top of the cliff. **Descent:** Walk off left. **Rack:** Stoppers and small to large cams.

MIDDLE SECTION

The first two climbs, Route 8 and Route 9, are on the right side of a huge alcove around the buttress east of Swamp Slabs. Look for a faint trail that thrashes through the oak brush to the base of the wall.

8. **C. W. Hicks (Direct)** (II 5.11) 4 pitches. Sustained and intriguing crack climbing. **Pitch 1:** Climb a flared, dark-streaked crack (5.11-) up a smooth wall to a belay ledge. No pro to start the pitch. Often lots of lichen. **Pitch 2:** Scramble up broken blocks left to the base of a large, left-facing corner system. **Pitch 3:** Work up the clean, open corner to a slot through a roof. Strenuous moves lead up and out the slot. Hand jam above the slot to a small belay ledge on the right. **Pitch 4:** Climb a crack up left from the belay and step across left to a hand crack. Jam the awkward crack (5.9) above to a chimney. Continue up the narrow chimney (5.6) to a belay atop the cliff. **Descent:** Walk east along the top of the cliff and do 3 double-rope rappels down *Coke Bottle*. **Rack:** Stoppers and small to large Friends.

9. **Magnolia Thunder Pussy** (II 5.9-) 4 pitches. First free ascent by Karl Karlstrom, David Lovejoy, and Scott Baxter in 1971. A 1960s restaurant on The Hill in Boulder, Colorado, as well as some flakes on pitch 3, inspired the route's name. Classic and highly recommended. Was originally rated 5.8. Begin down right from Route 8 below a shallow chimney. **Pitch 1:** Jam and stem up double cracks (5.9-) in the back of the square, shallow chimney to a blocky roof. Turn the roof on the right or left (both 5.9-). The right exit, a hand crack, is more fun and protects better. The left side involves a mantle into an off-width. Belay on a good ledge. **Pitch 2:** Scramble up left and back right over broken blocks to the base of a right-angling, left-facing corner. **Pitch 3:** Climb cracks up the corner (5.7) to a roof and the flakes for which the route was named. Interesting and precarious chimneying leads out left through a slot and up to a good belay ledge with a tree. **Pitch 4:** Easy cracks lead up right over blocks to a right-facing corner. Climb the hidden chimney (5.5) above to the crag summit. **Descent:** Walk east along the top of the cliff and do 3 double-rope rappels down *Coke Bottle*. **Rack:** Mostly a generous selection of medium to large cams.

10. **Green Savior** (II 5.8+) 4 pitches. First ascended in 1968 by Scott Baxter and Tom Taber. The original 1973 guide calls this "A status symbol climb in the Basin." It still doesn't get many ascents with its off-width crux pitch. The name came from a tied-off tree on the top pitch that stopped Taber after a fall. The "Green Savior" is now dead. Begin left of the prow of the prominent buttress. **Pitch 1:** Climb a brushy crack up right to a small ledge. Step right and climb easy cracks to a belay

GRANITE MOUNTAIN
MIDDLE SECTION

walk-off to rappels →

.6
chimney

.9   hands

chimney
.5

.7

.10+

.7

8   9

3rd class

.8+
OW

var.
.8

.5

.9-

hands

.11

.9-

8

9

10

.9

.10-

var.

10

ledge. **Pitch 2:** *The Crisco Way* variation makes a better 2nd pitch and keeps the route harder. Move left over some blocks and climb a flared, 50' chimney (5.8) to a horizontal crack. Hand traverse right to a good belay on Comfort Ledge beneath a flared, off-width crack. The original pitch climbs easy cracks and ledges to a featured crescent crack/ramp, which heads up right (5.5) to a horizontal crack with a bundle of rap slings. Traverse left to Comfort Ledge. **Pitch 3:** The infamous crack pitch! Work up the tight chimney (left side in) to a fixed piton. Thrutch through the off-width bulge (5.8 or harder) above to a small belay stance below a big chimney. **Pitch 4:** Jams and edges (5.7) lead into the box chimney. Chimney up with back and knees to a rest spot, then on to a good belay ledge. Get small pro in piton scars in the lower chimney. **Descent:** Walk east along the top of the cliff and do 3 double-rope rappels down *Coke Bottle*. **Rack:** A wide range of gear including Stoppers and small cams, plus lots of big stuff including extra large Camalots.

11. **Kingpin** (III 5.10) 5 pitches. An airy and committing classic. Begin below an obvious, left-facing dihedral. **Pitch 1:** Climb broken cracks and corners to a slanting crack/ramp. Stem and jam (5.8) up the left-facing dihedral to a belay up left atop a flake. **Pitch 2:** Work up the progressively steeper dihedral (5.10) to a hanging belay stance at the top and just right of a small roof. A variation starting pitch (Route 11a on topo) is *Cinnamon Girl* (5.10), up the bolted face right of pitches 1 and 2. **Pitch 3:** Climb a thin, right-facing corner (5.7) that becomes a crack. Belay up left on an exposed, narrow ledge. **Pitch 4:** Face climb (5.9) vertical rock above the left side of the shelf to a horizontal break. Traverse left and then follow cracks and corners up left to a good belay ledge below a slanting corner. **Pitch 5:** Climb the right side of a sharp flake in the corner (5.8). Continue up the corner to a summit belay. **Descent:** Walk east along the top of the cliff and do 3 double-rope rappels down *Coke Bottle*. **Rack:** Wires and a generous selection of small to large cams.

12. **Waterstreak Delight** (III 5.10) 2 pitches. This edge and smear route makes an alternative face climbing start to Route 13. Begin just left of the huge left-facing dihedral in the center of the wall. **Pitch 1:** Move up left on an easy slab to a horizontal crack. Continue up the face above past 4 bolts (5.9 above last bolt) to a 2-bolt, semihanging belay. **Pitch 2:** Engaging face climbing (5.10) works up steep rock past 5 bolts before easing off. Join the *Coatimundi Whiteout* flake crack and jam up to an easy traverse to the right and a 2-bolt belay ledge. Climb the last 3 pitches of Route 14 to the crag's summit. **Rack:** Stoppers and a selection of medium and large Friends.

Climbers on the second pitch of *Coatimundi Whiteout* (III 5.9), Swamp Slabs at Granite Mountain.

13. **Coatimundi Whiteout/Candyland Finish** (III 5.9) 5 pitches. The crag's ultraclassic, must-do route. It is best to finish up with *Candyland* and keep the grade 5.9. The regular route traverses left under the Great Roof at 5.11 before climbing an easy groove to the summit. Begin in the middle of the wall beneath a huge, left-facing dihedral. **Pitch 1:** Climb up right (5.8) along a flake to the dihedral. Face climb and lieback the dihedral crack to a 2-bolt belay stance on the left. **Pitch 2:** Work up the dihedral to a small ledge with a bolt above it. Jam, lieback, chimney, and face climb up the large corner crack (5.8+) to an obvious traverse (5.7) that leads left 20' to a left-facing flake crack. Climb the fun crack to a small roof, then traverse right to a 2-bolt belay on a ledge. Watch rope drag on this pitch—use lots of runners. A good variation climbs the upper crack (5.9) instead of traversing. **Pitch 3:** Cruise a short, easy ramp crack (5.4) to a spacious ledge under the huge Great Roof. **Pitch 4:** Simply one of Arizona's wildest pitches! Climb a corner to the base of the 50-foot-wide roof and make a hand traverse (5.7) right past some fixed pitons and a bolt to an airy belay perch on the right side of the roof. **Pitch 5:** Work straight up the exposed, thin crack system above (5.9-) and past an ear roof. Jam the

crack up left to a final, right-angling crack (5.7) and a belay on top of the cliff. **Descent:** Walk east along the top of the cliff and do 3 double-rope rappels down *Coke Bottle*. **Rack:** Good selection of Friends, mostly medium and large, and a set of Stoppers.

14. **Candyland** (III 5.10-) 5 pitches. Another stunning, must-do line for the crack aficionado. The route ascends the prominent crack system right of *Coatimundi Whiteout*. Begin just right of the crack. **Pitch 1:** Face climb to a large flake. Jam around the flake and into the crack above. Work up the crack (5.9) to a bolt and jam the off-width crack above (5.10-) to a 3-bolt belay stance on the left. **Pitch 2:** Climb the crack (5.9) to a 2-bolt belay at the base of a ramp. **Pitch 3:** Lieback up the ramp crack and jam a spectacular crack (5.9) to a belay ledge directly under the Great Roof. **Pitch 4:** A great pitch! Climb a short crack and do an airy hand traverse (5.7) along a crack right under the roof, passing some fixed pins and a bolt, on your way to a belay ledge out right of the roof. **Pitch 5:** Jam a thin crack (5.9-) and pass a small roof on the left. Follow the crack up left and finish up a right-angling crack in a corner (5.7) to a belay on top of the cliff. **Descent:** Walk east along the top of the cliff and do 3 double-rope rappels down *Coke Bottle*. **Rack:** Wires and a generous selection of Friends, mostly medium and large.

15. **Classic** (II 5.7) 4 pitches. Well traveled and classic. This excellent route ascends a prominent dihedral system up the west side of The Flying Buttress, a large blocky pillar on the right side of the wall. Hike up the trail to its high point by some boulders. The line is directly north of here. The 1st pitch can be done two ways. The best line for the experienced leader is via *Crack Lover's Variation*; otherwise there is an easier start to the left. Both pitches are described. **Pitch 1:** For *Crack Lover's Variation* (5.8), locate an obvious splitter hand crack left of a left-facing corner. Jam this excellent crack (5.8 to start, then easier) to a spacious belay terrace with trees. Otherwise, scramble left through the oak brush to the base of a right-facing dihedral. Climb onto a block and belay. Work up the left crack on the side of a flake pillar to a traverse (5.6) right into a shallow hand crack. Climb to the belay terrace with trees. **Pitch 2:** Climb the obvious, wide chimney crack (5.4) to a good belay stance. **Pitch 3:** Work up a deep, V-shaped dihedral to a long, traversing roof. Jam past it on the left (5.7) to a second roof (5.6). Make a tricky step over and follow a right-diagonalling crack up a blank face to an okay belay stance atop The Flying Buttress. **Pitch 4:** To do the last pitch, shimmy down an edge to start. Alternatively, you can continue up the corner bypassing the "trick step" and then using the 1st bolt on the *High Exposure* pitch and a large Friend at

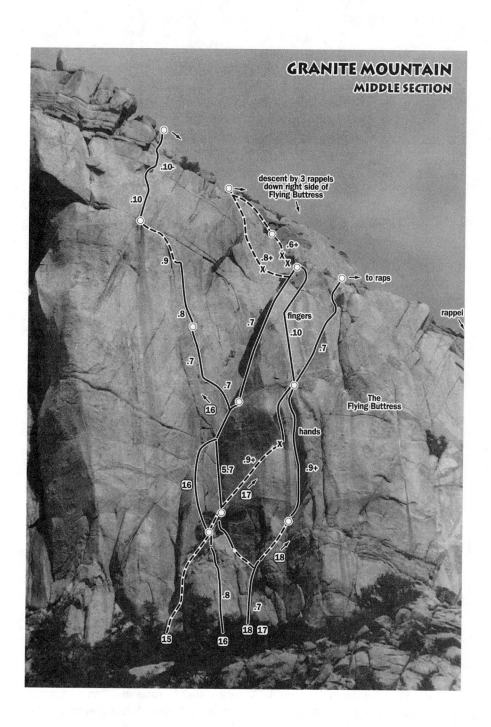

GRANITE MOUNTAIN
MIDDLE SECTION

.10-

descent by 3 rappels
down right side of
Flying Buttress

.10

.6+
.9   X   X
.8+ X
X

to raps

.8   rappel

fingers
.7   .10

.7
.7

16   The
Flying Buttress

hands
X
16   5.7   .9+   .9+

16   17

18

.8   .7

15   16   18 17

your feet for a belay anchor. (If you don't want to do pitch 4, go east through a hole and across a ledge to the rappel station atop *Coke Bottle*.) There are two exits off the buttress. Most *Classic* parties do the *High Exposure Exit* (5.6+). Move right and belay on the right side of the ledge. Climb up and right past 3 bolts to a gully. Scramble up and belay where convenient. *Beaver Cleaver* (5.8+) goes up left past a bolt to a short corner (5.7). Belay above a chockstone. **Descent:** Make 3 rappels down *Coke Bottle*. **Rack:** Stoppers and a good assortment of medium to large Friends.

16. **Slammer Jam** (III 5.10) 5 pitches. Beautiful, airy climbing on the steep wall left of *Classic*. The route begins at the second belay on *Classic*. The preferred way to reach this belay is by climbing both pitches of *Crack Lover's Variation*. For an easier start, climb the first 2 pitches of *Classic* (see Route 15's description). **Pitch 1:** For *Crack Lover's Variation* (5.8), find the obvious splitter hand crack left of a left-facing corner. Jam this fun crack (5.8) to a good belay by a tree. **Pitch 2:** Jam the crack directly behind the tree (5.7). When it reaches the top of the pillar, climb up right along a crack to *Classic's* second belay. **Pitch 3:** Jam a crack (5.7) to the base of a thin, right-facing corner. Traverse up left to another crack and then follow it (5.7) up to a traverse (5.8) leading right to a small belay stance above the right-facing corner. **Pitch 4:** Jam a splitter crack to a step left (5.9) into a short left-facing corner that arches to an exposed belay ledge. **Pitch 5:** Work up the right-facing corner (5.10-), which becomes a splitter crack. Traverse right (5.10a) under the small roof above and follow the crack to summit belay ledges. **Descent:** 3 double-rope rappels down *Coke Bottle*. **Rack:** Stoppers, TCUs, and Friends.

17. **Reunion** (II 5.10-) 4 pitches. First ascent by Scott Baxter and Karl Karlstrom in 1971. A fine tick for visitors. The best route combination is to do the first 2 pitches of *Said and Done*, the finger crack pitch of *Reunion*, then finish up *Beaver Cleaver*. Begin just right of *Crack Lover's Variation* below an obvious open book. **Pitch 1:** Work up the broken, left-facing dihedral with liebacks and stems (5.6) to a large belay ledge with trees. **Pitch 2:** Climb a short way up the main crack in the huge dihedral above to a hanging ramp. Face climb up right on the ramp (5.9+) to a stance with 1 bolt and a poor nut placement below a small thumb/dihedral. Belay here or continue up the lieback on the left side of the thumb (strenuous 5.9+) and belay on top at the base of a beautiful finger crack. **Pitch 3:** A dream pitch! Jam a thin, arching finger crack (5.10-) that splits the steep wall. Follow it up right to a belay atop The Flying Buttress. **Pitch 4:** Do either *High Exposure Exit* (5.6+) or *Beaver Cleaver* (5.8+) to the summit. *High Exposure* face climbs up

right (5.6+) past 3 bolts to a gully and a higher belay ledge. *Beaver Cleaver* works directly up the face past a bolt (5.8+) to a right-facing corner (5.7). Pass a chockstone and find a belay. **Descent:** 3 double-rope rappels down *Coke Bottle* on the right side of The Flying Buttress. **Rack:** Mostly small and medium stuff including Stoppers, TCUs, and Friends.

18. **Said and Done** (II 5.9+) 4 pitches. First free ascent in 1971 by Rusty Baillie and Jack Hauck. Just another classic Flying Buttress crack line. For a 3-star route, climb the first 2 pitches of *Said and Done* and the finger crack pitch on *Reunion*, then finish up *Beaver Cleaver*. Start just right of Route 17. **Pitch 1:** Move up a crack that arches up right (5.7) to an obvious right traverse along a broken rock band. Belay at a small stance from gear and a single bolt. **Pitch 2:** Lieback up a left-facing corner (5.9+) that becomes a good hand crack and leads up the right side of a thumb pillar. Belay atop the pillar (same as *Reunion*). **Pitch 3:** Climb the right-angling open book up right (5.7) to the top of The Flying Buttress. **Pitch 4:** Climb one of the 2 exit pitches—*High Exposure Exit* or *Beaver Cleaver*—to the top of the wall. (See *Reunion* for description). **Descent:** 3 double-rope rappels down *Coke Bottle*. **Rack:** Stoppers and a good selection of medium to large cams.

RIGHT SECTION

Past The Flying Buttress, there is another large right-facing dihedral, which forms the right side of the buttress. *Coke Bottle* (5.7) climbs the dihedral in three pitches to the top of the buttress. Descend *Coke Bottle* via three double-rope rappels. *Twin Cracks* (5.12a) works up thin double cracks on the left wall of the dihedral. The steep, slabby wall right of the large dihedral offers several routes, the best of which is *Falling Ross*.

Walk west along the brushy trail at the base of the cliff to the white wall right of the large dihedral. Route 19 ascends the left side of this wall.

19. **Falling Ross** (5.10) 2 pitches. First ascent by Larry and Becky Treiber in 1969. Superb jamming. The route was named for Paul Ross, one of Larry's partners. Begin at the base of the large open dihedral (*Coke Bottle*). **Pitch 1:** Climb a short way up the main dihedral crack to a dead tree. Face climb out right and follow flakes and cracks up to a small, triangular roof. Jam a finger crack (5.9+ at start) that arches up right (some vegetation). Follow to the second left-angling crack. Exit left up this crack (5.9) to another crack system that angles up right to a horizontal crack. Traverse right to a hand crack over a bulge and belay on the terrace with trees. **Pitch 2:** Move the belay left of the trees. Jam the obvious, sustained splitter hand crack (5.10) to a small

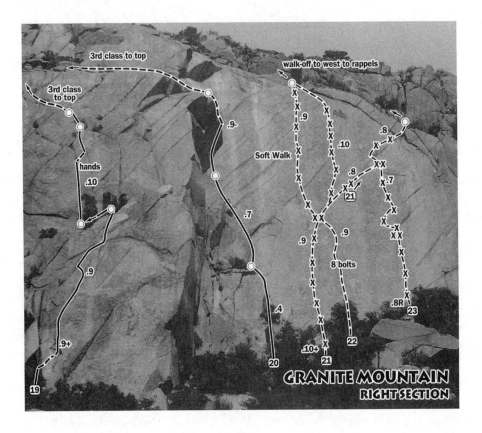

roof. Traverse right to another crack. Jam up (5.9) past a small tree to cracks that lead to a belay ledge. **Pitch 3:** Jam a thin crack (5.10-) for 45'. **Descent:** Scramble up and left in a class 3 gully to the crag summit. Make 3 double-rope rappels down *Coke Bottle*. **Rack:** Good assortment of Stoppers, TCUs, and Friends with extra hand-sized.

20. **Chieu Hoi (II 5.9)** 3 pitches. First ascent by Scott Baxter and Karl Karlstrom in 1971. The route ascends a prominent, right-facing dihedral on the left side of the immense, blank slab on the right side of the cliff. Begin below the dihedral. **Pitch 1:** Climb the dihedral (5.4) to a good belay ledge. **Pitch 2:** Continue up the dihedral, beginning with a hand crack/lieback above the belay to large flakes. Finish up wider cracks to a spacious ledge with trees. **Pitch 3:** Lieback the thin crack (5.9-) up a superb, right-facing dihedral to an obvious hand traverse left (5.9). Belay on a good ledge. A variation, *Short Man*, continues up the dihedral (5.8) to a point where you can traverse left and downclimb a crack (5.6) to the same belay. This variation is very scary for the

second. **Descent:** Scramble class 3 left along ramps and gullies to the top of the crag, then do 3 double-rope rappels down *Coke Bottle*. **Rack:** Stoppers and small to large Friends.

21. **Thin Slice** (II 5.10d R) 3 pitches. First ascent by Marty Woerner and John Diaz in 1971. Sustained face climbing with a scary, runout crux to the 1st bolt. Start uphill to the right of Route 20 below the left line of bolts. **Pitch 1:** Thin, hard-to-read face climbing (5.10d) to 1st bolt. Continue up easier but still thought-provoking face climbing on flakes, edges, and smears to a 2-bolt belay anchor in a scoop. 6 bolts. An alternative start begins at the base of *Chieu Hoi*. Climb up right past a bolt (5.10-) and join the route at the 2nd bolt. **Pitch 2:** Work up right along a right-angling seam past two bolts and a fixed piton. Step right and belay on *Bleak Streak*'s upper belay ledge. Look for some tricky below-the-feet wire placements on this pitch. **Pitch 3:** Face climb up left to a bolt, then back right past a bolt. Make tricky friction moves under a roof. Exit through a crack and belay above. (*Soft Walk Variation* makes a good, direct finishing pitch 2 rated at 5.9. From the first belay, move up left over a steep headwall past a bolt to a diagonal seam. Work back right and follow flakes left of a water streak to a prickly pear cactus on a narrow ramp. Climb up left and belay at the pine tree above the wall. 6 bolts.) **Descent:** Scramble up Class 3 rock above the belay to the top of the wall. Make 3 double-rope rappels down *Coke Bottle,* or hike east and south around the east buttress of the crag and then back along the base of the cliff to your packs. **Rack:** Quickdraws and some small Stoppers and RPs.

22. **For Pete, Thanks** (II 5.10a) 2 pitches. Continuous face climbing up the center bolt route. Begin below the middle line of bolts, right of Route 21. **Pitch 1:** Face moves (some 5.9) lead straight up past 8 bolts to Route 21's 2-bolt belay. **Pitch 2:** Work up right along a seam and then up the face past 6 bolts (.10a). Above the last bolt, angle up left to the last bolt of *Soft Walk*. Then go left to a narrow groove/ramp with a prickly pear cactus. Clip the bolt on the headwall and climb to the obvious pine tree above and belay. 7 bolts. **Descent:** Scramble up class 3 rock above the belay to the top of the wall. Make 3 rappels down *Coke Bottle,* or hike east and south around the east buttress of the crag and then back along the base of the cliff to your packs. **Rack:** Quickdraws and some small gear.

23. **Bleak Streak** (II 5.8 R) 3 pitches. The right-hand face route. Recommended, fun moves, but very scary getting to the 1st bolt. Some accidents have occurred. Begin uphill and right of Route 22 by an oak tree. **Pitch 1:** Pull up onto the top of an indistinct block/pillar and follow a right-angling seam (5.8 R/X crux) to the 1st bolt about 35'

up. Don't deck here because it's a groundfall! It may be possible to rig some pro in a small crack or in an empty bolt hole (chopped bolt) by the pillar. Continue above past 2 more bolts (5.7), then angle up left to a 3-bolt, semihanging belay. If you fall off the crux moves, you'll probably end up in a tree. **Pitch 2:** Work out left to a bolt, then climb back right above the belay to another bolt. Climb up right past 2 more bolts (5.7) to a belay ledge with a 3-bolt anchor. Expect steep edging and 5.7 moves above bolts. Pitches 1 and 2 can be combined into a 160' lead to avoid the foot pain of the semihanging belay. **Pitch 3:** Climb up left to a bolt and then traverse right along a groove/seam past a bolt to an overlap. Traverse right under the overlap to a large crack. Pull over the overlap and belay above on a ledge. **Descent:** Scramble up class 3 rock above the belay to the top of the wall, hike east and south around the east buttress of the crag, and then back along the base of the cliff to your packs. **Rack:** Quickdraws and some small to medium Stoppers, TCUs, and Friends.

KING DOME

OVERVIEW

King Dome perches on a lofty ridge high above Poland Creek and its steep canyon atop the Bradshaw Mountains. The immense, south-facing dome, at 6,200 feet, yields a selection of excellent, bolt-protected face and slab routes, along with some fine crack climbs. The crag, composed of hard, flawless granite, is darkened by occasional water streaks and broken by dihedral systems. The one- and two-pitch face routes are generally sewn up with 3/8-inch bolts and bolted belay and rappel anchors. Occasional runouts are found on easier sections.

Descent: The descent is accomplished by rappelling the routes with double ropes, although some of the crack routes require walking off. **Rack:** A dozen quickdraws and two 165-foot ropes are all that is needed for a day of sport climbing. All the crack routes require a rack of Stoppers and small to large cams.

Climbing history: The first climbing done in the Crown King area was on Castle Rock, a small quartzite cliff south of town, in 1974. The obvious King Dome didn't see a recorded ascent until 1988, when Ted Olson, Phil Falcone, and James Graves jammed a few of the best crack lines and bolted the first route, *The Final Solution*. In the 1990s, the rest of the lines were bolted and climbed by Olson, Falcone, Richie Eastman, and Marty Karabin. *Death by Agave*, the dome's hardest route, was put up by Mike Covington and Jay Anderson in 1993.

The Crown King area is packed with Arizona's early mining history. The town of Crown King, now a small vacation hamlet, was once a thriving community. The Crown King Mine, up a draw north of town, brought a frenzy of gold diggers to the Bradshaw Mountains. The mine, established in 1870, produced more than $1.5 million in gold ore. The town boomed, with more than 500 buildings, plus electricity and phone service, by the end of the century. After gold profits declined, Crown King fell into a long funk until it was rediscovered. The general store and saloon have been in business for more than a century and are worth a visit after a day of cragging. The ghost town of Cleator, on the road up to Crown King, began as Turkey Creek Station in 1864 and is one of the oldest settlements in central Arizona. The road between Cleator and Crown King was originally a railroad route built by Chinese laborers.

TRIP PLANNING INFORMATION

General description: An immense granite crag, laced with excellent, bolted face routes, in the Bradshaw Mountains.

Location: Central Arizona, northwest of Phoenix.

Camping: An excellent primitive campsite is located off the rough road above the dome. Otherwise, primitive camping is available in Prescott National Forest, including a few good spots off Crown King Road (Forest Service Road 259) northeast of the cliff. Also, there are some national forest campgrounds in Horsethief Basin, southeast of Crown King.

Climbing season: October through April is best. Almost all the routes are south-facing and get lots of sun, making it a great winter crag. Climbing, despite the high elevation, is just about unbearable on any hot day during the other half of the year.

Restrictions and access issues: The dome is in Prescott National Forest. There are currently no restrictions or access problems. Pick up after yourself and look after the crag so we can keep it that way.

Guidebooks: *Crown King Rock Climbing Guide* by Marty Karabin, 1997 is a fold-out guide with good topos and descriptions to King Dome, Roadside Wall, and Fool's Gold Wall.

Nearby mountain shops, guide services, and gyms: None. Check in Prescott and Phoenix for gear, guides, and gyms.

Services: Very limited services in Crown King. Plan on having a full tank of gas, all your supplies, and water. Be sure to check out the classic Crown King General Store and Saloon. Prescott has the nearest complete services. Otherwise, try Cordes Junction, the intersection of Interstate 17 and Arizona Highway 69.

Emergency services: Call 911.

Nearby climbing areas: Nearby crags along the Crown King Road include Fool's Gold Wall above milepost 24 (*Steel Monkey*, 5.7 and excellent fun), a bunch of short walls at milepost 26, and the Roadside Wall just past milepost 26. Check Marty Karabin's fold-out, *Crown King Rock Climbing Guide*, for topos and descriptions to these walls. Castle Rock is a quartzite crag south of Crown King. *Phoenix Rock II* has route descriptions and directions. The Jacuzzi

Spires, east of Interstate 17 at Exit 238, is an obscure but good area with multipitch routes in Tonto National Forest. Check *Phoenix Rock II* for route descriptions and directions. Prescott area crags include the Granite Dells, Thumb Butte, Groom Creek Boulders, Granite Mountain, The Promised Land, Sullivan Canyon, Verde River crags.

Nearby attractions: Historic Crown King, Crown King Cemetery, Prescott National Forest recreation sites, Castle Creek Wilderness Area, Prescott, Granite Mountain Wilderness Area.

Finding the dome: King Dome is above Crown King Road (Forest Service Road 259) west of Interstate 17. Take Exit 259 off I-17 (Bloody Basin Interchange) about 3 miles south of Cordes Junction. Drive west 3.5 miles on a gravel road to Cordes, a road junction with a couple of houses. Turn left (south) and drive 6.4 miles on the gravel road to a Y-junction. Keep right and drive another mile to FR 259. Make a right (west) turn here and drive west on the dusty gravel road for a total of 26 miles from the interstate to a parking area on the left just past milepost 26 and a road cut. King Dome is the obvious, large cliff to the northeast. Allow about one-and-a-half hours of driving time from Phoenix to this parking area.

Scramble up through underbrush and past numerous small cliffs and boulders to the base of the dome. There isn't a trail, so pick the best way up. A good place to start is just down east of the parking area. Hike up a bouldery draw and then bushwhack up left to the cliff. Be sure to wear long pants; this hike is a total thrash. Hiking time to the cliff's base is about 45 minutes.

If you have a four-wheel-drive vehicle, a 2.5-mile driving approach begins in the town of Crown King, which is another mile up the road from the parking area, and ends atop the dome. If there is any snow at Crown King, do not attempt this drive because it will be impassable. At Crown King, turn right, cross the creek to the general store, and take the first right. This dirt road heads northeast past old houses and cabins to an obscure junction by a house on the right. If you get to the church you've gone too far. Turn right on this hidden road and put your vehicle in four-wheel-drive. Follow this rough, single-lane, dirt track for a couple of miles to a short road that heads right to the camping plateau and the top of the dome. A short trail begins at the camping area, heads southwest, and scrambles down the west side of the dome to its base. Allow 15 minutes hiking time. Another trail accesses a two-rope rappel station on the east side of the dome's summit slabs and a class 3 gully descent route farther east.

KING DOME

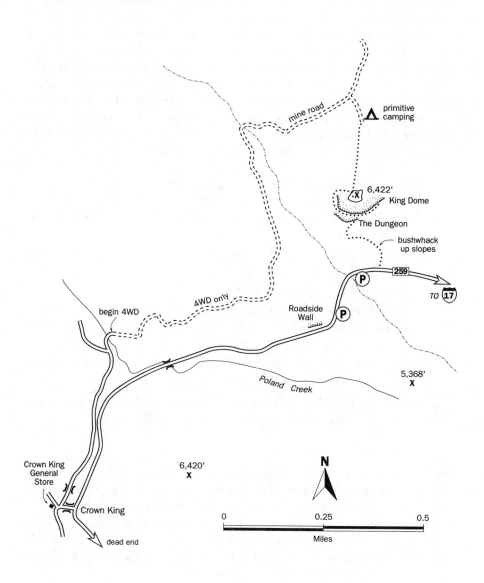

mine road

primitive
camping

6,422'
King Dome

The Dungeon

bushwhack
up slopes

259

P

TO 17

begin 4WD

4WD only

Roadside
Wall

P

5,368'
X

Poland Creek

Crown King
General
Store

6,420'
X

Crown King

dead end

N

0   0.25   0.5

Miles

THE DUNGEON

The routes on The Dungeon, the lower slab below the southwest corner of King Dome, are described first. The Dungeon is the lower apron on the left side of the dome. A ledge system marks the top of the face. Access it from the top by hiking down a trail along the left side of the cliff, or scrambling across the ledge above and following a good trail down the east side of the face. **Descent:** The easiest descent off the routes is by walking off the ledge to the right of the upper anchor and then scrambling back down a good trail to the cliff's base. Or, you can rappel from a two-bolt anchor on the bottom side of an overhang that is just above the big ledge system at the top of the cliff. Leave carabiners on the bolts and retrieve them later. Routes are described left to right.

1. **Return of the Falcon** (5.10a) A hard, bouldery start to a right-angling lieback and the 1st bolt 20' up. Edge up the bolted face. 4 bolts to 2-bolt anchor. **Descent:** A 2-rope rappel 120' from anchors, or walk off to the right.

2. **Dungeon Master** (5.10b/c) A boulder problem start, then up the slab to anchors. 5 bolts to 2-bolt anchor. **Descent:** A 2-rope rappel 120' from the 2-bolt anchor or walk off to the right.

3. **Perfect Victim** (5.10a) A fun route with good moves up the well-protected face. 6 bolts to 2-bolt anchor. **Descent:** A 2-rope rappel 120' from anchors or walk off to the right.

4. **The Rack** (5.9) Work up a long way to the 1st bolt, then cruise. 3 bolts to a tree anchor. **Descent:** Walk off to right.

5. **Iron Maiden** (5.8) On the right side of the slab. 3 bolts to a tree anchor. **Descent:** Walk off to right.

KING DOME

This large, south- and west-facing granite dome boasts a superb selection of bolted friction and face climbs. The massive, upper chunk of granite forms the bulk of King Dome. A ledge system lies below all the routes. Access the crag from the top by scrambling down a trail on the left (west) side. After the thrash approach from the road, it's best to access the ledge below the wall from the right side of The Dungeon. The routes on the main dome are described left to right from the far left (west) side of the crag.

THE DUNGEON AND KING DOME

6. **Kingsnake Crossover** (5.10a) No topo. The farthest route on the west side of the dome. Work up a left-angling hand crack past a bolt to its end. Step up right past another bolt into another crack/groove system. Jam to the rounded summit and belay off a tree. **Descent:** Scramble down the trail on the west side to the route's base. **Rack:** Large wired nuts and a good selection of small and medium cams.

7. **All Jazz and No Juice** (5.10b) No topo. Good sport line on the face just left of a deep chimney. Climb the face just right of a prow. Pass the small roof on the left. 9 bolts to 2-piton anchor. **Descent:** Rappel 140' with double ropes to the base.

8. **The Black Plague** (5.9) No topo. The slabby face immediately left of a leaning, off-width crack. Climb the face to a ledge and belay. Scramble up easy rock to the top. 6 bolts to ledge belay. **Descent:** Walk off to the west.

9. **The Split Cracks** (5.10a) Just right of a large, right-facing dihedral. Follow a hand crack to its end and move right past a bolt into another crack system. Continue up the thin crack to a 2-cold shut anchor. 75'. **Descent:** Rappel 75' to the base. **Rack:** Wires and small to medium cams.

10. **Living on the Edge** (5.10c) 3-star sport route up the outer edge of a prominent buttress. Edge up right and climb the exposed, blunt arête to anchors right of the arête. 7 bolts to 2 cold-shut anchor. **Descent:** Rappel or lower 75'.

11. **Death by Agave** (5.12b) 2 pitches. **Pitch 1:** Work up a left-facing flake to strenuous jamming up a steep finger crack. Carefully move past an agave and finish up a bulging, wide finger crack to a ledge belay below a chimney. **Pitch 2:** Work up the corner chimney to the summit and a 2-bolt belay anchor. **Descent:** Rappel 140' with double ropes from 2-bolt anchor. **Rack:** Wires and a generous selection of small to medium cams.

12. **The Peasant** (5.8) 2 pitches. **Pitch 1:** Edge up a slab and move left to a large, perched boulder. Pull around the right side and thrash left through a tree to a belay below a prominent, off-width crack. **Pitch 2:** Jam a dirty hand crack on the face right of the off-width to the top and a tied-off tree belay. **Descent:** Scramble right along a ledge system to Route 16's anchors and rappel 165' to the ground with double ropes, or make 2 single-rope rappels (80' each) from anchors. **Rack:** Small to large cams.

13. **Flight of the Falcon** (5.6 R) A good, easy trad route. Begin at the same place as Route 12 below an open book. Climb the corner and a slab to a stance, then right up cracks to a bolt. Continue up right to a ledge and climb a narrow, right-angling corner to a 2-piton anchor on a high ledge. 165'. **Descent:** Rappel 165' with double ropes from 2-piton anchor. **Rack:** Wires and a generous assortment of mostly small and medium cams and nuts.

14. **Runaway Train** (5.9) A long, slab pitch up the wall right of the right-angling corner. 11 bolts to 2-piton belay. 160'. **Descent:** Rappel 165' with double ropes from 2-piton anchor (same as Route 13).

15. **From Dimples to Pimples** (5.10b) A great, shorter route. Begin just right of Route 14. Climb a short, right-facing corner and then face climb above to an anchor below and right of a thin, right-facing corner. 5 bolts to 2-piton anchor. 80'. **Descent:** Rappel 80' from 2-piton anchor.

16. **Unfinished Business** (5.9+) 2 pitches. Excellent and fun face climbing. **Pitch 1:** Climb a left-angling groove and then up the slabby face to anchors. 9 bolts to 2-piton anchor. 80'. **Pitch 2:** Step left and work up a thin, right-facing corner to its top. Lieback and jam the right-angling corner above and then an easy slab to a 2-piton anchor at a horizontal crack. **Descent:** Two rappels (80' each) to the ground or a double-rope rappel for 165'. **Rack:** For pitch 2, small to medium nuts and cams.

17. **Tales of the Unexpected** (5.10b) Recommended. Fun edges and smears up a long, dark face. After the last bolt, move up right to a 2-bolt anchor. 9 bolts to 2-bolt chain anchor. **Descent:** Rappel 120' with double ropes.

18. **Kings and Queens and Guillotines** (5.10c) Sporty face climbing leads to an eyebrow-shaped roof. Pull past and finish up a well-protected headwall to a 2-bolt anchor. 10 bolts to 2-bolt chain anchor. **Descent:** Rappel for 120' with double ropes.

19. **Court Jester** (5.10a) 2 pitches. **Pitch 1:** Face climb up right along a right-angling seam past 7 bolts in a shallow corner to a 2-bolt anchor on a ledge. 70'. **Pitch 2:** Traverse left to a bolt, then up a headwall to anchors up left on a slab (same anchors as Route 17). 5 bolts to 2-bolt chain anchor. **Descent:** Rappel 120' with double ropes to the ground.

20. **It's Good to Be the King** (5.10b) 2 pitches. **Pitch 1:** Face climb (5.9) for 70' past 7 bolts to a 2-bolt anchor on a ledge. **Pitch 2:** Move right and climb up (5.10b) past 4 bolts on a headwall to easier rock and a belay from boulders atop the cliff. 110'. **Descent:** Walk off.

21. **The Peasants Are Revolting** (5.10b) Marty Karabin calls it a "classic slab route." Begin off the left side of a ledge system. Face climb directly up past 5 bolts to a stance. Work up right onto a 3-bolt headwall and finish up a final, easy slab topped with anchors. 8 bolts to 2-bolt anchor. **Descent:** Rappel 140' with double ropes.

22. **Full Armor** (5.10b/c) A long, well-protected sport lead. Start right of Route 21 on the ledge. Climb past 2 bolts to a small ledge on the left side of a large flake, then up a long, varnished face to slab anchors (same as Route 21). 13 bolts to 2-bolt anchor. **Descent:** Rappel 140' with double ropes.

23. **The Final Solution** (5.10d) Begin off the far right side of the ledge system. Climb the right side of a flake to a ledge on top. Work up the slabby face above between two large gray spots to the upper slab. Angle up left on easy rock to Route 21's anchors. 5 bolts to 2-bolt anchor. **Descent:** Rappel 140' with double ropes. **Rack:** Wires and small to medium cams.

24. **Dragon Slayer** (5.10c) Superb and recommended. On the far right side of the cliff. Edge up the slab right of the large, gray spot to a tree belay above the left-facing dihedral. 9 bolts to tree belay. **Descent:** Rappel 140' with double ropes from Route 23's anchors.

25. **Red Dragon** (5.9+) A fine climb up the obvious, left-facing dihedral on the right (east) side of the dome. Belay from a tree above the dihedral. **Descent:** Rappel 140' with double ropes from Route 23's anchors. **Rack:** Good selection of gear including wires and small to large cams.

OTHER PRESCOTT AREAS

OVERVIEW

There are a lot of other climbing areas around Prescott, in addition to The Granite Dells, Granite Mountain, and King Dome. Most of these areas offer good cragging on small cliffs. Rock types include granite, quartzite, and basalt. Most of the crags have a combination of sport and traditional routes in a wide variety of grades, as well as topropes and many boulder problems. For more information on these lesser-known areas, contact one of Prescott's climbing shops for topos, directions, and guidebooks.

THUMB BUTTE

Thumb Butte, a volcanic plug that towers to the west over Prescott, offers an excellent selection of devious face and clean crack routes up to 250 feet long. Most of the best lines ascend the shady north face, making the butte a good getaway on warm days. The cliff, lying in Prescott National Forest, is easy and quick to get to from town. The butte's rock is better than it appears at first glance, with crisp edges, sinker pockets, and occasional jugs. Some bolted sport lines are found, but most routes require gear placements between bolts. A few classics include *Sunshine Slab* (5.6), *Yellow Edge* (5.8), *Pickle Relish* (5.9), *Mecca* (5.9), *Thunder Roof* (5.10a), and *Acrobatic Flying* (5.12a). Find maps, route descriptions, and topos in pioneering climber Rusty Baillie's comprehensive guidebook, *Thumb Butte*, available in mountain shops in Prescott.

SOUTHERN GRANITE MOUNTAIN WILDERNESS

After the peregrine falcon began its comeback in central Arizona and Granite Mountain was closed to climbing for half the year, Prescott climbers began exploring the many small crags scattered across the south part of the Granite Mountain Wilderness Area. Some very fine routes were established, making it a good alternative when the main cliff is closed in spring. Lizard Head, the obvious, bullet-shaped formation south of Trail 261, yields some little-known gems. Rusty Baillie and David Lovejoy put up most of the routes in the 1970s. Some of the best routes are *Why Oh Why* (5.9), *The Great White Way* (5.10), and the classic *West Ridge* (5.6). Waves of Rock, a good-looking slab west of Clark Springs (Trail 40), has some great beginner lines including *Hang Ten* (5.4) and *Banzai* (5.6). Ask in Prescott for information on these cliffs.

GROOM CREEK BOULDERS

The Groom Creek Boulders, scattered in the pine woods south of Prescott, is one of Arizona's best bouldering areas. The jumbled, granite boulders yield numerous problems that range from V0 to V8, with lots of classics in the lower bouldering grades. Marty Karabin's fold-out topo guide lists 106 problems on

40 boulders. Good ticks include *Rayan's Fave* (V0), *The Brat Pack* (V3), *The Wave* (V0+), *The Wave Arête* (V2), and *Classic Crack* (V2). Sand and pine needles under the problems make landings safe if you forget the crash pad. Bill Cramer's *Prescott Bouldering Guide*, available in local shops, details most of Groom Creek's problems along with lots of other bouldering opportunities around Prescott.

The relatively high elevation, 6,200 feet, makes Groom Creek a good choice whether it's winter or summer. The compact area is on public land in Prescott National Forest.

Finding the boulders: Drive into Prescott on Gurley Street. Turn south on Mt. Vernon Street before you drop down a hill to downtown Prescott. Outside of Prescott, the street becomes the Senator Highway. Follow the paved road for 6.7 miles to a dirt road on the left marked "Camp Wamatochick." Turn left (east) here and park at an obvious parking area just off the highway. Walk north along forested Trail 307, a hiking and mountain biking trail, for a few hundred feet. The boulders are straight ahead below and right of the power lines. After the trail bends right, look for a climber's path that heads left through the open woods to the first boulders. If you don't have a guidebook, explore around. The problems are obvious on the many boulders.

SULLIVAN CANYON

North of Prescott, the Verde River meanders across wide Chino Valley before slicing eastward through layers of basalt in Sullivan Canyon. In the canyon below Sullivan Lake, there is a fine climbing area with short cracks and excellent stone. The smooth, compact basalt makes for painless jamming up its vertical cracks on the 50-foot-high cliffs. Many of the faces have also been climbed using crisp edges and small pockets. This is a no-bolt area, so come prepared to either lead with a rack or toprope the routes to maximize the pump factor. Sullivan Canyon is a good, sunny winter climbing area.

Five developed areas are found in Sullivan Canyon. Goff's Buttress, on the east end of the north cliff, offers some of the canyon's longest routes up steep crack systems. The Cyclops Eye area, on the north cliff just west of the gas pipeline that spans the canyon, has many hard face climbs. On the south cliff are three main areas. Morgan Ranch is at the east end of the south cliff. Access it from the parking lot on the north rim and descend a trail through broken limestone and across the river. You'll find lots of good cracks and steep arêtes. The other two areas—Petroglyph Area and Twin Cracks Area—are on the south cliff to the west of the gas pipeline. Approach these areas by parking at the dam and hiking down the canyon to the base of the cliff, or by walking along the south rim and rappelling in. The Petroglyph Area, just east of a bridge, has a good assortment of moderate cracks. Don't climb on or near the petroglyphs. Farther east, locate the Twin Cracks Area, a north-facing cliff with some fine, moderate cracks and a few hard face climbs.

Farther east of Sullivan Canyon are more basalt cliffs with both bolted face routes and crack climbs. Information, topos, and directions to these cliffs are found in Josh Gross's guidebook, *Verde Basalt,* available in Prescott mountain shops.

Finding the cliffs: Drive north from Prescott or south from Ash Fork/Interstate 40 on Arizona Highway 89. If you're driving from the north, turn southeast at the small town of Paulden and follow a road down to Sullivan Lake. From Prescott and the south, drive 13.25 miles north of the airport to a historical marker at Del Rio Springs. Turn right here and drive north to the dam at Sullivan Lake. Park in a lot at the dam on the west side of the road. Reach the north cliffs by hiking along the rim across state trust land to the far east side of the cliffs. Descend through broken limestone to the canyon floor. To access the south cliffs, hike right along the rim and rappel in, or hike down the south side of the canyon from the dam. The land south of the canyon is private property.

THE PROMISED LAND

The Promised Land is an excellent sport climbing area with over 30 bolted routes on horizontally banded quartzite along Granite Creek northeast of Prescott and the town of Chino Valley. The area is remote and somewhat hard to find, but it's well worth the effort. The area is divided into three main areas—Solomon, Valerie's Book, and Star Trek. Ask around in Prescott for topos to the cliffs—a guidebook is sometimes available to the area. To reach The Promised Land, drive almost 4 miles east of Chino Valley and Arizona Highway 89 on Perkinsville Road. Turn north and drive 5.6 miles on a series of rough, dirt roads. A high-clearance or four-wheel-drive vehicle is nice to have on these roads.

FLAGSTAFF AREA

OAK CREEK OVERLOOK

OVERVIEW

The Oak Creek Overlook is a spectacular viewpoint perched high above the confluence of Oak Creek and Pumphouse Wash on the edge of the Mogollon Rim south of Flagstaff. The Overlook is justifiably popular with tourists, who stop to marvel at the dramatic views into the abrupt canyons. Native American vendors sell turquoise jewelry to the tourists, and rock climbers come to jam up what is probably northern Arizona's most popular crag.

The Overlook, a 0.5-mile-long basalt cliff band that rims the canyon, offers climbers numerous crack routes from 30 to 80 feet long within a five-minute walk from the parking lot. A few face routes—mostly topropes—climb blank faces and arêtes between crack systems. The Overlook, unlike the steeper cliffs at nearby Paradise Forks, offers climbers a wide range of moderate routes with about half the climbs under 5.10. Be advised, though, that most visiting climbers find that the 5.6 to 5.10 traditional routes here and elsewhere in northern Arizona have conservative ratings. It's best to lead the routes here rather than toprope because of loose rock along the rim and because many of the trees on the top of the cliff are close to death from being used for toprope anchors.

Climbing history: The Overlook was one of the first climbing areas developed in northern Arizona. Flagstaff's famed Syndicato Granitica, a loosely formed climbing club, began regularly climbing here in 1971. Local hardmen Scott Baxter, Lee Dexter, and Tom Taber climbed many of the cracks in the 1970s, leaving only a handful of thin crack and face climbing problems for 1980s climbers to pursue. The three classic cracks on the Trinity Cracks Sector, protected by early nuts, were jammed in 1972.

This south-facing cliff, a mere 20 minutes south of Flagstaff, boasted over 100 routes a few years back, but Coconino National Forest has since closed the cliff directly below the vista point at the Oak Creek Overlook to climbing. This was done mainly to protect climbers at the cliff's base from falling objects, including rocks and full soda cans, hurled by unwitting tourists above, and to

FLAGSTAFF CLIMBING AREAS

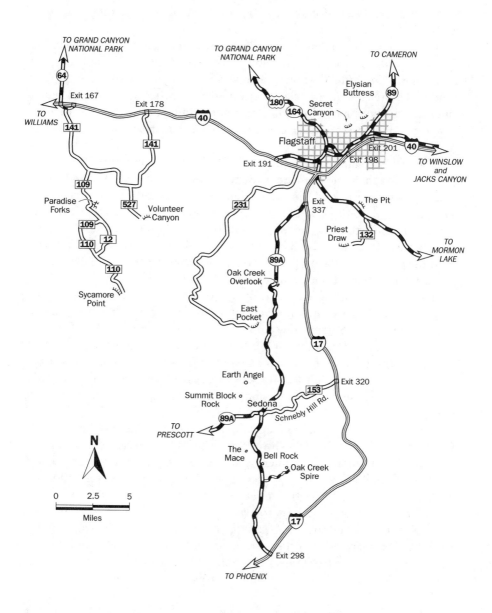

TO GRAND CANYON
NATIONAL PARK

TO GRAND CANYON
NATIONAL PARK

TO CAMERON

64

Exit 167

Elysian
Buttress

89

TO
WILLIAMS

141

Exit 178

180

Secret
Canyon

164

40

Flagstaff

Exit 201

40

141

Exit 191

Exit 198

TO WINSLOW
and
JACKS CANYON

109

Paradise
Forks

527

Volunteer
Canyon

231

Exit
337

The Pit

Priest
Draw

132

TO
MORMON
LAKE

109

110

12

89A

Oak Creek
Overlook

110

Sycamore
Point

East
Pocket

17

Earth Angel

Exit 320

Summit Block
Rock

153

Sedona

Schnebly Hill Rd.

N

89A

TO
PRESCOTT

The
Mace

Bell Rock

Oak Creek
Spire

0   2.5   5

Miles

17

Exit 298

TO PHOENIX

prevent the tourists from falling off the cliff while watching the climbers below. Rangers will ticket climbers who violate the ban. However, the cliffs behind (east of) the restrooms and information booth on the east side of the parking area are still open. They are easily reached by following a climber's trail that runs east along the rim for about 200 yards to an obvious descent gully on the east end of the cliff band.

Before venturing down to the cliffs, take a moment to walk around the Overlook and view the canyons below. Oak Creek Canyon is a transition zone between the Colorado Plateau to the north and the arid Sonoran Desert to the south. The area's dramatic elevation differences create a jumbled mosaic of climates and an amazing number of plant communities from the towering ponderosa pine forest on the canyon rims to the chaparral and cacti on the dry slopes below.

The rock formations exposed in Oak Creek Canyon, easily viewed from the Overlook, are the same formations found below the rim of the Grand Canyon. The climber's rimrock is a hard, erosion-resistant basalt that was spewed as vast lava flows from the San Francisco Peaks to the north. Below the basalt is the Kaibab Limestone, deposited in a shallow sea 225 million years ago. Next, there is the cliff-forming Coconino Sandstone, which preserves fields of ancient sand dunes, and finally, on the canyon floor, there is the Supai Formation, a 280-million-year-old floodplain deposit.

The Overlook, at an elevation of 6,400 feet, offers year-round climbing weather. Some locals claim the Overlook yields more climbable days than any other Arizona crag. Summer days can be hot, but the south-facing cliff falls into comfortable shade by midafternoon. Afternoon thunderstorms are common in July and August. Autumn offers the best weather, with cool, crisp days. Sunny winter days often yield shirtless cragging, while the forest above is blanketed in snow. It can be bitterly cold and windy at the cliff's edge, but pleasantly warm at the base and on the cliff out of the wind.

The cliff, 10 miles south of Flagstaff, lies just east of the parking lot at Oak Creek Overlook off Arizona Highway 89A. The lot is often crowded with tourist cars and RVs in summer. In winter, if the overlook parking area is closed, park in the small pullout on the opposite side of the highway and walk 200 yards farther. There are public restrooms at the parking area, but no water.

All the cracks can be led. Try to avoid toproping at the Overlook. If you do toprope, use extreme care when setting your anchors, pad the rope where it runs over the sharp edge of the cliff, and avoid knocking rocks and boulders from the loose rim onto climbers at the cliff's base. Falling rock is the greatest objective danger here. Also watch out for wasps that inhabit many of the cracks.

Rack: All the routes at the Overlook require gear. Bring a varied rack that includes sets of RPs and Stoppers and double sets of Friends to #3.5 or Camalots to #3. Few cracks require a large piece like a #4 or #5 Camalot. Look at your proposed line and rack up accordingly. Topropers should bring an extra rope

OAK CREEK OVERLOOK

Trinity Cracks Sector · Jungleland Sector · Orange Out Sector · Duck Soup Sector · Cliff top Trail · descent · base trail

for tying off trees, as well as padding to protect the rope running over the cliff's edge. A helmet is a good idea, especially for belaying at the base due to the loose rock along the cliff rim. Bring an extra rope for a rappel line to avoid walking back to the base after each climb.

TRIP PLANNING INFORMATION

General description: Excellent and easily accessible crack climbing on a 20- to 80-foot basalt cliff that overlooks Oak Creek Canyon.

Location: North-central Arizona, just south of Flagstaff.

Camping: Several excellent national forest campgrounds (fee sites) are located in Oak Creek Canyon, south of the Overlook along Arizona 89A. Pine Flats Campground is the most convenient. Other campgrounds and cheap motels are plentiful in Flagstaff along Old Route 66.

Climbing season: Year-round. Spring and fall are best, with warm, sunny days. Summers can be hot, but the cliff is shaded in the afternoon. Winters are great, depending on the snowfall. The south-facing cliff is a good heat-trap on sunny winter days.

Restrictions and access issues: No climbing is allowed on the Overlook from the restrooms south and west to the highway. Tourists toss rocks and themselves off the cliffs here, making a dangerous situation even worse. Rangers will cite violators of the ban. The parking lot at the Overlook is sometimes closed in winter. Park at a highway pullout and hike from there.

Guidebooks: *A Cheap Way to Fly* by Tim Toula, 1991 is a good, no-frills guide that covers the Overlook, as well as many other northern Arizona crags. Look for a complete guide to the Overlook to be published soon.

Nearby mountain shops, guide services, and gyms: Aspen Sports, Babbitt's Backcountry Outfitters, Mountain Sports, Peace Surplus, Popular Outdoor Outfitters, Troll Mountaineering, and Vertical Relief Rock Gym (Flagstaff); Canyon Outfitters (Sedona).

Services: All services are found in Flagstaff, including cheap motels, lots of restaurants, and an interesting downtown area.

Emergency services: Call 911. Flagstaff Medical Center, 1200 North Beaver Street, Flagstaff, AZ 86601, 520-779-3366 or 800-752-2332; Walk In Clinic, 4215 North U.S. Highway 89, Flagstaff, AZ 86004, 520-527-1920.

Nearby climbing areas: Pumphouse Wash (*Ultimate Finger Crack* and *Ultimate Dihedral* are good), Oak Creek Canyon (the classic routes *Book of Friends* and *Dresdoom*, and the Oak Creek Waterfall area, with over 150 basalt routes); Sedona area (The Mace and many other soft sandstone nightmares); Paradise Forks (Arizona's best crack preserve!); Volunteer Canyon; East Pocket; Sycamore Point; Le Petit Verdon (limestone clip-ups); Elysian Buttress; and Mount Elden West (bouldering and short routes). Outstanding bouldering is found at several areas around Flagstaff, including Priest Draw, Buffalo Park, Gloria's Rocks, and West Elden.

Nearby attractions: Sedona area, San Francisco Peaks, Sunset Crater National Monument, Wupatki National Monument, Walnut Canyon National Monument, Museum of Northern Arizona (Flagstaff), Grand Canyon National Park, Navajolands, Meteor Crater.

Finding the crags: Drive south from Flagstaff to the junction of Interstates 40 and 17 on the south side of town. Head south on I-17 (Milton Road turns into I-17) for a couple of miles to Exit 337 (Oak Creek Canyon/Sedona). Turn right (west), then left (south) onto Arizona 89A and drive south through the pine forest for 8.5 miles to a sign that says "Oak Creek Viewpoint." Turn left (east) here and park in the large parking area. The gate enclosing the parking area is closed from 5:30 P.M. until 8 A.M. If there is any chance you will be climbing after 5:30 in the afternoon, park in the pullout across the highway or your car will be locked in.

To reach the cliff, walk east on a climber's trail along the canyon rim for a few hundred yards to an obvious trail that scrambles down to the east end of the cliff band. Walk right (west) along the cliff's base to access the routes.

OAK CREEK OVERLOOK

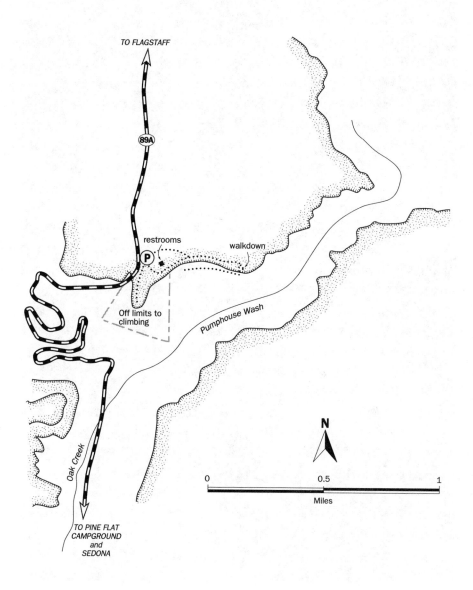

TO FLAGSTAFF

89A

restrooms

walkdown

P

Off limits to climbing

Pumphouse Wash

Oak Creek

N

0   0.5   1

Miles

TO PINE FLAT
CAMPGROUND
and
SEDONA

OAK CREEK OVERLOOK
"GRIFFO" AND "BUSH RUSH"

3rd class

OAK CREEK OVERLOOK
"NORMALLY 3 RURPS" AND "DUGALD'S ROUTE"

1. **Griffo** (5.6) At the bottom of the descent trail, walk right (west) to a good-looking, southeast-facing wall. Climb atop a pointed boulder and work into a shallow, left-facing corner with good liebacks. Continue up the corner to the top. 40'.

2. **Bush Rush** (5.9) Begin left of pointed the boulder at the cliff's base. Face climb up to a thin hand crack. Follow the finger and thin hand crack over a bulge to easier climbing and the top of the cliff. 45'. **Rack:** Small to medium Friends and Stoppers.

3. **Normally 3 Rurps** (5.6) Walk west around a blocky prow from Route 2 on a ledge trail for 75'. Start by a prominent juniper. Climb a crack system up broken blocks to a small roof. Continue around the corner right on easy rock to a juniper on the rim. 60'. **Rack:** Stoppers and cams to 2".

4. **Dugald's Route** (5.10-) Begin just left of Route 3. Jam over a small roof via a flared crack in a right-facing corner. Continue up corner with yellow lichen to a second roof, then undercling and lieback over into a scoop. Head up an obvious crack to the top. 60'. **Rack:** Stoppers, a set of cams, and runners.

DUCK SOUP SECTOR

5. **Burger King** (5.9-) Not climbed enough. Walk west on the trail at the base of the cliff for 50' from Route 4 past a broken cliff section. This route ascends a blocky buttress behind some oak trees. Face climb up the outside of the buttress to its top. Continue up easier rock behind to the rim. 70'.

6. **Obediah** (5.9-) Start 3 cracks and about 10' left of Route 5. Jam with left hand and face climb with right up a left-leaning, black crack. Above, move right on flakes past a bush onto a sloped ledge. Jam left in good cracks up a blocky arête to the rim of the cliff. 70'.

7. **Cakewalk** (5.12-) Often toproped. Walk left from Route 6 to a large boulder. Scramble 20' up easy rock to a belay ledge below an obvious, left-facing corner. Jam and stem up a thinning crack in the corner (5.12-). Above, the crack widens for good jams and handholds to the rim. 60'. **Rack:** RPs and a rack of cams.

8. **The Horn** (5.8) Begin 15' left of Route 7 on the lower ledge atop boulders. Thrutch up the obvious, off-width crack above. Easier but still wide cracks lead to the top of the cliff by a horn-like projection. Belay off a pine tree. 60'.

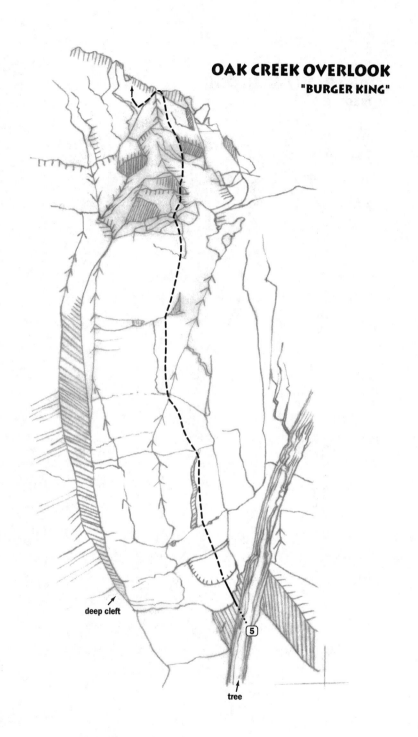

OAK CREEK OVERLOOK
"BURGER KING"

deep cleft

⑤

tree

OAK CREEK OVERLOOK

"OBEDIAH"

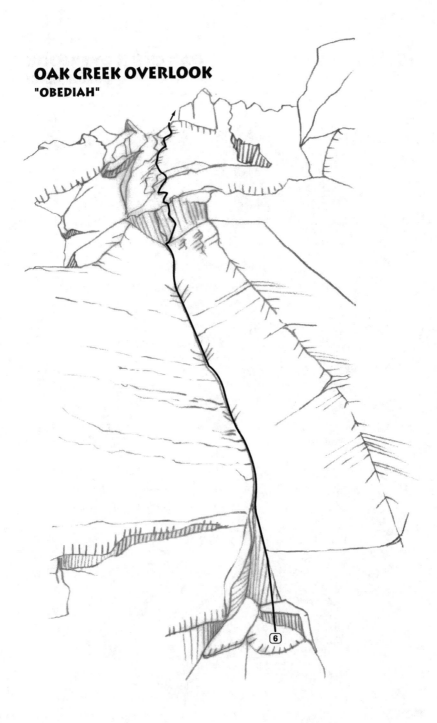

9. **George's Niche** (5.8) Just left of Route 8. Work up a short, overhanging off-width to a block on a small stance. Pleasant off-width climbing leads up good rock to a broken finish. Belay from a pine tree 60'.

10. **Duck Soup** (5.6) A fun moderate with tricky protection. Begin at ground level next to the large boulder and behind a juniper. Climb easy rock into a double crack system. Stem and jam up the cracks to a tree belay. 70'.

11. **Burnt Buns** (5.8) Locate a dead tree snag on a ledge left of Route 10. Scramble up 20' to a broken ledge right of the snag. Jam the obvious finger crack in the shallow corner above to the rim. 70'. **Rack:** Cams up to #5 if you use the right crack; otherwise, small gear.

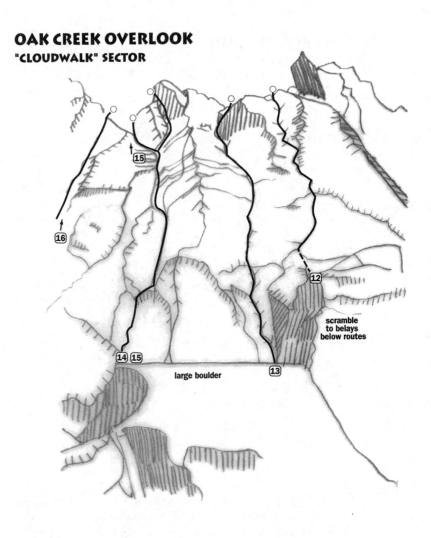

12. **Crackup** (5.9-) Scramble 30' onto a ledge left of the dead tree. Climb the finger and hand crack up the black slab above. 45' from ledge.

13. **Cloudwalk** (5.9+) 5' left of Route 12 on the ledge. Follow the thin face seam up and left to cactus on a small ledge. Finish on easier rock to the rim. 45' from ledge. **Rack:** RPs and Friends to #1.

14. **Wanderlust** (5.9+) Walk left along the cliff's base to a prominent juniper against the cliff. Move up easy rock to a stance below a broken corner. Climb broken rock with double cracks. Keep right onto a smooth face split by a hand crack. The thinning crack leads higher to obvious, black roof blocks. Exit right. 70'.

15. **Pegleg II** (5.8) Same start as Route 14. Keep left up the blocky corner with double cracks to blocky roofs. Turn lower roof on the left with a hand crack. 70'.

16. **Pegleg I** (5.9-) Begin 10' left of Route 15 on a ledge with agave plants above a juniper. Climb broken rock past an agave to a slab and left-facing corner. Continue up to a steep, black, left-facing corner. Follow it up and into a right-facing corner at the top. 50' from ledge.

ORANGE OUT SECTOR
Reach this sector by hiking west along the cliff's base for about 100-feet past a section of loose, vegetated cliffs. There are some good routes here.

17. **Answered Prayers** (5.9) A fun stemming route. Belay on the ground or at the base of a corner. Scramble up to a ledge behind a tall juniper growing out of a crack and begin on the ledge's right side below the obvious, black-streaked dihedral. Climb broken rock into the dihedral. Stem, jam, and lieback the thin crack to the top. See if all your prayers are answered. 70'. **Rack:** Wires, TCUs, and mostly small Friends.

18. **Sparky and the Firedog** (5.10-) Scramble up easy rock to the ledge behind the juniper. Belay here or from the ground. Awkward liebacks and jams lead up steep rock into a nice, right-facing corner. Jam and lieback a crack to the rim. 70'. **Rack:** Wires, TCUs, and Friends.

19. **Penicillin Debut** (5.11+) A toprope problem just left of Route 18. Pumpy face climbing up the orange streak on a black wall leads to easier climbing up a lower-angle arête.

20. **Orange Out Direct** (5.9+) One of the crag's best routes. Begin by scrambling 30' up easy rock to a broken ledge system. Jam an excellent hand crack up a left-facing corner to the base of the large, blocky roofs. The finish is surprisingly easy but wildly exposed! Hand jam up and over a roof to an overhanging slot. Chimney up the slot with good pro in the crack to a belay on the left at a prominent juniper on the rim. 70'. **Rack:** A good assortment of Friends including doubles from #1 to #2.

21. **Agent Orange** (5.11-) Climb easy rock 30' to a broken ledge. Climb up and into a left-facing corner 6' left of Route 20. Follow a thin crack up the corner and over the left side of a blocky roof. Continue face climbing to a thin crack and the rim left of a juniper and belay. 70'. **Rack:** Wires, TCUs, and Friends.

OAK CREEK OVERLOOK
ORANGE OUT SECTOR

354

Albert Newman on *Orange Out Direct* (5.9+) at Oak Creek Overlook.

22. **Orange Julius** (5.11-) Belay at cliff's base. Move up easy, broken corners for 30' to a ledge. Continue up steeper broken rock (hard to protect) to a slab broken by a thin crack. Hard edging leads to a thin crack. Belay by the juniper up top. This juniper is almost ready to fall off—watch out. 80'. **Rack:** Mostly Stoppers and RPs.

23. **Mint Julep** (5.9) Belay at the cliff's base. Climb easy corners for 30' to a ledge. Steep, shattered rock (hard to protect) leads to a narrow, right-facing corner. Face climb, jam, and stem the corner to a final easy slot left of the juniper on the rim. Look for a key fingerlock at the high crux. 80'. **Rack:** Wires, Aliens, and Friends.

24. **Morning's Mourning** (5.8) A classic hand crack. Climb easy rock 30' to a ledge with cacti. Work over broken blocks to a superb, right-facing corner system. Jam and lieback the excellent crack to the top. 80'. **Rack:** Stoppers and up to a Friend/Camalot #3.

JUNGLELAND SECTOR

Walk west along the cliff's base about 100 feet to the base of a tan wall lined with thin dihedrals. The first route begins on the right.

25. **Amateur Hour** (5.9) Start behind 2 large scrub oaks and left of a large dihedral with jagged cracks. Belay from the ground or scramble up to the base of the dihedral. Climb up the broken dihedral above to a large block, then angle left into a good crack in a right-facing corner. Jam hands and fingers up left to a broken crack system below a pointed roof. Go left of the roof to the rim. Or go straight and get a heel hook and hang upside down. **Rack:** Stoppers, TCUs, and cams to #2.

26. **Long Walk** (5.8) Just left of Route 25. Move up easy crack systems left of twin oaks to a large, broken ledge. Serious climbing begins off the right side of the ledge. Jam an off-width crack up an obvious, right-facing corner to the top. 60'.

27. **Fifty-Second Street** (5.11- TR) A toprope problem up an arête left of Route 26. Same start as *Long Walk* to the ledge. Toprope the prominent arête above. The first 20' are toughest, then cruise.

28. **Not Fade Away** (5.11d) Scramble up easy rock to a ledge, then stem and edge up a thin crack in a left-facing corner. **Rack:** RPs, small wires, TCUs.

29. **Jungleland** (5.11d) Start 6' left of Route 28 on a ledge. Hard stemming up a thin crack in a right-facing corner to the rim belay. 60'. **Rack:** Lots of small gear.

OAK CREEK OVERLOOK
JUNGLELAND SECTOR

27

26

25

28

31   30

29

33

32 31

30
31

3rd class

30. **Magical Mystery Tour** (5.11-) Another good one! Access a ledge below the route by climbing an easy, left-angling corner and stepping up right to the ledge. Jam and lieback up a thin crack and flakes in a right-facing corner left of a white streak. Continue up the crack system, then up left to a tight corner finish. 60'. Watch for wasps in summer. **Rack:** Small Stoppers, TCUs, and Friends to #2.

31. **Devil's Deed** (5.9) Same start as Route 30. Climb to the left side of the ledge. Work up a shallow right-facing corner for 15'. Step right into a good hand crack. Follow up right to a tight corner and the top. 60'. **Rack:** TCUs and up to a #3.5 Friend.

32. **Angel's Delight** (5.7) Begin at the cliff's base and climb broken rock up left in a shallow left-facing corner system to arête 40' up. Keep right up an obvious dihedral to an upper, overhanging finish. **Rack:** Up to a #3 Friend.

33. **Gingerbread** (5.7) Begin 10' left of Route 32 and right of a small juniper. Work up a shallow, black corner 20' to a roof. Move left over the roof and follow broken corners above to a small ledge. Continue up an excellent crack in a left-facing corner. Finish at a skyline juniper on the rim.

TRINITY CRACKS SECTOR

Walk west along the trail at the base of the cliff about 50 feet to the base of an obvious arête with three hand cracks splitting the wall of the arête.

34. **Jelly Roll** (5.8) Begin at a large juniper tree below and right of the obvious arête/prow. Climb the tree until you can step into an off-width crack. Climb a short slab to ledges. Stem up an easy corner and move right onto a ledge with a tree about 30' up. Jam the fist/off-width crack above and continue to the rim.

35. **Mint Jam** (5.7) Begin left of the juniper tree. Climb 15' up a slab to a ledge and an easy corner. Keep left, following double cracks up a left-facing dihedral to the top. This exit is tricky and 5.8.

36. **Isaiah** (5.9) Excellent and classic. The prominent crack right of the arête. Begin same as Route 35 or do the bouldery direct start (5.10-) by climbing thin cracks below the arête to a ledge at the base of a hand crack. Either way, jam the beautiful, overhanging hand crack up the brown wall. Exit right over a blocky roof to a final hand jam finish. 80'. **Rack:** Lots of hand-sized Friends.

OAK CREEK OVERLOOK
TRINITY CRACKS SECTOR

direct
start

37. **Right Trinity Crack** (5.10) The first of 3 hand cracks splitting a brown wall left of the prominent arête. Scramble onto boulders at the base of the face and belay. Climb flakes and cracks below *Left Trinity* and traverse right on flakes above a large roof to the crack nearest the arête. Jam the superb hand crack up and left to a large roof. Pull over the roof on blocks (5.9). Finish the crack (5.9) to a juniper tree on the rim's edge. 80'.

38. **Middle Trinity Crack** (5.10) Another great hand crack. Begin same as Route 37 but traverse right to the base of the middle crack. Jam the hand crack to a large roof. Hand traverse right and exit over a roof via blocks and a hand crack (5.9) to the belay at the juniper. 80'.

39. **Left Trinity Crack** (5.10-) Same start as other Trinity Cracks. Jam the hand crack to a large roof. Move right under the roof and pull over (5.9) on blocks to a hand crack (5.9) finish and the juniper belay at the rim. 80'. **Rack:** Friends up to #.5 with multiple #1.5s.

40. **Grunt 'n Dangle** (5.7) First it's a grunt, then it's a dangle! Work up an off-width in a right-facing dihedral, then hand traverse right under a roof and over the Trinity Cracks, continuing right to a ledge and up a 5.7 exit to the rim.

41. **Red Wagon** (5.8) A thin hand crack up the left wall of a large dihedral. Scramble up to boulders at the base and belay. Jam a sweet, thin hand crack up a steep face to blocky finishing moves. 70'.

THE PIT (AKA LE PETIT VERDON)

OVERVIEW

The Pit, also known as Le Petit Verdon, offers the best sport climbing routes in the Flagstaff area. Here, a series of broken, south-facing cliffs composed of steep Kaibab Limestone on the north side of Walnut Canyon offers hours of enjoyment for pocket aficionados. Almost all of the 140 or so routes are single-pitch, bolted sport routes that range in difficulty from 5.9 to 5.13d, with the majority being 5.10 and 5.11. Most of the cracks have also been done, but seldom see action due to their loose nature. Local climbers have climbed almost everything worth bolting here, leaving very few new route possibilities beyond some link-ups.

The area is literally a ten-minute drive and five-minute hike from Flagstaff, making it a good place to go for a quick pump. While the cliffs, at an elevation of 6,900 feet, offer year-round climbing, the prime season is March through November. Spring and autumn days are usually sunny but the air is cool. Summer days are often too hot for comfortable climbing on the sun-baked cliffs. Almost

THE PIT (AKA LE PETIT VERDON)

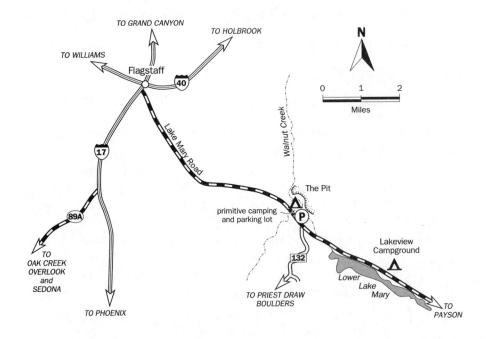

all the crags, however, are in the shade by 2 P.M. Summer evenings are excellent. Sunny winter days are also primo. Routes can be very busy on weekends, particularly the popular classics like *Mr. Slate* and *Popeye Meets the Burrito Master*.

Climbing history: The area's first routes followed crack lines and were put up by Alex McGuffie and Mike Lawson in the early 1980s. With the onset of the sport climbing revolution and rap bolting, rapid development at The Pit began in the autumn of 1987 by Flagstaff locals, who found that the canyon's limestone was surprisingly hard. Using a variety of ethics and styles, climbers, including Jim Symans, Kyle Copeland, Barry Ward, Jim Gaun, and Leo Henson, bolted and climbed many of today's classic routes. Later climbers, including Rob Miller, who wrote the area guidebook, established the harder routes and various link-ups.

Rack: The Pit is a sport climbing area. Most routes require only a rack of a dozen quickdraws and a 165-foot rope. Some of the longer routes on the White Wall need more draws and a 200-foot rope to safely lower off. **Descent:** From most routes, descent is by rappelling or lowering from permanent anchors. Some routes, however, do not have permanent anchors. Topropes are easily set on many routes. Use the bolted hardware whenever possible as the main anchor, and nearby trees only as backups to avoid damaging their trunks.

TRIP PLANNING INFORMATION

General description: More than 100 sport routes (mostly bolted) ascending a series of compact limestone cliffs in lower Walnut Canyon.

Location: North-central Arizona, just southeast of Flagstaff.

Camping: A free, primitive campground (Coconino National Forest) at the parking area is open spring through fall. Bring water and pack out all your trash. Stays are limited to 14 days. Other primitive camping is available on nearby national forest land. Public and private campgrounds are in the Flagstaff area. Good camping includes Oak Creek Canyon to the south, below the Overlook, and Sunset Crater National Monument, northeast of Flagstaff.

Climbing season: Year-round. Spring and fall offer the best cranking weather. Winter sun warms the crags nicely. Summer days can be hot, but the cliffs go into the shade by early afternoon.

Restrictions and access issues: None currently. The area is in Coconino National Forest. Follow existing trails to the cliff—taking shortcuts causes erosion. Watch for poison oak on the floor of Walnut Canyon. Don't remove lowering carabiners at anchors or steal another climber's quickdraws left on routes still being worked! This is the Wild West, partner. Expect a public hanging if you're caught stealing gear.

Guidebooks: *Climbing Guide to The Pit* by Robert Miller, 1996, is the comprehensive guide to the area. It's available in local shops. *A Cheap Way to Fly* by Tim Toula, 1991, is an older, no-frills guide to the area, as well as to other northern Arizona crags.

Nearby mountain shops, guide services, and gyms: Aspen Sports, Babbitt's Backcountry Outfitters, Mountain Sports, Peace Surplus, Popular Outdoor Outfitters, and Vertical Relief Rock Gym (Flagstaff); Canyon Outfitters (Sedona).

Services: All services are found in Flagstaff, including cheap motels, lots of restaurants, and an interesting downtown area.

Emergency services: Call 911. Flagstaff Medical Center, 1200 North Beaver Street, Flagstaff, AZ 86601, 520-779-3366 or 800-752-2332; Walk In Clinic, 4215 North U.S. Highway 89, Flagstaff, AZ 86004, 520-527-1920.

Nearby climbing areas: Priest Draw (excellent bouldering), Oak Creek Overlook, Pumphouse Wash, Oak Creek Canyon (classic routes *Book of Friends* and *Dresdoom*, and the Oak Creek Waterfall area, with over 150 basalt routes), Sedona area (The Mace and many other soft sandstone nightmares), Paradise Forks (Arizona's best crack preserve!), Volunteer Canyon, East Pocket, Sycamore Point, Elysian Buttress, Mount Elden West (bouldering and short routes).

Nearby attractions: Sedona area, San Francisco Peaks, Sunset Crater National Monument, Wupatki National Monument, Walnut Canyon National Monument, Museum of Northern Arizona (Flagstaff), Grand Canyon National Park, Navajolands, Meteor Crater.

Finding the crags: The Pit is 7 miles from downtown Flagstaff. To get there from downtown, drive south on Milton Road (which turns into Interstate 17) and make a right turn (west) on Forest Meadows Road. Drive 1 block and turn left (south) on Beulah Road, which is Arizona Highway 89A (to Sedona). Drive south a few blocks, go under Interstate 40, and turn left (east) on Lake Mary Road. This road is also reached by exiting from north-bound Interstate 17. Drive southeast on Lake Mary Road for 5.7 miles to a left turn just past the second cattleguard and the city limits sign. Follow this dirt road about 0.3 mile through a free national forest campground to a large parking area and trailhead. If the gate is closed, park on the road and walk north to the trailhead.

Walk north on Sandy's Canyon Trail (Trail 137) from the north end of the parking lot to a junction. Keep right and walk out to the canyon rim opposite the cliffs. A good trail switchbacks down the canyon slopes to the canyon floor. Follow the trail across the streambed. The trail bends left and follows the bottom of the canyon below the cliffs. Several short side trails climb the north slopes to the base of the cliffs. The first trail ascends to The Bulldog and The Oven. A second trail scrambles up to Mall Wall and White Wall. Stay on all trails to minimize erosion and watch for poison oak, especially along the trail on the canyon floor. Total approach time from the car to the cliffs is ten minutes.

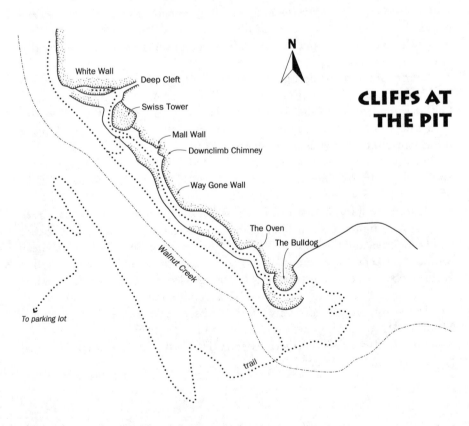

CLIFFS AT THE PIT

THE PIT

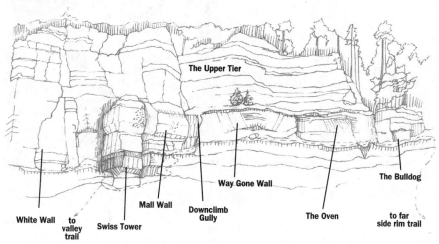

The Upper Tier

Way Gone Wall

The Bulldog

Mall Wall

Downclimb
Gully

White Wall   to
            valley
            trail

Swiss Tower

The Oven

to far
side rim trail

THE BULLDOG

This is the first sector encountered on the right side of the main cliff's lower tier. Follow the right-hand trail up from the canyon floor. It climbs up right of this cliff band and then traverses left on a ledge system along the base of the cliff. The routes are short. Toprope anchors can be easily set up from bolt anchors and a tree atop the cliff. Routes are described right to left above the trail.

1. **Blackboard** (5.9) This toprope is on the right side of the cliff. Use a single-bolt anchor and back it up with a tree. Good pocket and edge climbing up the dark face.

2. **Why Be** (5.11b) Good, bouldery moves past 2 bolts on a blunt prow to a tree anchor. Walk off right.

3. **Yappin' Chihuahua** (5.9) Usually toproped. Jam a crack up a tight corner left of a roof. Keep left at the top to a 1-bolt chain anchor.

4. **One Beer Shy of a Total Lunar Eclipse** (5.9) Short, popular, and fun. Edge up gray rock 10' left of the crack. 3 bolts to 2-bolt chain anchor.

THE PIT
THE BULLDOG

THE OVEN

The Oven, the next sector above the trail left of a broken corner system, bakes in the summer sun but is good in the afternoon and evening. The routes are short and powerful testpieces. Routes are listed right to left above the trail.

5. **Microwave** (5.11c) Left of a broken corner system. Thin edging up the right side of a tawny buttress. 3 bolts to 2-bolt chain anchor. 30'.

6. **Body Language** (5.12a) Follows a dark streak up the right side of the steeply overhanging, tan wall. Thin, powerful face climbing leads over a crux bulge into a short, left-facing corner. 4 bolts to 2-bolt chain anchor.

7. **Rage** (5.13b) A Jim Symans route that hasn't seen a second ascent. May be harder than 5.13b! Technical, pumpy edging up the tan face left of a water streak to a committing dyno. 4 bolts to 2-bolt chain anchor. The anchors on the lip of the roof are in the middle of a hard move. If the route was extended to the top of the cliff it might be 5.14.

8. **Terminal Vector** (5.13b) A sustained pumpfest! Swing up pockets to a left-angling crack. Work up the crack past a hard clip to anchors just left of the big roof. 7 bolts to 2-cold shut anchor. The other bolts that head over the big roof is a fantasy project that probably won't go without chipping.

9. **Tugena** (5.12c/d) Follow pockets and edges over a bulge and up an overhanging, gray streak. 5 bolts to 2-cold shut anchor (same anchor as Route 8).

10. **The Crucifix** (5.13c/d) The Pit's hardest offering. Savage crimps and sidepulls up the very steep wall just left of *Tugena*. Finish at the top of a small, triangular roof. 5 bolts to 2-bolt chain anchor.

11. **Crown of Thorns** (5.13c) A tough link-up. Begin on Route 9 and after 3 bolts, work up left and finish past Route 10's last 2 bolts. 5 bolts to 2-bolt chain anchor.

12. **Resurrection** (5.13b) Another thuggish link-up. Move past Route 10's first 3 bolts, traverse right, and pump past Route 9's last 2 bolts. 5 bolts to 2-cold shut anchor.

13. **Running Man** (5.12b) Make a dash for the finish on solid, technical moves just left of Route 10. A crimpy start leads to thin edges. 4 bolts to 1-bolt chain anchor.

14. **Put Your Fingers in My Pocket** (5.10d) Up dark stone right of a dihedral. More technical edges that require careful planning and a good head. Don't blow either clip—you'll deck! 2 bolts to a tree anchor.

THE PIT
THE OVEN

to 2 bolt
chain anchor

to anchors above

to anchors

THE PIT
THE OVEN

WAY GONE WALL

Superb limestone and great routes are found on this wall, which lies above the trail at the base of the cliff. Routes are described right to left from the dihedral.

15. **Gumbo Millennium** (5.11b) On the left wall of a big dihedral. Crank over a crux bulge to a technical slab. Use cheater stones to start if you're short. 3 bolts to 2-bolt chain anchor.

16. **Boltering** (5.13a) Start 10' left of Route 15 and just right of a big roof. Boulder over a bulge to a vertical finish. The runout to the 2nd bolt is moderate, but don't fall. 2 bolts to 2-bolt chain anchor.

17. **Minor Threat** (5.12b) Begin on the far left side of the big roof off some boulders. Climb onto a standing flake at the base and use a right sidepull/undercling to clip the 1st bolt. Strenuous and contorted moves power up the streak above to the cliff's lip. 4 bolts to 2-bolt chain anchor. 30'.

18. **Excaliber** (5.12c) A local classic. Begin left of a gray streak and stick-clip the 1st bolt. A powerful, bouldery start leads to a sprint up good edges on great rock. 3 bolts to 2-bolt chain anchor in groove. 30'.

19. **Fresh Squeezed** (5.13a) Squeezed in just left of Route 18. Dicey edges and crimps up a black streak to *Excaliber*'s anchors. 3 bolts to 2-bolt chain anchor.

20. **The Energizer** (5.12a) Another continuous, classic face climb on white rock. Crimps lead to a good rest at the 2nd bolt. Finish over a pumpy roof. 5 bolts to 2-bolt chain anchor.

21. **God Walks Among Us** (5.12b) Powerful edging moves past 3 bolts to a 2-bolt chain anchor.

22. **Jongleur Grey** (5.11a) Easily set up as a toprope. A bouldery start and strenuous final moves. 3 bolts to 2-cold shut anchor. Lower slowly to avoid rope jam in a groove at the top of the cliff.

23. **Secret Agent Man** (5.10d) Usually toproped off slings from Route 22's anchors. Face moves past 2 bolts. No anchor.

24. **Downclimb 101** (5.5) An easy chimney on the left side of the wall that is used as a downclimb from the terrace above.

MALL WALL

From the chimney (Route 24), continue walking left along the trail at the base of the cliff past a small buttress until the trail ends on a spacious, sloping ledge below the pocket-riddled Mall Wall. Several excellent and popular routes ascend the lower wall to anchors. Routes are described from right to left.

25. **Rave On** (5.10c) This long and excellent route goes to the top of the semi-detached pillar. Begin on the right side of the ledge and just left of a deep chimney. A few technical moves lead up black stone to some broken shelves. Follow corners (5.8) above up the right side of the pillar. 7 bolts to a 2-bolt anchor.

26. **Gotta Move** (5.11d) Begin left of Route 25 below a thin overlap. Edge, crimp, undercling, and pull pockets on white to black limestone to a good ledge with anchors. Lower from here or continue up Route 27 on the wall above. 4 bolts to 2-bolt anchor (chain and cold shut).

27. **Hops and Barley** (5.11c) Pocket climbing up the bulges above the ledge atop Route 26 gets you to anchors in black rock below the top of the pillar. 4 bolts to 2-bolt anchor.

28. **Popeye Meets the Burrito Master** (5.10d) Can be done in 2 pitches or as a single, long rope-stretcher pitch. The 1st pitch is 5.9 and utterly classic—a Pit must-do! The 2nd pitch is not worth doing. Begin on the base ledge. **Pitch 1:** Grab lots of great pockets to a stance with anchors 45' up. 4 bolts to 2-bolt chain anchor. **Pitch 2:** Continue up steep corners above the chains past 5 more bolts to a 2-cold shut anchor. 100' to top anchors.

29. **Moonlight Madness** (5.11a) Climb the 1st pitch of *Popeye* to the chained stance. Move left and swing over a series of bulges past 5 bolts to a 2-bolt chain anchor.

SWISS TOWER

This four-sided, semidetached pinnacle offers some of The Pit's best routes, which are all bolted and include lowering anchors. The routes are on the southeast and southwest faces. Reach the base of the tower by following an access trail up slopes above the main canyon trail or by scrambling down from Mall Wall. Routes are described from right to left, beginning with the arête on the right.

THE PIT
MALL WALL AND THE
SOUTHEAST FACE OF
SWISS TOWER

30. **Mr. Slate** (5.10b) An ultraclassic with supreme pocket pulling. Begin on a ledge on the right side of the southeast face below the obvious arête. Climb pockets and edges to a final bulge problem. Lower from anchors above a ledge just below the summit. 6 bolts to 2-bolt chain anchor. 70'.

31. **Sister of Mercy** (5.12c) Start 10' left of Route 30. Good pocket climbing up the vertical wall to a big roof. Stretch through holds over the roof to a nasty crimp finish. 8 bolts to 2-bolt chain anchor (same as Route 30).

32. **True Value** (5.11a) A great route that offers payment in pump. Brilliant pocket moves lead up the Swiss cheese wall to some technical edges and the roof. Pull over on airy holds and cruise to a ledge with anchors. 8 bolts and drilled pitons to 2-bolt chain anchor.

33. **Shark Bait** (5.11d) Begin below the obvious prow/arête. Pockets over a roof to start, then up left of a small roof. Edge up the arête to the 4th bolt. Climb up right and follow technical, exposed rock right of the arête to anchors. 7 bolts to 2-bolt anchor with lowering biners (leave in place!).

34. **Purple Shark** (5.12a) A recommended classic. The start is the same as *Shark Bait*. Pockets over a roof to a horizontal crack, then testy edge moves up the arête. At the 4th bolt, keep left and climb to the base of a large roof. Clip a bolt on the lip and air it out on steep, thuggish rock to anchors above a ledge. 6 bolts to 2-bolt chain anchor.

35. **As Nasty as They Want to Be** (5.12c) No topo. Begin just left of Route 34. Swing over a 5' roof to get the blood going. Follow pockets up left to technical edges on smooth, tan rock. Strenuous reaches lead over the second big roof to a crack finish. Step right onto a ledge to Route 34's anchors. 8 bolts to 2-bolt chain anchor.

36. **Don't Feed the Agave** (5.11c) No. Topo. Local guidebook author and activist Rob Miller says this one is "kind of cool." Begin on the far left side of the tower at the base of a deep chimney. Move out right on unprotected pockets (don't fall and feed the agave!) to the 1st bolt below a horizontal break. Continue up the left side of an arête to a big roof. Yank over on good but pumpy holds and work up right to anchors. 6 bolts to 2-bolt anchor with slings. A variation finish, *Jesus Thinks You're a Jerk* (5.11c), heads left above the roof to a 2-cold shut anchor.

Rob Miller hangs it out on *Mr. Slate* (5.10b) on Swiss Tower.

WHITE WALL

White Wall, an immense, east-facing cliff of pale limestone, has The Pit's longest and most exposed routes. Reach the base of the wall from Swiss Tower by following the trail along a terrace to a ledge below the routes. A short trail also accesses the wall from the main path along the canyon floor. Use the belay bolt on the ledge to safeguard your belayer. Routes are listed right to left above the ledge.

37. **Mordor** (5.10d) This route ascends a buttress flanked by large cracks. Climb good pockets and edges to a final crux at a small bulge (keep left). Find anchors up left of the ledge above. 8 bolts to 2-bolt anchor. 80'.

38. **Total Recall** (5.13b) Long, sustained, and brilliant—an endurance testpiece. Begin on the ledge left of a deep crack. Edge, crimp, and deadpoint up the steep, white wall. Look for rests. 11 bolts to 3-bolt chain anchor. 95'. Use a 200' rope for lowering.

39. **The Joker** (5.12c/d) Classic and beautiful face climbing. Work up left on slightly overhanging rock to the 2nd bolt. Move back right to the 3rd bolt and edge up to a steep crux bulge. Crank through on strenuous moves to a final, exhilarating runout and the anchor. 8 bolts to 3-bolt chain anchor. 85'.

40. **Total Joker** (5.13a) A good link-up of Routes 38 and 39 for locals who've already sent them. Climb up left above *Total Recall*'s 4th bolt and finish up *The Joker*. 8 bolts to 3-bolt chain anchor.

41. **No Joke** (5.13a) Another enduro link-up for locals. Begin up *The Joker* but exit right at the 4th bolt and traverse onto *Total Recall*. Clip and go to the anchors. 11 bolts to 3-bolt chain anchor. 95' long. 200' rope needed for lowering off.

42. **Stone Free** (5.13a) Airy and committing. Begin at the base of the prow, below and down left from the belay ledge at the base. Hard climbing leads up the face right of the prow. 10 bolts to 2-bolt chain anchor.

43. **Shock Treatment** (5.11c) Up the left side of the prow. Rob Miller recommends long draws to cut rope drag. Begin up *Stone Free* but move left and around the prow at the 4th bolt. 7 bolts to 2-bolt anchor.

Farther left of White Wall are more good sectors, including Bedrock, The Shooting Gallery, and Nose Rock, with almost 30 excellent routes. To the right of the described cliffs are other good crags, including The Sun Tower, with a good selection of moderates; Lost in the Woods; The Looney; and Live Wire Spire.

THE PIT
WHITE WALL

95'
XXX

85'
XXX

XX

80'
XX

40
41

43

39
41

38 40

37

42

all bolts not shown

Consult Rob Miller's comprehensive area guidebook for the complete beta on these crags. Farther down the canyon from The Pit are a couple of good, east-facing, basalt cliffs with crack routes and topropes.

PARADISE FORKS

OVERVIEW

The Mogollon Rim, one of Arizona's most distinctive natural features, twists 200 miles across Arizona from the New Mexico border to the town of Williams and separates the south edge of the Colorado Plateau from the desert basin and range province to the south. West of Flagstaff, a vast ponderosa pine forest blankets the rolling countryside between the volcanic San Francisco Peaks and the twisting rim of wild Sycamore Canyon. Paradise Forks, the junction of Gold and Silver Canyons, lies at the head of the canyon.

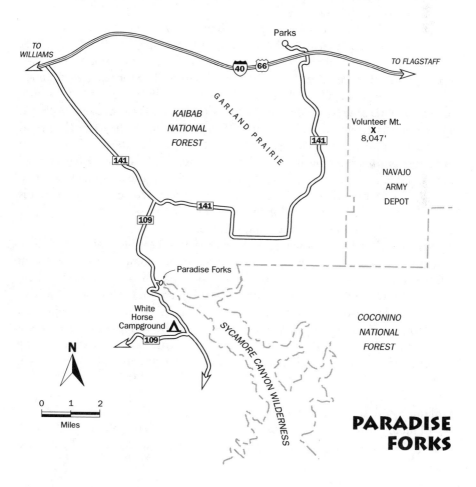

The cliffs that line these two canyons harbor one of America's best compact crack climbing areas on smooth, fine-grained basalt. The basalt, deposited in thick lava flows from volcanoes to the north, offers difficult crack climbs up to 70 feet long on clean, aesthetic rock. There is probably nowhere else in the country with the superb quality and sheer number of crack routes in such a condensed area. More than 160 routes, most between 5.10 and 5.13, line the vertical cliffs.

First-timers at Paradise Forks will find the routes and the ratings stiff compared to other areas. This is a place where it's hard to fake it. Getting up most Forks routes requires solid crack climbing skills because few edges or pockets are found on the cliffs. Besides impeccable crack technique, climbers here must be competent at placing gear and have a good sense of commitment. As at most crack climbing areas, the harder routes are finger cracks or seams that require difficult stemming. Paradise Forks is not a beginner area. Even the moderate routes seem hard. Leading a 5.10 here is not like leading a 5.10 at a sport area like Jacks Canyon. When you come, have a healthy respect for the grades and be ready to get spanked.

The Forks is also one of the most traditional areas in the United States. This is a bastion of conservative climbing ethics, with an emphasis placed on style of ascent and clean climbing. The canyon has had only two bolted routes— *Americans at Arapiles* and *Australians at the Forks*. The former was chopped after one ascent (but rebolted by John Mattson in 1998) and the latter sports only two bolts. Due to the smooth nature of the rock faces, the few potential sport routes left are of outstanding difficulty. For now, they remain proud topropes. Climber impacts have been further minimized by the use only of clean protection, rather than pitons and other fixed anchors. Battles have been waged over chalk, although now all but a few hardcore locals use it. Still, chalk often seems unnecessary when you're jamming on a crisp Arizona afternoon. This commitment to style, respect for the rock, and purity of ascent has kept the cliffs at Paradise Forks unspoiled and pristine.

The top of the cliffs, however, is another matter. Leading many routes here is a difficult and serious proposition; hence many climbers toprope them. Climbers also have to set up rappel lines to access the canyon floor. These activities have led to degradation of the environment on top of the cliffs, with the erosion of topsoil, loss of plant cover, and damage to trees used as anchors. Concerned climbers have met with Forest Service officials regarding the erosion problem. Hopefully, in the future, some sort of erosion control walls will be constructed of native materials along the tops of popular walls. In addition, climbers have discussed setting some designated rappel stations at key areas. Thus far, it appears unlikely that the Forest Service will initiate these projects without a widespread climber appeal.

Climbing history: Paradise Forks was unknown to climbers until 1979, when local pioneer Scott Baxter, along with Jim Whitefield and Bruce Sell, checked out a rumor of a hidden canyon out by White Horse Lake. The trio walked down a dry watercourse and came upon Silver Canyon. Shortly afterward, Baxter and Larry Coats did the area's first line *Born Under a Bad Sine* and then *Mayflower*. The active Forks climbers carefully guarded this new, secret area, swearing climbers to secrecy and supposedly blindfolding others on the drive to the crag. In the early 1980s, most of the area's classic lines went up by local activists, including Paul Davidson, Tim Coats, John Gault, Gordon Douglas, and Ross Hardwick.

In 1986, rap bolting came to the Forks. John Mattson, a strong Flagstaff climber, bolted *Americans at Arapiles*, a technical and demanding route up double arêtes. Mattson snared the route's only lead ascent before someone chopped the bolts. Meanwhile, the refinement of TCUs at Steve Bryne's shop Wired Bliss in Flagstaff allowed the safe protection of thin cracks and provided further impetus for new routes in the later 1980s. The best lines were snared by Tim Toula, Jim Waugh, Steve Bryne, Barry Ward, and John Mattson. With almost all the possible lines having been climbed, Paradise Forks quieted down and nearby developing sport climbing areas like The Pit saw all the action. Some of the last remaining problems finally fell to Mattson in the late 1990s when he free climbed an old aid line on The Gold Wall, calling it *Pacing the Cage* (5.13b), and completed *The Serpent* (5.12a X), a sporty arête with little gear. Mattson has also established several other outstanding thin crack masterpieces.

Today, Paradise Forks is usually quiet, especially on weekdays. Weekends can, however, get a little frenzied with lots of climbers vying for toprope anchors or queuing up for the classic cracks. If that's the case, you might want to head to some of the other cliffs not detailed in this guide, like White Wine Wall or Sine Wall. Pick up a copy of David Bloom's *Paradise Forks Rock Climbing* for the complete beta on all the routes at the Forks. Climbing in this fragile canyon environment is a true wilderness experience. Please show great respect for the privilege of climbing here.

Few objective dangers are encountered at Paradise Forks. However, use caution on your rappels and do not knock any loose rock off the top of the cliffs. If you're toproping, use an extra rope for setting up your anchor off of multiple trees. Use sling runners on trees for rappels or topropes to avoid damaging the bark. Be aware that a fine dirt is often on the walls and in the cracks after heavy rain or in springtime.

Rack: A standard Forks rack should include a set of wired nuts, a set of TCUs, and two sets of cams. A few large cams and some extra finger to hand sizes will complete your rack. On the hard routes, plan on using lots of small stuff—RPs, slider nuts, and ball units. Bring two ropes—one for climbing and one for setting up a fixed rappel line. Long runners are good for tying off trees for rappel and toprope anchors. Because the rock is smooth and not abrasive, you decide whether to tape.

TRIP PLANNING INFORMATION

General description: Popular and excellent, single-pitch crack routes ascending sheer basalt walls at the junction of two canyons.

Location: North-central Arizona, southwest of Flagstaff.

Camping: Camping is now prohibited at the trailhead parking lot. Primitive camping is available on nearby public lands, including several secluded and free campsites within a half-mile of the Forks. The nearest public camping is at Whitehorse Campground in Kaibab National Forest, two miles south of the Forks on Forest Service Road 109. There are water and pit toilets at this fee campground. If you're primitive camping, bring your own water and dispose of human waste properly. If you must have a fire, use an existing fire ring whenever possible and only pick up dead wood from the ground. Make sure the fire is completely out before leaving the site. Wildfires are a real threat during the dry months of May and June. Camping is prohibited within a quarter-mile of water sources to keep access open for wildlife.

Climbing season: The best seasons are spring and fall. April through June brings warm, sunny days with occasional storms. Autumn brings cool, sunny days that are ideal for hard cranking. Summer days can be very hot, and afternoon thunderstorms regularly occur in July and August. Sunny winter days are excellent. Winter access is a problem most years when snow closes the road. Every few winters, however, low snowfall keeps access to the crags open.

Restrictions and access issues: The area is in Kaibab National Forest and on the edge of Sycamore Canyon Wilderness Area. Forest Service issues here concern soil erosion and compaction, damage to vegetation, human waste disposal, damage to cultural resources, and overcrowding. The use of power drills is prohibited. The local ethic is that bolting routes is unacceptable. Please abide by this consensus. Only one bolted route currently exists at the Forks, and it has only two bolts. These face climbs, mostly arêtes, are toprope problems. Avoid placing rappel ropes directly around tree trunks. Instead, use a sling around the trunk. There are no bolted rappel stations. Local climbers may be establishing designated rappel stations in the near future as a way to alleviate damage to trees and vegetation along the rim of the canyon. Use existing trails to the rim and along the cliff's base. Do not cut down or damage trees and vegetation, including lichen, on the approach trails or the cliffs. Pick up all trash, including tape and cigarette butts. Do not leave human waste in the canyon or near the tops of routes. Use the restroom at the parking lot.

Guidebooks: *Paradise Forks Rock Climbing* by David Bloom, Falcon Publishing/Chockstone Press, 1995, is the comprehensive guide to the Forks. *A Cheap Way to Fly* by Tim Toula, 1991, offers topos and Tim's route recommendations.

Nearby mountain shops, guide services, and gyms: Aspen Sports, Babbitt's Backcountry Outfitters, Mountain Sports, Peace Surplus, Popular Outdoor

Outfitters, and Vertical Relief Rock Gym (Flagstaff); Canyon Outfitters (Sedona), and Flagstaff Mountain Guides (Williams).

Services: All services are found in Williams and Flagstaff.

Emergency services: Call 911. Flagstaff Medical Center, 1200 North Beaver Street, Flagstaff, AZ 86601, 520-779-3366 or 800-752-2332; Walk In Clinic, 4215 North U.S. Highway 89, Flagstaff, AZ 86004, 520-527-1920.

Nearby climbing areas: Sycamore Point (Tim Toula calls it "The Land of a Thousand Climbs"), Parks Wall (bouldering), Volunteer Canyon (two-pitch basalt routes in Sycamore Canyon Wilderness Area), East Pocket Rocks (basalt cliffs), the Overlook, Oak Creek Canyon (classic routes *Book of Friends* and *Dresdoom*, and the Oak Creek Waterfall area, with over 150 basalt routes), Sedona area (The Mace and many other soft sandstone nightmares), The Pit (limestone clip-ups), Elysian Buttress, Mount Elden West (bouldering and short routes).

Nearby attractions: Grand Canyon National Park, Sedona area, San Francisco Peaks, Sunset Crater National Monument, Wupatki National Monument, Walnut Canyon National Monument, Museum of Northern Arizona (Flagstaff), Navajolands, Meteor Crater.

Finding the crags: From Flagstaff and points east, drive west on Interstate 40 to Exit 178 (Parks Road). Drive south from the interstate on Garland Prairie Road (Forest Service Road 141). This gravel road is often rough, with washboards. After 9.7 miles, the road makes a sharp right in the middle of Garland Prairie, a large, open grassy area. After 13.8 miles, turn left on FR 109 and drive south for 3.4 miles to a spur road on the left. Turn left (east) and drive 0.25 mile to the trailhead parking area.

From Williams and points west, drive east on Interstate 40 to Exit 167 (Garland Prairie Road). Drive southeast on Garland Prairie Road (FR 141) for 6.7 miles to FR 109. Turn right (south) on FR 109 and drive south for 3.4 miles to a spur road on the left. Turn left (east) and drive 0.25 mile to the trailhead parking area.

From the trailhead, walk east past the outhouse and descend a short hill onto a flat, piney area. Go right (south) on a climber's path to The Three Yogis and The Gold Wall. Go left on the main trail, which leads to the waterfall area atop Silver Canyon. Walk south along the top of the west side of the cliff to access The Pillow Wall and The Prow. Hike around the top of the waterfall to the top of the east side of the cliff to access The Davidson Wall and Sine Wall. Take time to scope out the walls from cliff top before descents. **Descent:** Rappel to the base of the walls from a convenient tree. It's best to leave a fixed rope for the day.

PARADISE FORKS

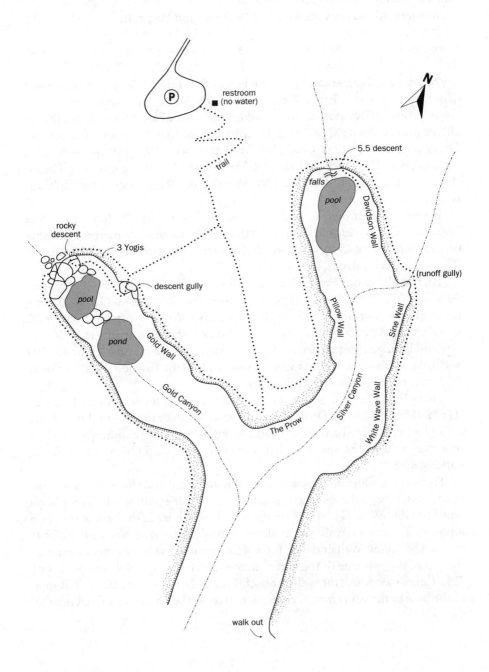

P

restroom
(no water)

N

trail

5.5 descent

falls

pool

Davidson Wall

rocky
descent

3 Yogis

descent gully

(runoff gully)

pool

Pillow Wall

Sine Wall

pond

Gold Wall

Gold Canyon

The Prow

Silver Canyon

White Wave Wall

walk out

THE THREE YOGIS

These three excellent routes make a good introduction to thin jam cracks at Paradise Forks. They are on the sunny north side of Gold Canyon, the left canyon fork, between the two waterfalls of Sycamore Falls and above Upper Gold Pond. Access the cliff by walking down the trail from the parking area. At the base of the hill, follow a faint trail right (south) for about 100 yards to the top of the cliff. Reach the cliff's base by scrambling down a loose gully system to the left (east) or by downclimbing polished rock steps to the right (west). Several trees set just back from the rim make good toprope anchors. Routes are listed left to right from the cliff's base, which is very water polished.

1. **Laughing** (5.9) Fun, varied climbing. The left-hand corner system. Slick lieback moves work into a slightly overhanging, left-facing corner with good handholds and stems. Watch for some loose rock. At the ledge, traverse left or better yet, climb a short crack to the right and reach the rim.

2. **Hopping** (5.9) The middle corner. Awkward hand jams to a thin finger crux. Continue up crack above the ledge to the rim.

3. **Dancing** (5.9+) A thin, right-facing corner with an overhanging finger jam crux. Step left on the ledge and finish up a moderate crack.

THE GOLD WALL

An assortment of steep crack lines of varying grades ascends this south-facing cliff on the north side of Gold Canyon above Gold Pond and east of The Three Yogis. All but the first five routes are reached by a rappel from the canyon rim to the floor. It's best to fix a rappel line for the day by slinging a tree and rappelling after climbing each route. It can be busy on weekends, so share the rappel with other parties to avoid damaging trees and vegetation on top of the cliff. Reach the first three routes by rapping off a rimrock tree to a ledge partway down the cliff. Scope out the wall before climbing by walking around to the south rim of the canyon. If you toprope the routes, use gear placements along the rim for the main anchor, with a tied-off tree as a backup to avoid damaging the trees and rimrock vegetation. Routes are listed left to right.

4. **Fogdish** (5.8) Begin on a wide ledge above the northwest corner of Gold Pond (reach by rappelling from the rim or scrambling in from the west on loose ledges). This shortie, one of the "easiest" Forks cracks, liebacks and jams a committing finger crack in a 15' right-facing corner to a ledge. Continue up easier rock to the rim. **Rack:** Small to medium cams and Stoppers.

PARADISE FORKS
THE GOLD WALL

tree belay

belay on ledge

fingertips

4 5 6

8

7 9

385

5. **Grievous Angel** (5.9) A neglected classic. Start off the right side of a ledge. Straightforward hand and foot jamming up an enjoyable hand crack in an open corner leads to easier climbing up broken ledges. **Rack:** Medium and large cams including a #3.5 Camalot for a wide section.

6. **Waterslip Down** (5.10-) Rap to a ledge above the pond. Begin off the far right side of a wide shelf. Make an airy step right off the shelf into a thin finger crack. Jam the finger to thin hand crack for 30' to easier climbing over broken rock. **Rack:** Small to medium cams.

7. **Liquid Sky** (5.11- TR) A proud toprope! Set up TR anchors and rappel to the edge of Gold Pond. Face climb up corners and edges to a roof, turn on the right, and bear-hug up the double arêtes to a ledge below the rim. The arêtes can also be reached by traversing right (5.10+) from the ledge where Route 6 begins.

8. **Supercrack** (5.9+) Superb and varied jamming up a right-facing corner. Rappel down the corner from the rim to a small ledge with a bush above chunky rock. Work up the widening crack—hands to fist to off-width (10" to 12") to squeeze chimney—to the rim. **Rack:** Mostly large stuff. A large Camalot up high keeps the excitement level down, but it's still run-out.

9. **Acid Test Crack** (5.12-) This one will severely test your finger strength. Begin below the left side of the wall above the pond. Face climb up a somewhat loose crack (hard to protect) past a flare to a small stance. Strenuous fingertip jams and liebacks up a shallow left-facing corner to more finger jams to a rimrock pine.

10. **East of Eden** (5.10-) Classic and popular. Face climb up a loose, blocky corner past a small roof to a clean, right-facing corner. Jam a short, thin hand crack in the corner to a sloping stance. Jam and bridge up twin finger cracks to the rim.

11. **Emotions in Motion** (5.11) Start 15' right of Route 10. Jam a loose hand crack to a ledge with bushes. From the left side of the ledge, work up a tips crack (5.11) in a shallow, right-facing corner to a small, blocky stance. Continue up right to a flake system, past a hanging scrub oak, and finish up a thin finger crack to the rim just right of a gnarly, old juniper.

12. **King Fissure** (5.11+) Begin 20' right of Route 11 below a small pedestal. Take the crack on the right side of the pedestal, just left of a smooth face. Above the pedestal, head straight up a hand crack in a right-facing corner to a spacious ledge atop a pillar. After resting, step left on the ledge and stem and jam a fingertip crack to the rim.

PARADISE FORKS
THE GOLD WALL

stem

.9

.10
LB

.9+

17

15

16

14

388

13. **Goldfinger** (5.11) A superb but strenuous testpiece. Use the same start as *King Fissure*, or for a more entertaining but hard-to-protect start, begin a few feet and 2 cracks right of Route 12. Follow the crack to the base of a right-facing corner. Alternatively, jam the *King Fissure* crack to the pedestal ledge and move up the corner above for about 10' to an obvious traverse right on good flakes and edges to the base of a clean, right-facing corner. Head up the steep corner with stems and fingertip jams in twin cracks to a good rest ledge atop a pillar. Move to the right from the stance and jam a pumpy, overhanging, thin hand crack to the rim.

14. **T. L. Bush** (5.10) Begin about 70' right of Route 13 and just left of a small, whitish pillar at the cliff's base. Work up a thin crack with face holds and face climb over a small, leaning roof. Lieback up the obvious openbook above to a ledge on the right. From the left side of the ledge, make airy jams to a broken ledge. Easier ground up right leads to the rimrock.

15. **Hatchet** (5.10) Start by the small pillar at the cliff's base. Face climb the corner crack behind the pillar and out right over a small roof. Move up right onto a cramped, sloping stance and surmount a bulge to twin cracks. Fingerlocks, thin hand jams, and face moves lead up the right-hand crack.

16. **Rush 'n' Arête** (5.9+) The next crack right of *Hatchet*. Stem up a blocky corner onto a sloping stance. Continue stemming up the left-facing corner above to a small ledge. Entertaining face moves up the left-leaning arête above gain the rim. The arête is hard to protect; plug pro in a crack to the right to keep the fear factor in check!

17. **Standard Forks 5.8** (5.9) It's still hard at 5.9. Begin around a corner and right of Route 16. Climb loose, blocky rock up left to a short, right-facing corner and an exposed stance shared with *Rush 'n' Arête*. Move up right on big flakes into an open book. Stem to top.

THE PROW

The Prow is the wedge of basalt that divides Gold and Silver Canyons and forms the Forks. Some of the area's best lines ascend the east-facing wall of The Prow, making it popular and busy, especially on weekends. Approach by following the trail down the hill from the parking lot. Keep left on the good trail to the canyon rim and follow a path along the rim of Silver Canyon right (south) to the top of the cliff. Or follow a trail from the top of The Three Yogis and The Gold Wall east to the top of The Prow. Set up a fixed rappel line on either side of the wall to access the bottom of the cliffs. Routes are described left to right from the base of the cliff or right to left from the top of the cliff. It is difficult to

Pieter Dorrestein belays Issac Shaffer on a Paradise Fork classic, *The Prow* (5.11-).

figure out which routes are which from the top. Walk along the rim to the opposite side of the canyon to check the routes out before rappelling and climbing. The first route is directly south of the ponderosa pine tree on the rim. There are five good, shorter routes left of Route 18.

18. **Americans at Arapiles** (5.12+) A spectacular but controversial route that was bolted and led by John Mattson and subsequently chopped. He rebolted it in 1998. Begin by rappelling down to a ledge left (right if you're on the rim) of The Prow. The route climbs the impressive south-facing wall and arête above. Start at the left arête, then face climb up right on thin edges to the right arête. Powerful palming moves lead up the arête before moving left to finish up the left arête.

19. **The Prow** (5.11-) A must-do, classic Forks crack. Begin directly below The Prow and a semi-detached pillar. There are two starts. The left crack is 5.8 and the right off-width crack is 5.10. Above the pillar, jam a 5.11 thin hand crack (perfect for small hands) up the beautiful, right-facing corner to the rim.

20. **Mutiny on the Bounty** (5.11+/.12-) Sustained fingers and stems. Start a few feet right of the small pillar. Jam a finger crack (5.11-) to a broken ledge. Step up left to a higher stance. Fingertip jams and liebacks coupled with wide stems get you up the soaring, left-facing corner with twin cracks. End at the prominent pine on the rim.

21. **Sail Away** (5.12-) Great route—if you can do it! Grade is dependent on hand size. Begin on *Mutiny* and climb to the first ledge. Step to the right side of the broken ledge and climb a thin crack up a left-facing corner with vicious fingerstacks. As the crack widens, it becomes tight hands. End at the rimrock pine tree.

22. **Jolly Roger** (5.10) Real-life jamming! Start 15' and two crack systems right of *Mutiny*. Face climb up the obvious, flared crack to a small roof. Grope up and over on good edges and continue up double cracks in the left-facing corner using finger to fist jams.

23. **Ship of Fools** (5.10-) Start in the next crack right of Route 22. Climb necky face moves up a thin seam to a small stance with a bush below a right-facing corner. Jam and stem the gorgeous corner.

24. **Pilgrim's Progress** (5.10-) Begin at the crack right of Route 23. Jam and face climb a hand crack to a broken ledge with loose rock and small bushes. Continue up twin cracks in a right-facing corner.

25. **Mayflower** (5.9) The first route on The Prow and the second at the Forks. Start about 20' right of Route 24 by a fallen fir tree. From the top of a block, jam a short finger crack to a ledge atop twin pillars.

PARADISE FORKS
THE PROW

TR

.12

thin hands

.12-

.11-

stem

18

20

21

25

28

alt.

.8

OW

.10

19

20

22

23

24

26

27

25

Make awkward face moves up left from the left side of the pillars onto a scooped stance. Launch up the wide hand crack in a right-facing corner and end at a prominent rimrock juniper tree.

26. **Mayflower Direct** (5.11+/.12-) This direct start to *Mayflower* is a superlative testpiece. Begin left of Route 25 below a clean, right-facing corner. Stems and pumpy liebacks get you up the corner to a final bulge. Continue up *Mayflower* from the scoop.

27. **I Want Your Sex** (5.12+ TR) Another direct start—call it the *Mayflower Madam*. Use powerful face moves and palming on the magnificent, sharp arête between Route 25 and Route 26.

28. **Fool's Game** (5.9) Popular classic. Same start as *Mayflower*. Jam a finger crack to the top of twin pillars. From the left side of the pillar ledge, jam the right-facing corner above. Watch for some loose blocks partway up.

PILLOW WALL

This northeast-facing wall, up Silver Canyon from The Prow, offers a selection of popular Forks moderates. The cliff, which receives lots of shade on warm days, can be very busy with topropers and leaders on weekends. Reach the cliff by following the trail down from the parking lot toward the falls at the head of Silver Canyon. Turn right (south) and follow the trail on top of the cliff about 150 feet to the top of the wall.

It's difficult but not impossible to set up toprope anchors from gear in cracks along the cliff's edge. Use one of the pines as a backup anchor. Avoid using the trees themselves for toprope and rappel anchors in order to mitigate damage to the trunks and the already beaten ground surface along the top of the cliff. To climb and rappel, set up a day's rap line with an extra rope to either side of the cliff. Before climbing any of the routes, walk around to the opposite side of the canyon and scope the routes out. Routes are listed left to right from the base of the cliff or right to left from the top of the cliff. All routes are about 50 feet long.

29. **Pillow Stuffing** (5.7) One of the area's easiest routes. Begin on the left side of Pillow Wall below an obvious, shallow chimney. Stem up the chimney using cracks in the back to a blocky finish.

30. **Short Sheeted** (5.11) A lichen-covered face with thin face moves and a flared finger crack.

31. **Pillow Fight** (5.10) A fun, left-leaning crack that narrows from fists to hands to an upper finger section.

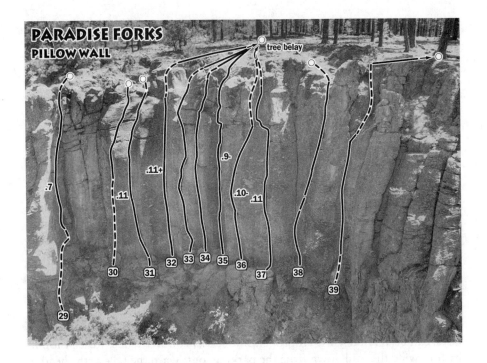

32. **Davidson Dihedral** (5.11+) A classic corner climb. Steep, strenuous finger crack up a perfect dihedral. Gotta crack climb this one!

33. **Pillow Talk** (5.9) Wide hands and fists up an obvious crack.

34. **Geekus Amongst Us** (5.9-) Just right of Route 33. Flared finger to hand crack.

35. **Pillow Case** (5.9-) Jams and stems up a left-facing corner.

36. **Ivory Snow** (5.10-) A flared finger crack to final moves over blocks.

37. **Marilyn Chambers Crack** (5.11) Okay, who remembers Ms. Chambers? Begin off a pedestal ledge. A boulder problem start up a thin finger crack leads to some flared hand jams. Finish with more fingers.

38. **Crack-a-Pogo** (5.9+) Twin cracks up a corner system. Keep in the right crack up high.

39. **Chlorox** (5.8+) Another crack-in-corner climb.

DAVIDSON WALL

The wall, named for Forks activist Paul Davidson, yields a superb selection of testpiece cracks for the aspiring crackmaster. The west-facing cliff, shady on warm mornings and sunny on cool afternoons, is on the east side of Silver

Canyon, just down the canyon from Silver Pond and the waterfall. Reach the cliff by following the trail from the parking lot down a hill and through a pine forest to the water-polished watercourse above the falls. Cross here, using caution if water is present, and walk east and southeast along the edge of the canyon until you are above the cliff.

Scope the cliff first, though, by walking along the west canyon rim to the top of Pillow Wall. Note the location of a stepped gully on the left (north) end of the wall. This makes a good fixed rappel route. Watch for loose rock in the gully. Routes are described left to right from the bottom of the cliff or right to left from the top.

40. **Torpedo** (5.10+) Quality jamming. Begin on the far left side of the wall, down and right of a dark, stepped, pour-off gully and behind a small tree among broken boulders. Climb a short, blocky, left-facing corner and enter a stem box with two thin finger cracks. Jam the cracks until they begin to diverge. Step right into the right-hand crack and move up right to a small stance. Jam straight to the top via double hand cracks. A variation finish steps right from the stance and follows a right-angling flared hand crack (5.11-).

41. **Jane Fonda Workout** (5.12-) An excellent stemming workout but hard to protect. Start about 20' right of Route 40 and right of some boulders. Climb a thin crack with some face holds to a sloping ledge. Acrobatic stems, small edges, and fingertip liebacks lead up the thin seam above to double finger cracks. Keep left up high to a right-facing corner.

42. **Loose Lips** (5.10+) Same start as Route 41. Climb the thin corner to sloping ledge. Step out right into a hand crack up the left side of a pillar. Jam to a ledge atop the pillar. Continue up a finger crack to the rim.

43. **Australians at the Forks** (5.12-) Recommended face climbing up the only bolted route here. Same start as Route 41. Move up the corner to the sloping ledge. Traverse right and swing up a stellar, rounded arête past 2 bolts to a good ledge atop a pillar. Finish up the finger crack above. A harder, R-rated start begins just right and moves up thin cracks to the base of the arête.

44. **Three Turkeys** (5.11) Start behind a boulder 15' right of Route 41. Jam and stem a crack up a short, left-facing corner to a small roof. Lieback out left. Jam and face climb up thin cracks and finish up a flared hand crack.

45. **Retard's Recess** (5.10+) Begin on a large boulder a few feet right of Route 44. Make face moves up to a sloping ledge. Jam and stem up double hand cracks, one in a right-facing corner and the other up the left wall.

var.

.11.

.10+

fingers

thin

41

42

.12-

X

X

43

40

.10+

.12-R

var.

44

45

46

41 42

43

43

PARADISE FORKS
DAVIDSON WALL

Manual Rangle leads *Kingfolia* (5.10+) on Paradise Fork's Davidson Wall.

46. **Paradise Lost** (5.12-) Paradise will be regained, but only if you get up this wickedly exciting route! Climb a thin crack up and right under a blocky roof. Continue up the beautiful, right-facing corner with sustained and pumpy finger jams.

47. **The Equalizer** (5.13a R) A John Mattson classic that was first led by placing gear. It has been repeated with pre-placed pro—only a few are equal to this demanding lead. Begin right of a large boulder at the base of the cliff. Hard face climbing up a shallow, left-facing corner leads to sustained, sequential stemming up a stem box with two thin seams that pinch off to hard finishing moves. The route requires long reaches with gear below your feet and impeccable technique.

48. **Watusi** (5.12-) Begin about 3' right of Route 47. Follow a thin crack up right into an open corner. Continue to a small, flat rest stance up right. Stem and jam thin double cracks to a roof; turn on the left.

49. **Bach's Celebration** (5.12) Another leg-spreading stem problem. Start right of graffiti that says "I am the Master." Thin cracks in a short corner lead to a roof. Turn the left side of the roof and enter a stem box up a right-facing corner. Stem up the corner to a pillar ledge on the left. Use face holds up right from a tree to a flared pod. More face moves lead to the rim.

50. **The Flake** (5.12- R) Same start as Route 49. At the roof, go right and climb a thin crack a few feet before moving left and mantling onto a small ledge. Sustained face climbing leads to a final stem box.

51. **Bladerunner** (5.11+) Begin just right of a large boulder. Climb a shallow, right-facing corner into parallel, twin finger cracks. Stem and jam up right to a small stance. Finish up a hand crack.

52. **Kingfolia** (5.10+) Same start as *Bladerunner*. Move up a thin corner before face climbing up right to the base of a wide hand crack in a shallow, left-facing corner. Jam the crack to the top of a small pillar. Continue up left via a thin crack in a left-facing corner.

53. **Queenfolia** (5.10) Quality. Climb *Kingfolia* to the top of the pillar. Fun face moves on jugs lead up right on a flake to a hand crack.

54. **Kingkinkus** (5.11-) Begin a few feet right of Route 51. Work up a wide crack to face edges that move up right to lichen-covered rock below a short, right-facing corner. Follow a thin, left-slanting crack that joins *Queenfolia*'s final hand crack.

PARADISE FORKS
DAVIDSON WALL

PARADISE FORKS
DAVIDSON WALL

tie off trees for anchors

53

55

hands

.9

52

54

56

55. **Queenkinkus** (5.11) Climb Route 54 and instead of going left, stem up right in a shallow, left-facing corner.

56. **Brown Derby** (5.9+) Walk about 15' right of Route 54 and begin off boulders below a short, right-facing corner. Climb the corner up and left to a prominent, small roof. Lieback and jam the left side of the roof. Follow a good hand crack to easier climbing on broken rock.

SEDONA SPIRES

OVERVIEW

Sedona, a trendy resort town and art colony, sits amidst the spectacular sandstone country of lower Oak Creek Canyon. The canyon begins at the Mogollon Rim to the north and plunges southward through an abrupt defile lined with magnificent sandstone walls before widening at Sedona. The Sedona area forms a transition zone between the Colorado Plateau to the north and the arid Sonoran Desert to the south, with plants and animals from both areas mingling together. Towering sandstone cliffs, sculpted by erosion into spires, buttes, buttresses, and soaring walls, surround Sedona and form a geologic and scenic marvel that attracts tourists, hikers, and rock climbers.

It also attracts crystal hunters, spiritual seekers, and other New Agers who search for enlightenment in this cosmic red rock country. The psychic author Page Bryant wrote in 1981 that Sedona was our planet's "heart chakra," a place filled with more vortices or Earth-energy emanation sites than anywhere else. A vortex is a natural energy spot that discharges three kinds of energy—an electric or positive charge, a magnetic or negative charge, and an electromagnetic or balanced charge. These charges are measurable with electronic instruments. Some of the area's largest vortices are Cathedral Rock, Boynton Canyon, Bell Rock, and the man-made Medicine Wheel vortex on Schnebly Hill Road. Climbers will undoubtedly find vortices on their chosen pinnacles, and perhaps even some inner peace after a vertical brush with death.

Geologists call Sedona's ruddy sandstone, deposited in a desert some 275 million years ago, the Schnebly Hill Formation. This thick sandstone ranges in quality from very good to very bad. Some sections are compact and reliable for climbing, while others are composed of soft and brittle rock more akin to dried brown sugar. Tim Toula, who wrote the area's comprehensive guidebook, calls the rock "sandy, friable, hollow, unprotectable, choked with loose blocks." The climbing here is similar to that at other sandstone areas like Colorado's Garden of the Gods. The climbers used to granite or limestone crags will find fragile dinner plate–sized flakes, sandy friction footholds, crumbling edges, and rubble-filled chimneys. But they will also find some wild, exciting routes that

SEDONA SPIRES

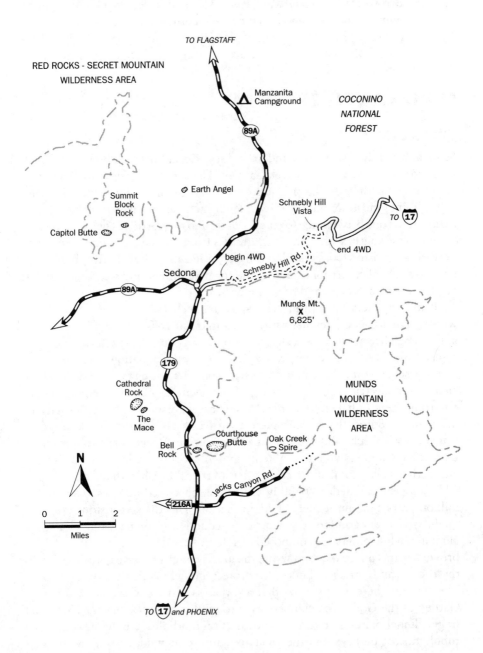

RED ROCKS - SECRET MOUNTAIN
WILDERNESS AREA

TO FLAGSTAFF

Manzanita
Campground

COCONINO

NATIONAL

FOREST

89A

Earth Angel

Summit
Block
Rock

Schnebly Hill
Vista

TO 17

Capitol Butte

end 4WD

begin 4WD

Sedona

Schnebly Hill Rd.

89A

Munds Mt.
X
6,825'

179

MUNDS

MOUNTAIN

Cathedral
Rock

WILDERNESS

The
Mace

AREA

Courthouse
Butte

Oak Creek
Spire

Bell
Rock

N

Jacks Canyon Rd.

216A

0   1   2

Miles

TO 17 *and PHOENIX*

finish atop airy summits with stunning views. Many of the area's newer routes in Oak Creek Canyon are on excellent sandstone.

Climbing history: The ancient Sinagua Indians made the first ascents in the Sedona area, edging up chiseled holds on steep slabs to reach their lofty cliff aeries. Some of their remote sites, hidden in the cliffs, are only accessible by Class 5 climbing or via rappel. The late 1950s saw the first ascents of a few Sedona classics when several California climbers traveled through the area. Bob Kamps first noted The Mace on a postcard while on a northern Arizona trip. In 1957, Kamps, along with Dave Rearick, TM Herbert, and Yvon Chouinard, stopped in Sedona on a desert climbing trip. On Sunday, December 30, Chouinard went to Mass at the local church. The other three decided that they weren't going to wait around for the end of Mass and set off to The Mace. A few hours later they were perched atop the summit, celebrating the first ascent of this Arizona classic. Kamps also did first ascents of a few other routes. The prolific Fred Beckey was also active here.

The 1960s were relatively quiet here, with few new routes going up. The 1970s and 1980s, however, became the golden age of Sedona rock climbing. A handful of climbers, including Scott Baxter, Karl Karlstrom, Ross Hardwick, Steve Grossman, Tim and Larry Coats, Glenn Rink, and Tim Toula, began systematically ticking off the area's spires and best-looking crack lines. Noteworthy ascents were Baxter and Hardwick's long route up Earth Angel in 1975 and The Acropolis by Baxter and the Coats brothers. Kamps, Herbert, and Don Wilson first climbed Oak Creek Spire in the early 1970s. Nomadic climber Ed Webster put up the spire's classic route in 1978. On Summit Block Rock, *Dr. Rubo's Wild Ride* was first jammed by Scott Baxter and Larry and Tim Coats in 1983.

With most of the spires already climbed, the 1990s brought hard crack and aid climbing on new walls to the Sedona area and Oak Creek Canyon. Flagstaff climbers, including David Bloom and John Mattson, have ascended multipitch routes with 5.13 finger cracks as well as dozens of bolted sport and traditional crack routes on some of Sedona's better sandstone walls.

Climbing is possible year-round in Sedona and Oak Creek Canyon. The best time is during the spring months of April and May and from October until the middle of December. Expect moderate temperatures and usually dry conditions. Summer days can be too hot. Get an early start and climb in the shade. Isolated, heavy thunderstorms regularly occur on July and August afternoons. Keep an eye out for bad weather moving in and avoid lightning by retreating from the summits. Winter days are often too cold for comfort, but they can also be very pleasant.

Lots of objective dangers are found on the Sedona spires. These include loose blocks and boulders, removable handholds, bad bolts, bad and hard-to-find protection, questionable anchors, and heinous approaches filled with catclaw acacia, Spanish bayonet, and cactus. Wear a helmet. Climb softly. Place lots of gear. Back up all anchors. Replace rappel slings. And as Tim Toula notes, "Don't fall! To fall on a route here is sheer stupidity." Keep in mind that many of Sedona's classic routes are rated conservatively, especially if you are unaccustomed to sandstone climbing.

Use soft rock-climbing techniques to guarantee that you'll come back for another sandstone adventure. Pull down, not out, on flakes and handholds, use stemming moves and mantles, blow sand off dicey footholds before weighting your foot, watch for loose blocks and boulders, and don't fall. Protection is often hard to judge. When in doubt, sew it up. That way at least one piece might hold a fall. Tri-Cams and hexentric nuts often work better in cracks than camming devices. Never trust a single bolt for an anchor. Always back it up for safety and a long life. Belay and rappel anchors are being replaced with modern bolts and rappel chains on many of Sedona's well-traveled routes.

Rack: A standard rack for Sedona includes two sets of Friends or similar camming devices, a set of wired Stoppers, a selection of hexentric nuts and Tri-Cams, a few off-width pieces, and two 165-foot ropes. Bring extra webbing for replacing worn or dried rappel slings. On the described routes, climbers do not need a bolt kit to replace or add bolts or fixed pitons.

TRIP PLANNING INFORMATION

General description: Soft sandstone routes ascending an assortment of spectacular towers in the red rock country around Sedona.

Location: Central Arizona, Sedona area.

Camping: Best campgrounds are the national forest ones in Oak Creek Canyon. These five campgrounds—Pine Flats, Cave Springs, Bootlegger, Banjo Bill, and Manzanita—are open from mid-May through mid-September. Good primitive campsites are found along the Schnebly Hill Road east of Sedona.

Climbing season: Year-round. Spring and autumn are the best seasons. From March through May, expect good climbing weather with moderate temperatures and variable winds. October to mid-December is also excellent. Summers are usually hot, with daily highs in the 90s. Climb in the morning and pick shady routes. Watch for severe thunderstorms and lightning in July and August. Winters from mid-December through February are unpredictable, with rain, snow, wind, and sunshine. Average winter temperatures are in the 50s.

Restrictions and access issues: None currently. While all the towers are on national forest land, some of the approaches cross private property. Use discretion and keep a low profile. Many of the popular climbs are in designated wilderness areas. Also, pick up after yourself—your mother is not here to do that for you.

Guidebooks: *A Better Way to Die: Rock Climber's Guide to Sedona and Oak Creek Canyon* by Tim Toula, Falcon Publishing/Chockstone Press, 1995, is a no-frills guide to the Sedona spires and Oak Creek Canyon.

Nearby mountain shops, guide services, and gyms: Canyon Outfitters (Sedona); Aspen Sports, Babbitt's Backcountry Outfitters, Mountain Sports, Peace Surplus, Popular Outdoor Outfitters, and Vertical Relief Rock Gym (Flagstaff).

Services: All services are found in Sedona including lots of lodging choices and excellent restaurants.

Emergency services: Call 911. For rescues, call 911 for the Sedona Fire Department.

Nearby climbing areas: Oak Creek Overlook, Pumphouse Wash, Oak Creek Waterfall area, Schnebly Hill Crag, Paradise Forks, Granite Mountain, Granite Dells, Thumb Butte, Sullivan Canyon, The Promised Land.

Nearby attractions: Sedona, Schnebly Hill Road, Red Rocks-Secret Mountain Wilderness Area, Slide Rock State Park, Oak Creek Canyon, Sycamore Canyon Wilderness Area, Munds Mountain Wilderness Area, Montezuma Castle National Monument, Tuzigoot National Monument.

THE MACE

The Mace, a 300-foot-high sandstone pinnacle, is one of Arizona's most popular tower climbs. The *Original Route*, put up in 1957 by Californians Dave Rearick, Bob Kamps, and TM Herbert, climaxes with an exciting and exposed step-across move over a gaping chimney to the highest summit. The other highlight is the long jump back to the lower summit (about 10 feet across and 10 feet down), although now it can be avoided by rappelling directly off the top. The route, following cracks and chimneys, is generally well protected with solid belay stances and anchors. Allow at least half a day to approach, climb, and rappel the route, although the route has been climbed in one-and-a-half hours car to car.

Finding the tower: From the intersection of Arizona Highway 89A and 179 in Sedona, drive 3.6 miles southeast on Arizona 179 to Back of Beyond Road. Make a right (southwest) turn here and drive 0.6 mile west to an obvious parking area and trailhead on the left. Hike south up the Cathedral Rock Trail for just over 1 mile to the base of The Mace. The route is on the north side of the tower, facing the parking lot. Hiking time is 20 to 30 minutes.

1. **Original Route** (5.9+) 5 pitches. Begin on the right side of the north-

THE MACE

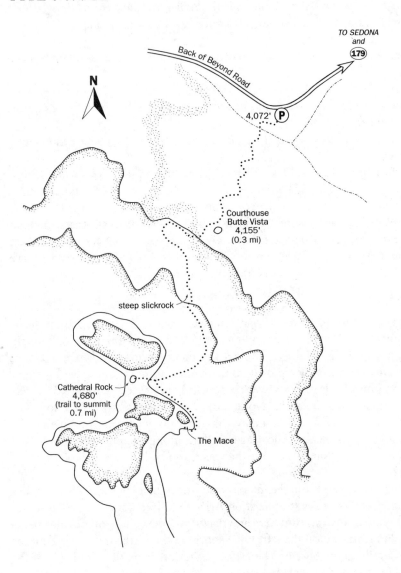

N

TO SEDONA
and
(179)

Back of Beyond Road

4,072' (P)

Courthouse
Butte Vista
4,155'
(0.3 mi)

steep slickrock

Cathedral Rock
4,680'
(trail to summit
0.7 mi)

The Mace

SEDONA SPIRES
THE MACE

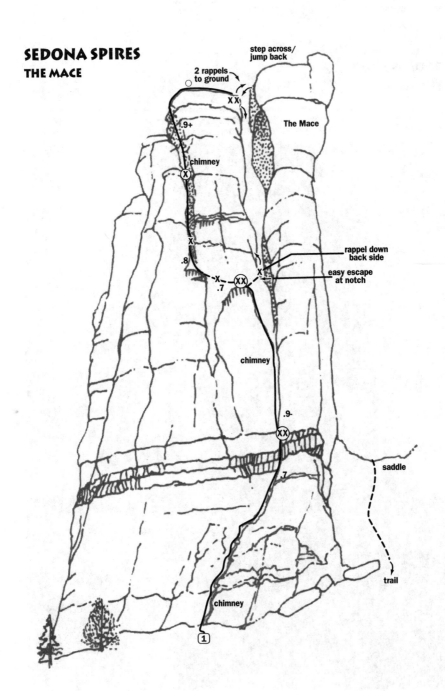

SEDONA SPIRES
THE MACE

step across/
jump back

2 rappels
to ground

X X

The Mace

.9+

chimney

X

X

.8

rappel down
back side

X

easy escape
at notch

X (XX)

.7

chimney

.9-

XX

saddle

.7

trail

chimney

1

east face below a right-angling groove. **Pitch 1:** Climb up right in the wide groove (5.6) to a band of gray limestone that forms a roof. Pull over the roof (5.7) by stemming to a good belay ledge and a 2-bolt anchor. **Pitch 2:** Jam a hand crack (5.9) that becomes a chimney. Work up left in a 5" to 6" crack (#5 Camalot) on the right side of a pillar to an exposed ledge with a 2-bolt belay atop the pillar. **Pitch 3:** Make an airy face traverse left (5.7) past a bolt into a deep chimney/crack. Squeeze up the system (5.8) to a belay ledge with an eyebolt. **Pitch 4:** The crux pitch. Stem up the chimney above to an off-width (4") crack (5.9+) on the right wall that leads to the lower summit. A #4 Camalot and bolt protects the crux. **Pitch 5:** A memorable pitch! Step across the airy gap and climb up and right past a flake (5.8). Move up right to the summit and sign the register. **Descent:** 2 double-rope rappels to the ground from the lower summit. First though, make the exciting jump 10' back across the abyss to the lower summit or rap from bolts. **Rappel 1:** Rappel 120' from bolt anchors on the edge of the lower summit down the gap between the towers to a notch. **Rappel 2:** Scramble down left in the notch and rappel with double ropes from bolt anchors 110' to the ground. **Rack:** A good rack is a full set of Camalots (or equivalent) including a #5 for pitch 2, some small cams, a selection of medium to large wired nuts, and 2 ropes.

OAK CREEK SPIRE

The *North Face* route offers good crack and chimney climbing up Oak Creek Spire, also known as Rabbit Ears. This classic "eared" spire is on the south edge of Lee Mountain southeast of Sedona and east of The Mace. Some locals consider this a better route than The Mace. Jim Waugh calls it "a good adventure climb." There is some loose rock. Use care not to knock any off and wear a helmet.

Finding the spire: From the intersection of Arizona Highways 89A and 179 in Sedona, drive 7.3 miles southeast on Arizona 179 to Jacks Canyon Road in Oak Creek Village. Turn left (east) and drive 2 miles to a right turn. Drive through a gate and park in the designated lot at Jacks Canyon Trailhead. Jacks Canyon Trail (Trail 55) begins here.

There is an alternative parking area 0.7 mile farther east on Jacks Canyon Road. Drive to a parking area and trailhead on the right just before Pine Valley Estates, a housing development. Cross the fence and hike east to join Jacks Canyon Trail.

Jacks Canyon Road is also easily reached from Interstate 17. Take Exit 298 and follow Arizona 179 north for 7 miles to Jacks Canyon Road. Turn right (east.)

OAK CREEK SPIRE

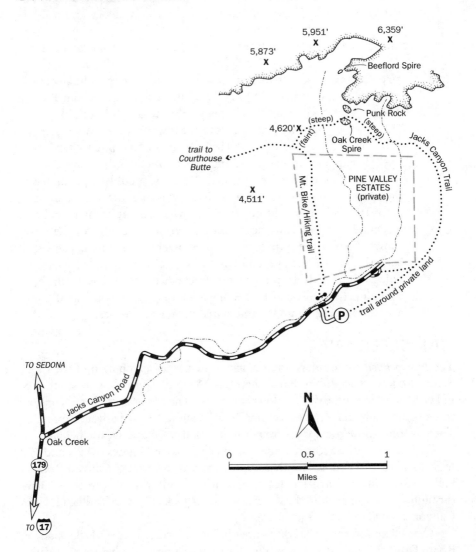

5,951' X

6,359' X

5,873' X

Beeflord Spire

Punk Rock

4,620' X (steep)

(faint)

(steep)

Oak Creek Spire

Jacks Canyon Trail

trail to Courthouse Butte

Mt. Bike/Hiking trail

PINE VALLEY ESTATES (private)

X 4,511'

trail around private land

P

N

TO SEDONA

Jacks Canyon Road

Oak Creek

179

TO 17

0   0.5   1

Miles

SEDONA SPIRES
OAK CREEK SPIRE

3 raps down East Chimney

.9

.8

.9

move belay

.8+

2

trail

From the designated lot at the trailhead, follow Jacks Canyon Trail, an abandoned road, northeast and north around the houses, then locate another path that heads northwest to the spire. Hike west through underbrush (nasty catclaw acacia!) to a path that winds up to the base of Oak Creek Spire. If you find the climber's trail to the spire, you'll avoid most of the bushwhacking. Scramble up to the saddle north of the spire. The route ascends a crack system on the right side of the north face. Total approach time is one hour.

2. **North Face** (III 5.9) 5 pitches. Begin from the saddle north of the spire on the right side of a pillar and left of a bush. **Pitch 1:** Cruise up obvious cracks on the right side of the pillar (5.8+) to a large ledge with a tree. 60'. **Pitch 2:** From the tree, scramble right on the ledge, then up and left (class 3) to a natural belay at the base of a thin crack. 50'. **Pitch 3:** Difficult, thin moves (5.9) right off the belay lead to a lower-angle crack. Grunt up (5.8-) the obvious flaring chimney to a belay above the chimney in twin cracks. 90'. **Pitch 4:** Continue up cracks, passing several ledges. Jam a hand crack (5.9) on the right wall to the lower summit. 90'. Pitches 3 and 4 can be combined with a 200' rope. **Pitch 5:** Muster up the courage to leap across the 100-foot-deep, 4-foot-wide chasm below you to a small ledge with great handholds and no footholds. Move up left then back right (5.8) to the summit. 60'. **Descent:** 3 rappels down the *East Chimney* route. Rappel 1: Do a 2-rope rappel from the summit 150' down the wide chimney to a short, loose scramble to the 2nd rappel station. Rappel 2: Do another 2-rope rappel to a ledge with anchors. Rappel 3: Do a 2-rope rappel to the base of the *East Chimney*. **Rack:** A generous selection of gear with medium to large Stoppers and double sets of cams to 4". A big piece for an off-width is useful. Also bring extra webbing for the rappel slings.

SUMMIT BLOCK ROCK

An excellent and popular climb up a semi-detached tower with a top-heavy block summit just north of Coffee Pot Rock and northwest of Sedona. The route was first ascended in 1983 by Scott Baxter and Larry and Tim Coats. The tower, on the east side of a large, clifflike amphitheater, blends into the cliffs from many angles. The west-facing route gets lots of sun, making it a good winter climb.

Finding the tower: From the intersection of Arizona Highways 89A and 179 in Sedona, continue west on Arizona 89A for 1.8 miles to Coffee Pot Road and a traffic light. Turn right (north) and drive a total of 0.8 mile north to a Forest Service parking area between Caswell Drive and Little Elf Drive. To get

SUMMIT BLOCK ROCK

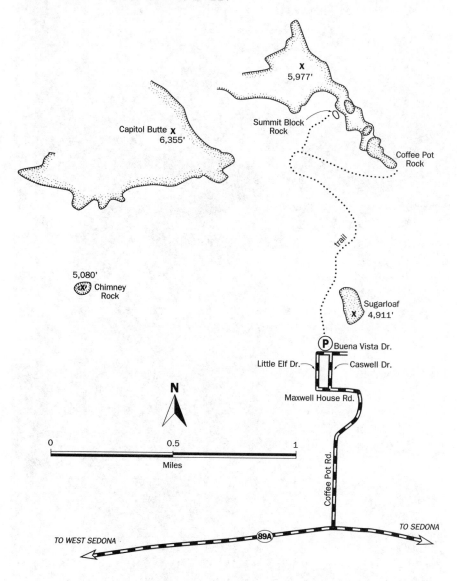

SEDONA SPIRES
SUMMIT BLOCK ROCK

XX 150'
to notch

.9

.7
X–X–X
X

.9
hands

.8+

3

there, first drive north on Coffee Pot Road, then make the obvious left turn onto Maxwell House Road. Drive a short distance and turn right on Caswell Drive. Follow Caswell for a couple of blocks to Buena Vista Drive. Turn left and into a gravel parking lot on the right, the trailhead for Coffee Pot Trail. The top of the spire is visible to the northeast.

Hike north on a good trail around the west side of Sugarloaf, a rounded butte on the right. The trail works north and then follows a sandstone bench east around the amphitheater. Scramble up the slopes below the cliffs to the base of the west-facing spire. Allow about half an hour to approach the spire.

3. **Dr. Rubo's Wild Ride** (II 5.9+) 4 pitches. A classic line up the southwest face of the tower. Begin left of a deep chimney. **Pitch 1:** Jam a crack to a band of limestone. Jam and stem through (5.8+) and belay at a stance with 1 piton above. **Pitch 2:** Jam a 3" hand crack (5.9+) up the corner above. Up higher, the difficulty (5.7) eases. Belay on the shoulder. **Pitch 3:** Make an airy traverse up right (5.7) past 4 fixed pitons to a belay ledge. **Pitch 4:** From a tree, climb up left to a bolt and mantle. Easier face climbing leads to the summit. **Descent:** From the summit anchors, make a 2-rope rappel for 150' to a saddle between the spire and the main wall. Scramble down the back side of the saddle and walk back around the spire to your packs. **Rack:** 2 sets of Friends to #3.5. An extra #3 is nice.

EARTH ANGEL

This almost 1,000-foot-high tower is tucked into a canyon northwest of Sedona. The tower features the Sedona area's longest route, a 6- to 8-pitch line up cracks and chimneys on the spire's west face. The spectacular and airy route, put up by Scott Baxter and Ross Hardwick in 1975, is considered by many Sedona aficionados as one of the best spire climbs. Plan on a full day to approach, climb, and descend the tower.

Finding the tower: From the junction of Arizona 179 and 89A in Sedona, drive north on Arizona Highway 89A for 0.4 mile to Jordan Road. Make a left turn on Jordan Road and drive 1.3 miles north to a parking area at the road's end. Hike up the drainage in Mormon Canyon for about 3 miles. Earth Angel is in a side canyon to the right. Scramble up to the base of the west face to the route.

Martha Morris belays Albert Newman on the first pitch of *Dr. Rubo's Wild Ride* (5.9+) on Summit Block Rock.

SEDONA SPIRES
EARTH ANGEL

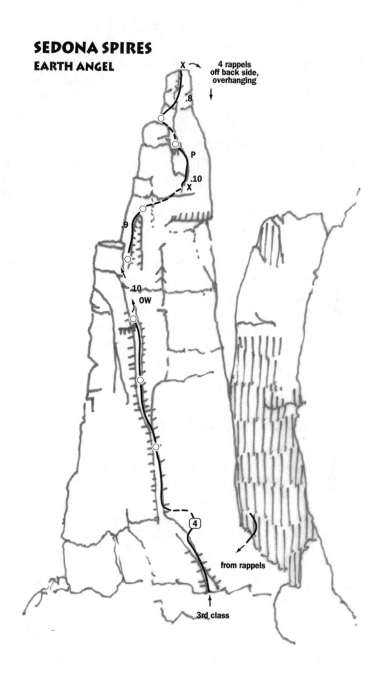

X

4 rappels
off back side,
overhanging

.8

P

.10

X

.9

.10

OW

4

from rappels

3rd class

4. **Earth Angel** (IV 5.10) 6 to 8 pitches. One of Arizona's longest spire routes up a spectacular tower. Expect airy face climbing, off-widths, and chimneys. It's a full-day adventure. Pitches 2 and 3 are often combined into a single 240' pitch. To start, scramble up a gully on the west side of the tower to a flat ledge and set up the 1st belay. **Pitch 1:** Climb a crack and make a traverse (5.6) left to a chimney system and belay. **Pitches 2 and 3:** Climb the sandy chimney (5.7) to a belay ledge on the left. **Pitch 4:** Move out right past a bolt into a right-facing corner. Work up a classic, off-width crack (5.10) to a belay stance. **Pitch 5:** Climb a nice, left-facing corner (5.9) on the left side of a rotten pillar to a belay atop the pillar. **Pitch 6:** Move up right over several shelves to a bolt below a right-angling, right-facing corner. Follow the corner up right (5.10) past a fixed piton, then face climb to a belay by a chickenhead. **Pitch 7:** Face climb up left to a good ledge. **Pitch 8:** Follow a crack up right (5.8) to the summit. **Descent:** Make 4 double-rope rappels down the back side of the tower. Rappel 1: Rappel 130' from a chickenhead and a bolt to a ledge. Rappel 2: Rappel 165' from a thread and a fixed nut to a 2-bolt chain anchor. Rappel 3: Rappel 130' to a large ledge and traverse right to a small tree. Rappel 4: Rappel 80' from the tree to the ground. **Rack:** Stoppers, TCUs, a double set of Friends, and off-width pro to 5". A #5 Camalot is nice to have but not necessary.

OTHER SEDONA SPIRES AND ROUTES

There are lots of other spires and buttes with routes up them in the Sedona area. Many are worthwhile and classic adventures. Many others are loose, grungy, and deadly. For more information, pick up Tim Toula's *A Better Way to Die: Rock Climber's Guide to Sedona and Oak Creek Canyon.* Toula says, "recommending a route here is like handing a bottle of nitro to an epileptic friend. I would rather leave it up to your judgment." Here are some favorite and classic routes:

1. **Princess Spire** (5.10+) 2 pitches. A spectacular route up a small spire near Midgley Bridge.

2. **Queen Victoria** (5.7) 3 pitches. Up cracks and faces on the east skyline to a great summit above Schnebly Hill Road.

3. **Screaming Besingi** (5.8) 2 pitches. A superb route up a classic chimney on the east face.

4. **Streaker Spire** (5.7) 3 pitches up an airy pinnacle in the Church Spires.

5. **Bell Rock** (5.8) A single pitch up a blocky butte with a great summit view.

6. **Original Route** (5.9) 4 pitches. On Coffee Pot Rock. Toula ca. "neat mountaineering route."

7. **Castles in the Sand** (5.11d/12a) A spectacular, 5-star, horizontal hand crack established by John Mattson.

8. **Coyote Tower** (5.10) East of Bell Rock. A well-protected neoclassic put up by John Burcham in 1998.

OAK CREEK CANYON

There are lots of good sandstone routes on the cliffs above Oak Creek north of Sedona. Consult Tim Toula's comprehensive area guide for details and topos. Recommended routes are *Book of Friends* (excellent off-width and chimney) and the six-pitch *Dresdoom,* with superb face climbing up an R-rated arête. Flagstaff activists have put up numerous new crack and sport routes in the late 1990s. Inquire locally for route information.

There is an excellent basalt crack climbing area, similar to Paradise Forks, in the upper canyon at Oak Creek Waterfall. To reach the area, park at the Encinoso Picnic Area. Walk north on the highway to another parking spot, then hike up a brushy drainage for about half an hour to the obvious amphitheater above and east of the highway. About 75 crack routes, mostly 5.10 and 5.11, line the cliffs. Toula's guide offers topos, names, and ratings.

Another basalt area with a stunning view of Sedona and Oak Creek Canyon sits atop the Schnebly Hill Road. Drive up the rough road from Sedona to the canyon's east rim and park at an obvious parking area on the north side of the road. Follow a trail along the canyon rim north for almost half a mile to a southwest-facing basalt cliff with several fun crack and face routes.

JACKS CANYON

OVERVIEW

Jacks Canyon, which begins from shallow drainages on the Mogollon Rim in central Arizona, twists northeast through rounded hills and high volcanic mesas to the Little Colorado River at Winslow. The canyon, virtually hidden from nearby Arizona Highway 87, is walled by stair-stepped limestone cliffs and floored by a cobbled streambed lined with shady cottonwood trees. It's no wonder, given the canyon's hidden character and relative remoteness from Arizona's population centers, that the place remained devoid of rock climbers until the 1990s. Now, over just a few years, Jacks Canyon has become one of the state's premier sport climbing areas. Jacks offers almost 300 bolted routes, a wide variety of grades with a plethora of moderate routes, quick access to the cliffs from the rimrock camping area, and good year-round cranking weather.

JACKS CANYON

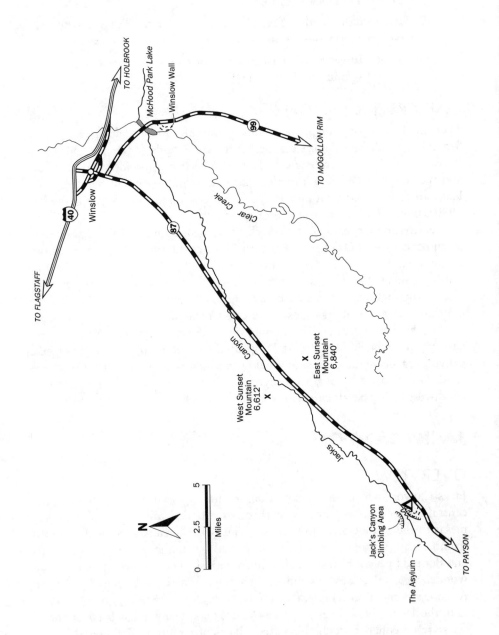

TO HOLBROOK

McHood Park Lake

Winslow Wall

99

TO MOGOLLON RIM

Clear Creek

Winslow

40

TO FLAGSTAFF

87

Canyon

West Sunset
Mountain
6,612'
X

East Sunset
Mountain
6,840'
X

Jacks

Jack's Canyon
Climbing Area

The Asylum

TO PAYSON

N

0   2.5   5

Miles

The canyon's cragging area, also called Moenkopi (a Hopi word that means "Place of Running Water") by the area developers, is divided into six distinct areas: Lower Moenkopi, Casino Cliffs, The Main Wall, Swiss Wall and White Gang Wall, Cracker Jack Cliffs, and High Life Wall. Farther up the canyon The Asylum, a separate area with lots of hardman routes, is being developed by Phoenix climbers. All of the areas are packed with side-by-side routes so you can work your way down the cliff through a succession of grades.

The routes are characterized by vertical to overhanging, finger-friendly limestone with lots of pockets, edges, sidepulls, jugs, and even the occasional hand jam. The limestone here is strange, with occasional bands of coarse sandstone deposited in the finer-grained rock matrix. The cliffs that rise out of the creekbed, like The Main Wall, begin with roofs and bulges formed by flash floods and heavy spring runoff that undercut the cliffs. The other cliffs above the usually dry creekbed tend to be vertical and harbor many of the best moderate lines.

All the routes at Jacks Canyon are well bolted with 3/8-inch bolts and cold shut lowering anchors. Most of the lines follow natural features, with bolt placements at good stances or rest holds. Hangers are often recessed to prevent spinners. Loose blocks and flakes have been cleaned so very little loose rock is encountered, especially on the popular routes. There are, however, enhanced and chipped holds and drilled pockets on many of the canyon's routes (The Asylum is the exception), particularly the harder lines, including those on The Main Wall and White Gang Wall. These manufactured holds raise serious ethical debates about the validity of these routes and the conservation of the climbing area. All visiting climbers need to carefully consider the chipping issue and its impact on our sport and make up their own minds about ethics.

Climbing grades are notoriously soft and inconsistent at Jacks Canyon. This is the place where you might want to tick that first 5.11 lead. Be advised that the grades here can vary as much as two or three letter grades from routes at other Arizona areas like Mount Lemmon or Queen Creek Canyon. The grades up the canyon at The Asylum are more accurate and stiffer.

Climbing history: Jacks Canyon is one of Arizona's newest climbing areas. Before the 1990s, Jacks was a lonely canyon, first inhabited by the ancient Anasazi Indians. Later, a few cowboys rode along its dusty pinyon pine–studded rim in search of stray cattle. That all changed in 1993, when Diedre Burton and Jim Steagall, looking for new rock to develop, found virgin cliffs in this secret canyon 30 miles southwest of Winslow. They dubbed the place Moenkopi and set to work cleaning and bolting routes on The Main Wall, beginning with aptly named *Genesis*. Over the next few years other climbers, including Stephen and Melissa Tucker, Matt Embring, Chris Hahn, and Bryan Fife, toproped, bolted, and redpointed most of the canyon's routes. In 1997, Embring and other Phoenix climbers began developing their own area, The Asylum, farther southwest up the canyon, putting up many hard 5.13 routes.

Jacks Canyon, at 6,200 feet, is a year-round climbing area. Shaded or sunny routes are easily found on either side of the canyon. Like everywhere else in Arizona, spring and autumn offer the best conditions. From March to May and from September to November, expect generally clear, warm, sunny days, with highs between 60 and 80 degrees. Spring snowmelt on the mountains to the south often floods the canyon floor for a few weeks, limiting access to the cliffs. Winter offers surprisingly good weather, with cool but sunny days and scant snowfall. Expect daily highs in the 40s and 50s, but cold nights. Summer is often hot, although shaded climbs abound. Summer high temperatures are usually in the 80s and 90s. Carry plenty of water to stay hydrated. Afternoon thunderstorms often occur in July and August, usually on the higher Mogollon Rim to the south. Keep an eye out for flash floods raging through the canyon. During late spring and early summer, there can be lots of mosquitoes until pools of water dry up. Bring bug dope to ward off the hordes.

There is convenient and currently unregulated primitive camping in the pinyon pine forest above the canyon's east rim. Increasing use and abuse by climbers is impacting this fragile desert area. Camp only in existing sites. Use existing fire rings and bring your own firewood to avoid stripping the surrounding forest of scarce wood. Dispose of human waste properly by burying it at least six inches deep and packing out your toilet paper in a plastic bag. Follow existing trails to and from the cliffs from the parking area to minimize impact and erosion. Pick up all of your litter, including cigarette butts, tape scraps, and anything left by unaware low-lifes.

Rack: A dozen quickdraws and a single 165-foot (50-meter) rope is sufficient for most routes. A clip-stick is useful for clipping the first bolts on many of the harder routes, particularly the overhanging starts on The Main Wall. Be aware that the cold shut anchors on some routes are open or unwelded. These are very weak. Don't toprope off them. **Descent:** For all routes, descend from cold shut lowering anchors.

TRIP PLANNING INFORMATION

General description: More than 200 fun, bolted sport routes ascending the limestone walls of a remote, twisting, high desert canyon.

Location: Central Arizona, south of Winslow.

Camping: Free, primitive camping is available on the rim above the canyon. Bring water, dispose of human waste properly, and pick up and pack out all trash, including toilet paper. Build fires only in established fire rings to minimize impact.

Climbing season: Year-round. Spring and fall are best with warm days and cool nights. Summer highs reach the 90s, but there are shady walls in both morning and afternoon. Watch for flash floods up the canyon after summer thunderstorms. Winter days can be excellent because the canyon is sheltered from the wind, and the sun warms the rock. Snow accumulation is low. Spring snowmelt can flood much of the canyon floor, although many routes are still accessible.

Restrictions and access issues: None currently. The area is in Coconino National Forest. Increasing climber use is impacting this fragile, high desert area. Preserve the area and access by following responsible, low-impact camping, climbing, and hiking protocol.

Guidebooks: *Jacks Canyon Sport Climbing* by Diedre Burton and Jim Steagall, 1997, is the comprehensive guide and was published by the canyon's main developers.

Nearby mountain shops, guide services, and gyms: None. Closest shops and gym are in Flagstaff: Aspen Sports, Babbitt's Backcountry Outfitters, Mountain Sports, Peace Surplus, Popular Outdoor Outfitters, and Vertical Relief Rock Gym.

Services: Nearest services, including two grocery stores and several restaurants and motels (cheap climber rates), are in Winslow, 30 miles to the north. Nearest water and pay phone are behind the fire station, 8 miles south of the canyon. Turn off Arizona 87 at milepost 306.

Emergency services: Call 911. There's an emergency room at 1501 North Williamson Avenue in Winslow.

Nearby climbing areas: Winslow Wall, Petrified Forest National Park boulders, Canyon Diablo, The Pit, Oak Creek Overlook, Paradise Forks, and other Flagstaff areas. Check *A Cheap Way to Fly* by Tim Toula for beta on most of these areas.

Nearby attractions: Mogollon Rim, Meteor Crater, Tonto Natural Bridge State Park, Fort Verde State Historic Park, Montezuma Castle National Monument, Sedona, Walnut Canyon National Monument, Flagstaff attractions.

Finding the crags: From Interstate 40 in Winslow, take Exit 253 (North Park Drive) and turn south. Drive 1 mile south and turn left (east) on Second Street, then drive a few blocks to the marked right (south) turn for Arizona Highway 87. Turn right and drive 30 miles to mile 313.7 (just past mile marker 314). Make an obvious right turn (west) off the highway onto a dirt road and pass through a gate.

From Phoenix and southern Arizona, drive north on Arizona 87 through Payson. Continue north on Arizona 87 for 34 miles over the scenic Mogollon Rim to mile 313.7 and turn left (west) onto the dirt road. This junction is also easily reached from Interstate 17. Allow about two-and-a-half hours driving time from Phoenix.

After closing the gate behind you, follow a series of dirt roads for a total of 1.2 miles to the campground and trailhead on the east rim of Jacks Canyon. To get there, drive 0.1 mile and turn right, drive 0.2 mile and turn left, and then drive 0.2 mile and turn right. Continue 0.7 mile to the trailhead and park.

The trailhead is just west of the main group of campsites. Look for a stone-lined trail that heads northwest. Follow the path along the top of the mesa for a few hundred yards to the canyon rim. The trail switchbacks down to the floor of the canyon opposite Casino Cliffs. At the bottom of the canyon, an obvious trail goes to Casino Cliffs, while a left turn onto a trail on the canyon floor leads to The Main Wall.

JACKS CANYON CLIFFS

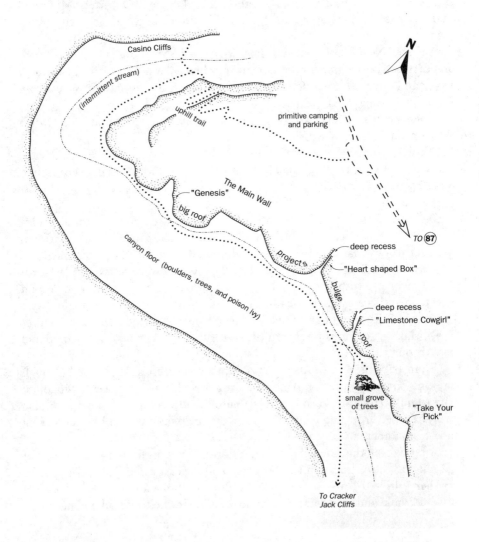

CASINO CLIFFS

This vertical cliff, on the west side of the canyon, lies immediately west of the canyon access trail from the parking area. The east-facing cliff receives winter sun in the morning and summer shade in the afternoon. This is a good place to get acquainted with cranking at Jacks Canyon, with a good assortment of moderate routes up to 50 feet high. Routes are listed right to left. The first routes are on a buttress up and right behind some trees. The boulders below the first wall have lots of problems, plus toprope anchors. Consult the comprehensive guidebook on Jacks Canyon for details on names and ratings.

1. **Ante Up** (5.8) Pockets and edges up black stone. 3 bolts to 2-bolt anchor.

2. **Maverick** (5.10a) Short route, short crux. 3 bolts to 2-bolt anchor.

3. **Unknown** (5.10) Thin moves up a steep, black slab. 4 bolts to 2-bolt anchor.

4. **Black Jack Crack** (5.10b) Puzzling moves along a thin crack. 4 bolts to 2-bolt anchor.

5. **Queen of Jacks** (5.10b) Boulder problem start up the buttress to an easy slab finish. 6 bolts to 2-bolt anchor.

6. **Let It Ride** (5.10a) A technical, slabby start (crux) to right-angling groove. 5 bolts to 2-bolt anchor.

7. **One-Armed Bandit** (5.10a) An arête right of a chimney. Great pulling up the right side of the arête past a prominent white spot. Do it one-handed on toprope just for fun! 5 bolts to 2-bolt anchor.

8. **Big Spender** (5.11c) Left of the chimney. Cruise to the bulging black rock crux between the 3rd and 5th bolts. 5 bolts to 2-bolt anchor.

9. **Deal from the Bottom** (5.11b) Superb limestone. A crimpy boulder problem start leads to a black vertical wall. 5 bolts to 2-bolt anchor.

10. **Winner Takes All** (5.10b) Interesting technical moves past a couple of horizontal cracks to a white spot. 5 bolts to 2-bolt anchor.

11. **Progressive Slots** (5.6) Great beginner's lead and popular toprope. It's just plain fun! Climb excellent rock with ledgy holds. 6 bolts to 2-bolt anchor.

12. **Fist Full O'Dollars** (5.10a) Sidepulls and edges up the arête right of a chimney. 5 bolts to 2-bolt anchor.

13. **Royally Flushed** (5.11c/d) Power up the low crux to more relaxed moves up high. 6 bolts to 2-bolt anchor.

14. **Take the Money and Run** (5.11c) Begin under the obvious roof. Thin moves to an undercling under the roof. Pull over on crimps to a jug. 6 bolts to 2-bolt anchor.

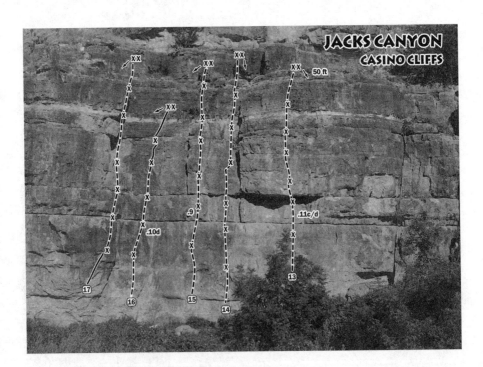

15. **Mickey Goes to Vegas** (5.9) A popular Jacks classic that's a great warm-up and all-around good time. Follow a right-angling flake system to the left side of the obvious roof. Note the Mickey Mouse ears under the roof. Step up right to anchors. 6 bolts to 2-bolt anchor.

16. **Roll the Dice** (5.10d) Precarious face moves up great rock to a crack. 5 bolts to 2-bolt anchor.

17. **Dealer's Choice** (5.10c) A thin, lieback crack in a right-facing corner. 6 bolts to 2-bolt anchor.

18. **High Roller** (5.12a) Pockets and edges up steep, tan rock to an ebony, slabby finish. 6 bolts to 2-bolt anchor

19. **Hold or Fold** (5.12b/c) Powerful crimps and edges to the roof. Continue over strenuous bulges. 6 bolts to 2-bolt anchor.

20. **Read 'em and Weep** (5.12c) Underclings and layaways up overlaps to the roof and upper bulges. 6 bolts to 2-bolt anchor.

21. **Wild Card** (5.12a) Excellent climbing up the tan wall to the roof. 5 bolts to 2-bolt anchor.

22. **Lady Luck** (5.12a) Continuous pocket and edge moves up and over a bulge. 5 bolts to 2-bolt anchor.

23. **Ten the Hard Way** (5.10d) A sustained edgefest! This is a bona fide

5.10 route. Lieback up a crack to great pockets and edges. 5 bolts to 2-bolt anchor.

24. **Circus Circus** (5.6) A fun one for the kiddies. Follow jugs right of a wide crack. 5 bolts to 2-bolt anchor.

25. **Easy Money** (5.7) On the right-hand face of a pillar. Begin with liebacks up a flake crack for 15', step left, and swing up big holds. 4 bolts to 2-bolt anchor.

26. **Card Shark** (5.11c) Up the prow of the pillar. Thin, slabby moves to a bulge. 4 bolts to 2-bolt anchor.

27. **Ace in the Hole** (5.10b) In the shady Grotto chimney left of Route 26. An undercling to fingertip liebacking start leads to sustained but easier movements. Don't pitch and scrape your back on the outside wall. 5 bolts to 2-bolt anchor.

28. **One for the Money** (5.12d) A Casino toughie. Bouldery moves up mono pockets to a horizontal break lead to cruise climbing. 6 bolts to 2-bolt anchor.

29. **Poker Face** (5.11) Lieback left up flakes to a bulge to a slab ending. 7 bolts to 2-bolt anchor.

30. **Crack Dealer** (5.11a/b) Thin crack with jams, stems, and face holds. 7 bolts to 2-bolt anchor.

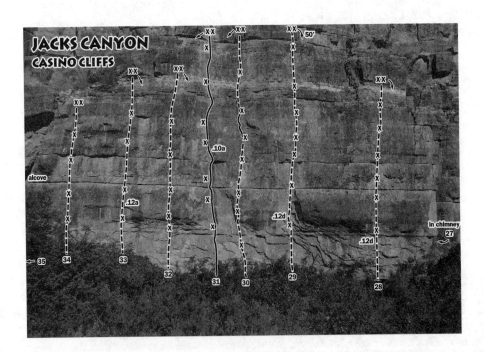

31. **Sports Book** (5.10a) Classic. Hard for those sport weenies not versed in jam techniques—if you can't jam it, stem it. Follow the bolted hand and finger crack up a shallow, left-facing corner. The 1st bolt is high and it's kind of tricky getting to it. 7 bolts to 2-bolt anchor.

32. **Lost Wages** (5.12c/d) Pull over a bulge on some drilled pockets to a steep headwall. 5 bolts to 2-bolt anchor.

33. **Lucky Streak** (5.12a) Steep, pumpy moves up black and tan rock. 4 bolts to 2-bolt anchor.

34. **Texas Holdem** (5.11b) Right of an alcove/chimney. Follow pockets up a black bulge. 4 bolts to 2-bolt anchor.

35. **Gamblin' Fever** (5.11b) Just left of the chimney. Climb tan rock to a high crux. 4 bolts to 2-bolt anchor.

Follow the trail at the base of the cliff farther left to a few more routes, including *Bet on Black* (5.9), *Double or Nothin'* (5.9), *Slots O' Fun* (5.10a), and *Edge Your Bets* (5.10a). The guidebook *Jacks Canyon Sport Climbing* has topos.

THE MAIN WALL

The west-facing Main Wall lies just up the canyon from Casino Cliffs on the opposite side of the canyon and has more than 60 routes for the hardman/woman. Most lines check in at 5.11 and 5.12, with only a handful of moderates. The bulging and overhanging cliff receives afternoon sun for winter climbing and morning shade for summer pumps. From the trail intersection east of Casino Cliffs, turn left on the trail and walk a few minutes to the cliff's base. Routes are described left to right.

36. **Genesis** (5.10d) The first route encountered on the cliff and second route bolted in Jacks Canyon. Begin right of a deep chimney. Great climbing from the very beginning. Work up pocketed rock to a pumpy roof finale. 6 bolts to 2-bolt anchor (open cold shuts).

37. **Unknown** (5.12a) Powerful moves over several roofs to anchors on top of the cliff. 5 bolts to 2-bolt anchor.

38. **Power Trip** (5.11c) Under the right side of the big roof. Long, strenuous moves to anchors under the roof. 4 bolts to 2-bolt anchor.

39. **Unknown** (5.11) On the left side of the left wall of a huge dihedral. Diagonal up left along bolts to anchors at a break. 5 bolts to 2-bolt anchor (open cold shuts).

40. **Two Hands for Beginners** (5.11b) You need both hands to grip edges on this left-angling line up vertical rock. 5 bolts to 2-bolt anchor (open cold shuts).

JACKS CANYON
THE MAIN WALL

41. **Last Episode** (5.10d) Just left of the chimney crack. Fun, but thought-provoking moves up pockets. Keep left up high to avoid the chimney. 4 bolts to 2-bolt anchor.

42. **Sacrificial Lizard** (5.11b) November 1, 1993—the first route established at Jacks Canyon. Up the wall right of the big dihedral. Crimps and edges up the vertical wall to a final bulge. 6 bolts to 2-bolt anchor. (Note: There is a new 5.11 just right of Route 42.)

43. **Tales from the Grypt** (5.11c) One of the canyon's longest offerings. Lower bulge to long vertical headwall. 10 bolts to 2-bolt anchor.

44. **Twist of Cain** (5.12a) Up a prow just left of a deep chimney. Pockets and edges up overhanging rock. 6 bolts to 2-bolt anchor (open cold shuts).

45. **Glued, Screwed and Tattooed** (5.12?) Up steep overlaps right of the chimney. 5 bolts to 2-bolt anchor.

46. **Hand Job** (5.12a) A quality route. Hand jams up cracks in overlaps to a pocketed crux over bulge. 5 bolts to 2-bolt anchor.

47. **Unknown** (5.12) Just right of Route 46. Angle up right on overhanging rock over several small roofs. 5 bolts to 2-bolt anchor.

Walk east along the cliff's base past several projects on the steep wall above to a deep, recessed alcove. One of these projects was sent by Eric Scully at 5.13c. Afterward, the route's bolter chopped the bolts and filled in all the drilled holds in order to rebolt, redrill it, and make it easier.

48. **Haul of Flame** (5.13b) A long and excellent line left of the alcove. Strenuous and pumpy. It gets hard right away—climb over the overhanging bulge and move up the steep wall above to a good rest at a horizontal crack. Pull roofs above to finish at anchors below a ledge. 12 bolts to 2-bolt anchor.

49. **Evil Offspring** (5.12d) A classic, hard route. Same start as Route 48. Work up the bulge to the roof edge. Follow pockets and edges right along the lip. Pull up right and finish up on the right side of an arête. 11 bolts to 2-bolt anchor (open cold shuts). Have a spot on the traverse moves, especially when clipping.

50. **Evil Tweak** (5.13a) An Eric Scully hybrid that begins on *Evil Offspring* and traverses up right to finish on *Trick or Tweak*. 11 bolts to 2-bolt anchor.

51. **Unpopular Mechanics** (5.12d) Another good pumpfest with a big dyno. Begin below an arête at the left side of the deep alcove. Swing up the roof to a block at the lip. Climb up left and edge up the right side of the arête to anchors. 7 bolts to 2-bolt anchor (open cold shuts).

Noah Hannawalt on the hard classic *Evil Offspring* (5.12d), The Main Wall at Jacks Canyon.

52. **Unpopular Tweak** (5.13a) A link-up of *Unpopular Mechanics* and *Trick or Tweak*. Climb Route 51 to the 4th bolt, then traverse up right past a bolt and join Route 53. 8 bolts to 2-bolt anchor.

53. **Trick or Tweak** (5.12d) Another quality Moenkopi classic. Left of a chimney up the left wall of the deep recess. Undercling and sidepull up overlaps to a mono move. Thin, small pockets above to anchors under the big roof. 6 bolts to 2-bolt anchor.

54. **Trick Mechanics** (5.12c/d) The combination of *Trick or Tweak* and *Unpopular Mechanics*. 7 bolts to 2-bolt anchor.

55. **Mighty Morphin** (5.11b) Good fun! Right of a chimney on the right wall of the alcove. Pumpy start up bulging wall to fun slab moves to anchors under the roof. 5 bolts to 2-bolt anchor (open cold shuts).

56. **Cry Baby** (5.12a) Quality moves. Stiff pocket pulling to a horizontal break. Then good pockets to anchors under the big roof. 5 bolts to 2-bolt anchor (open cold shuts).

57. **Total Lack of Jump** (5.12a) Up the right side of the deep recess. Deadpoint over a series of roofs to a horizontal crack. Continue up to anchors under a small, triangular roof. 4 bolts to 2-bolt anchor.

The following routes, rising out of the cobbled streambed, are right of the deep recess.

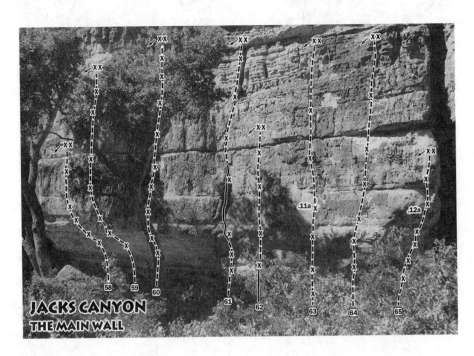

JACKS CANYON
THE MAIN WALL

58. **The Thin Thin** (5.13?) Pockets and edges over a bulge to the base of a roof and on to a lip encounter. Edge up the thin, technical wall above. 5 bolts to 2-bolt anchor.

59. **Cowgirl Diplomacy** (5.12c/d) Recommended. Pull up a bulge to a horizontal roof and past a manufactured pocket. Motor up the steep, pocketed headwall. Have a spot down low when clipping. 7 bolts to 2-bolt anchor.

60. **Shortest Straw** (5.12a) After a boulder problem start, angle up right over a bulge to excellent, slabby, black wall. Stick-clip bottom bolts to protect the hard start. 9 bolts to 2-bolt anchor.

61. **Pretty Pasties** (5.11b) Begin on the left side of a big roof. Stick-clip 1st bolts, then swing up crux moves over a bulge. Continue up a crack in a short, right-facing corner to good pockets. 7 bolts to 2-bolt anchor.

62. **Kolaric Energy** (5.11b) Stick-clip bottom bolts. Start on cheater stone unless you're really tall. Cruxy moves over a bulge lead to easy climbing up a pocketed wall. 4 bolts to 2-bolt anchor.

63. **Bull in a China Shop** (5.11a/b) Start off cheater stones again. Encounter a hard bulge to a big roof, then cruise up excellent flakes on the vertical wall. 6 bolts to 2-bolt anchor.

64. **Path of Desperation** (5.11d) Cheater stone start. Desperate moves over a crimpy bulge, then pockets. 6 bolts to 2-bolt anchor (open cold shuts).

65. **Swiss Arête** (5.12a) Up an overhanging prow left of a deep chimney. Steep pocket pulling (some chipped and drilled) up the holed Swiss cheese prow. 6 bolts to 2-bolt anchor (open cold shuts).

66. **Heart Shaped Box** (5.11d) On the wall immediately right of a deep chimney. Undercling up right to a final headwall test. The back wall is off! 9 bolts to 2-bolt anchor (open cold shuts).

67. **Natural Born Driller** (5.12) Up overhanging overlaps with drilled pockets to pockets and flakes up the vertical wall. 8 bolts to 2-bolt anchor (open cold shuts). Same anchor as Route 66.

68. **Fluffy** (5.12d) Short and steep. Clip the belay bolt, then pull up edges on overhanging bulges to a headwall finish. Anchors below the obvious, horizontal break. 5 bolts to 2-bolt anchor. Burton and Steagall's guidebook recommends long draws on 3rd and 4th bolts.

69. **System in Ruins** (5.12) Left of a crack/chimney system. A steep bulge to technical, vertical rock. 6 bolts to 2-bolt anchor.

70. **Limestone Cowgirl** (5.11d) A good 5.11d. On the left side of the next buttress and just right of a narrow chimney. Pumpy moves up flakes on overhanging bulges lead to thin moves with pockets and edges up

JACKS CANYON
THE MAIN WALL

71 73
XX

75
72 74
70
77
XX

76
XX

XX

XX

.12a

.12c

.12b

70 71

72

all bolts not shown

73 76 77

78

79

the technical wall right of the crack. Left wall is off—if you stem left into the dihedral it's 5.11b. 5 bolts to 2-bolt anchor (open cold shuts).

71. **Ropin' the Wind** (5.12d) A hybrid route. Start up *Limestone Cowgirl* and head right at 3rd bolt past another bolt. Pull a bulge on pockets, then up excellent stone on the left side of a prow. 8 bolts to 2-bolt anchor.

72. **Blazing Saddles** (5.13c) A canyon classic. Stick-clip the 1st bolt and start off a cheater stone stack. Climb out overlaps using flake underclings. Keep left on a bulge at the 3rd bolt and finish up pocketed rock right of a blunt arête. 6 bolts to 2-bolt anchor.

73. **Back in the Saddle** (5.12d) Climb past 3 bolts on a big bulge, then embark up left on an traverse past 5 bolts. Finish up vertical rock. 10 bolts to 2-bolt anchor.

74. **Saddle Up** (5.12d) A link-up line. Begin up Route 73, keep left at bolt 3, then finish up *Blazing Saddles*. 7 bolts to 2-bolt anchor.

75. **Blazing Cowgirl** (5.12c) A 3-route link-up. Start on *Limestone Cowgirl*, work up right at the 3rd bolt past 2 bolts and finish up *Blazing Saddles*. 7 bolts to 2-bolt anchor.

76. **Under Attack** (5.12a) Quality climb time. Work over a large bulge by underclinging flake overlaps. Keep right to good edges at the top of the bulge. Reach through on good pockets up excellent stone. 6 bolts to 2-bolt anchor.

77. **Under the Cowgirl** (5.12d) A triple combination if you've done all the others. Begin with *Under Attack*, veer left at the 3rd bolt, make a long, diagonal traverse up left past 4 bolts and finish up with *Limestone Cowgirl*'s vertical tech moves. 10 bolts to 2-bolt anchor.

78. **Friendly Fire** (5.12c) Watch out! It's not as friendly as you think. Clip a directional bolt and climb over white bulges on edges to good holds below an upper bulge. Continue up pockets and edges left of a short arête. 6 bolts to 2-bolt anchor (open cold shuts).

79. **Sweet Dreams** (5.12b) Up the severely overhanging, right side of a buttress and left of deep chimney. Pocket cranking up the steep prow. 5 bolts to 2-bolt anchor (open cold shuts).

80. **Bone Crusher** (5.12b) Right of a deep, dark chimney. Pockets and edges over a tan bulge to a black headwall left of a double roof. 7 bolts to 2-bolt anchor (open cold shuts).

81. **Zone of Exclusion** (5.12a) Interesting moves up steep, tan rock to anchors under the double roof. 3 bolts to 3-bolt anchor (2 open cold shuts).

82. **Sandman** (5.11b) Continuous and technical moves guarantee you won't fall asleep. Work up overlaps to a small, right-facing corner. 4 bolts to 2-bolt anchor (open cold shuts).

83. **Serpentine** (Project) Over a bulge below the right side of double roofs. 3 bolts to 2-bolt anchor.

84. **Pockets of Resistance** (5.12c) Clip a directional, then climb up on pockets and edges over a bulge to a horizontal break. Swing over the roof (right side of double roofs), then up to a narrow ledge with anchors. 5 bolts to 2-bolt anchor.

85. **This Old Route** (5.11b) It was born in 1994 so it's not really that old! A bouldery start leads to a crack in a thin, right-facing corner to slabby finishing moves. 5 bolts to 2-bolt anchor (open cold shuts).

86. **Kindest Cut** (5.12b) A bulge start to sidepulls up a tan wall. 7 bolts to 2-bolt anchor.

87. **Hooked on Pockets** (5.12d) No topo. Good, continuous pocket pulling. Good pockets to start up the tan wall. Difficulty relents above 4th bolt. 7 bolts to 2-bolt anchor.

88. **Honed Improvement** (5.12a) No topo. Same start as Route 87 but veer right above 1st bolt. Pockets and layaways to a corner finish. 5 bolts to 2-bolt anchor (open cold shuts).

89. **Twisted Sister** (5.12c) No topo. Begin behind trees. Climb left above the 1st bolt, then up the right side of a prow. 6 bolts to 2-bolt anchor.

90. **State of Panic** (5.11c) No topo. Start is shared with Route 89. Go right after the 1st bolt up a flake to a black slab. 5 bolts to 2-bolt anchor.

91. **Male Basher** (5.12b) No topo. Small grips for girls. Start behind trees. Up thin crimps and pockets (chiseled) to a slabby, black finish. 5 bolts to 2-bolt anchor (open cold shuts).

92. **Pocket Runt** (5.11c/d) No topo. Begin behind trees and just left of a large log. Cruxy face moves to the 3rd bolt, then a technical face. 5 bolts to 2-bolt anchor (open cold shuts).

93. **Blackened** (5.10a) No topo. Short and popular. Start right of the log. Thin face moves up a black, slabby crack. 4 bolts to 2-bolt anchor (open cold shuts).

94. **Bats in the Belfry** (5.11a) Right of the obvious chimney. Up a broken crack system. 5 bolts to 2-bolt anchor.

95. **Windchill** (5.10a) Right of Route 94 on the left side of a dihedral. Slab and face moves up good rock. 5 bolts to 2-bolt anchor.

96. **Take Your Pick** (5.10a) Just left of the big corner. A steep start to a juggy slab. 5 bolts to 2-bolt anchor.

Farther up Jacks Canyon are more developed cliffs, including the Swiss Wall, White Gang Wall, Cracker Jack Cliffs, and High Life Wall. Topos and route information are found in *Jacks Canyon Sport Climbing*. The White Gang Wall, a five-minute walk from The Main Cliff, offers several steep, hard 5.12 and 5.13 routes with drilled pockets up an overhanging white cliff. The Cracker Jack Cliffs, on the north side of the canyon on the next creek meander, has many excellent routes on great limestone. This cliff sector is a haven for moderate climbers, with ten 5.10s, nine 5.9s, two 5.8s, and a stellar 5.5. The High Life Wall offers some of the longest routes at Jacks, with most in the 5.11 and 5.12 range.

OTHER FLAGSTAFF AREAS

OVERVIEW

The Flagstaff area is blessed with an abundance of climbing areas. Almost all the areas are composed of basalt, a volcanic rock deposited as lava. Most areas also offer short routes up to half a pitch in length. Some cliffs have a mixture of bolted and traditional routes, while others are gear cracks, toprope crags, or bouldering areas. Farther afield, there are more crags, cliffs, and domes in northern Arizona. Most of these are seldom visited and offer superb opportunities for wilderness climbing adventures and new routes. Check out Tim Toula's guidebook *A Cheap Way to Fly* for directions and topos to many of the Flagstaff crags. His book *Rock 'N Road* has a detailed listing of northern Arizona climbing areas.

ELYSIAN BUTTRESS

Elysian Buttress, perched on the north side of a wide amphitheater on the east flank of Mount Elden just north of Flagstaff, has a good, five-pitch (5.9) route up its 300-foot-high middle buttress. The route is easily accessed from town and makes an exciting afternoon adventure. Scott Baxter, Karl Karlstrom, and Erik Powell first climbed the classic route in the early 1970s. The line was originally rated 5.7, but a lot of climbers say it's more like 5.9. Be advised, too, that much of the gear is small wires and RPs.

Finding the cliff: Drive north from downtown Flagstaff on US Highway 89. Just after you leave the north side of town, look for the first forest service road on the left. The road is south of the buttresses, so keep right at the junction toward the cliff. Park where convenient. Hike cross-country for about 30 minutes to the base of the middle buttress. A cairn marks the start of the route.

1. **Elysian Buttress** (III 5.7+) 5 pitches. **Pitch 1:** Climb a short pillar, then up a shallow groove to a bulge. Face climb left (5.7) around the bulge and climb cracks to a belay stance. **Pitch 2:** Face climb up right (5.6) to an easy, slanting crack system that leads up left to a belay by a tree.

Pitch 3: The Skyline Pitch. Climb out right across shelves and then face climb (5.7) up the skyline to a belay stance. **Pitch 4:** Climb a right-facing corner to an overhang (5.7). Belay above. **Pitch 5:** Face moves lead up left (5.6) to an easy ramp that angles up right to the top of the cliff. **Descent:** Descend to the west past the first gully and buttress and then down the second main gully system. **Rack:** RPs, a set of Stoppers, and Friends to 3".

SECRET CANYON

This hidden canyon, tucked on the south flank of Mount Elden directly north of Flagstaff, yields a good selection of more than 50 sport and traditional routes on a tilted 60-foot-high band of dacite. David Bloom wrote a guidebook to the area, which is usually available in local mountain shops. The trail up to the cliffs is very steep. Tim Toula calls it a "sport climber's death trudge."

O'LEARY PEAK

There are more than 70 crack routes on basalt cliffs on the northwest slope of the 8,916-foot-high O'Leary Peak immediately north of Sunset Crater National Monument. This somewhat remote and unknown area yields some great crack climbing in a beautiful setting that overlooks the surrounding volcanic field at Sunset Crater, the San Francisco Peaks, and the broad sweep of the Navajo Reservation. The undeveloped area, with routes up to 100 feet long, is in Coconino National Forest.

Finding the cliffs: Drive north from Flagstaff on US Highway 89 to the turnoff to Sunset Crater National Monument. Turn right and drive east. After a few miles, look for Forest Service Road 545A. Turn left (north) on this dirt road and follow it for 3 miles as it steeply climbs to the summit of O'Leary Peak. After enjoying the spectacular, 360-degree view, look down the north side and locate the cliffs. Descend a few hundred feet to the base of the cliffs. There is no guide to this adventure area—you're on your own.

GRAND FALLS

Grand Falls, lying on the Navajo Indian Reservation northeast of Flagstaff, is a spectacular waterfall along the Little Colorado River. The intermittent falls usually runs only in spring or after heavy rains; otherwise it's usually just a trickle. Avoid the area during heavy runoff. The area is best known for its outstanding boulder problems on the hueco-covered limestone boulders downstream from the falls. More than 60 problems have been established. There are almost 30 routes, mostly following cracks, on the sandstone cliffs around the waterfall. Flagstaff climbers have named many of the routes. Ask around in Flagstaff for the beta. Tim Toula lists some of the classics on his website *www.rocknroad.com*, including *Little Colorado Crack* (5.11), *Big Colorado Crack* (5.12), and *Hershey's Disaster* (5.10).

PRIEST DRAW

The limestone bouldering area in Priest Draw, southeast of Flagstaff, is one of northern Arizona's best bouldering sites. Many problems of varied difficulty ascend bulges and roofs on boulders and small crags in the shallow, piney canyon. Also, there are some good, pumpy traverses.

Finding the boulders: Drive south from Flagstaff on Arizona Highway 89A to Sedona. Just out of town, turn left (east) on Lake Mary Road and follow it for 6 miles. Just past the cattleguard and the left turn for The Pit, look for Forest Service Road 132 on the right. Turn right (west) on FR 132 and follow it for about 3 miles to a fork. Go right on FR 235 and follow it a short distance. The boulders are visible in the obvious wash. Park, hike, and crank.

OAK CREEK WATERFALL AREA

The Oak Creek Waterfall area is a huge amphitheater of basalt cliffs on the steep east slope of Oak Creek Canyon below the Overlook. This is a superb climbing area, with lots of hard, traditional crack routes similar to Paradise Forks. Most of the routes are 5.10 and 5.11, although there are a few harder and easier lines. Routes are up to 120 feet long, and most have rappel anchors. The approach from Arizona Highway 89A is a brushy, uphill, 30-minute hike. Consult Tim Toula's *A Better Way to Die: Rock Climber's Guide to Sedona and Oak Creek Canyon* for a map, topos, and brief descriptions for 52 routes.

VOLUNTEER CANYON

Volunteer Canyon is a cliff-lined finger canyon in Sycamore Canyon Wilderness Area southeast of Paradise Forks. The basalt cliffs have a selection of routes up to two pitches in length—northern Arizona's longest basalt routes. The canyon is just off Forest Service Road 527, 4 miles southeast of FR 141, the eastern approach road for the Forks. Tim Toula's guidebook *A Cheap Way to Fly* has a map and topo for seven routes.

SYCAMORE POINT

Sycamore Point, one of northern Arizona's most scenic viewpoints, overlooks the rugged beauty of Sycamore Canyon. The deep canyon is rimmed with a long, erosion-resistant cliff band of basalt, forming a climbing area with virtually unlimited potential. The area is nicknamed "The Land of a Thousand Climbs." Tim Toula advises in his guide *A Cheap Way to Fly* to "Pick a line and go for it!" The south-facing cliff band west of the viewpoint has seen the most action. Locals usually toprope many of the routes to maximize cranking time; otherwise, plan on rappelling in and climbing back to the rim. Expect lots of good cracks and face climbs. Watch for loose rock and rattlesnakes. There are excellent camping spots on the rim near the point.

Finding the cliffs: Follow driving directions to Paradise Forks. From the Forks, continue south on Forest Service Road 109 past White Horse Lake. Follow the road west to FR 110 and turn left (south). Follow this good dirt road (and signs for Sycamore Point) for about 8 miles to Sycamore Point. There are good routes on the cliffs ten minutes west of the parking area.

EAST POCKET

Expect more great basalt climbing at East Pocket, a remote, south-facing cliff perched atop the west side of Oak Creek Canyon. There are lots of good crack climbs up to 80 feet long. Classics include *Alley of Aeolus* (5.9+ hand crack), *Pocket Change* (5.11+), *The Pod* (5.11), and *Finger Socket Pocket* (5.11 finger crack). Look in *A Cheap Way to Fly* for a topo and descriptions for 18 routes.

Finding the cliffs: It takes at least one-and-a-half hours on back roads to drive from Flagstaff to East Pocket. Pick up a map of Coconino National Forest to figure out the best way to get there. Briefly, follow Forest Service Road 231 from the west side of Flagstaff. FR 231 runs southwest through pine forests to the rimrock, then bends around the top of the West Fork of Oak Creek before trending southeast toward East Pocket. When you reach a locked gate below a fire tower, park on the north side of the road. Hike south for about 20 minutes up a rocky four-wheel-drive track to the top of the cliff. Downclimb to the base at the west end of the cliffs.

THE ASYLUM

The Asylum is a sport climbing area just up the canyon from Jacks Canyon that is being developed by Phoenix climbers. Because this is a developing area, only a small amount of information is given here. There are lots of bolted 5.12 and 5.13 routes at The Asylum, along with a selection of easier warm-up climbs. Areas include The Grotto, The Main Wall, and the Upper Tier. Recommended routes include *Natural Prozac* (5.11d) and *To Air is Human* (5.12a). Unlike neighboring Jacks, almost none of the routes here have drilled pockets or enhanced holds, nor are the climbs overgraded. Expect hard pulling here. Inquire in Flagstaff or Phoenix for directions and topos to the cliffs.

WINSLOW WALL

The Winslow Wall is an excellent sandstone climbing area along East Clear Creek, southeast of Winslow. The hidden wall is located in a narrow canyon that slices sharply into the almost featureless plain. There are routes on both the east and west walls in the canyon. The canyon is often flooded with snowmelt in spring or after heavy rainstorms. This is a primitive climbing area—come ready to explore. It might take you some time to find the right cliffs because there are lots of cliffs in the canyon and lots of roads on the rim, making it an adventure just reaching the place!

Finding the cliffs: Exit Interstate 40 in Winslow and drive into town. Go south on Arizona Highway 87 toward Jacks Canyon. About 1 mile south of town, go left (east) on Arizona 99. Drive 4.5 miles to a picnic area at McHood Park Lake. Drive another mile past a fence and over a cattleguard. Take a right past the cattleguard at 4.9 miles onto the first dirt road and follow over some hills before turning left and driving 0.25 mile to a parking area on the canyon rim. Hike southeast from the parking lot about a quarter-mile to an obvious gully. Downclimb into the canyon. The west wall is on the opposite side of the canyon, while the east wall is the one below the parking area. Most parties rappel in and leave a fixed line in place for the day.

WEST WALL

The west wall offers some three-star, classic crack climbs. Routes are listed from left to right.

1. **King Snake** (5.9) Stem and jam a long, right-facing dihedral. **Descent:** Rap the route with double ropes from a 2-bolt anchor.

2. **Hangin' Judge** (5.12) A classic finger crack up a 185-foot streaked face that is done in 3 pitches. **Pitch 1:** A 5.7 crack to a ledge. **Pitch 2:** Work up the ½-inch crack (5.11+). Above, it widens to 1¼-inch. Keep right at the Y up a crack (5.10) to a belay stance. Escape by traversing right (5.7) or climb pitch 3. **Pitch 3:** Work up the 6-inch crack in a left-facing corner to the canyon rim. **Descent:** Scramble down right to a 2-bolt rap anchor. Rappel 80' to the canyon floor.

3. **Black Juju** (5.8) A 2-pitch route up dark corners.

4. **Stick It** (5.10) A 2-pitch left-facing corner with a fist and off-width crack and an eagle's nest. Most parties rap from anchors after the outstanding 1st pitch.

5. **Dark Star** (5.10-) 2 pitches. **Pitch 1:** A lightning-bolt crack up the right side of a black tower that ranges between 5" and 12". **Pitch 2:** Face climb up right (5.10-) and follow a left-angling corner to the canyon rim.

6. **American Beauty** (5.10+) 2 pitches. **Pitch 1:** Climb a hand crack up a varnished corner to a belay. **Pitch 2:** Continue up the crack to a left-facing corner that arches left. Stem past the arching roof (5.10+) and continue up the left-facing corner to the rim.

EAST WALL

The east wall also offers a selection of superb cracks. Routes are listed from right to left.

7. **Cruise Control** (5.9) South of the descent gully. A thin crack up a left-arching corner.

8. **Route 1** (5.7) A slabby, right-facing corner south of the descent gully.

9. **Fallen Angel** (5.10) Jam a crack out of a cave.

10. **Plunge Line** (5.9) A thin hand crack left of Route 9.

11. **Stranger in Paradise** (5.10) Jam the right-hand of two parallel cracks.

12. **Flood Gates** (5.9 R) A right-angling, thin crack left of a cave.

13. **The Womb** (5.7) North of the parking area. Wiggle up inside a womblike chimney.

NORTHERN ARIZONA

GRAND CANYON NATIONAL PARK

OVERVIEW

The Grand Canyon, Arizona's most famous and beloved landmark, is an awesome gash that stretches 277 miles from just south of the Utah border through northwestern Arizona to the Nevada border. The canyon is a stunning feature that exposes almost two billion years of the earth's geologic history in the sweep of an eye, from the piney canyon rims to the sun-scorched, inner canyon walls. The canyon, protected as Grand Canyon National Park, casts an elusive spell on its visitors. From an airy perch on the canyon rim, there is a sense of limitless space. Canyon and sky merge at a distant horizon. The canyon, chiseled by millennia of relentless, running water from the Colorado River, is filled with an impressive natural architecture of buttes, temples, cliffs, buttresses, escarpments, and abrupt chasms. It offers a strong sense of place that stuns the first-time viewer to silence and reverence.

The canyon's many visitors have long been surprised and captivated. One of the first Anglos to view it, U.S. Army Lieutenant Joseph Ives, deemed the canyon "altogether worthless . . . Ours has been the first, and will doubtless be the last, party of whites to visit this profitless locality . . . intended by nature to be forever unvisited and undisturbed." Later visitors were kinder. Naturalist John Burroughs called it "The world's most wonderful spectacle, ever changing, alive with a million moods." In 1903, President Teddy Roosevelt noted that the canyon was "the most impressive piece of scenery I have ever looked at . . . It is beautiful and terrible and unearthly." Five years later, Roosevelt created Grand Canyon National Monument, the forerunner of today's national park.

The Grand Canyon, perhaps the world's greatest example of erosion, lies like an open book whose pages document almost half the earth's history. In each different stratum, there is evidence of the changing and evolving landscape—the uplift and subsequent erosion of immense mountain ranges, the inundation of land by vast seas, great fields of sand dunes spread by persistent winds, belching volcanoes and lava flows, and the grand development of life in the sea and on land.

GRAND CANYON

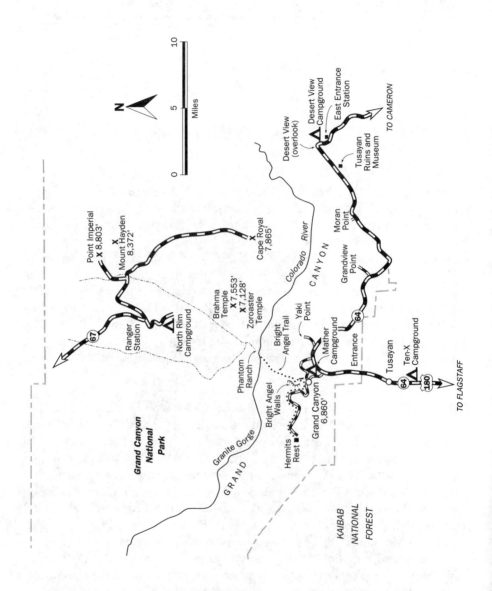

Point Imperial X 8,803'
X Mount Hayden 8,372'
Cape Royal X 7,865'

Ranger Station
North Rim Campground
67

Brahma Temple X 7,553'
Zoroaster Temple X 7,128'

Colorado River

CANYON

Phantom Ranch

Bright Angel Trail

Yaki Point

Bright Angel Walls

Granite Gorge

GRAND

Grand Canyon Park National

Grand Canyon 6,860'

Hermits Rest

Mather Campground

Moran Point

Grandview Point

64

Entrance

Tusayan

Ten-X Campground

64

180

TO FLAGSTAFF

KAIBAB NATIONAL FOREST

Desert View Campground
East Entrance Station
Desert View (overlook)
Tusayan Ruins and Museum

TO CAMERON

N

0 5 10
Miles

Climbing history: Despite the Grand Canyon's endless sandstone and limestone ramparts and cliff bands, little technical climbing has been done in the park except for the backcountry temples and towers, including Mount Hayden and Zoroaster Temple, and a few climbing areas along the South Rim Road. Nontechnical routes reach the top of most of the 125 or so named temples within the canyon. Many of the summits were first climbed by intrepid canyoneer Harvey Butchart.

Zoroaster Temple, named for a Persian prophet who founded the religion of Zoroastrianism, is a 500-foot-high pyramid of Coconino Sandstone below the North Rim. The monolith was first climbed by Phoenix climbers Dave Ganci and Rick Tidrick, who, despite hot temperatures, heavy packs, and the long desert approach, reached the lofty summit on September 23, 1958 via the route *Northeast Arête*. Atop the flat summit, they erected a 5-foot-high cairn. Zoroaster's other route was climbed in 1980 by Dave Ganci, John Annerino, and George Bain, with Annerino leading the last pitch, an off-width, at midnight with a flashlight in his mouth.

There is more climbing in Grand Canyon on the Kaibab Limestone cliffs just below the South Rim. Both toprope and lead routes are found below Twins Overlook east of Grand Canyon Village. The most accessible cragging is at a small area on the limestone cliffs northwest of Bright Angel Lodge and Grand Canyon Village and above the Bright Angel Trail. Beginning in 1991, routes on four different cliff sectors just below the rim were climbed and bolted on lead by area climbers and park rangers.

These routes, protected with both bolts and gear, are accessed from the Rim Trail west of Grand Canyon Village. Climbers should keep a low profile and remember that climbing on public lands is a privilege, not an inalienable right. There are no current climbing regulations or restrictions in the park, but adhere to the following rules. All bolts should be hand drilled; power drills are not permitted. Extensive cleaning of rock and vegetation should be avoided. Avoid visual impact by using camouflaged bolt hangers and rock-colored slings. Follow the existing access trails along the tops of the cliffs and the short descent paths to the bases of the cliffs to avoid erosion. As difficult as it may seem, avoid knocking rocks down from the cliff bands—Bright Angel Trail, a popular hiking trail, is below the cliffs. The described routes were bolted on the lead. Climbers are encouraged to follow this ground-up tradition.

Rack: Plan on carrying a full rack that includes sets of Friends, TCUs, and Stoppers. Some sport routes require only quickdraws. Long slings and locking carabiners should be carried for setting up toprope anchors on top of the cliffs.

Descent: Walk off most routes. A few routes have lowering anchors.

TRIP PLANNING INFORMATION

General description: A selection of both sport and traditional routes on Kaibab Limestone cliffs above Bright Angel Trail on the South Rim of the Grand Canyon and some remote multi-pitch temples.

Location: Northern Arizona, north of Flagstaff.

Camping: The large Mather Campground on the South Rim is operated by the national park. A limited number of sites is available on a daily basis during busy times of the year. Check at the campground entrance for site availability—they usually go quickly. Reservations can be made in advance through BIOSPHERICS by calling 800-365-2267. A free shuttle will take you out to the trailhead for the crag from the campground. Other campgrounds include Desert View Campground at the park's east entrance and Ten-X Campground, a Forest Service campground off Arizona Highway 64, 2 miles south of Tusayan. There is also free, primitive camping off any one of the many forest service roads south of Tusayan.

Climbing season: Climbable weather is found year-round. Best seasons are spring and fall. Summer days can be hot, with temperatures over 90 degrees. The east-facing cliffs are in shade during the afternoon, however, allowing for pleasant climbing. Winter days are often very cold and snowy, but warm, sunny days occur.

Restrictions and access issues: Climbing here, as on all other public lands, is a privilege. Don't abuse it. The following regulations are in effect at the Grand Canyon. Sensible bolting is allowed, but power drills are not. Extensive cleaning of climbs, including the removal of vegetation and lots of loose rock, is prohibited. Don't climb in visible tourist areas or below lookout points. Additionally, follow existing trails to and from the climbing area and don't trundle or knock rocks off—they could tumble all the way down to popular Bright Angel Trail below.

Guidebooks: Information on Zoroaster Temple and Mount Hayden is found in *Adventuring in Arizona* by John Annerino, Sierra Club Books, 1991. Other route information on the temples, as well as a photocopied handout for Bright Angel Walls, is available at the backcountry office.

Nearby mountain shops, guide services, and gyms: Aspen Sports, Babbitt's Backcountry Outfitters, Mountain Sports, Peace Surplus, Popular Outdoor Outfitters, and Vertical Relief Rock Gym (Flagstaff); and Canyon Outfitters (Sedona).

Services: All services are at Grand Canyon Village on the South Rim, as well as at Tusayan just south of the park on Arizona 64. Mather Campground has a laundry and coin-operated showers. Nearby, there is a general store and grocery, post office, and bank.

Emergency services: Call 911. Grand Canyon Clinic, 502-638-2551 or 502-638-2469, offers 24-hour emergency services.

Nearby climbing areas: Brahma Temple, Commanche Point Pinnacle, Cameron Boulders, the Overlook, Oak Creek Canyon, Sedona area, Paradise Forks, The Pit, Elysian Buttress, Mount Elden West.

Nearby attractions: San Francisco Peaks, Sunset Crater National Monument, Wupatki National Monument, Walnut Canyon National Monument, Museum of Northern Arizona (Flagstaff), Navajolands, Meteor Crater.

BRIGHT ANGEL WALLS

There are some good, short routes, both traditional and bolted, on these east-facing cliff bands west of Bright Angel Overlook.

Finding the cliffs: The four walls described here are located on the cliff band below the West Rim Trail between the Bright Angel Trailhead to the east and Trailview Overlook to the west. Take the Village Loop free shuttle bus to its westernmost point at the West Rim Interchange where the Bright Angel Trail begins and the West Rim Loop shuttle takes off. Or, park in the lot at the Maswik Transportation Center and Backcountry Office to the south of the interchange and walk north to it.

From the interchange/shuttle stop, walk west on the paved Rim Trail for almost 0.25 mile. At the trail's first switchback, locate a narrow path that leads straight or north below a short cliff band. Follow this path to a point that overlooks Wailing Wall. A small cave is up to the left. Scramble left to the cave and downclimb 10 feet onto the Traverse Ledge. An exposed trail contours north along this ledge, accessing the four cliff sectors. Stay on the trail to reach all the cliffs and be extremely careful not to dislodge loose rocks, which could roll all the way down to Bright Angel Trail below.

WAILING WALL

Wailing Wall is the first crag encountered after leaving the paved west Rim Trail. After leaving the main trail at the first switchback, walk a short distance to a point that overlooks the Wailing Wall amphitheater. A short downclimb below a shallow cave leads to Traverse Ledge. The first six routes are on the upper tier above the ledge, while Routes 7 through 17 are on the cliff band below the ledge. Reach the lower routes by following Traverse Ledge north to an obvious descent gully. Scramble down to the base of the lower cliffs. Take care not to dislodge loose rocks on the descent. Routes on both cliff tiers are described left to right.

1. **Roof Left** (5.6) Climb a banded slab left of an obvious, slanted roof on the rim of the cliff to a tree anchor.
2. **Roof Right** (5.6) Pull up the slab broken by horizontal cracks on the right side of the big roof to a tree anchor.

BRIGHT ANGEL WALLS

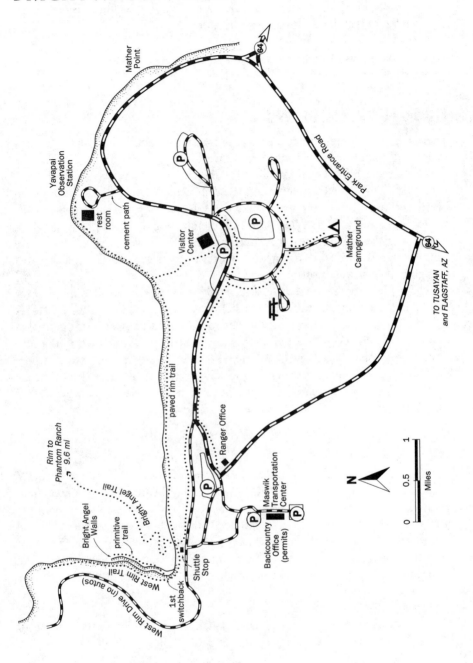

Mather Point

Yavapai
Observation
Station

rest
room

cement path

Visitor
Center

Park Entrance Road

Mather
Campground

TO TUSAYAN
and FLAGSTAFF, AZ

paved rim trail

Rim to
Phantom Ranch
9.6 mi

Ranger Office

Bright Angel
Walls

primitive
trail

Bright Angel Trail

Maswik
Transportation
Center

Backcountry
Office
(permits)

West Rim Trail

West Rim Drive (no autos)

1st
switchback

Shuttle
Stop

N

0   0.5   1

Miles

3. **Wail Pod** (5.10) A vertical crack/groove with 1 bolt. Step right at the top to a 2-bolt chain anchor.

4. **Orca the Killer Wall** (5.10-) Good face moves up a tan wall to a black bulge. 3 bolts to 2-bolt chain anchor.

5. **A Fine Whine** (5.11) Crimps and edges right of Route 4 to the last bolt, then traverse left to Route 4's anchors. 5 bolts to 2-bolt chain anchor.

6. **For Crinoid Out Loud** (5.11) A left-leaning crack with a fixed piton. Go to a rimrock tree anchor or traverse left to Route 4's chain anchors.

LOWER WAILING WALL

The next two routes are on an excellent black face covered with fossils below an overlook point. The two-bolt anchor is accessible from a big ledge for setting up a toprope. Scramble down the descent gully and go right (south) along the cliff's base to the black face.

7. **Right to a Peel** (5.10) Fun climbing! The left route on the face. Work up a black streak to a small roof. Pull past a bolt to a large, right-facing flake (medium Friend and stopper crack) and a ledge. Continue over a bulge to anchors. 2 bolts to 2-bolt anchor.

8. **Black Bawl** (5.9) Recommended. Up right from Route 7. Face climb to a small roof, then move up left past the right side of a bulge to a face finish and anchors on a ledge. 1 bolt and 2 fixed pins to a 2-bolt anchor.

9. **Easier Than Jackie** (5.7) An easy slab right (south) of the descent gully. Toprope off a tree.

The following routes are on a buttress below Traverse Ledge. Reach by scrambling down the descent gully and go left (north) to the base of the cliff's face.

10. **No Name Slab** (5.3) A short crack up a short slab just right of the descent gully. Belay from a single-bolt anchor.

11. **Rip Off** (5.8) Begin off a ledge right of the gully. Work up a shallow corner to a bulge. 2 bolts to a 1-bolt anchor on a ledge above.

12. **Lieback and Enjoy It** (5.10-) Start off the right side of a ledge. Climb up right to a fixed piton, then lieback a flake to a bolt. Finish on fossil holds. 1 piton and 2 bolts. Belay from a 1-bolt anchor.

13. **Tip Off** (5.9) Edge up flakes in a right-facing corner to the single-bolt belay anchor.

View from top of Bright Angel Trail.

14. **So So Security** (5.11-) Climb the excellent, black slab past 1 fixed pin and 2 bolts between corners. Finish atop the left-facing corner at a single belay bolt.

15. **Cinch Up** (5.6) A left-angling crack up the big, left-facing dihedral. Belay at a single bolt.

16. **Holey Terror** (5.10-) Step right of Route 15 on a ledge to start. Move up to a short, right-angling crack (medium Friend). Swing up a headwall past a bolt to a shelf. Climb a short corner up left to a 2-bolt chain anchor.

17. **Cold Shoulder** (5.10+) Walk out the airy ledge right of Route 16 to a belay bolt. Climb up left under a roof to a bolt on a ledge. Work up a headwall past a bolt to easier rock and a tree belay anchor.

FLAILING WALL

Follow Traverse Ledge north and around an airy corner to another amphitheater. There are two routes on the short, steep cliff above the ledge. The rest of the routes are on cliffs below the trail. Downclimb an obvious gully in the middle to reach them.

18. **Arm and Hammer** (5.12) On the upper tier above the trail. Climb an easy slab, clip a bolt by a crack, and pull over a black bulge along a left-slanting crack. 2 bolts to tree anchor.

19. **Beetle of the Bulge** (5.12) Short and powerful. An easy slab start to a bolt in a black water streak. Finish up a groove to loose rock and a tree anchor.

20. **Manly Bulge** (5.10+ R) On the right side of the steep cliff right (south) of the downclimb gully. Climb shallow, right-facing corners to a bolt in the crux bulge. Belay or lower off from a pinyon pine tree.

21. **Macho Do About Nothing** (5.8) Just right of Route 20. Corners and ledges to a bolt in the black crux bulge. Belay from the pinyon pine.

The following routes are all on the lower cliff tier left (north) of the descent gully. Routes are listed left to right along the cliff's base.

22. **Studly Do-Right** (5.9) A fun, left-facing flake system to a tree belay.

23. **Nautilus Workout** (5.10) Flakes and short corners to a bolt in a bulge.

24. **The Pink Panter** (5.10) Start off the right side of a ledge. Work up right to a bolt and mantle onto a shelf below a small roof. Climb up left past 2 bolts and pull over a bulge to a tree belay.

25. **A Yucca Minute** (5.11) Begin down right from Route 24. Face climb 15' to a bolt. Climb up a right-facing flake system to a tree belay. **Rack:** Stoppers and small to medium Friends.

26. **Zingin' in the Rain** (5.12) A bouldery start to a small roof. Continue over bulges to the 3rd bolt. Angle up right over excellent limestone. 6 bolts to 2-bolt chain anchor.

27. **Unknown** (5.12) Begin 15' right of Route 26. Difficult moves past 3 bolts on good limestone. Edge up left to the 4th bolt on Route 26 and finish up right. 6 bolts to 2-bolt chain anchor.

28. **Too Big For Your Bridges** (5.10) Stem and pull up a water groove to a bolt. Head up an easier chimney above to a juniper belay tree.

29. **Surface Tension** (5.10) Quality climbing. Start off a boulder at the base of the cliff right of the groove. Edge up excellent stone studded with fossils. 5 bolts and 1 fixed piton to tree belay. Use caution on the loose rock above the cliff when setting up the belay.

30. **Preying Mantles** (5.11) Another good one! Begin just right of a twisted pinyon pine. Climb straight up past the left side of a black, eyebrow-shaped roof to the left side of a long roof that caps the cliff. Lower from a bolt here or continue to a tree belay. 5 bolts to tree belay.

View from head of Bright Angel Trail.

MEDIVAC WALL

Continue along the Traverse Ledge around the promontory above the right side of Flailing Wall. Past the promontory, the trail edges along a narrow ledge above a northwest-facing cliff. There are three routes below the trail here. Move along the ledge to a downclimb move and onto another ledge. A steep gully with a dead tree in it offers a tenuous descent to the base of an east-facing wall with several more routes. A path switchbacks up through scree above the wall to a short cliff band and the paved Rim Trail above, easy exit to top from here.

31. **Loch Ness** (5.11) This unfinished, left-most route is on the steep, black slab below the trail. Looks really good but needs 1 more bolt.

32. **Godliness** (5.9) The left line up the black slab. Excellent climbing on fossil holds past 2 bolts to a 2-bolt chain belay. Easy to set up as a toprope from the access trail.

33. **Cleanliness** (5.9) The right-hand twin to Route 32. More fun edging up the black slab. 2 bolts to 2-bolt anchor. Also easy to toprope.

34. **Billy Crystal** (5.7) This line is right of the downclimb gully. Way easier than it looks! Begin just left of a pinyon pine on a ledge at the cliff's base. Pull up great rock past 2 bolts to a tree belay.

35. **Learning Curve** (5.11+) One of the area's best routes. Start right of the pinyon pine and Route 34. Power over a crux bulge past 3 bolts. Continue up the slabby wall to a tree anchor. 5 bolts to tree anchor.

36. **Just for the Trilobit** (5.9) Go right from Route 35 on a ledge to an obvious, right-facing corner. Climb flakes up the corner with wires and TCUs for pro to a 2-bolt chain anchor on the left.

37. **Rain of Terror** (5.11-) Start just right of the corner. Climb a slabby face past 4 bolts to a 2-bolt chain anchor up left.

CRUMBLIN' WALL

This exposed wall perches high above the canyon north of the Medivac Wall. Reach it by following Traverse Ledge above Medivac Wall to an obvious downclimb groove/gully that angles northeast. A huge, flat roof is right of the gully. Walk north along a narrowing ledge to reach the routes. Use extreme caution on the ledge—the drop-off is extreme and fatal.

38. **Ruskie Business** (5.10) 2 pitches. Begin from a belay bolt on the narrow ledge. **Pitch 1:** Move up right past big blocks onto a ledge with a small pinyon pine 20' up. Work up past 2 bolts, then traverse left past a bolt under a gray, leaning roof to a crack belay. **Pitch 2:** Climb the obvious crack above to ledges and a belay tree.

39. **Warren Piece** (5.12) A spectacular, unfinished route up the exposed overhanging wall above the ledge. Walk out the flat, very exposed ledge to a large boulder. Swing up and right on pocketed limestone past 3 bolts. Continue to a horizontal break and a kneebar rest. Work over a black, streaked bulge to a bolt with a lowering carabiner. 6 bolts.

40. **The Urge to Purge** (5.10) Follow the ledge until it ends around the corner below a large dihedral. Jam and face climb up cracks in the openbook corner. **Rack:** A couple of sets of Friends.

ZOROASTER TEMPLE

Zoroaster Temple is dramatic and one of the most photographed features in Grand Canyon National Park. Despite its visibility from the nearby North Rim and the tourist hordes on the South Rim, 7,123-foot-high Zoroaster is a remote, backcountry peak that requires at least three days to approach (one day), climb (one day), and return to your car (one day). Along the way, you can expect to hike more than 30 miles and gain and lose 20,000 feet of elevation.

The flat-topped monolith itself is more than 500 feet high and is composed of Coconino Sandstone and Kaibab Limestone.

Remember that climbing Zoroaster Temple is a true backcountry adventure. Expect the unexpected. Carry lots of water. Take your time to figure out the approach. Buy and carry topographic maps of the canyon and the trail systems. And check at the South Rim Backcountry Office for information on the temple and to pick up a camping permit. It's a good idea to call in advance. Remember, too, that weather is fickle in northern Arizona and a backcountry rescue would be difficult and costly.

Finding the temple: These directions are for the approach from the South Rim. Drive north from Flagstaff on US Highway 180 for 50 miles to its junction with Arizona Highway 64. Continue north on US 180/Arizona 64 for another 27 miles to the South Rim of the Grand Canyon.

The hike begins at the Bright Angel Trailhead on the west side of the South Rim Village. Descend Bright Angel Trail for 9.6 miles to Phantom Ranch. Cross the river on a suspension bridge and hike up the North Kaibab Trail for 1 mile to its junction with Clear Creek Trail. The last water source you can count on is at Bright Angel Campground. Fill all your bottles here. Follow Clear Creek Trail as it switchbacks up to the Tonto Platform. After about 1.5 miles, look for the first major drainage, Sumner Wash, that intersects the trail below the east side of Sumner Butte. The wash is unnamed on the topo map. A large tiñaja or rainwater basin below the trail here is sometimes filled with water in spring and fall—but don't count on it.

Leave the trail here and hike up Sumner Wash to an obvious break (a prominent chimney) in the mostly continuous 500-foot-high band of Redwall Limestone. Switchback up to the base of the broken chimney/gully system. Avoid the first part of the chimney by traversing out of it on the right (east) and climbing easy rock back to it 50 feet higher above a large chockstone. Pass a Class 4 headwall on the left up higher and then scramble up loose rock to the top of the Redwall cliffs. The climbing here is Class 4. Use a rope if you feel at all insecure with a heavy pack. Loose rock also abounds. Use caution. There is a good bivy spot east of the top of the gully.

Above the gully, you're on the Hermit Platform. Hike eastward up talus to some short cliff bands of Supai Sandstone. Traverse north, with occasion cairns to mark the way, to several short Class 3 chimneys. Keep on the top of the ridge as much as possible until you reach the base of the main Supai cliff. Traverse left (north) along an exposed trail below the cliff to a steep bowl below Zoroaster's large north face. Look for the easiest route up through the cliff band. This is mostly Class 4 climbing with occasional technical moves. The line is marked with rappel slings and occasional cairns. A rope offers comfort on this exposed section.

Above the cliff band, angle up loose talus slopes composed of Hermit Shale to the base of the temple. To reach the route *Northeast Arête*, continue northeast to the saddle between Brahma and Zoroaster Temples. The saddle makes a great, flat bivouac spot, but it will take most parties a full day of hiking (13 miles) to reach it. The route *Southwest Face* is reached by traversing left (east) below the Coconino Sandstone wall, past the southeast ridge, and under the towering southwest face. The route begins at the first obvious crack in the center of the face.

41. **Northeast Arête** (III 5.9- A0) 6 pitches. First ascent by Dave Ganci and Rick Tidrick in 1958. Classic climbing up pretty good Coconino Sandstone to one of Arizona's best summits. The route follows a broken system of cracks and corners up the temple's northeast ridge. **Pitch 1:** Climb a crack (5.5 A0) left of a large rockslide scar to a ledge belay. **Pitch 2:** Move up a right-angling crack system (5.7) that becomes a smooth, hard-to-protect chimney to a ledge belay. **Pitch 3:** Climb cracks and faces up right and past a flake (5.7). Continue up a crack and ramp to a belay ledge on the right. **Pitch 4:** Jam a long crack (5.8) to a small ledge. **Pitch 5:** Traverse right on a friction face past 2 bolts and

GRAND CANYON NATIONAL PARK
ZOROASTER TEMPLE "NORTHEAST ARETE"

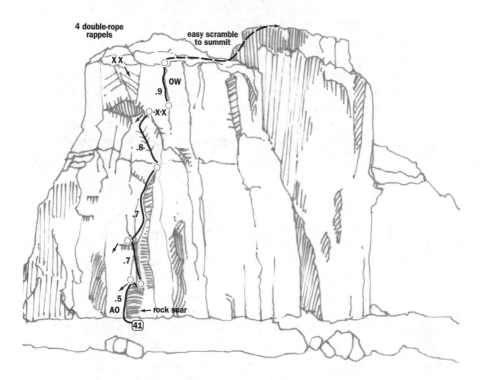

climb a chimney past a ledge to a small belay ledge on the right. **Pitch 6:** Work up a strenuous off-width (5.9 R) to the top of the route and the summit ridge. Scramble south along the ridge to an easy 80' band of limestone cliffs that guards the flat summit. **Descent:** 4 double-rope rappels down the route. For rap 1, find a 2-bolt anchor north of the top of pitch 6. Rappel back to the top of pitch 4. For rap 2, rappel to anchors on a ledge left of the flake on pitch 3. For rap 3, rappel to the ledge atop pitch 1. For rap 4, do a short rappel from a tree through the rockslide scar to the ground. **Rack:** A full rack to a #4 or #5 Camalot, 2 ropes, and extra slings for the rappel stations. Also, some old carabiners with smooth gates for clipping old bolt hangers that are too small for new 'biners. (If you want to do a public service, replace those old bolts with modern ones.) A helmet is also a good idea.

42. **Southwest Face** (III 5.9+) 6 pitches. First ascent by George Bain, Dave Ganci, and John Annerino in 1980. A superb wilderness climbing adventure up the huge southwest face. Begin at the obvious crack system in the middle of the face. **Pitch 1:** Climb ledges to a short, left-facing corner that leads to a traverse left under a roof to a ledge belay. **Pitch 2:** Face climb up grooves and slabs (5.7) to a stance. **Pitch 3:** Move left under a small roof to a short, left-facing corner that becomes a right-facing corner (5.9). Belay up right on a ledge. **Pitch 4:** Face climb up right and then back left (easy class 5) to a long right-facing dihedral (5.8). **Pitch 5:** Make The Twilight Traverse—a long, run-out friction traverse to the right (5.9+ R) to a rotten, left-facing corner system. Belay right of a large roof on a sloping, loose ledge. **Pitch 6:** Scratch up a long, strenuous off-width and chimney crack (5.8 R) to the top. **Descent:** Easiest rappel route is 4 double-rope rappels down the *Northeast Arête*. See Route 41's descent description for details. **Rack:** A full rack from Stoppers to a #4 or #5 Camalot, 2 ropes, extra slings for the rappel stations, and helmets. Some larger off-width pro like Big Bros are useful.

MOUNT HAYDEN

Mount Hayden is a prominent, isolated temple directly below the Point Imperial Overlook on the North Rim of the Grand Canyon. The 8,372-foot-high peak is actually on the east side of the Kaibab Plateau. This lofty sky island is easier and less time-consuming to climb than the multi-day expedition that Zoroaster Temple requires—but you still can't sleep in if you plan to climb it! The peak can be climbed in a full day by a competent party. Several routes ascend Mount Hayden. The described route *Pegasus* is the best and most popular line, but be prepared for some stout climbing. The easier *Original Route* ascends cracks and corners up the south face. Camping is available at the North Rim.

Free, primitive camping is found in Kaibab National Forest several miles north of the park boundary.

Finding the temple: Drive to Jacob Lake in northern Arizona on US 89A from Fredonia to the northwest or US Highway 89 south of Page to the east. Turn south in Jacob Lake and drive south on Arizona Highway 67 to Grand Canyon National Park. Past the entrance station, drive almost to the North Rim. Look for a marked scenic drive that turns left (east). Follow this to a left turn toward Point Imperial. Park at the overlook.

From the overlook, walk north along the rim several hundred yards, dropping into the first probable descent route—an obvious gully that drops steeply east. Although the gully is steep and rugged, you shouldn't have to rappel. Descend the gully for about 1,000 feet to the base of the Coconino Sandstone

GRAND CANYON NATIONAL PARK
MOUNT HAYDEN, "PEGASUS"

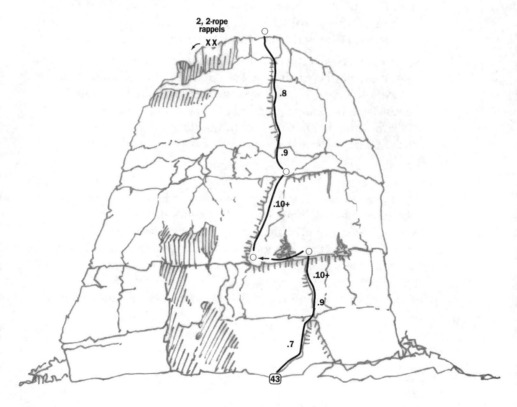

layer. Traverse through dense thickets of brush along the cliff's base until you're opposite Mount Hayden. Descend along a ridge of red Supai Sandstone to a saddle below the tower. Scramble up to the base and contour around to the east face. *Pegasus* angles across the east face. Allow two hours for the approach and even longer for the arduous uphill trek back to your car.

43. **Pegasus** (II 5.10+) 3 pitches. The route was first climbed by Paul Davidson and Jim Haisley in 1984. Considering the nature of the rock and the grand exposure, this route will likely seem stiff for the grade. All bolts should be considered suspect. Begin just right of the east face's center. **Pitch 1:** Climb the left side of a short pillar (5.7) to a ledge. Jam a 1-inch crack (5.9) up right, then up left along a strenuous quarter-inch crack (5.10+) to a good belay ledge. **Pitch 2:** Scramble left along the ledge to the base of a corner. Climb the long, right-angling corner (5.10+) to a belay stance. **Pitch 3:** Climb a right-facing corner to a hand crack (5.9). Work up left along the crack (5.8) to the summit. Scramble up to the flat summit block. **Descent:** Make 2 double-rope rappels from anchors on the southeast corner of the spire. Or make 3 rappels with double ropes off trees down the route. The first rap is off a sapling that teeters on the edge—scary! **Rack:** A selection of Stoppers, TCUs, and cams to 3.5", plus extra webbing for rap slings.

44. **South Face Original Route** (5.7–5.8) No topo. 3 or 4 pitches. This is a good route up the south face. Start above a yucca. Bouldery moves lead to a lower-angle crack system. Belay at bolts after 150'. From here, make 2 or 3 short pitches via several variations (5.7 and 5.8) to reach the summit. **Descent:** Rap this route or rap down the east face. **Rack:** A wide selection of gear including a big piece (this is desert climbing).

45. **North Face** (5.8 A1 or 5.10) No topo. First free ascent was by Stan Mish and friends. This route ascends what Flagstaff climber Albert Newman calls "the ooh-ahh crack system" that is viewed from the rim overlook. Begin by bouldering through loose rock past a fixed piton before reaching better rock. Cruise up the spectacular chimney, encountering some surprising moves, before reaching the summit. **Descent:** Rappel the route or rap down the east face. **Rack:** A couple of sets of cams including extras in the larger sizes for the chimney.

VIRGIN RIVER GORGE

OVERVIEW

Northwestern Arizona is a rough, empty landscape filled with ragged mountain ranges, lofty plateaus, broad basins, and abrupt canyons. The Virgin River, originating atop the 9,000-foot-high Markagunt Plateau, slices through immense sandstone layers in Zion National Park, meanders past St. George in southwestern Utah, and cuts sharply through tilted limestone strata in the Virgin Mountains of extreme northwestern Arizona, forming the Virgin River Gorge before draining into the Overton Arm of Lake Mead. Virgin River Gorge, traversed by busy Interstate 15, offers sport climbers some of America's most difficult rock climbs on towering limestone cliffs above the highway. The gorge's walls, despite their proximity to the asphalt, form Arizona's most remote climbing area. The cliffs are actually inaccessible from any Arizona roadway. The only roads leading here come from neighboring Utah and Nevada.

Almost all of the climbing in Virgin River Gorge is on the immense, black-streaked, tan cliffs in the lower canyon. The main cliff group, including popular Mentor Wall, Planet Earth Wall, and Blasphemy Wall, looms above the south side of the freeway. Mentor Wall features *Mentor*, an overhanging jug haul considered to be the best 5.12 in the canyon. The adjoining Planet Earth Wall is laced with some long endurance routes, including two 5.14s—*Planet Earth* and *Horse Latitudes*. Farther east is the almost 200-foot-high Blasphemy Wall. This sleek sweep of limestone offers eight 5.13s and three 5.14s, including *Necessary Evil* (5.14c), one of the country's most difficult routes. The north side of the canyon features more cliffs and caves. These include Sun Wall and Sun Cave, on the wall directly north of the parking area, and Fossil Cave, a 120-foot-high cave of arching limestone, which yields a selection of burly, overhanging lines.

Climbing in the gorge, or the VRG as climbers call it, is a somewhat urban experience. The crags, straddling the edges of two wilderness areas, tower above Interstate 15. This major four-lane highway is constantly busy with traffic rumbling between Salt Lake City to the north and Las Vegas and Los Angeles to the southwest. If you sit at the base of the cliffs after a morning of relentless crimping, you can count an average of ten cars and trucks a minute speeding below, or about one every six seconds. After spending a day here, the highway roar fades into a kind of unobtrusive white noise. You tune out the industrial sounds and attune yourself instead to your own inner rhythms and the silence of the limestone.

VRG is basically a three-season climbing area. The area's generally mild winter weather and absence of measurable snowfall make it an ideal winter destination. Winter daytime highs often climb into the 60s. Cooler days can, however, be downright chilly because the cliffs are shaded all day in winter and

VIRGIN RIVER GORGE

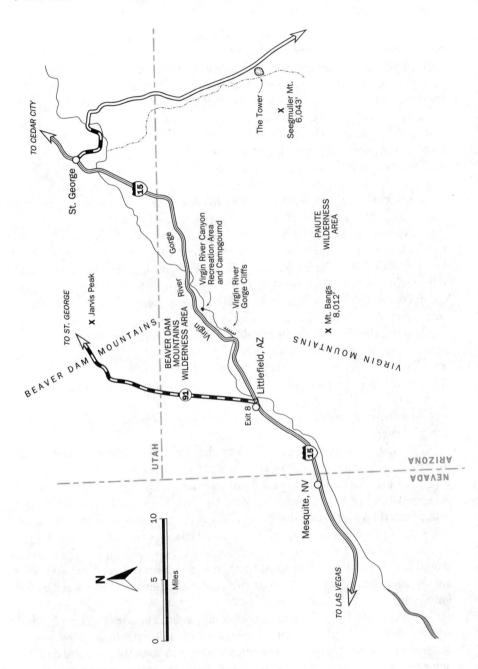

a brisk wind often sweeps up the canyon. January can be too cold, but December and February usually offer excellent climbing weather. If it is cold, check out Sun Cave and Fossil Cave for warmer conditions. March and April are also great months, although days can be hot and afternoons breezy. October and November are good, too. The summer months from May through September are baking hot, with daily high temperatures often topping the century mark. The cliffs do get lots of summer shade though. Plan to climb early in the morning during these scorching months.

Climbing history: Virgin River Gorge is a crag of the 1990s. It was developed as bolted sport climbing finally came of age in the United States and it became the locale of some of America's hardest routes. Although countless climbers had passed the gorge along the interstate, no one had really checked out the potential of the huge walls in the lower canyon until northern Utah climbers Boone Speed, Vince Adams, and Jeff Pederson stopped in 1989. Within a week, they had bolted VRG's first lines up Paradigm Wall and the next week they started on Blasphemy Wall's immaculate limestone. Speed bolted and climbed *The Fall of Man*, while Pederson created *Dark Boy* 15 feet to the right.

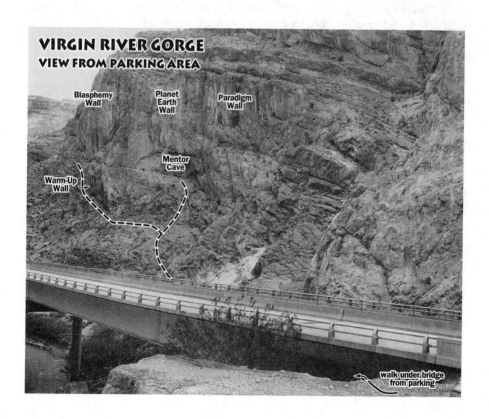

These initial forays turned other climbers on to the gorge's vast potential for hard routes. Tom Gilje bolted *Mentor* from the ground up, creating an instant classic that was more accessible to most climbers than the surrounding 5.13s. American Fork pioneer Bill Boyle added *High Flames Drifter*, while Scott Frye climbed *Dude* and *Don't Call Me Dude* in the early 1990s.

Blasphemy Wall, with its long technical masterpieces, became a playground for Boone Speed, who bolted and redpointed two 5.14s—*Route of all Evil* and *F-Dude*. His crimpy direct start to *Route of All Evil* was finally climbed by kid wonder Chris Sharma in 1998, who dubbed it *Necessary Evil* and rated it 5.14c, making it one of America's hardest lines. *Planet Earth* and *Horse Latitudes*, two of the other VRG 5.14s, were established and climbed by Randy Leavitt. Leavitt, who routinely drove here for a weekend of climbing from his Southern California home, almost single-handedly cleaned, bolted, and climbed all the routes in the overhanging Fossil Cave on the north side of the canyon. Another route activist here was Tim Wagner, who put up several excellent routes on Blasphemy Wall. Lots of overhanging limestone still remains here for future projects, requiring only a handful of bolts and hangers and a lot of endurance and crimping strength.

Rack: All the gorge routes are bolted sport climbs. Bring 20 quickdraws and a 200-foot (60-meter) rope. **Descent:** Lower off or rappel. There are midpoint anchors on the longer pitches.

TRIP PLANNING INFORMATION

General description: Numerous bolted sport routes ascend the overhanging limestone cliffs above Interstate 15 in Virgin River's deep desert canyon.

Location: Northwest corner of Arizona, 25 miles southwest of St. George, Utah.

Camping: The Bureau of Land Management (BLM) maintains a good, but sometimes noisy campground at a rest area in the Virgin River Gorge, just south of St. George. Snow Canyon State Park has an excellent 36-unit campground (fee) with showers, 8 miles north of St. George off Utah Highway 18. There are many places for primitive camping in the surrounding desert. Keep a low profile and pick up after yourself.

Climbing season: Fall, winter, and spring. Winter has climbable temperatures almost every day, with highs regularly in the 50s. Low temperatures rarely dip below freezing. Fall and spring are also excellent, although it can be hot. There are some shaded climbs. Summers are hot. Daily highs usually exceed 100 degrees. Climbing at the lower elevation crags is almost impossible.

Restrictions and access issues: Most of the crags are on BLM land and currently have no restrictions. Use common sense, however, by keeping impact to a minimum. Park in designated areas, camp only in existing primitive sites, and use climber trails to the bases of the cliffs whenever possible. Be sure to pick up all your trash and any that was left previously, including cigarette butts and tape. Leave all wildlife alone. It is illegal to pick up and traumatize desert tortoises. Also, watch for chuckwallas in cracks and scorpions in pockets.

Guidebooks: *Too Much Rock, Not Enough Life: A Sport Climbing Guide to St. George and Southwestern Utah* by Todd Goss, Paragon Climbing Guides, 1996 is a topo guide to all the major sport crags in the St. George area, including nearby Virgin River Gorge. Rockfax is publishing a guide to the limestone areas around Las Vegas, as well as Virgin River Gorge and southwestern Utah. Randy Leavitt is writing the section on Virgin River Gorge.

Nearby mountain shops, guide services, and gyms: Outdoor Outlet, 1062 East Tabernacle, St. George, UT; 801-628-3611 or 800-726-8106. Todd Goss with Paragon Climbing Instruction, 801-673-1709, offers basic and intermediate climbing courses, as well as guiding services and area climbing tours.

Services: All visitor and climber services are in St. George, including restaurants, motels, groceries, and gas. Winter motel rates can be very cheap. Check around for deals.

Emergency services: Call 911. Dixie Regional Medical Center, 544 South 400 East, St. George, UT; 801-634-4000 or 800-326-4022.

Nearby climbing areas: The Tower. Just over the border in Utah, there are lots of climbing areas, including Pioneer Park Bouldering Area, Black Rocks, Cougar Cliffs, Turtle Wall, The Green Valley Gap, Gorilla Cliffs and Simeon Complex, The Diamond, The Wailing Wall, The Cathedral, Zion National Park, Kolob Canyons, The Overlook, Cetacean Wall, and Cedar City areas.

Nearby attractions: In Arizona: Virgin River Gorge, Beaver Dam Mountains Wilderness Area, Paiute Wilderness Area, Arizona Strip, Grand Canyon National Park, Toroweap Point, Pipe Spring National Park.

In Utah: Pine Valley Mountain Wilderness Area, Zion National Park, Smithsonian Butte Back Country Byway, Virgin River Narrows, Kolob Canyons, Kolob Arch (largest in world), Cedar Breaks National Monument, Joshua Tree Natural Area (farthest north Joshua tree area).

Finding the crags: The Virgin River Gorge is split by Interstate 15 in the far northwest corner of Arizona. The gorge is accessed via the interstate from Las Vegas to the south (90 miles) and from St. George to the north (25 miles).

Parking for the climbing area in the gorge is near interstate milepost 13, which is 13 miles from the Arizona and Nevada border. Parking is allowed only in a large roadside pullout on the north side of the highway and on the west side of a long bridge. Parking is not allowed on the south side before the highway bridge. If you are heading north on I-15, continue 5 miles up the highway past milepost 13 to an exit at milepost 18. Exit, cross the highway, and drive west to the parking area. Pay attention at milepost 14. The highway crosses a long bridge and the parking area is immediately past it.

VIRGIN RIVER CLIFFS

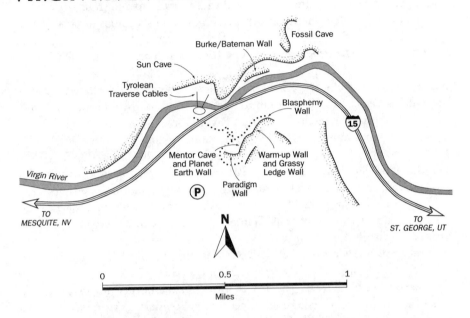

To reach the cliffs, walk under the bridge and follow a climbers' trail that zigzags up a steep hillside to the Mentor Wall area on the right side of the main cliff.

MENTOR WALL

This is the triple-roofed, overhanging wall on the right side of the main cliff. The first route is on a buttress down and right from the Mentor Cave. Routes are described right to left.

1. **Unknown** (5.10d) A bad route. 5 bolts to 2-bolt chain anchor.

2. **Brutus** (5.11b) 7 bolts to 2-bolt chain anchor.

3. **Corrosion** (5.12c) 8 bolts to 2-bolt chain anchor.

4. **Mars** (5.13b) 8 bolts to 2-bolt chain anchor.

5. **Bowser Wowser** (5.13a/b) 16 bolts to 2-bolt chain anchor.

6. **Bowser** (5.12d) 11 bolts to 3-bolt chain anchor.

7. **Subterfuge** (5.13a) Powerful and excellent. This route finishes up *Mentor's* final roof to its anchors. 10 bolts to 3-bolt chain anchor.

VIRGIN RIVER GORGE
MENTOR WALL AND PARADIGM WALL

to chains   to chains   to chains

Paradigm Wall

13 12

3rd class

11

10

3rd class

4

3

5 4   3 2

1

all bolts not shown

VIRGIN RIVER GORGE
MENTOR WALL AND PARADIGM WALL

Paradigm Wall

to chains

3rd class

Mentor Cave

50'

478

8. **Mentor** (5.12b) The cliff's mega-classic, must-do route. Most popular route at VRG. Put up on lead by Tom Gilje. Begin at the right side of the cave. Climb up and out of the cave on polished jugs, a leg-thread rest, and a pull-up bar, to a vertical finish. 9 bolts to 3-bolt chain anchor.

9. **Sensory Overload** (5.13b) 14 bolts to 2-bolt chain anchor.

PARADIGM WALL

This wall is above and right of Mentor Cave. All the routes begin on a big ledge below the wall that is reached by climbing Route 1. Routes are described right to left.

10. **The Hunger** (5.12d) 7 bolts to 2-bolt anchor.
11. **Dim** (5.12c) 6 bolts to 2-bolt anchor.
12. **Velvet Underground** (5.12c) 8 bolts to 2-bolt anchor.
13. **Paradigm** (5.12c) 8 bolts to 2-bolt chain anchor.

PLANET EARTH WALL

The Planet Earth Wall is the immense sweep of slightly overhanging limestone left of Mentor Cave. All the routes begin off a sloping ledge left of the cave. Belay bolts are placed along the ledge for anchors. Routes are described right to left from Mentor Cave. Carry more quick draws than you think you'd need. All bolts not shown.

14. **Quick Fixe** (5.11d) Popular pump. 5 bolts to 2-bolt anchor.
15. **Hell Comes to Frogtown** (5.13d) 6 bolts to 2-bolt anchor.
16. **Surrender Dorothy** (5.12d) 7 bolts to 2-bolt anchor.
17. **Project** (5.13?) 20 bolts to 3-bolt anchor.
18. **Don't Believe the Hype** (5.12a) 7 bolts to 2-bolt anchor.
19. **Project** 5 bolts to 2-bolt anchor. No topo.
20. **Dirt Cowboy** (5.12c) 10 bolts to 2-bolt chain anchor.
21. **False Witness** (5.13a) No topo. Start on *Dirt Cowboy*. At its anchors, go left to the 1st bolt of *Captain Fantastic*, then head up right to finish 20' right of *Captain Fantastic's* anchors. 17 bolts to 2-bolt chain anchors.
22. **Captain Fantastic** (5.13c) Excellent. Belay from a bolt on the slab below the route. Climb *Dirt Cowboy* for 70', go up 1 bolt above its chain anchors, and work up left on good holds another 50' to a 2-bolt chain anchor. 16 bolts to 2-bolt anchor.

Ian Spencer-Green resting with a leg-thread rest on the most popular route at Virgin River Gorge, *Mentor* (5.12b).

23. **Planet Earth** (5.14a) A Randy Leavitt endurance testpiece. 15 bolts to 2-bolt anchor.

24. **Horse Latitudes** (5.14a) A long endurance route. 15 bolts to 2-bolt anchor.

25. **Joe Six-Pack** (5.13a) Randy Leavitt calls this "one of the best 5.13s in the VRG." A good on-sight route for the grade. A long route up the left margin of the wall. 12 bolts to 2-bolt chain anchor.

26. **Redneck** (5.12b) 7 bolts to 3-bolt anchor.

27. **Deliverance** (5.13a) 8 bolts to 3-bolt anchor.

WARM-UP WALL

This short, northwest-facing wall is up and left (east) from Mentor Cave. Follow a trail along the cliff's base that passes under the wall en route to Blasphemy Wall. Routes are described right to left.

28. **Corporate Slut** (5.9) 6 bolts to 2-bolt chain anchor. 50'.

29. **Spook** (5.11c) 4 bolts to 2-bolt chain anchor. 45'.

30. **Call Me Mike** (5.11a) 4 bolts to 2-bolt chain anchor. 45'.

31. **Lyme Disease** (5.10c) 4 bolts to 2-bolt chain anchor. 45'.

32. **Smoked Chub** (5.10b) 5 bolts to 2-bolt chain anchor. 45'.

GRASSY LEDGE WALL

These routes are on the black-streaked wall above the obvious, grassy ledge above Warm-Up Wall. Access them by Class 3 scrambling up a crack and groove system left of the wall and right of Blasphemy Wall. Routes are described right to left.

33. **Shyster Myster** (5.11d) 4 bolts to 2-bolt anchor.

34. **Bugger Bill** (5.12b) 5 bolts to 2-bolt anchor.

35. **Catalyst** (5.11c) 2 pitches. **Pitch 1:** 5 bolts to 2-bolt anchor. **Pitch 2:** 8 bolts to 2-bolt anchor.

36. **Dead on the Phone** (5.11d) 5 bolts to 2-bolt anchor.

BLASPHEMY WALL

This huge, black-streaked wall offers a selection of long, excellent routes that

VIRGIN RIVER GORGE
WARM-UP WALL AND GRASSY LEDGE WALL

3rd class

35

36

35   34   33

Grassy Ledge Wall

Planet Earth Wall

to Blasphemy Wall

32

31
cave   30

29   28

Warm-Up Wall

to
Mentor Cave

include some of America's hardest lines. Reach the wall by scrambling up a trail that follows the base of the cliff left of Planet Earth Wall. Routes are described right to left.

37. **Erotic Jesus** (5.13a) 13 bolts to 2-bolt anchor.

38. **Bloody Mary** (5.11d) 8 bolts to 2-bolt anchor.

39. **Swear to God** (5.13b) 8 bolts to 2-bolt anchor.

40. **Don't Call Me Coach** (5.13c/d) 8 bolts to 2-bolt anchor.

41. **Open Project** (5.13+?) 9 bolts to 2-bolt anchor.

42. **Necessary Evil** (5.14c) This direct start to Route 43, first climbed by Chris Sharma, is one of the hardest routes in the country. 11 bolts to 2-bolt anchor.

43. **Route of All Evil** (5.14a) A Boone Speed masterpiece. Start up the first 3 bolts of Route 44 and then move up right, edging and pulling past many bolts up the slightly overhanging wall. 11 bolts to 2-bolt anchor.

44. **Don't Call Me Dude** (5.13c) 11 bolts to 2-bolt anchor.

45. **Dude** (5.13c) It's harder if you're short. 11 bolts to 2-bolt anchor.

46. **F-Dude** (5.14a) Classic. An ultraendurance crimpfest that links the cruxes of *Dude, Dark Boy,* and *Fall of Man.* A redpoint usually takes at least half an hour of hanging out. 14 bolts to 2-bolt anchor.

47. **Dark Boy** (5.13b) Long reaches, underclings, and pumpy slopers to a vertical finish. 12 bolts to 2-bolt anchor.

48. **Fall of Man** (5.13a/b) The first route on Blasphemy Wall. Powerful, technical climbing leads to thin, continuous moves on overhanging and vertical rock to a slab crux at the 12th bolt. 15 bolts to 2-bolt anchor. 130'.

49. **High Flames Drifter** (5.12c) 6 bolts to 2-bolt anchor.

50. **I Saw Jesus at the Chains** (5.13a) You'll hang on so long that you'll see him too! 13 bolts to 2-bolt anchor.

OTHER NORTHERN ARIZONA AREAS

OVERVIEW

Northern Arizona is the state's empty quarter. Most of the uninhabited land is rough, lonely country punctuated by high plateaus, rock-rimmed mesas, wide valleys, and sheer canyons. There is lots of climbing still to be done out there in the Arizona outback. A few are listed below.

The northeast quarter of the state is part of the Navajo Indian Reservation. There is lots of excellent sandstone climbing on the "Rez," but most of it is illegal. Ask permission first from the government of the Navajo Nation in Window Rock or from the local grazing permit holder. Otherwise, it's climb at your own risk. Possible penalties for illegal ascents include the confiscation of equipment and cars, fines, and jail sentences. Now that's real adventure climbing!

THE TOWER (aka THE PHALANX OF WILL)

The Tower is a remote, monolithic, 200-foot-high limestone thumb hidden at an elevation of 3,300 feet in Dutchman Draw in far northwestern Arizona. Glen Burke, who discovered the airy spire in 1996, made the first ascent of the tower with Todd Perkins via a 5.6 crack up the northwest side. Since then, more than 20 bolted routes have been established on the formation's three overhanging faces, most in the extreme 5.12 and 5.13 grades. Expect long, pumpy pitches with technical, crimpy moves. All the routes are bolted, with lowering anchors. Classics are *A Fossil of Man* (5.13c/d) up a 140-foot arête and *Pompetus Vision* (5.12d). There is also lots of great bouldering in the canyon around The Tower. This place is a wilderness alternative to the noisy Virgin River Gorge. The Tower is on Bureau of Land Management public land. Primitive camping is available at Dutchman Draw, but bring water. This is definitely a three-season climbing area. Sunny winter days offer the best cranking weather. Spring and fall are also very pleasant. Summer is an inferno.

Rack: Bring 24 quickdraws and a 200-foot (60-meter) rope. *Too Much Rock, Not Enough Life* by Todd Goss, is a comprehensive guidebook to The Tower, Virgin River Gorge, and all the excellent cliffs around St. George, Utah. The book has a map and topos to The Tower. The guide is available at the Outdoor Outlet in St. George. A topo guide also appeared in *Rock & Ice* #86.

Finding the cliff: From Interstate 17 and St. George, exit onto Bluff Street and drive north to the second stoplight at 700 South. Turn right (east) onto 700 South and follow it to River Road. Turn right (south) onto River Road and follow it across the Virgin River. Just past the bridge, take a left turn onto 1450 South. Follow this paved road for 5.5 miles, then continue for 10.5 more miles on a gravel road to the end of the improved road. You will need a four-wheel-drive vehicle for the last 1.5 miles to The Tower. The rough road enters a wash. Follow the wash for 1 mile to another wash on the left. Go left up this wash for 0.5 mile to the obvious formation.

TOOTHROCK

Toothrock is a huge, toothlike sandstone formation hidden in an isolated desert canyon near the Colorado River and Marble Canyon in northern Arizona. The main bulk of the 6,158-foot Toothrock is composed of Wingate Sandstone sitting atop loose layers of Chinle Sandstone and capped by relatively solid Navajo Sandstone. This almost 2,000-foot-high monolith offers climbers three of the wildest and scariest big walls in Arizona.

The 20-pitch *Lost Love Route* (V 5.9 A3) was established by Spencer McIntyre and George Bain over four days in February, 1977. Eric Bjornstad's guide *Desert Rock* describes the route as "characterized by rotten sandy rock with Volkswagen-size boulders, frequent rockfall and intricate routefinding." Consult *Desert Rock,* now out-of-print, for a full route description.

The 11-pitch *East Buttress* (VI 5.10 A2) was climbed by Dougald MacDonald and Paul Gagner in early January, 1997. The route, attempted twice by Arizona climbers in the 1980s, follows Toothrock's obvious right-hand buttress. The route begins with some dangerous scrambling up the lower bands of rotten Chinle Sandstone.

Finding the formation: Drive north from Flagstaff on US Highway 89 to Bitter Springs. Go left on US 89A and continue north to the town of Marble Canyon on the west side of Navajo Bridge. Turn right (north) on Lee's Ferry Road, drive about 2 miles to Cathedral Wash, and park off the road. Toothrock is about 2.5 miles west up the wash in a huge, sandstone amphitheater. Hike up the wash to a talus slope just before a dry waterfall. Climb the talus and follow an old road to Lowrey Spring at the base of the tower.

MONUMENT VALLEY

Monument Valley, straddling the Arizona and Utah border north of Kayenta in northeastern Arizona, is one of the most famous and scenic areas on the entire Colorado Plateau. The area, on the Navajo Indian Reservation, has a stunning assortment of spires, buttes, and mesas composed of de Chelly Sandstone. Monument Valley saw many early ascents of its sheer towers, including The Three Sisters and The Totem Pole, by pioneer desert climbers like Layton Kor and Fred Beckey. Now, most of the spires are definitely off-limits to climbers, although ascents still occur. It's best to ask permission from the local grazing permit holder before climbing any of the towers; otherwise, it's climb at your own risk. The valley is a Navajo Tribal Park.

There are excellent routes just over the border in Utah on Stagecoach, King on a Throne, The Rabbit and The Bear, and Shangri-la. Shangri-la, a large blocky tower, offers a superb route (IV 5.10 A0) that begins on its north side and ends up chimneying through the formation to finish up the south face. Jacobs Ladder, a thin 300-foot spire, and Eagle Rock Spire (III 5.9 A3+) are nearby on the north side of Eagle Mesa.

The Arizona side of Monument Valley offers the best routes. These are also the most risky to climb. Layton Kor and Steve Komito first climbed the Left Mitten Thumb in the 1960s. The 5-pitch *East Route* (III 5.6 A2) follows crack systems up the east face. The Right Mitten Thumb was first summited by a serious aid route in the late 1960s by Tom Ruwitch and Bill Mummery. The summit is a narrow edge that the climbers had to straddle with 400 feet of air on each side. The Banditos from Phoenix made a subsequent ascent via *Right Thumb* (III 5.9+ A3) in 1984. The Three Sisters, lying on the southeast end of Mitchell Mesa, have all been ascended by a variety of routes.

Nearby is The Totem Pole—the most spectacular spire in Arizona, if not the world. The spire, probably the thinnest and tallest freestanding formation in the world, is 400 feet high and between 25 and 40 feet in diameter. Steve Roper described it in a 1970 *Ascent* magazine as "a fearsome red shaft, so thin and precariously built that the thought of climbing it sends shudders through the body." Climbing it is, of course, strictly prohibited, although the Pole was featured prominently in the movie *The Eiger Sanction*, as well as in numerous advertisements. California climbers Mark Powell, Don Wilson, Bill (The Dolt) Feuerer, and Jerry Gallwas snagged the first ascent in June 1957. The party aided up cracks using wide aluminum channel pitons made for the ascent by Feuerer. The *Northwest Face* (III 5.7 A4) saw several more ascents until the fifth in 1975 by Ken Wyrick and Eric Bjornstad. The pair was hired to climb the spire for *The Eiger Sanction*, and part of the deal with the Navajo Nation was that the route would be completely cleaned of fixed anchors. This action led to the establishment of *Never Never Land* (III 5.10 A2) in 1979 by The Banditos on the back side of the tower. This is the route that climbers use now for underground ascents.

AGATHLA

Agathla, a massive volcanic plug composed of basalt and tuff-breccia, lies just off US Highway 163 between Monument Valley and Kayenta. The name Agathla is derived from the Navajo word "Aghaa'la" meaning "Piles of Wool," and the peak figures in Navajo mythology. The Shiprock-like mountain offers several routes for climbers. The best and most popular route is *West Face* (III 5.7), a mountaineering-type route that was first climbed by Herb Conn, Ray Garner, and Lee Pedrick in May 1949. This is probably the easiest route to climb surreptitiously on the Navajo Reservation. Ask for permission from the local grazing permit holder if you want to make it legal. Otherwise, climb at your own risk. The following description is merely for entertainment—you're on your own, partner.

Finding the formation: Agathla towers east of US 163 at milepost 400, about 7.5 miles north of Kayenta. Park in a scenic pullout, study the obvious west face, and hike cross-country to its base.

West Face (III 5.7) 7 to 9 pitches. The left side of the peak is basalt, while the right side is tuff-breccia. On the left skyline where the two formations meet is an obvious, deep notch. This is the 3rd prominent notch from the left. Begin below this notch. **Pitches 1 to 5:** Climb loose basalt blocks up the steep wall to the notch. Most of this is easy 5th class climbing with occasional 5.7 moves. **Pitch 6:** From the notch, descend 20' into a narrow gully and follow it up another 120' to another notch. **Pitches 7 and 8:** Climb west onto the main ridge and follow it for 200'. **Pitch 9:** Climb to an exposed notch, work up a wall above and belay. Continue up 200' of Class 4 scrambling to the summit. **Descent:** Downclimb back to the top of the headwall above the upper notch. Leave the ascent route here and downclimb 150' of Class 4 rock to the east. Make a double-rope, 100-foot rappel into a large talus gully. Descend the gully for several hundred feet until you see an obvious notch to your left. This is the lowest of the 3 notches seen from the parking area. Scramble up to the notch and make 4 rappels down the wall below to the base of the west face. **Rack:** Sets of Stoppers and Friends, runners, extra slings for the rappel stations, and 2 ropes. A helmet is a good idea too.

SPIDER ROCK

Spider Rock, an 800-foot-high tower tucked away in Canyon de Chelly in northeastern Arizona, is reputed to be the tallest freestanding spire in the world. The tower is in Canyon de Chelly National Monument, a spectacular preserve of ancient Anasazi ruins on the Navajo Indian Reservation. Climbing Spider Rock is prohibited, partly because it figures in Navajo religion. Legend says the Spider Lady, the Navajo equivalent of the Bogeyman, lives atop the rock and when children misbehave, nearby Whispering Rock tells the Lady and she crawls down from her rocky aerie. She catches the children and carries them back to the summit where she devours them, leaving their bones to gleam in the sun. The leached, white rocks on Spider Rock's summit are the remains of the bones.

Californians Don Wilson, Jerry Gallwas, and Mark Powell made the first ascent of Spider Rock over 3 days in March 1956. Their route, graded 5.8 A3, ascended one of the first major desert towers ever to be climbed. Wilson later wrote, "We felt that we would not only be pioneering a new route, but also writing a new chapter in the history of rock climbing in the Southwest." The spectacular line was climbed several times before the Navajos banned further ascents. Todd Skinner and Tom Cosgriff free climbed the route at 5.10d in 1983, finding the crux an off-width near the summit. The nine-pitch route begins on the east side below a deep cleft that separates the main tower from a subsidiary summit. Climb cracks and chimneys to the top and then make six rappels down.

If you do decide to climb Spider Rock, remember that it's very illegal and serious consequences confront climbers who are caught. Eric Bjornstad notes in the old guidebook *Desert Rock*: "WARNING Spider Rock is sacred to the Navajo, and climbing it would very likely result in trouble of some kind, certainly a fine." It's best to respect the religious beliefs of the Navajo and leave Spider Rock to the Spider Lady.

OTHER CLIMBING AREAS

There are lots of other climbing areas scattered across northern Arizona and the Navajo lands. These areas are reserved for adventure climbers—those who want to head out to the empty spaces on the map and find enlightenment. Consult Tim Toula's *Rock 'N Road* for beta on off-the-beaten-track places and Eric Bjornstad's out-of-print *Desert Rock* for details about remote Navajo routes.

There are a few good areas around Kingman in northwestern Arizona. The 600-foot-high Hualapai Wall and Walnut Creek Wall loom above deep canyons on the west flank of the Hualapai Mountains south of Kingman. The Hualapai Wall, formed of excellent gneiss with lots of positive holds, has several routes up to six pitches long. Two large towers, Lost Angel of the Desert and Eagle's Nest, are detached from the main wall and offer some excellent backcountry crack climbs. Walnut Creek Wall is a beautiful, north-facing dome composed of dark granite. *A Dream of White Whales* (III 5.8) is a good, five-pitch line up the smooth center of the slab. Bring lots of TCUs and wires to protect the route. These routes are best visited during the cooler months. There are supposed to be lots of Mojave rattlesnakes in the boulderfields below the cliffs.

Hackberry Dome is an excellent, gleaming white dome north of Seligman and old US Highway 66. Supposedly, as many as 50 routes have been done on the hard granite apron by members of the Syndicato Granitica and students from Prescott College. The dome is northwest of Hackberry off Antares Road.

APPENDIX A:

FURTHER READING

A Better Way to Die: Rock Climber's Guide to Sedona and Oak Creek Canyon, Tim Toula, Falcon Publishing/Chockstone Press, 1995.

A Cheap Way to Fly, Tim Toula, 1991.

A Rock Jock's Guide to Queen Creek Canyon, Marty Karabin, 1995.

Adventuring in Arizona, John Annerino, Sierra Club Books, 1991.

Backcountry Rockclimbing in Southern Arizona, Bob Kerry, Backcountry Books of Arizona, 1997.

Beardsley Boulder Pile Rock Climbing Guide, Marty Karabin. A fold-out topo guide.

Climbing Guide to The Pit, Robert Miller, 1996.

Crown King Rock Climbing Guide, Marty Karabin, 1999. A fold-out topo guide.

Desert Rock, Eric Bjornstad, Chockstone Press, 1988. Out of print.

Dromedary Peak Rock Climbing Guide, Marty Karabin. A fold-out topo guide.

East Windy Point, Marty Karabin. A fold-out topo guide.

Groom Creek Bouldering Guide, Marty Karabin. A fold-out topo guide.

Hiking and Climbing Guide to Lookout Mountain, Marty Karabin. A fold-out topo guide.

Ice Castles Rock Climbing Guide, Marty Karabin. A fold-out topo guide.

Jacks Canyon Sport Climbing, Diedre Burton and Jim Steagall, 1997.

Paradise Forks Rock Climbing, David Bloom, Falcon Publishing/Chockstone Press, 1995.

Phoenix Rock: A Guide to Central Arizona Crags, Jim Waugh, Polar Designs, 1987. Out of print.

Phoenix Rock II, Greg Opland, Falcon Publishing/Chockstone Press, 1996.

Pinnacle Peak, Marty Karabin. A fold-out topo guide.

Prescott Bouldering Guide, Bill Cramer, 1998.

Rock 'N Road: Rock Climbing Areas of North America, Tim Toula, Falcon Publishing/Chockstone Press, 1995.

Squeezing the Lemmon: A Rock Climber's Guide to the Mt. Lemmon Highway, Eric Fazio-Rhicard, 1991.

Superstitions Select Volume 1, Greg Opland, Steel Monkey Publishing, 1998.

Thumb Butte, Rusty Baillie, 1991.

Too Much Rock, Not Enough Life: A Sport Climbing Guide to St. George and Southwestern Utah, Todd Goss, Paragon Climbing Guides, 1998.

Verde Basalt, Josh Gross, 1997.

APPENDIX B:

RATING SYSTEM COMPARISON CHART

YDS	British	French	Australian
5.3	VD 3b	2	11
5.4	HVD 3c	3	12
5.5	MS/S/HS 4a	4a	12/13
5.6	HS/S 4a	4b	13
5.7	HS/VS 4b/4c	4c	14/15
5.8	HVS 4c/5a	5a	16
5.9	HVS 5a	5b	17/18
5.10a	E1 5a/5b	5c	18/19
5.10b	E1/E2 5b/5c	6a	19/20
5.10c	E2/E3 5b/5c	6a+	20/21
5.10d	E3 5c/6a	6b	21/22
5.11a	E3/E4 5c/6a	6b+	22/23
5.11b	E4/E5 6a/6b	6c	23/24
5.11c	E4/E5 6a/6b	6c+	24
5.11d	E4/E5 6a/6b	7a	25
5.12a	E5 6b/6c	7a+	25/26
5.12b	E5/E6 6b/6c	7b	26
5.12c	E5/E6 6b/6c/7a	7b+	26/27
5.12d	E6/E7 6c/7a	7c	27
5.13a	E6/E7 6c/7a	7c+	28
5.13b	E7 7a	8a	29
5.13c	E7 7a	8a+	30/31
5.13d	E8 7a	8b	31/32
5.14a	E8 7a	8b+	32/33
5.14b	E9 7a	8c	33
5.14c	E9 7b	8c+	33

Sources: *Mountaineering: The Freedom of the Hills*, 6th Edition; *Climbing Magazine*, No. 150, February/March 1995.

APPENDIX C:
MOUNTAIN SHOPS, CLIMBING GYMS, AND GUIDE SERVICES

Flagstaff
Babbitt's Backcountry Outfitters
12 East Aspen Avenue
Flagstaff, AZ
520-774-4775

Flagstaff Mountain Guides
P.O. Box 2383
Flagstaff, AZ
520-635-0145
NAZClimb@aol.com

Peace Surplus
14 West Route 66
Flagstaff, AZ
520-779-4521

Sandstone Stairway (guide)
2400 North Kramer Street
Flagstaff, AZ 86001
520-774-7753

Vertical Relief Rock Gym
205 South San Francisco
    Street, Flagstaff, AZ
520-556-9909

Phoenix Area
Alpine Ski & Sports,
3320 East Roser Road
Phoenix, AZ 83040
602-268-2942

Alpine Ski & Sports
1753 East Broadway
Tempe, AZ 85252
602-968-9056

Arizona Hiking Shack
11649 North Cave Creek
    Road
Phoenix, AZ 85020
602-944-7723

Arizona Hiking Shack II
14036 North Scottsdale Road
Route 2, Scottsdale, AZ 85254
602-443-3721

Ascend Arizona
680 South Mill Avenue
Tempe, AZ 85282
602-495-9428

Desert Mountain Sports
2824 East Indian School Road
Route 4
Phoenix, AZ 85016
602-955-2875

Phoenix Rock Gym
2810 South Roosevelt
Suite 101, Tempe, AZ
602-921-8322

Recreational Equipment Inc.
    (REI)
1405 West Southern
Tempe, AZ 85282
602-967-5494

Recreational Equipment Inc.
    (REI)
12634 North Paradise Village
    Parkway West
Paradise Valley
AZ 85032; 602-996-5400

Venture Up Inc. (guide)
Phoenix, AZ
602-955-9100

The Wilderness
5130 North 19th Avenue
Phoenix, AZ 85015
602-242-4945

Wilderness Adventures (guide)
602-438-1800
www.wildernessadventures.com

Wilderness Re-Tread'em
(shoe resole)
5130 North 19th Avenue
Phoenix, AZ 85015
602-242-4945 or
800-775-5650

Prescott
Adventure Concepts (guide),
484 Whetstine Avenue
Prescott, AZ 86301
520-771-7641
www.spirit-works.com/
    adventure

Base Camp
142 North Cortez
Prescott, AZ 86301
520-445-8310

Granite Mountain Outfitters
320 West Gurley Street
Prescott, AZ 86301
520-776-4949

HGA Rock Climbing (guide)
Prescott, AZ
520-776-5937

Sedona
Canyon Outfitters Inc.
2701 West Highway 89A
Sedona, AZ
520-282-5293

Tucson
Bumjo's Climbing Shop
7445 East 22nd Street
Tucson, AZ 85710
520-751-4212

Rocks & Ropes Gym
330 South Toole
Route 450
Tucson, AZ
520-882-5964

Summit Hut
5045 East Speedway
Tucson, AZ; 520-325-1554

Winslow
Jungle Jym Rockwear Outlet
    Store
1221 East 3rd Street
Route 101
Winslow AZ; 520-289-4989

INDEX

A

E

Eagletail Mountains 287
Earth Angel 77
Earth Angel 418
Easier Than Jackie 457
East Cochise Stronghold, Batline Dome
    Batline 105
    Dikohe 105
    Unknown 105
East Cochise Stronghold, Cochise Dome
    Double Jeopardy 129
    Let's Make a Deal 129
    What's My Line 127
    What's My Line Direct 129
East Cochise Stronghold, Entrance Dome 109
East Cochise Stronghold, Out-of-Towners Dome 109
East Cochise Stronghold, Owl Rock
    Naked Prey 107
    Nightstalker 107
East Cochise Stronghold, Rockfellow Domes
    Abracadaver 122, 125
    Be All End All 119
    Cap'n Pissgums 119, 121
    Days of Future Passed 116, 118
    Endgame 118-19
    Forest Lawn 125, 127
    Interiors 121
    Jabberwock 125
    Knead Me 122
    Magnas Veritas 116
    Pair A Grins 125, 127
    Poetry in Motion 118
    Uncarved Block 121
    Welcome to the Machine 118
East Cochise Stronghold, Stronghold Dome
    Beeline 112
    Big Time 112
    Bounty, The 114
    Come and Get It 114
    End Chimney Left 109
    End Chimney Right 112
    Greasy Gizzards 113
    Reen's Rête 112
    Shake 'n' Bake 113-14
    Stage Fright 112
    Stand, The 114
    Unknown 114-15

    Wishbone 114
East Cochise Strongland, The Wasteland 107-9
East of Eden 387
East Pocket 446
Easy Money 428
Ego Trip 194
El Capitan Canyon 287
Electric Raguland 235
Electro Magnus 51
El Gato Grande D'Amore 262
Eliminator, The 285
Elysian Buttress
Elysian Buttress 443
Emerald, The 264
Emotions in Motion 387
Empire Strikes Back, The 297
End Chimney Left 109
End Chimney Right 112
Endgame 118-19
Endomorph Man 273
Energizer, The 370
Enga's First 233, 235
Entrance Dome 109
Equalizer, The 398
Erection Direct 225
Erotic Jesus 485
Even Cowgirls Get the Blues 228
Evil Offspring 433
Evil Tweak 433
Excaliber 370
Experiment in Terror 189

F

Face First 189
Fallen Angel 448
Falling Ross 325-26
Falling Stars 283
Fall of Man 485
False Witness 479
Fat Boy Goes to the Pond 273
F-Dude 485
Fearless Leader 180
Fear of Flying 279
Feast and Famine 250
Feeling a Little Thor 294
Fettuccini Afraido 227
Fifty-Second Street 356
Final Solution, The 336
Fine Whine, A 455
Fireball 76
Fire in the Hole 144
Firezone 77
Fist Full O'Dollars 426
Fistful of Pockets, A 230

5.8 Flu 229
Flagstaff area
    Asylum, The 446
    East Pocket 446
    Elysian Buttress 443-44
    Grand Falls 444
    Jacks Canyon 419-43
    Oak Creek Canyon 419
    Oak Creek Overlook 340-61
    Oak Creek Waterfall area 445
    O'Leary Peak 444
    Paradise Forks 377-401
    Pit, The 361-77
    Priest Draw 445
    Secret Canyon 444
    Sedona Spires 401-19
    Sycamore Point 445-46
    Volunteer Canyon 445
    Winslow Wall 446-48
Flailing Wall 458-61
Flake, The 398
Flakes of Wrath 252
Flatiron, The 216
Flight of the Falcon 335
Flood Gates 448
Floozie, The 285
Fluff Boys in Heat 233
Fluffy 437
Fluid Dynamics 250
Flyboy 55
Flying Chipmunk, The 285
Fogdish 384
Fool's Game 393
Footnotes 55
For a Few Pockets More 230
For Crinoid Out Loud 455
For Crying Out Loud 181
Forest Lawn 125, 127
For Pete, Thanks 327
Forrest Spires, The 216
Fortress, The
    Bay Tree Belay 231
    Bon-Bons in Space 230
    Bypass 230
    For a Few Pockets More 230
    Fistful of Pockets, A 230
    Freely Freaking 230
    Linear Accelerator, The 230
    Pocket Full of Rainbows 230
    South Side 230
    Stardust 231
Four Peaks 287
Fred 300
Freely Freaking 230
French Tickler 305
Fresh Squeezed 370

Y

Z

ABOUT THE AUTHOR

Stewart M. Green is a freelance writer and photographer living in Colorado Springs. He has written ten other books for Falcon Publishing, including *Rock Climbing Colorado, Rock Climbing Utah, Scenic Driving California, Scenic Driving Arizona,* and *Scenic Driving New England.* Stewart has more than 30 years experience as a climber and is also a leading climbing photographer with many photographs appearing in catalogues, advertisements, and national publications, including *Climbing, Rock & Ice, Sports Illustrated for Kids,* and *Outside.*

He is currently writing *Rock Climbing New England* for Falcon.

CLIMBING GLOSSARY

aid: using means other than the action of hands, feet, and body english to get up a climb

anchor: a means by which climbers are secured to a cliff

arete: an outside corner of rock

armbar: armlock: a means of holding onto a wide crack

bashie: a piece of malleable metal that's been hammered into a rock seam as an anchor: used in extreme aid climbing

belay: procedure of securing a climber by the use of rope

beta: detailed route information, sometimes move by move

bergschrund: gap where a glacier meets rock

bight: a fold (as in a bight of rope)

biner: see **carabiner**

bollard: a naturally constructed ice and snow anchor

bolt: an artificial anchor placed in a hole drilled for that purpose

bomber or **bomb-proof:** absolutely fail-safe (as in a very solid anchor or combination of anchors)

bucket: a handhold large enough to fully latch onto, like the handle of a bucket

cam: to lodge in a crack by counterpressure: that which lodges

carabiner: aluminum alloy ring equipped with a spring-loaded snap gate

ceiling: an overhang of sufficient size to loom overhead

chock: a wedge or mechanical device that provides an anchor in a rock crack

chockstone: a rock lodged in a crack

clean: a description of routes that may be variously free of vegetation, loose rock, or the need to place pitons; also the act of removing chocks from a pitch

cold shut: a relatively soft metal ring that can be closed

with a hammer blow; notoriously unreliable for withstanding high loads

crampon: framework of metal spikes that attach to climbing boots and provide traction on ice and snow

crimper: a small but positive edge

crux: the most difficult section of a climb or pitch

dihedral: an inside corner of rock

drag: usually used in reference to the resistance of rope through carabiners

Dulfersitz: a method of rappelling that involves wrapping the rope around the body and using the resulting friction to control speed

dynamic or dyno: lunge move

edge: a small rock ledge, or the act of standing on an edge

exposure: that relative situation where a climb has particularly noticeable sheerness

fifi: an un-gated hook used to quickly attach a climber to an anchor

figure-eight (figure-8): a device used for rappelling and belaying; or, a knot used in climbing

free, free climb, or free ascent: to climb using hands and feet only; the rope is only used to safeguard against injury, not for upward progress or resting

French technique: a method of ascending and descending low angle ice and snow with crampons

glissade: to slide down a snowfield on one's rump or feet

gobis: hand abrasions

hangdog: when a leader hangs from a piece of protection to rest, then

continues on without lowering back to the ground; not a free ascent

jam: wedging feet, hands, fingers or other body parts to gain purchase in a crack

jugs: holds secure as jug handles

lead: to be first on a climb, placing protection with which to protect oneself

lieback: the climbing maneuver that entails pulling with the hands while pushing with the feet

line: the path of weakness in the rock followed by the route

mantle: the climbing maneuver used to gain a single feature above one's head

monodoigts: very small holes or holds, about finger size

move: movement; one of a series of motions necessary to gain climbing distance

nut: same as a chock; a mechanical devise that, by various means, provides a secure anchor to the rock

on-sight: to climb a route without prior knowledge or experience of the moves, and without falling or otherwise weighting the rope (also on-sight flash)

opposition: nuts, anchors, or climbing maneuvers that are held in place by the simultaneous stress of two forces working against each other

pinkpoint: to lead (without falling) a climb that has been pre-protected with anchors rigged with carabiners

pins: pitons

pitch: the section of rock between belays

pitons: metal spikes of various shapes, hammered into the rock to provide anchors in cracks (also pins or pegs)

placement: the quality of a nut or anchor

protection or pro: the anchors used to safeguard the leader

prusik: both the knot and any means by which one mechanically ascends a rope

quickdraws: short slings with biners that help provide drag-free rope management for the leader

rappel: to descend a rope by means of mechanical brake devices

redpoint: to lead a route, placing and/or clipping protection as you go, without falling or resting on pro

RP: small nut used mostly in aid climbing

runout: the distance between two points of protection; often referring to a long stretch of climbing without protection

Screamers (Yates Screamers): load-limiting quickdraws that are sewn in such a manner as to lessen the impact of a fall on protection or anchors

second: the second person on a rope team, usually also the leaders belayer

self-arrest: a method of stopping a fall on steep snow or low-angle ice

sling or runner: a webbing loop used for a variety of purposes to anchor to the rock

smear: to stand on the front of the foot and gain friction against the rock across the breadth of the sole to adhere to the rock

stance: a standing rest spot, often the site of the belay

stem: to bridge between two widely-spaced holds

Supergaiters: gaiters that enclose the entire boot

thin: a climb or hold of relatively featureless character

toprope: a belay from an anchor point above; protects the climber from falling even a short distance

traverse: to move sideways, without altitude gain

verglas: extremely thin ice plastered to rock

wall or big wall: a long climb traditionally done over multiple days, but may take just a few hours for ace climbers

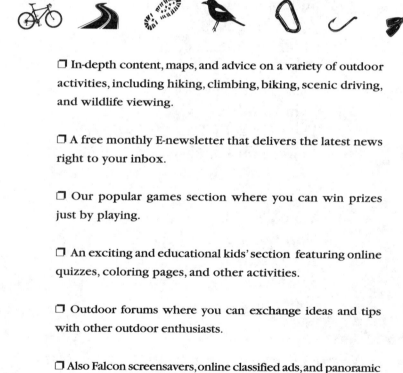

More Climbing Guides from Falcon and Chockstone Press

FALCON®

FALCON®

FALCON GUIDES® Leading the Way™

All books in this popular series are regularly updated with accurate information on access, side trips, & safety.

HIKING GUIDES

Best Hikes Along the Continental Divide
Hiking Alaska
Hiking Arizona
Hiking Arizona's Cactus Country
Hiking the Beartooths
Hiking Big Bend National Park
Hiking the Bob Marshall Country
Hiking California
Hiking California's Desert Parks
Hiking Carlsbad Caverns & Guadalupe
  Mtns. National Parks
Hiking Colorado
Hiking Colorado, Vol. II
Hiking Colorado's Summits
Hiking Colorado's Weminuche Wilderness
Hiking the Columbia River Gorge
Hiking Florida
Hiking Georgia
Hiking Glacier/Waterton Lakes
Hiking Grand Canyon National Park
Hiking Grand Staircase-Escalante
Hiking Grand Teton National Park
Hiking Great Basin
Hiking Hot Springs in the Pacific NW
Hiking Idaho
Hiking Maine
Hiking Michigan
Hiking Minnesota
Hiking Montana
Hiking Mount Rainier National Park
Hiking Mount St. Helens
Hiking Nevada
Hiking New Hampshire
Hiking New Mexico
Hiking New York

Hiking North Carolina
Hiking North Cascades
Hiking Northern Arizona
Hiking Olympic National Park
Hiking Oregon
Hiking Oregon's Eagle Cap Wilderness
Hiking Oregon's Mt Hood/Badger Creek
Hiking Oregon's Three Sisters Country
Hiking Pennsylvania
Hiking Ruins Seldom Seen
Hiking Shenandoah National Park
Hiking the Sierra Nevada
Hiking South Carolina
Hiking South Dakota's Black Hills Cntry
Hiking Southern New England
Hiking Tennessee
Hiking Texas
Hiking Utah
Hiking Utah's Summits
Hiking Vermont
Hiking Virginia
Hiking Washington
Hiking Wyoming
Hiking Wyoming's Cloud Peak
  Wilderness
Hiking Wyoming's Wind River Range
Hiking Yellowstone National Park
Hiking Zion & Bryce Canyon
Exploring Canyonlands & Arches
Exploring Hawaii's Parklands
Exploring Mount Helena
Exploring Southern California Beaches
Wild Country Companion
Wild Montana
Wild Utah
Wild Virginia

FALCON®

FALCON GUIDES® Leading the Way™

WILDLIFE VIEWING GUIDES
Alaska Wildlife Viewing Guide
Arizona Wildlife Viewing Guide
California Wildlife Viewing Guide
Colorado Wildlife Viewing Guide
Florida Wildlife Viewing Guide
Indiana Wildlife Vewing Guide
Iowa Wildlife Viewing Guide
Kentucky Wildlife Viewing Guide
Massachusetts Wildlife Viewing Guide
Montana Wildlife Viewing Guide
Nebraska Wildlife Viewing Guide
Nevada Wildlife Viewing Guide
New Hampshire Wildlife Viewing Guide
New Jersey Wildlife Viewing Guide
New Mexico Wildlife Viewing Guide
New York Wildlife Viewing Guide
North Carolina Wildlife Viewing Guide
North Dakota Wildlife Viewing Guide
Ohio Wildlife Viewing Guide
Oregon Wildlife Viewing Guide
Puerto Rico and the Virgin Islands WVG
Tennessee Wildlife Viewing Guide
Texas Wildlife Viewing Guide
Utah Wildlife Viewing Guide
Vermont Wildlife Viewing Guide
Virginia Wildlife Viewing Guide
Washington Wildlife Viewing Guide
West Virginia Wildlife Viewing Guide
Wisconsin Wildlife Viewing Guide

HISTORIC TRAIL GUIDES
Traveling California's Gold Rush Country
Traveling the Lewis & Clark Trail
Traveling the Oregon Trail
Traveler's Guide to the Pony Express Trail

SCENIC DRIVING GUIDES
Scenic Driving Alaska and the Yukon
Scenic Driving Arizona
Scenic Driving the Beartooth Highway
Scenic Driving California
Scenic Driving Colorado
Scenic Driving Florida
Scenic Driving Georgia
Scenic Driving Hawaii
Scenic Driving Idaho
Scenic Driving Indiana
Scenic Driving Kentucky
Scenic Driving Michigan
Scenic Driving Minnesota
Scenic Driving Montana
Scenic Driving New England
Scenic Driving New Mexico
Scenic Driving North Carolina
Scenic Driving Oregon
Scenic Driving the Ozarks including the
   Ouchita Mountains
Scenic Driving Pennsylvania
Scenic Driving Texas
Scenic Driving Utah
Scenic Driving Virginia
Scenic Driving Washington
Scenic Driving Wisconsin
Scenic Driving Wyoming
Scenic Driving Yellowstone & Grand Teton
   National Parks
Back Country Byways
Scenic Byways East & South
Scenic Byways Far West
Scenic Byways Rocky Mountains

To order any of these books, check with your local bookseller
or call FALCON® at **1-800-582-2665**.
Visit us on the world wide web at:
www.FalconOutdoors.com

FALCON®

ACCESS: It's every climber's concern

The Access Fund, a national, non-profit climbers' organization, works to keep climbing areas open and to conserve the climbing environment. Need help with closures? land acquisition? legal or land management issues? funding for trails and other projects? starting a local climbers' group? CALL US!

Climbers can help preserve access by being committed to leaving the environment in its natural state. Here are some simple guidelines:

- **STRIVE FOR ZERO IMPACT** especially in environmentally sensitive areas like caves. Chalk can be a significant impact on dark and porous rock—don't use it around historic rock art. Pick up litter, and leave trees and plants intact.

- **DISPOSE OF HUMAN WASTE PROPERLY** Use toilets whenever possible. If toilets are not available, dig a "cat hole" at least six inches deep and 200 feet from any water, trails, campsites, or the base of climbs. *Always pack out toilet paper.* On big wall routes, use a "poop tube" and carry waste up and off with you (the old "bag toss" is now illegal in many areas).

- **USE EXISTING TRAILS** Cutting switchbacks causes erosion. When walking off-trail, tread lightly, especially in the desert where cryptogamic soils (usually a dark crust) take thousands of years to form and are easily damaged. Be aware that "rim ecologies" (the clifftop) are often highly sensitive to disturbance.

- **BE DISCREET WITH FIXED ANCHORS** *Bolts are controversial and are not a convenience*—don't place 'em unless they are *really* necessary. Camouflage all anchors. Remove unsightly slings from rappel stations (better to use steel chain or welded cold shuts). Bolts sometimes can be used pro-actively to protect fragile resources—consult with your local land manager.

- **RESPECT THE RULES** and speak up when other climbers don't. Expect restrictions in designated wilderness areas, rock art sites, caves, and to protect wildlife, especially nesting birds of prey. *Power drills are illegal in wilderness and all national parks.*

- **PARK AND CAMP IN DESIGNATED AREAS** Some climbing areas require a permit for overnight camping.

- **MAINTAIN A LOW PROFILE** Leave the boom box and day-glo clothing at home—the less climbers are heard and seen, the better.

- **RESPECT PRIVATE PROPERTY** Be courteous to land owners. Don't climb where you're not wanted.

- **JOIN THE ACCESS FUND!** To become a member, make a tax-deductible donation of $25 or more.

The Access Fund

Preserving America's Diverse Climbing Resources
PO Box 17010 Boulder, CO 80308
303.545.6772 • www.accessfund.org